StarOffice For Linux® For Dummies®

StarOffice Function Toolbar Buttons

Button	Function
	Display previous document or URL
	Display next document or URL
	Stop loading current URL
	Load predefined home page
	Reload current URL or document
	Edit current document
	Open a document file
	Save the current document
	Send the current message via e-mail
	Print the current document
	Cut selected text or object from the current document and save it on the clipboard
	Copy selected text or object to the clipboard
	Paste text or object from the clipboard into the current document
	Display/hide Explorer window
	Display/hide Beamer window
	Display/hide Navigator window
	Display/hide Stylist window

StarDesktop Object Toolbar Buttons

Button	Function
	Display the contents of the directory one level higher on the directory tree than the current directory
	Display the detail view of the contents of the current directory
	Display the icon view of the contents of the current directory
	Display the Preview panel to preview the contents of the selected item
	Display the Description panel to show information about the selected item
	Display file extensions for all files and directories

StarWriter Object Toolbar Buttons

Button	Function
B	Make the selected text bold
i	Make the selected text italic
U	Underline the selected text
	Left align the selected paragraph
	Center align the selected paragraph
	Right align the selected paragraph
	Justify the selected paragraph
	Automatic numbered list formatting
	Automatic bullet list formatting

...For Dummies®: Bestselling Book Series for Beginners

StarOffice For Linux® For Dummies®

StarCalc Object Toolbar Buttons

Button	Function
	Apply Currency format to numbers in selected cells
	Apply Percent format to numbers in selected cells
	Apply Standard format to numbers in selected cells
	Add decimal to numbers in selected cells
	Delete decimal from numbers in selected cells
	Add borders to selected cells
	Select background color for selected cells

StarDraw and StarImpress Main Toolbar Buttons

Button	Function
	Edit points
	Select tool
	Change magnification of the display
	Create text objects
	Create rectangles and squares
	Create ellipses and circles
	Create 3-D objects
	Create lines and polygons
	Create arrows and lines
	Create connectors

StarSchedule Object Toolbar Buttons

Button	Function
	Create a new event
	Create a new task
	Display events for a single day
	Display events for a week
	Display events for a month
	Display events for a workweek
	Display events for a multiple workweeks
	Display events in a list
	Display/hide the Task List panel
	Display/hide the Calendar panel
	Display/hide the Details View panel

Cheat Sheet $2.95 value. Item 0576-9.
For more information about IDG Books, call 1-800-762-2974.

...For Dummies®: Bestselling Book Series for Beginners

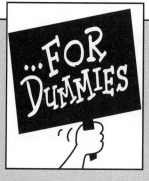

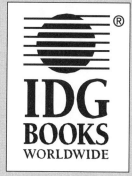

StarOffice for Linux® For Dummies®

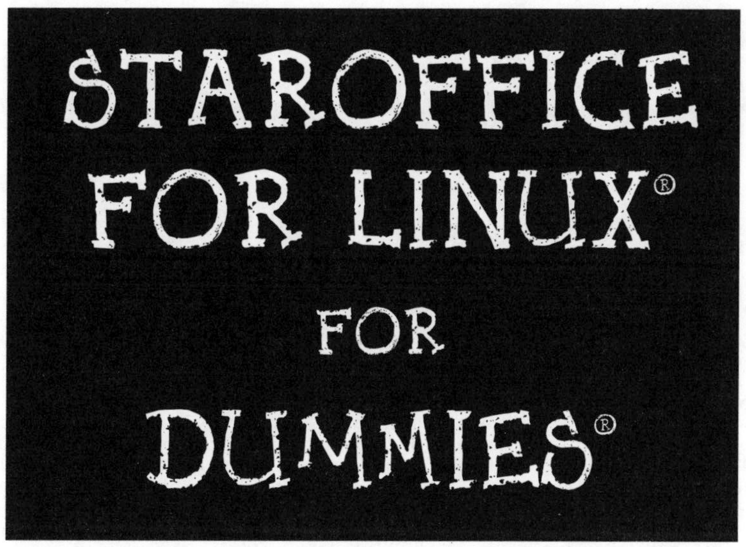

StarOffice for Linux® For Dummies®

by Michael Meadhra

IDG Books Worldwide, Inc.
An International Data Group Company

Foster City, CA ◆ Chicago, IL ◆ Indianapolis, IN ◆ New York, NY

StarOffice For Linux® For Dummies®

Published by
IDG Books Worldwide, Inc.
An International Data Group Company
919 E. Hillsdale Blvd.
Suite 400
Foster City, CA 94404
www.idgbooks.com (IDG Books Worldwide Web site)
www.dummies.com (Dummies Press Web site)

Library of Congress Catalog Card No.: 99-64909

ISBN: 0-7645-0576-9

Printed in the United States of America

10 9 8 7 6 5 4 3 2 1

1O/ST/QY/ZZ/IN

Distributed in the United States by IDG Books Worldwide, Inc.

Distributed by CDG Books Canada Inc. for Canada; by Transworld Publishers Limited in the United Kingdom; by IDG Norge Books for Norway; by IDG Sweden Books for Sweden; by IDG Books Australia Publishing Corporation Pty. Ltd. for Australia and New Zealand; by TransQuest Publishers Pte Ltd. for Singapore, Malaysia, Thailand, Indonesia, and Hong Kong; by Gotop Information Inc. for Taiwan; by ICG Muse, Inc. for Japan; by Norma Comunicaciones S.A. for Colombia; by Intersoft for South Africa; by Eyrolles for France; by International Thomson Publishing for Germany, Austria and Switzerland; by Distribuidora Cuspide for Argentina; by LR International for Brazil; by Galileo Libros for Chile; by Ediciones ZETA S.C.R. Ltda. for Peru; by WS Computer Publishing Corporation, Inc., for the Philippines; by Contemporanea de Ediciones for Venezuela; by Express Computer Distributors for the Caribbean and West Indies; by Micronesia Media Distributor, Inc. for Micronesia; by Grupo Editorial Norma S.A. for Guatemala; by Chips Computadoras S.A. de C.V. for Mexico; by Editorial Norma de Panama S.A. for Panama; by American Bookshops for Finland. Authorized Sales Agent: Anthony Rudkin Associates for the Middle East and North Africa.

For general information on IDG Books Worldwide's books in the U.S., please call our Consumer Customer Service department at 800-762-2974. For reseller information, including discounts and premium sales, please call our Reseller Customer Service department at 800-434-3422.

For information on where to purchase IDG Books Worldwide's books outside the U.S., please contact our International Sales department at 317-596-5530 or fax 317-596-5692.

For consumer information on foreign language translations, please contact our Customer Service department at 1-800-434-3422, fax 317-596-5692, or e-mail rights@idgbooks.com.

For information on licensing foreign or domestic rights, please phone +1-650-655-3109.

For sales inquiries and special prices for bulk quantities, please contact our Sales department at 650-655-3200 or write to the address above.

For information on using IDG Books Worldwide's books in the classroom or for ordering examination copies, please contact our Educational Sales department at 800-434-2086 or fax 317-596-5499.

For press review copies, author interviews, or other publicity information, please contact our Public Relations department at 650-655-3000 or fax 650-655-3299.

For authorization to photocopy items for corporate, personal, or educational use, please contact Copyright Clearance Center, 222 Rosewood Drive, Danvers, MA 01923, or fax 978-750-4470.

About the Author

Michael Meadhra is an author and consultant who began writing articles for software newsletters after several years in the corporate world. Now he writes books such as this one. He has written about topics such as Windows, office suites, graphics and presentation programs, the Internet, and online banking and personal finance management software. His list of credits has grown to more than 30 computer book titles and innumerable articles for magazines and software newsletters. Meadhra's other titles from IDG Books Worldwide, Inc., include *SmartSuite 97 For Windows For Dummies, Lotus SmartSuite Millennium Edition For Dummies,* and *Banking Online For Dummies*.

ABOUT IDG BOOKS WORLDWIDE

Welcome to the world of IDG Books Worldwide.

IDG Books Worldwide, Inc., is a subsidiary of International Data Group, the world's largest publisher of computer-related information and the leading global provider of information services on information technology. IDG was founded more than 30 years ago by Patrick J. McGovern and now employs more than 9,000 people worldwide. IDG publishes more than 290 computer publications in over 75 countries. More than 90 million people read one or more IDG publications each month.

Launched in 1990, IDG Books Worldwide is today the #1 publisher of best-selling computer books in the United States. We are proud to have received eight awards from the Computer Press Association in recognition of editorial excellence and three from Computer Currents' First Annual Readers' Choice Awards. Our best-selling *...For Dummies*® series has more than 50 million copies in print with translations in 31 languages. IDG Books Worldwide, through a joint venture with IDG's Hi-Tech Beijing, became the first U.S. publisher to publish a computer book in the People's Republic of China. In record time, IDG Books Worldwide has become the first choice for millions of readers around the world who want to learn how to better manage their businesses.

Our mission is simple: Every one of our books is designed to bring extra value and skill-building instructions to the reader. Our books are written by experts who understand and care about our readers. The knowledge base of our editorial staff comes from years of experience in publishing, education, and journalism — experience we use to produce books to carry us into the new millennium. In short, we care about books, so we attract the best people. We devote special attention to details such as audience, interior design, use of icons, and illustrations. And because we use an efficient process of authoring, editing, and desktop publishing our books electronically, we can spend more time ensuring superior content and less time on the technicalities of making books.

You can count on our commitment to deliver high-quality books at competitive prices on topics you want to read about. At IDG Books Worldwide, we continue in the IDG tradition of delivering quality for more than 30 years. You'll find no better book on a subject than one from IDG Books Worldwide.

John Kilcullen
Chairman and CEO
IDG Books Worldwide, Inc.

Steven Berkowitz
President and Publisher
IDG Books Worldwide, Inc.

Eighth Annual Computer Press Awards 1992

Ninth Annual Computer Press Awards 1993

Tenth Annual Computer Press Awards 1994

Eleventh Annual Computer Press Awards 1995

IDG is the world's leading IT media, research and exposition company. Founded in 1964, IDG had 1997 revenues of $2.05 billion and has more than 9,000 employees worldwide. IDG offers the widest range of media options that reach IT buyers in 75 countries representing 95% of worldwide IT spending. IDG's diverse product and services portfolio spans six key areas including print publishing, online publishing, expositions and conferences, market research, education and training, and global marketing services. More than 90 million people read one or more of IDG's 290 magazines and newspapers, including IDG's leading global brands — Computerworld, PC World, Network World, Macworld and the Channel World family of publications. IDG Books Worldwide is one of the fastest-growing computer book publishers in the world, with more than 700 titles in 36 languages. The "...For Dummies®" series alone has more than 50 million copies in print. IDG offers online users the largest network of technology-specific Web sites around the world through IDG.net (http://www.idg.net), which comprises more than 225 targeted Web sites in 55 countries worldwide. International Data Corporation (IDC) is the world's largest provider of information technology data, analysis and consulting, with research centers in over 41 countries and more than 400 research analysts worldwide. IDG World Expo is a leading producer of more than 168 globally branded conferences and expositions in 35 countries including E3 (Electronic Entertainment Expo), Macworld Expo, ComNet, Windows World Expo, ICE (Internet Commerce Expo), Agenda, DEMO, and Spotlight. IDG's training subsidiary, ExecuTrain, is the world's largest computer training company, with more than 230 locations worldwide and 785 training courses. IDG Marketing Services helps industry-leading IT companies build international brand recognition by developing global integrated marketing programs via IDG's print, online and exposition products worldwide. Further information about the company can be found at www.idg.com.

1/24/99

Author's Acknowledgments

It takes a team of talented people to produce a book such as this one, and I've been very fortunate to work with the publishing team at IDG Books Worldwide, Inc. Once again, they made the publishing process a pleasant and rewarding experience as they transformed my manuscript into the finished product you hold in your hands. Sherri Morningstar and David Mayhew, the acquisitions editors, deserve special credit for working with me to make this book a reality. And I especially want to thank Jeanne S. Criswell, project editor, for her patience and faith in me as the deadlines loomed near. I appreciate Shelley Lea's efforts to work out problems with figure captures under Linux. Thanks to copy editors Kim Darosett, Jerelind Charles, James Russell, Ted Cains, and Pam Wilson-Wykes for their work editing my prose. Thanks also to technical editor Drew Michaels for ensuring the book's technical accuracy. I also want to thank the IDG Books production staff that turned a rough manuscript into a finished book and the rest of the executives and staff at IDG Books whose work was essential to making this book possible.

My agent, David Fugate, of Waterside Productions, was instrumental in pulling this project together. Thanks, David!

My thanks to Oliver Petry of StarDivision for his work as liaison and for providing background information and access to beta software.

When time got short and schedules tight, some contributors stepped in to help get the manuscript finished on time. Duane Morin contributed to chapters in Part IV. Kate Wrightson and her writing partner Joe Merlino contributed to chapters in Part V and to Chapter 21. Thanks to you all! My friend Steve Rindsberg also deserves recognition for his invaluable technical assistance and contributions to several chapters.

Thanks also go to Douglas Montanus of Kinetic Corporation and Jacob Robert Wilkins of the Linux User Group at Speed Engineering School, University of Louisville, for their help in dealing with Linux-related issues that arose while I was working on this book.

Publisher's Acknowledgments

We're proud of this book; please register your comments through our IDG Books Worldwide Online Registration Form located at `http://my2cents.dummies.com`.

Some of the people who helped bring this book to market include the following:

Acquisitions, Editorial, and Media Development

Project Editor: Jeanne S. Criswell

Acquisitions Editors: David Mayhew, Sherri Morningstar

Copy Editor: Kim Darosett

Technical Editor: Drew Michaels

Associate Permissions Editor: Carmen Krikorian

Media Development Coordinator: Megan Roney

Editorial Manager: Rev Mengle

Media Development Manager: Heather Heath Dismore

Editorial Assistant: Jamila Pree

Production

Project Coordinator: E. Shawn Aylsworth

Layout and Graphics: Angela F. Hunckler, Barry Offringa, Brent Savage, Michael Sullivan, Brian Torwelle, Dan Whetstine

Proofreaders: Laura Bowman, Nancy Price

Indexer: Becky Hornyak

Special Help

Ted Cains, Jerelind Charles, Paul Levesque, James Russell, Pam Wilson-Wykes

---

General and Administrative

IDG Books Worldwide, Inc.: John Kilcullen, CEO; Steven Berkowitz, President and Publisher

IDG Books Technology Publishing Group: Richard Swadley, Senior Vice President and Publisher; Walter Bruce III, Vice President and Associate Publisher; Steven Sayre, Associate Publisher; Joseph Wikert, Associate Publisher; Mary Bednarek, Branded Product Development Director; Mary Corder, Editorial Director

IDG Books Consumer Publishing Group: Roland Elgey, Senior Vice President and Publisher; Kathleen A. Welton, Vice President and Publisher; Kevin Thornton, Acquisitions Manager; Kristin A. Cocks, Editorial Director

IDG Books Internet Publishing Group: Brenda McLaughlin, Senior Vice President and Publisher; Diane Graves Steele, Vice President and Associate Publisher; Sofia Marchant, Online Marketing Manager

IDG Books Production for Dummies Press: Michael R. Britton, Vice President of Production; Debbie Stailey, Associate Director of Production; Cindy L. Phipps, Manager of Project Coordination, Production Proofreading, and Indexing; Shelley Lea, Supervisor of Graphics and Design; Debbie J. Gates, Production Systems Specialist; Robert Springer, Supervisor of Proofreading; Laura Carpenter, Production Control Manager; Tony Augsburger, Supervisor of Reprints and Bluelines

◆

The publisher would like to give special thanks to Patrick J. McGovern, without whom this book would not have been possible.

◆

Contents at a Glance

Cartoons at a Glance

By Rich Tennant

page 177

page 349

page 317

The 5th Wave By Rich Tennant

AT 11:18 ON APRIL 25TH IN THE YEAR 2003, PC SOFTWARE AND HARDWARE REACHED A PERFECT APPLICATION-TO-MEMORY SYNCHRONICITY.

What the heck...?

page 249

page 279

The 5th Wave By Rich Tennant

"MY GIRLFRIEND RAN A SPREADSHEET OF MY LIFE, AND GENERATED THIS CHART. MY BEST HOPE IS THAT SHE'LL CHANGE HER MAJOR FROM 'COMPUTER SCIENCES' TO 'REHABILITATIVE SERVICES.'"

page 123

page 55

page 9

Fax: 978-546-7747 • E-mail: the5wave@tiac.net

Table of Contents

Introduction

Welcome to *StarOffice For Linux For Dummies.*

Actually, the name of this book is a little misleading. StarOffice *is* a computer program that provides the tools (for word processing, creating spreadsheets, creating databases, scheduling, drawing, preparing presentations, Web browsing, sending and receiving e-mail, getting the news, and more) that the typical office worker, student, or home user needs. And this book *is* about StarOffice. But it's not exclusively about using StarOffice on the Linux operating system. StarOffice for Linux is probably the best-known version of the program (that's why I mention it in the title), but StarOffice runs on a variety of other computer platforms, including Windows, and looks and works the same on all of them. So just about everything in this book applies equally well to StarOffice for Linux, Windows 95 or 98, Mac OS, Java, Solaris, and Windows NT.

Also, this isn't a book for dumb people. Far from it! This book is for smart people who are trying to use a strange new software program that may not do what they expect it to do or may do things in an unexpected way. When confronted with such a situation, you may momentarily feel like a dummy — or you may feel that the computer programmers are the dummies for making the program behave that way. This book helps you get past those times.

This book won't transform you into a StarOffice wizard overnight. It doesn't provide an exhaustive catalog of every command and feature available in the program. And it doesn't get bogged down with theoretical discussions of computers, office organization, or anything else. What it does do is give you the basics of how to use the tools available in StarOffice to get real work done.

About This Book

This book is a tool that you can pick up and use to find out how to do something. It's not a novel or a tutorial that you must start reading at Page 1 and proceed through the chapters in sequence. (Believe me, you aren't going to spoil the ending if you skip ahead and read part of Chapter 16 before you read Chapter 5.)

You can use the index or table of contents to look up a topic that interests you and then turn to that part of the book and read a few pages to discover how to use a StarOffice feature to accomplish something useful. Having done so, you can put down the book and get on with your work — and your life.

Oh sure, you can read this book straight through if you really want to, but that isn't necessary. You aren't going to miss anything critical by skipping a chapter. If one task or feature requires knowledge of something that is covered in another part of the book, cross-references in the text tell you where you can find the supporting material, if you aren't already familiar with it.

Foolish Assumptions

While writing this book, I made some assumptions about you, the reader. I tried very hard not to make too many assumptions because some of them would, inevitably, be wrong. But a few basic assumptions were necessary. Here's a summary of the assumptions that I made:

- **You own (or have access to) a personal computer capable of running one of the versions of StarOffice.** That computer most likely runs some flavor of Linux, or perhaps Windows, although a few of you may be using StarOffice on a different computer platform. (Actually, StarOffice looks and works essentially the same on all platforms. As a result, almost everything in this book still applies, regardless of the computer platform you use. It's just that Linux and, to a lesser extent, Windows get special attention in the text by virtue of being the most commonly used platforms for StarOffice.)
- **You're familiar with the basic parts of a computer (you can use the keyboard, and you know that the mouse doesn't have fur or eat cheese), and you can turn the system on.**
- **Your computer's operating system (Linux, Windows, or whatever) is installed, configured, and operating properly with the features (printing, Internet access, and so on) that you need.** Note that I don't assume that you did this work yourself, just that it has been done.
- **You can log in as a user and get X-Window System (or your system's Graphical User Interface) on-screen if it doesn't appear automatically.** A *Graphical User Interface (GUI)* is a fancy name for the system of icons and windows that enables you to control the computer with a mouse instead of typing arcane commands at a plain text prompt.

- **You've had at least a little experience using a computer with a Graphical User Interface before (probably Windows or a Macintosh), so you know how to do a few simple things like open and close windows and make selections in dialog boxes.** I don't assume that you like using computers (I do, but I don't assume that you do) or that you're particularly adept at using them — I just assume that I can skip the lesson that starts with "When you move the mouse thingy, the pointer on the screen moves, too."
- **You have acquired a copy of StarOffice, or you plan to do so.**
- **You want to use StarOffice to get some work done.** In other words, you need to write a report, analyze some numbers, draw a chart or diagram, prepare a presentation, surf the Web, read your e-mail, create a to-do list or appointment calendar, keep an address book or other database, or something of that sort.
- **You probably need to exchange documents, spreadsheets, and other files with people who use other programs, such as Microsoft Office (Word, Excel, PowerPoint), Lotus 1-2-3, and WordPerfect.**

How This Book Is Organized

This book is packed with information, but I try to make it easy to use by arranging that information in an accessible hierarchy. The book is divided into parts that correspond to the major kinds of tasks for which you use StarOffice (and the StarOffice tools that are designed to handle those tasks). Each part is divided into chapters, and the chapters are divided into sections and subsections.

If you're looking for information on a specific task, you may need to read only a single section to find out how to perform that task. If you're looking for a broader topic, you may need to read a few sections or perhaps a chapter or two. But regardless of the amount of information you seek, it will be chunked together in logical groups.

Part I: Getting to Know StarOffice

This part starts out with an introduction to the StarOffice program and an overview of what each of the StarOffice tools does. You discover how to find your way around in the program and how to use common elements that are in all the StarOffice tools. Next up is a more detailed introduction to the StarDesktop where you can organize your StarOffice documents and projects.

Part II: Working with Words in StarWriter

When your project calls for working with words, you need to use the StarOffice word processing tool, called StarWriter. This part starts out with basic word processing techniques, such as how to enter, edit, and format text and print a document. Then you discover how to add more sophisticated (and consistent) formatting to documents and how to use editing tools, such as search and replace, spell checking, and AutoCorrect. Also in this part, you find out how to save time by automating document creation and how to add tables, text frames, pictures, lines and borders, and rotated text to documents.

Part III: Calculating with StarCalc

For number crunching, StarOffice provides a tool called StarCalc. In this part of the book, you find out how to use StarCalc to create a simple spreadsheet — including how to navigate columns, rows, and cells and how to perform basic math operations. Then you discover how to use more complex functions and cell addressing and how to work with multiple sheets. Next, you find out how to add pizzazz to your numbers with formatting techniques. Finally, you focus on using StarChart to create charts — how to enter data, generate a chart, add labels, select or change a chart type, and add and manipulate 3-D effects.

Part IV: Impressing an Audience with Graphics and Presentations

According to the old saying, a picture is worth a thousand words. StarOffice includes tools that enable you to create and manipulate pictures and assemble those pictures (along with charts and text) into presentations. You find out in this part how to create drawings and diagrams and manipulate scanned images. You then discover how to create a slide show and arrange the slides in order. You also cover how to finish a presentation by adding transition effects, showing a presentation on-screen, and printing slides and handouts.

Part V: Scheduling Your Time and Tasks with StarSchedule

Keeping track of a hectic schedule is easier with a good calendar program. If you use StarSchedule, you won't forget important tasks or miss appointments. In this part, you discover how to set up a to-do list and how to prioritize and track tasks. You also find out how to schedule appointments and set alarms to nag (er, remind) you to get there on time.

Part VI: Managing Your Data with StarBase

StarOffice includes a built-in address book to help you keep track of your friends and associates. This part of the book shows you how to use the address book and also how to use the database program that lurks behind the address book. If you want to pursue database development, you can discover in this part how to create your own database (perhaps you want to catalog your extensive CD collection) and how to generate reports that organize the information you squirrel away in your database.

Part VII: Getting on the Internet

If you want to surf the World Wide Web or correspond with friends via e-mail, you don't have to leave StarOffice to do so; StarOffice includes all the tools that you need. This part shows you how to set up StarOffice for Internet access and how to use the built-in Web browser. You also find out about sending and receiving e-mail and participating in online discussions in newsgroups. For information on using StarOffice to create Web pages, see the bonus chapter on the Web at `www.dummies.com/bonus/staroffice`.

Part VIII: The Part of Tens

The Part of Tens is a tradition in *...For Dummies* books, and everyone seems to like the format of these chapters. So in this part, presented in the time-tested manner, is a collection of tips and tricks for successfully sharing information among the various StarOffice tools and for sharing StarOffice documents and files with users of Microsoft Office and other programs.

Appendix

Tucked away at the back of the book is information on how to install StarOffice, if you haven't already installed it before buying this book. I include installation instructions for the two most common computer platforms: Linux and Windows 95 or 98.

Conventions Used in This Book

Writing a computer book means writing instructions for how to issue computer commands. I've adopted a few conventions for representing those commands in the text of this book.

One of the most common ways to tell a computer program what you want it to do is to choose a series of commands from the program's menus by clicking the commands with your mouse. Describing those commands can make instructions long and cumbersome, so I often resort to a shortened instruction that uses the ⇨ symbol to seperate a series of menu choices. For example, an instruction to choose File⇨Save means to click File in the program's menu bar and then choose Save from the drop-down menu that appears.

You can invoke some commands and program features by pressing a special key combination on the keyboard. Key combinations provide fast shortcuts for frequently used commands. For example, the shortcut key combination for the command to save the current file is to hold down the Control (Ctrl) key and press the S key. Shortcut key combinations appear in the book as key names joined by the plus sign, like so: Ctrl+S.

When I give you instructions to type something specific, the text that you need to type appears in bold letters. So if the instructions read: type **~/Office50**, you need to type the bold-faced characters exactly as shown, including spacing and capitalization. Similarly, if I call attention to text that appears on-screen as a label or prompt, that text appears in a special monospaced font, like this: `system prompt`.

Icons Used in This Book

One of the cool things about a *...For Dummies* book is the icons that appear in the page margins beside selected paragraphs. The icons mark paragraphs that deserve special attention, either because the paragraph covers something important or because it includes information that you can skip. Here's a list of the icons used in this book and what they mean:

This icon flags the tips, tricks, and shortcuts that can make working with StarOffice easier and more convenient.

This icon marks the general principles and background information that you need to keep in mind as you use StarOffice.

This icon alerts you to potential traps and trouble spots. You get to benefit from my mistakes so you don't have to go through the painful experience of discovering why I stuck a warning in the text.

This icon serves as a geek alert, marking technical details and background information that may be interesting but aren't necessary for mere mortals to bother with.

This icon highlights places where you need to deal with the nitty-gritty details of the Linux operating system or where Linux-specific issues may impact how you use the program.

This icon points out the few instances where StarOffice behaves differently on the Windows platform or where Windows-specific issues may impact how you use the program.

Linux Configuration Used in This Book

The Linux operating system — the open source software (that is, free software) Unix clone for PCs — is, in some ways, a strange beast. Unlike computer operating systems that are developed and marketed by a single company, the typical Linux installation is made up of components from several different sources. The components are all built on the same core features of the Linux *kernel* (the core operating system), but the assortment of accessories that accompany the kernel can vary considerably.

In particular, the Graphical User Interface — the part of the system that enables you to use a mouse to interact with on-screen icons instead of typing obscure text commands — can vary in appearance and function. As a result, your screen may look a little different than the examples shown in this book. Most of the differences are purely cosmetic and have no affect on the way StarOffice operates. The location and appearance of the buttons in the title bar of the main StarOffice program window are probably the only differences that you may notice between your system and most figures or instructions in this book. In addition, you may need to adjust a few of the instructions marked with the Linux icon for your particular version of Linux, but those instances are rare.

The Linux community thrives on openness and free exchange of information. In the spirit of that openness, here is a summary of the Linux configuration that I'm using as I write this book:

- Red Hat Linux 5.2 — using the *Workstation* installation defaults
- XFree86 X-Window System

- KDE 1.1 desktop environment with the KWM window manager (the panel and taskbar are hidden in most figures)
- E-mail and primary Internet access (through a Proxy server) via an Ethernet connection to a TCP/IP-based local area network
- Dial-up Internet access (PPP) via a modem
- Printing via a PostScript printer (HP LaserJet 4MP)

Where to Go from Here

Now that the preliminary stuff is out of the way, you're ready to get started. You can begin by browsing through the book until something catches your eye. Or you can scan the table of contents for an interesting topic and begin reading the related chapter. Or you can look up a specific topic in the index and turn to the page where it is discussed and begin reading there. The approach that you choose depends on your personal style and what you want to accomplish right now. Just pick one and do it. The sooner you begin reading, the sooner you'll be able to use StarOffice to do something useful.

Part I
Getting to Know StarOffice

"Okay, make sure this is right. 'Looking for caring companion who likes old movies, nature walks, and quiet evenings at home. Knowledge of StarOffice for Linux a plus'."

In this part . . .

Get to know StarOffice with an overview of the program and an introduction to the various StarOffice tools and what they do. Discover the StarDesktop and the Explorer and Beamer windows that you can use to access the StarOffice tools and organize your documents.

Chapter 1

Working in the StarOffice Environment

In This Chapter

- Just what is StarOffice anyway?
- Launching StarOffice
- Checking out the tools in the StarOffice toolbox
- Working with StarOffice documents
- Comparing StarOffice to other office suites

When you first meet new coworkers, you usually find out a little bit about them and the roles you can expect them to play. Introductions typically go something like this: "This is Joe. He handles widget acquisitions. You need to work with him to make sure that you have enough widgets on hand."

Similarly, this chapter serves as your introduction to StarOffice. Just as the person introducing you to a group of coworkers probably starts off with a bit of background information about the group, this chapter starts with a brief overview of the StarOffice program as a whole. You discover how to launch the StarOffice program and find out about the assortment of StarOffice tools and what they do. Because most computer users are likely at some point to work with people who use different computer programs, this chapter also discusses how StarOffice deals with documents and files from some of the other popular office suites.

Introducing StarOffice — The Star of Your Virtual Office

StarOffice is an *office suite* — a program that provides an assortment of office productivity tools. In other words, StarOffice isn't just a word processor for creating letters, memos, and reports. It isn't just a spreadsheet program for working with rows and columns of numbers and formulas. And, it isn't just a program for preparing presentations. StarOffice is all these things and more. In fact, StarOffice provides tools for all the tasks that a typical office worker, student, home user, or small businessperson is likely to need. That makes StarOffice one *sweet* suite.

The StarOffice tools include the following:

- **Address book:** For keeping contact information for friends and coworkers
- **Chart-making tool:** For converting numbers into graphics
- **Database:** For managing data and generating reports
- **Drawing tool:** For creating diagrams and other vector graphics
- **E-mail client:** For reading and sending e-mail over the Internet or a local network
- **File utility:** For managing your documents and projects
- **Image tool:** For manipulating scanned images
- **Mathematical equation editor:** For adding equations and formulas to your documents
- **Newsgroup client:** For reading and posting articles in the Usenet newsgroups (e-mail based discussion groups) on the Internet
- **Presentation tool:** For preparing on-screen slide shows
- **Scheduling calendar:** For tracking appointments and to-do-list tasks
- **Spreadsheet:** For analyzing and manipulating numbers
- **Web browser:** For viewing World Wide Web pages
- **Web page and frame editor:** For creating your own Web pages
- **Word processing tool:** For creating letters, reports, and other text-based documents

StarOffice integrates all these tools into one program with a unified look and feel. The tools' wide range of features enables you to perform all your daily tasks without leaving the StarOffice environment. And the tools' consistent appearance and operation mean that after you know how to use one tool in the suite, you can easily figure out how to use the others.

Using StarOffice on different computers

StarOffice is a *cross-platform* program, which means that it's available in versions that run on more than one kind of computer. All the StarOffice versions for the different computer platforms look and act the same, although you must use the version that is designed for your kind of computer (for example, StarOffice for Windows 95 or 98 or StarOffice for Macintosh). Using StarOffice on a Linux machine is essentially the same experience as using StarOffice on a Windows-based computer or on a Macintosh, because StarOffice creates a working environment that is almost completely self-contained. When you're working in StarOffice, you hardly notice the underlying operating system of the computer you're using.

StarOffice is available for all the following computer operating systems:

- Java clients
- Linux
- Mac OS
- OS/2
- Solaris
- Windows 95 or 98
- Windows NT

The title of this book is *StarOffice For Linux For Dummies* because it focuses on the Linux version of StarOffice. You see this version of the program in all the figures and examples in this book. However, the other versions of StarOffice are so similar that almost everything in this book applies to StarOffice running on any computer platform.

Of course, some subtle differences exist between StarOffice versions running on the various computer platforms. Most of the differences crop up when you must interact with the computer's hardware (for example, you need to print something) or the computer's file system (for example, you need to open and save files). The availability and rendering of fonts is another area where aspects of the operating system are evident in the StarOffice environment. Other than those situations, almost all the platform-specific differences in the various StarOffice versions are cosmetic. For example, the buttons in the main StarOffice window title bar may look and act differently from one operating system to another (or from one Linux/X-Window System window manager to another, for that matter), but the windows and dialog boxes within StarOffice itself still look the same.

Using StarOffice in different countries

To many people in the United States, StarOffice seems like a relatively new product. Actually, StarOffice is no newcomer — on the contrary, it's a well-established program. StarOffice was developed in Germany by Star Division GbH and enjoys a strong following in Europe, where StarOffice is the corporate standard at many large companies and educational institutions.

The recent surge in interest in the Linux operating system has also focused attention on application programs — such as StarOffice — that run on Linux. The increased visibility that StarOffice enjoys as a Linux program afforded Star Division the opportunity to make a serious entry into the United States software market. As a result, the company opened an office in California to facilitate marketing StarOffice in the United States as well as across Europe.

Starting StarOffice

StarOffice is designed to take advantage of your computer operating system's *Graphical User Interface* (GUI). The GUI is what enables you to interact with the computer by manipulating on-screen windows and icons with a mouse instead of by typing commands at a prompt on a text-only screen. On a Linux-based computer, the GUI is called the *X-Window System,* and you need to make sure that the X-Window System is running before you attempt to start StarOffice.

Your computer may be configured to start the X-Window System automatically when you turn on the system. If so, you're ready to go as soon as you complete the standard login procedure by entering your user ID and password. Otherwise, you probably need to log in in text mode and then start the X-Window System manually by typing **startx** on the command line and pressing Enter. (The startx command is the most common way to start an X-Window System session on Linux systems. However, some systems use a different command or sequence of commands. Be sure to use the proper commands to start X-Window System on your computer.)

When the X-Window System desktop appears on your screen, it can take on any one of several different facades, depending on the window manager that you're using and the themes and other settings that are active on your system. I use the KDE desktop with its panel of buttons along the bottom of the screen and taskbar at the top. Your desktop (or background, or opening screen), on the other hand, may start out looking quite different. Perhaps you have a fancy background image and an assortment of icons arranged along the sides of the screen; or perhaps you have a taskbar at the bottom of the screen with a Start button at the left end. What window manager you use doesn't make much difference; StarOffice works the same in all of them.

The following steps assume that you already installed StarOffice. If you haven't installed the program yet, turn to the Appendix in the back of this book for information about installing StarOffice for Linux or for Windows 95 or 98. Then return here after you finish the installation. I'll wait for you, I promise.

After you log in to your Linux system and start the X-Window System, you're ready to run StarOffice. (Make sure that you log in under the same user ID that you used when you installed StarOffice.) Depending on the window manager that you use and the way that it's configured, you may be able to launch the StarOffice program several different ways, but one technique that works the same in just about every window manager is to follow these steps:

1. **Open a terminal window by running xterm or a similar program.**

   If you use the KDE desktop, you can open a terminal window by clicking the K button in the panel and then choosing Utilities⇨Terminal. If you use a different window manager, you may open a terminal window by clicking an icon or by right-clicking the desktop and making a selection from a pop-up menu. Use whatever technique is appropriate for opening a terminal window under your X-Window System window manager.

2. **Type** cd ~/Office51/bin **at the prompt in the terminal window and then press Enter.**

   This command changes the working directory to the directory where the StarOffice program is installed (cd ~/Office51/bin). If StarOffice is installed in a different directory on your system, make the appropriate changes in the command.

3. **Type** ./soffice **and press Enter to start StarOffice.**

   StarOffice is a large program, so it takes a little while to load. Be patient. In a moment, the StarOffice logo appears, followed by the main StarOffice program window displaying the StarDesktop, as shown in Figure 1-1.

If you install StarOffice on a system running KDE, the installation program automatically adds StarOffice to the K button menu. To start StarOffice, click the K button and choose Personal⇨StarOffice. You can create a desktop icon in KDE or GNOME that's linked to the command that starts the program (~/Office51/bin/soffice). You can then click that icon to start StarOffice.

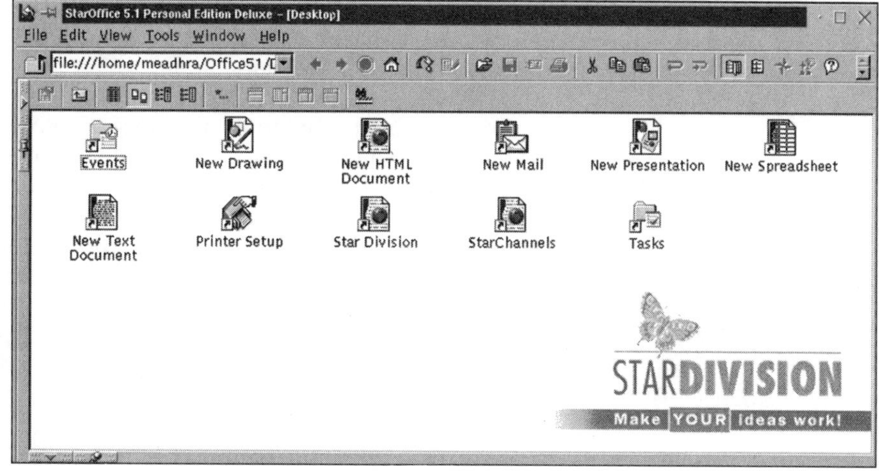

Figure 1-1: StarOffice normally starts with the StarDesktop.

The procedure for creating an icon to launch a program varies depending on what window manager you're using. Most window managers also enable you to add programs like StarOffice to their menus. Again, the procedure for doing so varies, depending on the specific window manager. Check out the documentation for your window manager to find out how to create icons and menu items.

Windows 95 or 98 users can launch StarOffice by clicking the Start button in the taskbar and then choosing Programs⇨StarOffice 5.1⇨StarOffice 5.1.

Getting to Know the Players in the StarOffice Lineup

Unlike office suites that are made up of several separate programs that you can (and often must) run individually, StarOffice is one integrated program. Within that program, you have an assortment of tools or modules at your disposal, which enable you to tackle different tasks.

Perhaps the best way to familiarize yourself with the StarOffice program and its features is to start with a brief introduction to each of the StarOffice tools and what they do.

StarDesktop

StarDesktop is what you see when you start the StarOffice program (refer to Figure 1-1). It creates a virtual computer desktop within the main StarOffice window. Just as your physical desktop is where you work with files, folders, and papers relating to your current projects, StarDesktop provides a central location to work with your computer files and folders.

StarDesktop is designed to be the master control center for your work in StarOffice. Icons on StarDesktop allow you to easily create new files and access other StarOffice features, and you can add your own icons to the StarDesktop for quick access to your ongoing projects. StarDesktop includes a built-in viewer that enables you to view the contents of files without opening them in a separate window. StarDesktop also includes a powerful file management utility, called Explorer, which lets you locate and work with files anywhere on your system.

For more information on using StarDesktop, see Chapter 2.

StarWriter

Working with text documents is probably the most common task for office workers, students, and home users alike. Whether you're preparing a sales proposal, writing a book report, or composing a letter to Aunt Jane, StarWriter — the StarOffice word processing program (shown in Figure 1-2) — can handle the job.

Of course, StarWriter includes all the basic text entry and editing features that you expect. StarWriter corrects your spelling errors and gives you access to the fonts and formatting tools that you need to make your documents look sensational. It also includes a wealth of more advanced features, such as styles and templates for easy formatting, and AutoPilots that automate creation of common documents. Part II of this book (Chapters 3 through 6) shows you how to use StarWriter with text documents.

If you need to create and edit your own Web page, StarWriter can handle that task as well. In addition to regular text documents in a number of file formats, StarWriter can also handle HTML documents with ease. Although creating Web pages in StarOffice is beyond the scope of this book, you can find information on this topic on the Web at `www.dummies.com/bonus/staroffice`.

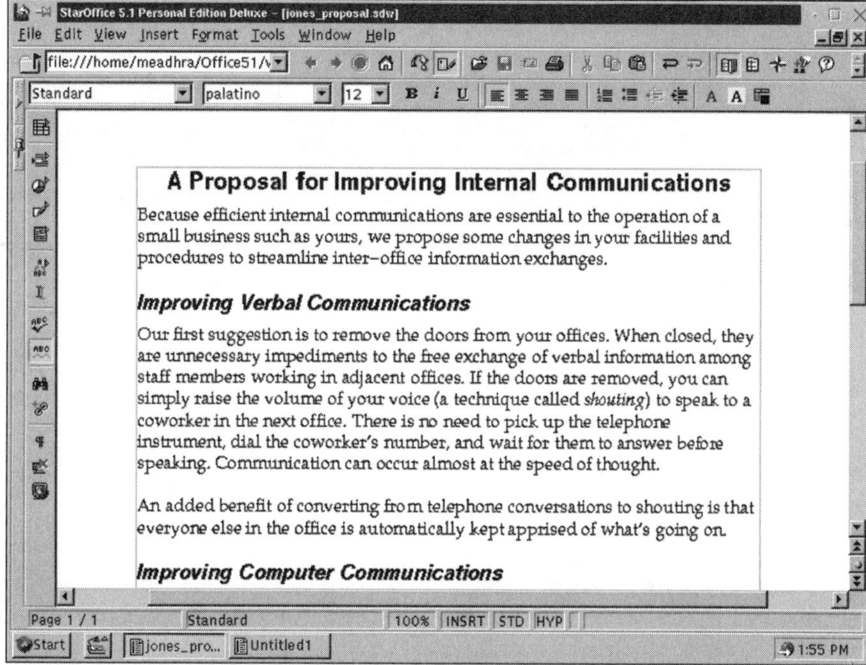

Figure 1-2: StarWriter shows you what your document looks like as you edit it.

StarCalc

If working with numbers is your thing, StarCalc (shown in Figure 1-3) is your tool. StarCalc is the StarOffice spreadsheet tool, which enables you to work with numbers, labels, and formulas arranged in rows and columns. Using StarCalc, you can do anything from constructing a simple table or invoice, to developing a budget or doing sophisticated financial analyses.

StarCalc supports multiple worksheets in each file, which makes building complex spreadsheet models a simple task. StarCalc also includes formatting features so you can turn your spreadsheets into attractive printed reports.

Part III of this book (Chapters 7 through 10) shows you how to work with spreadsheets using StarCalc.

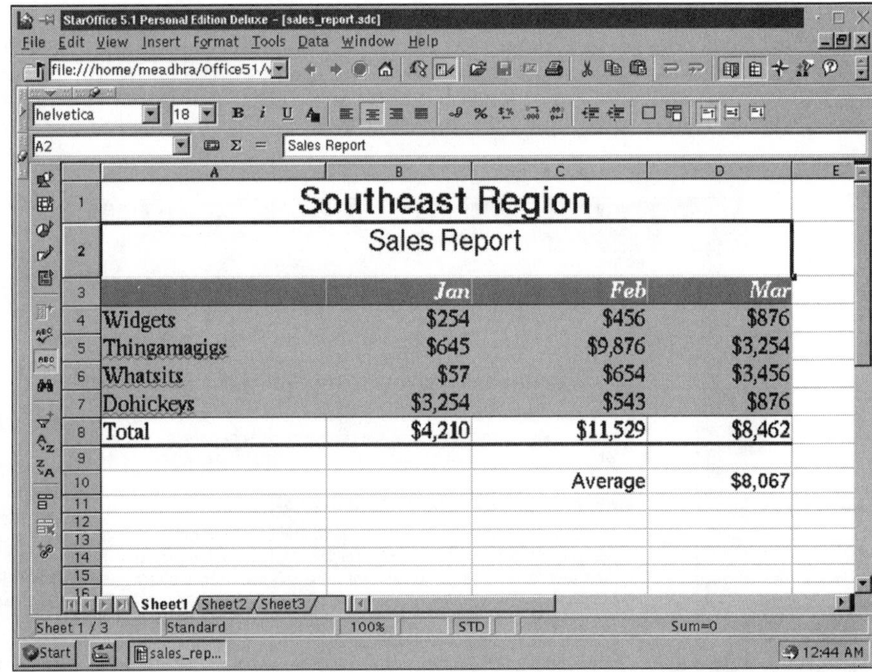

Figure 1-3: StarCalc is just the thing for preparing budget projections.

StarChart

Converting raw numbers into attractive charts is StarChart's job. You can choose from a variety of different chart types and variations to create a chart to impress your boss. StarChart even lets you add fancy three-dimensional effects to give your chart extra pizzazz, as shown in Figure 1-4.

Page ahead to Chapter 10 for information on how to create charts using StarChart.

StarDraw and StarImage

When you need to create or edit a picture, you don't have to exit StarOffice to do it. StarDraw is a powerful, easy-to-use drawing tool that anyone can use to create flowcharts and diagrams. If you have an artistic bent, you can use StarDraw to create logos and more sophisticated drawings.

If you need to manipulate bitmap images — scanned photos and the like — then StarImage is the tool for you. With StarImage, you can load an image (from a scanner or a file) and manipulate, edit, or retouch it, as shown in Figure 1-5. Artists can even use StarImage to create their own images from scratch.

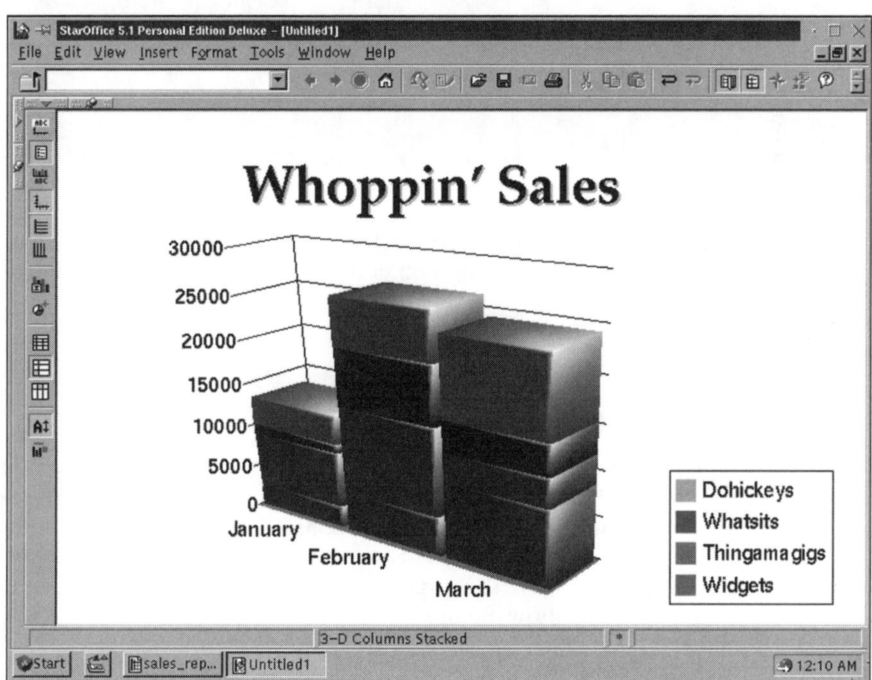

Figure 1-4: StarChart can create impressive 3-D effects.

Figure 1-5: StarImage lets you retouch your scanned photos.

You can find out how to use StarDraw to create drawings and diagrams in Chapter 11. For information on editing images with StarImage, head to Chapter 12.

StarImpress

When you need to impress an audience with a top-notch presentation, you can use StarImpress, the StarOffice presentation tool, to create and deliver an on-screen slide show. Create slides consisting of text, charts, and graphics and arrange them in order. Then complete your presentation with transition effects and timing. With StarImpress, you can deliver your presentation as an on-screen slide show and also support it with printed handouts of your slides.

See Chapters 13 and 14 for information on using StarImpress to create impressive presentations.

StarSchedule

Keeping up with a busy schedule can be tough, but the StarOffice calendar tool, StarSchedule (shown in Figure 1-6), can make it easier. You can use StarSchedule to keep track of tasks that you need to do; it shows the status, due date, and priority of those tasks. StarSchedule also keeps track of your appointments and important events, whether they are one-time events or recurring appointments. You won't have any excuse for being late to the big meeting if you use StarSchedule's reminder to alert you in advance of the upcoming event.

Check out Chapters 15 and 16 to find out how to use StarSchedule to track your tasks and events.

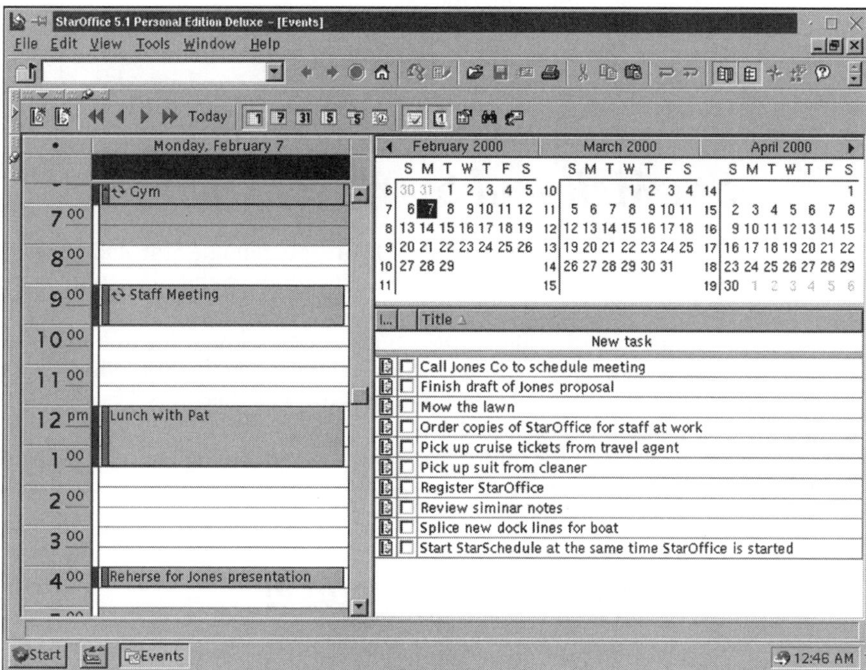

Figure 1-6: Plan your day with StarSchedule.

StarOffice Address Book

StarOffice includes a built-in Address Book where you can keep contact information for friends, family, and colleagues. The Address Book is designed to integrate with other StarOffice components so that you can quickly and easily locate contact information in the Address Book and insert that info into a letter, an e-mail message, or whatever. The combination of the StarOffice Address Book and the StarSchedule tool makes a fairly complete personal information manager (PIM) utility contained within the StarOffice program.

Find out how to use the StarOffice Address Book in Chapter 17.

StarBase

Who doesn't need to keep lists of data of some kind? Whether your data is a simple catalog of your music CDs or the product inventory for your small business, StarBase, the StarOffice database tool, gives you the features that you need to create a database, design data-entry forms, sort your information, and generate reports.

Part VI of this book shows you how to use StarBase to build a database and generate reports from it.

StarMail and StarDiscussion

StarMail is the StarOffice e-mail tool. You can use StarMail to send and receive messages via Internet e-mail accounts and also some kinds of corporate network e-mail accounts. StarMail supports threads to keep groups of messages on the same topic together as well as rules to automate the handling of incoming messages. StarDiscussion is the StarOffice tool that enables you to participate in Internet newsgroup discussions.

See Chapter 21 for information on accessing e-mail and newsgroups with StarMail and StarDiscussion.

StarOffice Web browser

When you're ready to surf the Web, you don't need to fire up a separate Web browser. StarOffice includes a built-in Web browser that enables you to view Web pages from the Internet or your local intranet Web server. The StarOffice Web browser, as shown in Figure 1-7, is easy to set up and simple to use, and it supports most of the features of the popular separate Web browser programs.

See Chapter 20 for more on browsing the Web from within StarOffice.

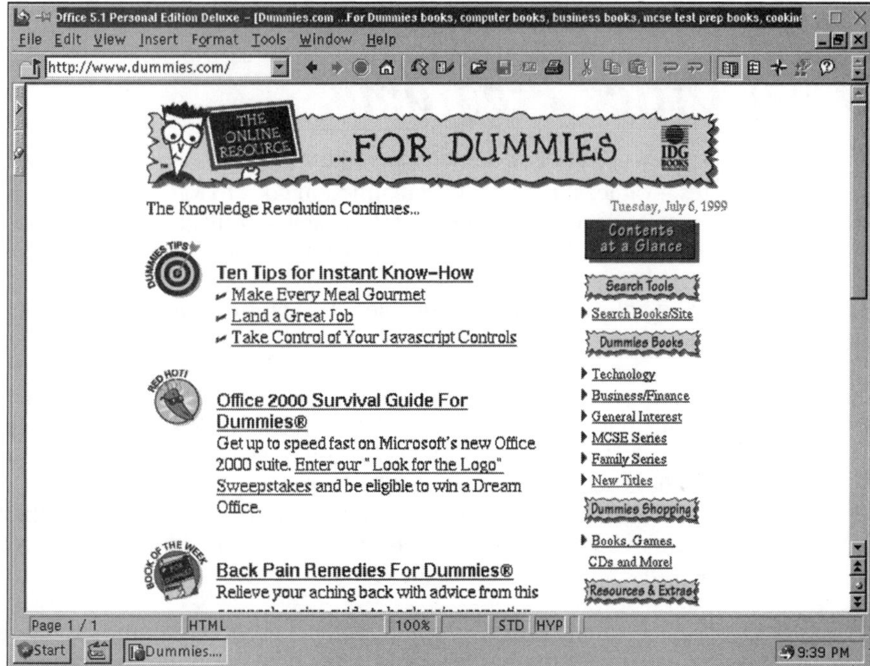

Figure 1-7: Surf the Web from within StarOffice.

Creating and Editing StarOffice Documents

While working in StarOffice, you can usually concentrate on the task at hand and let StarOffice automatically invoke the appropriate tool for whatever you want to do. For example, if you open an existing text document, StarOffice automatically launches StarWriter, the word processing tool, and loads your selected document for editing. If you create a new spreadsheet file, StarOffice launches its spreadsheet tool, StarCalc, with an empty worksheet loaded.

This feature means that you're free to organize and work with your files and documents in any way that is meaningful for you. You don't need to keep StarCalc files with the StarCalc tool and text documents with the StarWriter tool. Instead, you can group files together by project, date, topic, or whatever. StarOffice always knows which tool to use to open or edit a file, no matter where the file is located.

Comparing StarOffice to That Other Office Program

StarOffice is a very nice program, but it's not the market leader among office suites — at least not yet. That distinction goes to Microsoft Office. Because Microsoft Office is so ubiquitous, the likelihood is great that you may need to share files and documents with friends and coworkers who use Microsoft Office.

Sharing your files can be a problem if each program uses only its own file formats.

Fortunately, StarOffice makes sharing documents with Microsoft Office users a simple matter, because each of the key StarOffice tools can open and edit files created by its Microsoft Office counterpart. After editing a file in StarOffice, you can save the file in the corresponding Microsoft Office program format, so that Microsoft Office users can open and edit the file. In fact, you can even create a document from scratch in StarOffice and save the document in a Microsoft Office file format.

Table 1-1 summarizes how the StarOffice tools correlate to their counterpart programs in Microsoft Office and a few other popular programs.

Table 1-1 Comparison of StarOffice Tools with Other Programs

StarOffice Component	*Counterpart*	*File Exchange*
StarWriter	Microsoft Word	Exchanges files with several versions of Word
StarCalc	Microsoft Excel Lotus 1-2-3	Exchanges files with several versions of Excel plus some 1-2-3 files
StarImpress	Microsoft PowerPoint	Opens and saves PowerPoint files
StarSchedule	Microsoft Outlook Lotus Organizer	Imports tasks and appointments from both
StarDraw and StarImage	Microsoft PhotoDraw	Supports drawing and image formats that are compatible with a variety of popular graphics programs
StarMail and StarDiscussion	Microsoft Outlook Express	StarMail imports messages from Outlook Express

StarOffice Component	*Counterpart*	*File Exchange*
StarBase	Microsoft Access Lotus Approach	Uses the dBase file format, which is supported by most database programs
StarOffice Web browser	Microsoft Internet Explorer Netscape Navigator	Supports industry-standard HTML documents

Exchanging files between StarOffice and Microsoft Office programs isn't a flawless process — especially if you are also moving files from one platform or computer to another. For example, you may have problems with fonts that don't display or print properly on another system. StarOffice may not support all the features of its counterpart in Microsoft Office (such as the pivot table feature in Microsoft Excel). The reverse is also true. Some StarOffice formatting features aren't supported by the Microsoft Office counterpart programs. Expect to do some clean up work on documents that you exchange between StarOffice and Microsoft Office. However, basic documents and most of the commonly-used features survive the translation remarkably well.

Chapter 2

Exploring StarDesktop

In This Chapter

- Getting to know StarDesktop
- Arranging documents and icons on your desk
- Checking out the tools in the StarOffice toolbox
- Working with StarOffice documents

StarDesktop is the StarOffice home base. It's normally the first thing that you see when you start StarOffice, and it's the place you return to again and again as you work in the program. StarDesktop is where you organize your projects, create documents, open StarOffice tools, and do all the miscellaneous stuff that isn't covered by one of the major tools.

This chapter gets you better acquainted with StarOffice in general and StarDesktop in particular. You discover how to get around in the StarOffice environment and find out about StarDesktop features such as Explorer and Beamer. I also show you how to customize some StarOffice and StarDesktop features.

Getting to Know StarDesktop

Take a moment to look at your desk and note the tools and materials that you work with. (Okay, perhaps you should straighten up a bit first; then look at your desk.)

Your desk is your primary workspace — it's where you spread out your documents and other papers when you work with them. In addition to the documents that you're working on at the moment, you probably also have stacked on your desk (or within reach on a credenza or bookshelf) an assortment of other documents, file folders, and reference materials for various current projects. If you're like most people, your desk is also home to a variety of tools for doing your work. You have paper and pens for creating new documents and tools — such as a ruler or calculator — that you may need as you work on your various projects. Communications are important, too, so you probably have a telephone on your desk with a Rolodex organizer or phone book beside it and perhaps an inbox and outbox for papers.

Just as your physical desk provides a convenient work surface and a home for your various tools and materials, StarDesktop serves a similar function in the StarOffice environment. (Gee, what a remarkable coincidence that they named it Star*Desk*top.) StarDesktop is the first thing that you see when you launch the StarOffice program — it's the main work area. When you open and create documents with the various StarOffice tools, those documents appear in windows on top of (or within) StarDesktop. The document windows may temporarily obscure StarDesktop — just as your paper documents may obscure your desk — but it's always there underneath all the clutter of working documents.

StarDesktop is home to an assortment of icons that you can use to create new documents. You also find StarDesktop icons for Events and Tasks, for Printer Setup, and for Web sites. You can also add your own icons to StarDesktop to give you quick access to your documents and project folders, your e-mail inbox and outbox, and more. Although it's not obvious at first glance, StarDesktop also features built-in file viewers that enable you to preview the contents of various files and folders without opening the files themselves. In addition, StarDesktop gives you access to the Explorer and Beamer utilities for managing your files. And you can customize these utilities and other StarDesktop features to suit your own preferences.

When you launch StarOffice, it opens the StarOffice program window and displays StarDesktop along with a docked window for Tips (along the bottom), as shown in Figure 2-1. The title bar at the top of the window and the border around the edge are standard stuff and look like any typical program window on your system. It's what's inside the StarOffice window that makes the program unique.

StarDesktop occupies the work area of the main StarOffice program window. All the StarOffice tools share the title bar, menu bar, Function toolbar, and Task bar as well as the Explorer and Beamer windows and the Tips window (when they're displayed). The parts of the StarOffice window that are unique to StarDesktop are the StarDesktop Object toolbar and the StarDesktop workspace. As you use other StarOffice tools to work with documents and files, you open other windows. These document or tool windows appear on top of or within the StarDesktop work area and may hide StarDesktop from view, but StarDesktop is always there in the background.

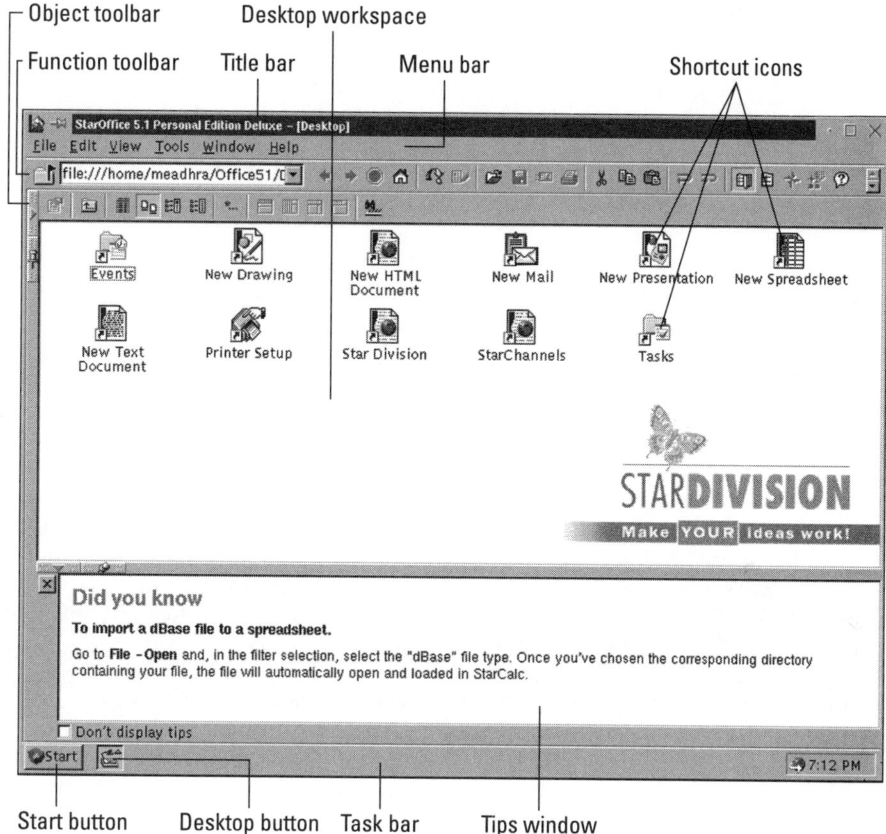

Figure 2-1: StarDesktop greets you when you launch StarOffice.

Figure 2-1 shows just one of several variations of the StarDesktop layout. You find out how to select other layouts and add icons and folders in the "Arranging your StarDesktop" section, later in this chapter. For now, the default layout is a good place to get acquainted with StarDesktop and the rest of the StarOffice program window.

To give yourself more working room on the StarDesktop, close the Tips window (click the Close "X" button in the upper-left corner of the Tips window). A cleaner workspace than the default StarOffice window, shown in Figure 2-1, results. If you don't want StarOffice to display the Tips window each time you open the program, check the Don't Display Tips option at the bottom of the Tips window before closing that window.

The title bar, the frame around the StarOffice window, and the buttons at each end of the title bar may look different on your system because the X-Window System window manager controls the appearance of those elements. However, those cosmetic differences don't affect the appearance and function of the elements inside the StarOffice window.

Title bar

You may as well start your get-acquainted tour of the StarOffice program window with the title bar at the top. The *title bar* identifies the StarOffice program and version and also displays `[Desktop]` to indicate that StarDesktop is currently active. When you open a document, the name of the document appears in the title bar in place of the desktop label.

The buttons at each end of the title bar typically control the size and placement of the StarOffice program window on your computer screen. The title bar buttons shown in Figure 2-1 were placed there by *KWM,* the window manager for the K Desktop Environment (KDE) that I use on my test system. Clicking the X button at the right end of the title bar closes the StarOffice program. Clicking the square button (next to the X button) switches the StarOffice program window between full-screen mode and a floating, resizable window. Clicking the dot (.) button minimizes (or iconifies) the StarOffice window. Clicking the StarOffice logo button at the left of the title bar displays a menu of window management commands. Clicking the push-pin button (next to the logo button) tells the StarOffice window to hold its position onscreen even if you take advantage of KDE's multiple virtual desktops to switch to a different desktop. (Refer to a book on KDE for more information about virtual desktops.)

If you use a different X-Window System window manager (or a different operating system), different buttons may appear in the StarOffice title bar, and they may function a little different from the preceding descriptions. But don't let that throw you. The buttons in the StarOffice title bar work just like the title bar buttons in other programs that you run on your system. Your window manager controls those buttons, and StarOffice doesn't do anything to cause them to behave in unexpected ways.

Menu bar

Immediately below the title bar in the StarOffice window, you find a menu bar (refer to Figure 2-1). The StarOffice *menu bar* follows the same conventions as menu bars in most other Windows, Mac OS, and Linux/X-Window programs, so you're probably familiar with its appearance and use. The menu names start with File on the left and end with Help on the right. If you click a menu name, StarOffice displays a drop-down menu of available commands. If you select a command from a menu (by clicking it), StarOffice carries out the selected command or opens a dialog box where you can make further selections. If you select (or just point to) some menu items, such as Toolbars on the View menu, a submenu of additional choices pops open.

The menu bar changes to display a slightly different selection of menu names, depending on what StarOffice tool is open and active. The standard menus — File, Edit, View, Tools, Window, and Help — are always available on the menu bar. However, when you're editing a text document with StarWriter, the menu bar also includes Insert and Format menus. Furthermore, when you're working with a spreadsheet in StarCalc, the menu bar includes the Insert and Format menus plus the Data menu; and when you're creating a presentation with StarImpress, the Presentation menu replaces the Data menu. You get the idea.

Function toolbar

The Function toolbar is the row of buttons that appears just below the menu bar (refer to Figure 2-1). This toolbar contains an address box just like the one that you're probably accustomed to seeing in a Web browser program. And guess what, the address box works just like the ones you find in popular Web browsers and in Windows Explorer on Windows 98 machines.

The address box displays the path and filename of the file that's displayed in the current window. When you're viewing StarDesktop, the address box shows the StarDesktop folder's address — the directory on your hard drive where StarOffice stores the files and shortcut links that appear on the desktop. When you're editing a text document in StarWriter, the address box shows the path and filename of the document file.

The reverse is also true. You can type a path and filename in the address box to tell StarOffice to open that file. If, instead of a filename, you enter the Internet address for a Web page, StarOffice switches to its Web browser mode and displays the Web page for you. (For more on Web browsing with StarOffice, see Chapter 20.)

To the left of the address box is the Bookmark button. (See Chapter 20 for information on using the Bookmark button.) To the right of the address box is an assortment of buttons that gives you easy one-click access to features and commands that you can use throughout StarOffice.

At any given time, some of the buttons on the Function toolbar may be *grayed out* to indicate that you can't use them with the currently open window. When you open a document or tool to which a button can apply, the button automatically assumes its normal coloration, instead of being grayed out. Clicking a normally colored button on the button bar immediately invokes the associated command.

Like toolbar buttons in many other programs, the buttons on the Function toolbar provide a quick and easy way to access commonly used StarOffice commands and features. Most of the toolbar buttons are nothing more than a faster, easier way to issue commands that are also available on the standard

StarOffice menus. However, a few buttons (for example, the first four buttons to the right of the address box: Back, Forward, Stop, and Home) have no counterparts in the standard menus — usually because the toolbar buttons are so much easier to use that the corresponding menu commands would be redundant. (The StarOffice menus are *user configurable,* so you can add the missing commands to a menu if you really want them. For more information, see the "Arranging your StarDesktop" section later in this chapter.)

The easiest way to find out what each button does is to point to a button with the mouse pointer and let the pointer hover over the button for a couple of seconds. When you do, a small box (sometimes called a *tool tip*) pops up under the pointer, showing the descriptive name of the button. Most of the names are self-explanatory.

If enough room isn't available to display all the buttons in the Function toolbar, a pair of arrow buttons appears at the right end of the toolbar. Clicking the down arrow displays another row of buttons to accommodate the overflow. Clicking the up arrow returns the top row of buttons to view.

The default location for the Function toolbar is immediately below the menu bar, as you see in Figure 2-1. However, the Function toolbar doesn't have to stay there. You can move the Function toolbar (and other StarOffice toolbars) to other locations within the StarOffice window, if you prefer. I show you how to move toolbars in the "Working with toolbars" section later in this chapter.

Object toolbar

Another row of buttons, called the Object toolbar, normally resides just above the desktop workspace (refer to Figure 2-1). Unlike the Function toolbar, which applies to all the StarOffice windows, the buttons in the Object toolbar are for commands and features that pertain directly to the associated window — in this case, StarDesktop.

The Object toolbar is normally attached to the work area, not to the menu bar. When you open documents in separate windows, a separate Object toolbar appears in each window — provided an Object toolbar is available for the StarOffice tool that you're using in that window. (Some of the StarOffice tools, such as the Web browser, don't have Object toolbars.) As you may guess, the buttons that appear in the Object toolbar vary depending on what StarOffice tool you're using in that window.

The StarDesktop Object toolbar, shown in Figure 2-2, contains the following buttons:

- **Properties:** Displays the Properties dialog box for the selected item
- **Up One Level:** Displays, on the desktop, the contents of the directory one level above the current directory (the current directory's parent directory)
- **Details:** Displays the contents of the desktop as a list with details instead of as large icons
- **Icons:** Displays the contents of the desktop as large icons
- **Preview:** Displays the Preview panel on the desktop, which enables you to preview the contents of the selected desktop object
- **Description:** Displays the Description panel on the desktop, which shows a detailed description of the selected desktop object
- **Show File Extensions:** Displays the filename extensions of desktop objects
- **Layout 1– Layout 4:** Selects one of four arrangements of the desktop objects, Preview panel, and Description panel (only available when the Preview or Description buttons are selected)
- **Multiple Search:** Modifies Desktop and Beamer searches to include more than a single filename

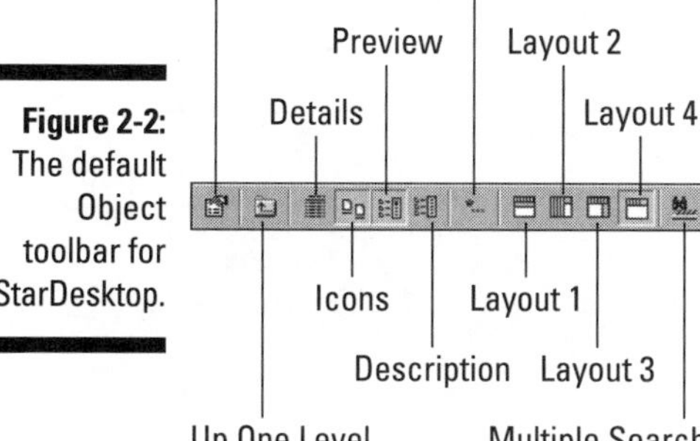

Figure 2-2: The default Object toolbar for StarDesktop.

For information on how to use many of these buttons, see "Arranging your StarDesktop," later in this chapter.

Main toolbar

Another important StarOffice toolbar is the Main toolbar that appears in the document windows of many of the StarOffice tools. No Main toolbar is available for StarDesktop, but because this toolbar is a major feature of tools such as StarWriter, I decided to mention the Main toolbar in this discussion of the other StarOffice toolbars.

The Main toolbar normally appears on the left side of the workspace in a document window, as shown in Figure 2-3. Like the Object toolbar, the Main toolbar is part of the document window, and the buttons on the toolbar vary, depending on which StarOffice tool you're using in the window. You can find information about using buttons on the Main toolbar for various StarOffice tools in the chapters about those tools.

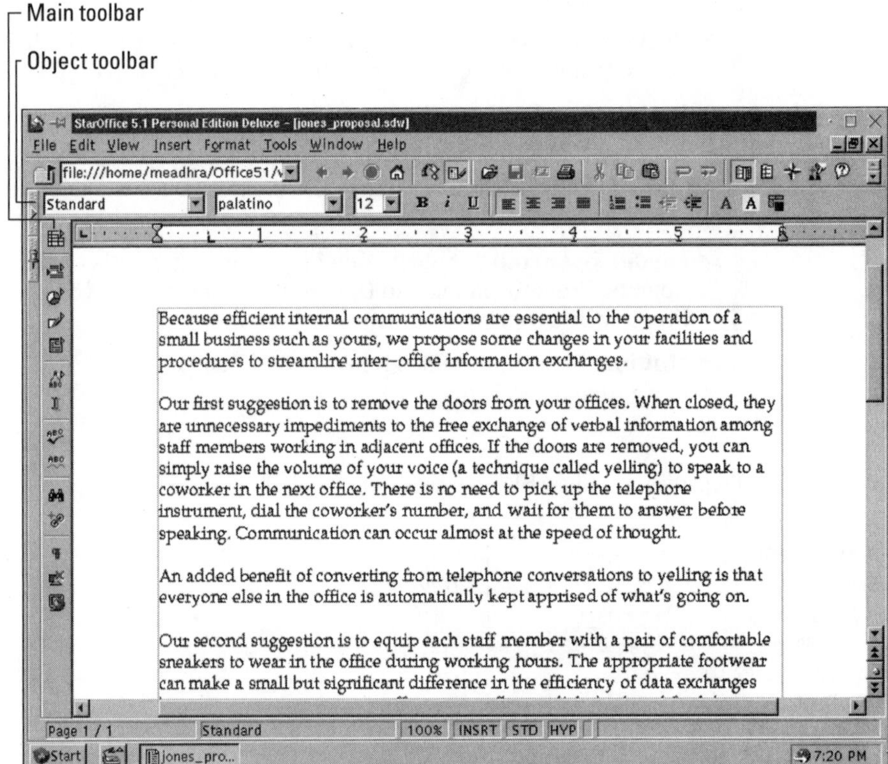

Figure 2-3: The Main toolbar is a prominent feature of a StarWriter window.

Task bar

The Task bar (refer to Figure 2-1) occupies a strip of screen real estate across the bottom of the StarOffice program window. Its name — Task bar — as well as its function are reminiscent of the Windows 95 or 98 taskbar. The StarOffice Task bar includes a Start button at the left end of the bar and a clock at the right end of the bar. Near the Start button is the Desktop button, which gives you instant access to StarDesktop no matter how many document windows are open on top of it.

When you open a document for editing, a corresponding button, shown in Figure 2-4, appears on the Task bar between the Desktop button and the clock. Clicking one of these document buttons brings the corresponding window to the forefront, restoring the window to its normal size if necessary — just like it does in Windows 95 or 98.

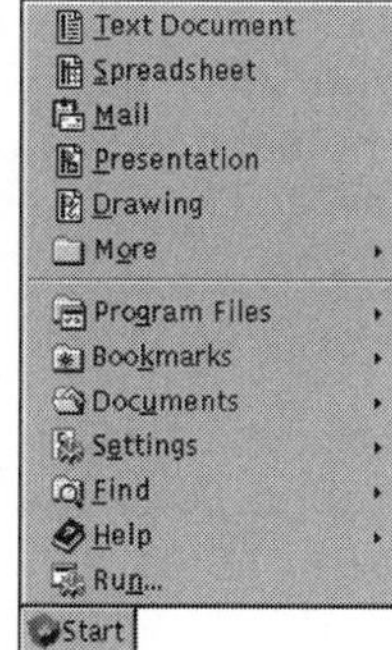

Figure 2-4: The Start menu ensures that document creation commands are always available.

If you click the Start button in the StarOffice Task bar, a Start menu pops up that is similar to the menu shown in Figure 2-4. (Now where do you suppose Star Division got that idea?) Selecting one of the commands from the top portion of the Start menu instructs StarOffice to create a new document of the selected type.

The commands and options available in the lower portion of the Start menu vary somewhat, depending on the system in which you're running StarOffice. The options vary because the program attempts to integrate some of your system commands with StarOffice-specific commands. For example, on the KDE-based test system I use, StarOffice is able to detect most of the programs listed on the K-button menu and make them available on the Program Files submenu of the StarOffice Start menu. That means quick, easy access to other programs without having to take steps such as minimizing the StarOffice window first. Pretty slick, huh?

One nearly hidden feature of the Task bar is something called the Quickstart bar. The Quickstart bar is the space between the Start button and the Desktop button on the Task bar. You can drag an icon from the desktop and drop it on the Quickstart bar to create a button that gives you instant access to whatever that icon does.

For example, if you drag the New Spreadsheet icon from the desktop and drop it on the Quickstart bar, you have a button that opens a new StarCalc window and creates a new spreadsheet document. Similarly, if you drag an icon for an existing document file from the desktop and drop it on the Quickstart bar, the resulting button opens that document file for editing.

Remember that the Task bar is always available anytime the StarOffice window is open, so the buttons in the Quickstart bar give you one-click access to the documents or features they represent without having to open a menu or display StarDesktop first.

Although the number of buttons you can have on the Quickstart bar is limited only by the length of the Task bar, bar buttons are small and display only an icon for the type of file they represent (such as a spreadsheet or text document). Quickstart buttons have no other labels to distinguish between, for example, a button that creates a new text document and one that opens an existing text document. This makes populating the Quickstart bar with too many buttons for the same type of file impractical.

The Quickstart bar is a handy feature, and you may well find it convenient to have Quickstart buttons for a few frequently used documents. But eventually, you may need to remove or replace a Quickstart button. To do so, just right-click the button that you want to get rid of and choose Remove from the pop-up menu. Poof, the button's gone.

The main desktop

The big, open workspace in the middle of the StarOffice program window is where you interact with StarDesktop. You can configure the desktop workspace a number of different ways, but the default setting is to display an assortment of large icons. Double-clicking an icon tells StarOffice to take the associated action, such as creating a new document.

When you install StarOffice, the program populates StarDesktop with a number of helpful icons. Among them, you find the following:

- **New Drawing:** Opens StarDraw and creates a new drawing file
- **New HTML Document:** Opens StarWriter and creates a new HTML document (Web page)
- **New Mail:** Opens StarMail and creates a new e-mail message
- **New Presentation:** Opens StarImpress and creates a new presentation file
- **New Spreadsheet:** Opens StarCalc and creates a new spreadsheet file
- **New Text Document:** Opens StarWriter and creates a new text document file
- **Printer Setup:** Opens the StarOffice printer setup utility

- **Star Division:** Connects to the Internet and displays the home page of the Star Division Web site
- **StarChannels:** Connects to the Internet and displays the StarChannels Web page

In addition to these standard icons, you can add a number of other useful icons to StarDesktop. For example, you can insert any of the following kinds of icons:

- **Database:** A link to a StarOffice database file
- **Folder:** A link to a directory on your hard drive or network
- **FTP Account:** Access configuration for an FTP server so you can set up StarOffice to download files using the File Transfer Protocol
- **IMAP Account:** A StarMail inbox for an IMAP e-mail account (Internet or intranet e-mail)
- **Link:** A link to any file or Internet address
- **News:** A StarDiscussion inbox for an Internet newsgroup account
- **Outbox:** An outbox for outgoing e-mail messages
- **POP3 Account:** A StarMail inbox for a POP3 e-mail account (Internet or intranet e-mail)
- **Search:** Predefined search criteria
- **Subscriptions:** A Web page that you can download and store on your hard drive for offline access
- **VIM Account:** A StarMail inbox for a VIM e-mail account (corporate LAN e-mail)

StarDesktop is really a directory on your hard drive, so if you store document files in the desktop directory, their icons appear in the StarDesktop work area. Conversely, you can copy or move documents to StarDesktop by dragging and dropping their file icons onto the desktop workspace. StarOffice then stores those files in the desktop directory.

In Windows, StarDesktop starts out with a different set of icons on the desktop. StarOffice detects the shortcut icons on your Windows 95 or 98 desktop and integrates them into StarDesktop in place of the standard StarOffice desktop icons. This feature is part of the Integrated Desktop. If you choose View⇨Integrated Desktop, StarOffice replaces the standard Windows 95 or 98 desktop with StarDesktop. StarOffice expands to occupy the full screen, and the StarOffice Task bar replaces the Windows 95 or 98 taskbar. To return StarOffice to a normal window, just choose View⇨Integrated Desktop again to deselect the feature.

Explorer

Explorer is the StarOffice built-in file management utility. It normally resides in a special collapsible window docked to the left side of StarDesktop. When Explorer is collapsed, it appears as an extra border on the left side of the StarOffice window and contains two thin buttons. (You can see it if you look closely at the left side of the screen in Figure 2-1.) If you click the Show button (the button with the arrow pointing toward the desktop), the Explorer window appears, as shown in Figure 2-5. When the Explorer window opens, the button that you used to open it changes into the Hide button. (The arrow on the button reverses direction.) If you click the Hide button, the Explorer window returns to its hidden position as a thin strip along the border of the window.

When you expand the Explorer window, it slides out in front of the desktop and any document windows that may be open, obscuring a portion of those windows. You can click the Stick button (the button with a push pin on it, located just below the Show/Hide button) to change the way the Explorer window interacts with the desktop and document windows.

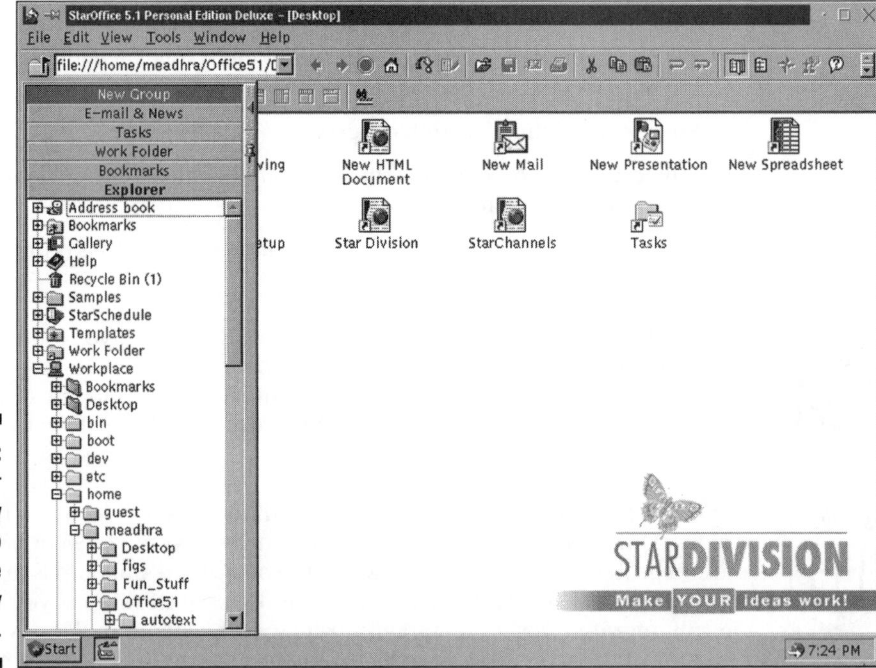

Figure 2-5: The Explorer window expanded to show the directory tree.

When the Explorer window is in *sticky* mode, StarOffice incorporates it into the desktop — the desktop workspace automatically shrinks to make room for the Explorer window, and the contents of the desktop workspace are rearranged to fit the smaller space. As a result, none of the desktop contents are obscured by the Explorer window when it's in sticky mode, but the Explorer window may be obscured by document windows floating over it because it becomes part of the desktop. Just click the push-pin button (Stick/Floating) again when you want to float the Explorer window over the desktop.

The contents of the Explorer window are subdivided into groups. Each group has its own header button, and clicking that button displays the contents of that group. (If you've used Microsoft Outlook and its Outlook bar, then you're familiar with this arrangement.) Each of the default groups contains a different kind of information, as summarized in the following list:

- **E-mail & News:** This group contains icons for your e-mail and newsgroup accounts as well as your outbox and other e-mail folders. Double-clicking an account icon opens the associated mailbox window.
- **Tasks**: You use the icons in this group to create new StarOffice documents. The icons work just like the corresponding StarDesktop icons — clicking an icon tells StarOffice to create a new document of the selected type (for instance, a text document or a spreadsheet) and display it in a new document window. The Tasks group in Explorer even includes icons for several document types that don't normally appear on StarDesktop.
- **Work Folder:** The icons in this group give you access to the subfolders and files in the default folder, defined as your preferred storage place for StarOffice documents. Clicking an icon in this group opens a document window to display the contents. If you click a folder icon, StarOffice displays the files and subfolders contained in that folder. If you click an icon for a document file, StarOffice opens that document for editing.
- **Bookmarks:** Web surfing is easy with fast access to your bookmarks in this Explorer group. StarOffice even gets you started with an assortment of preset bookmarks, neatly arranged into several subfolders. By default, the Bookmark group is displayed in hierarchical arrangement. To display the contents of a subfolder, click the plus (+) sign beside the icon. To view a bookmarked Web page, simply click its bookmark icon. StarOffice connects to the Internet (if necessary) and displays the page.
- **Explorer:** Yes, one of the Explorer groups is named Explorer. This group displays your system directory structure in an outline type of hierarchy that is sometimes called a tree structure. In Figure 2-6, the items starting with Address Book and going through Work Folder are direct links to your StarOffice resources. The Workplace branch of the tree gives you access to your system's entire directory structure.

  Using Explorer to navigate your system directories is a lot like using the left panel in a Windows 95 or 98 Windows Explorer window. The StarOffice Explorer window starts out showing the top-level directories.

You can click a plus sign (+) beside a directory item to expand that entry and show the subdirectories of that branch of the directory tree. With Explorer, you can drill down to subdirectories nested within subdirectories within subdirectories to see as much detail of your directory structure as you need. Clicking a minus sign (-) beside a directory entry collapses that branch of the tree to show less detail.

If you double-click a folder icon in Explorer, StarOffice opens a viewing window on the desktop to display the contents of the selected directory. Then you can work with the files and folders from the selected directory on the desktop. Double-clicking a file icon opens the file, and right-clicking a file icon opens a pop-up menu of other choices, such as Copy, Delete, and Rename.

Explorer shows directories and subdirectories, but not individual files within directories. To see individual files, you must display the contents of the selected directory in the desktop — or in the Beamer window. (See the "Beamer" section of this chapter for more details.)

You can turn the Explorer window on or off by choosing View⇨Explorer from the StarOffice menu. Disabling Explorer completely removes Explorer from the StarOffice window, unlike clicking the Hide button which simply reduces the Explorer window to its small, hidden size. Even so, Explorer is never far away. You can turn it back on by choosing the same command again.

To make Explorer more useful, you can create new groups in the Explorer window and rename or delete existing Explorer groups. You can populate the Explorer groups with icons of your choice and change how StarOffice displays those icons. The following list summarizes the Explorer customization options:

- **To create a new group:** Click the New Group button at the top of the Explorer window and enter a name for the group on the General tab of the Create New Group as Link dialog box. Click the Bookmark tab and enter the pathname of the folder you want the group to display in the Target URL box, and then click OK. StarOffice adds a group button to the Explorer window. Clicking that button displays the contents of the specified folder.
- **To remove a group from the Explorer window:** Right-click the group button and choose Remove Group from the pop-up menu that appears. After you confirm the action, StarOffice removes the group from Explorer.
- **To rename a group:** Right-click the group button and choose Rename Group from the pop-up menu that appears. StarOffice highlights the name on the group button. Type a new name and press Enter to record your change.

- **To add a folder icon to a group:** Right-click the background of the group and choose New⇨Folder from the pop-up menu that appears; then enter a name for the folder and click OK. StarOffice creates a new subdirectory of the directory displayed in that group and adds a link icon to the group.
- **To add a File Link icon to a group:** Right-click the background of the group and choose New⇨Link from the pop-up menu that appears, fill in the Properties of Link dialog box (be sure to check the Display in Explorer option on the Bookmark tab), and then click OK. StarOffice creates an icon in the group that is a link to the file or Internet address that you defined in the Link dialog box.
- **To change the way icons in a group are displayed:** Right-click the group button and choose Large Symbols, Small Symbols, or Hierarchical from the pop-up menu that appears. Choosing Large Symbols displays large icons for each item in the group (like the default display in the Tasks group). Choosing Small Symbols displays small icons for each item in the group (like the default display in the Bookmarks group). Choosing Hierarchical displays items in the group in an expandable outline or tree arrangement (like the default display in the Explorer group).
- **To update the display:** Right-click the group button and choose Update from the pop-up menu that appears. StarOffice updates the display in both the Explorer and Beamer windows. You use this option after changing the contents of a folder that has a feature or an outside program that doesn't cause Explorer to update its display automatically.

Beamer

StarOffice Beamer is the companion utility to Explorer. Like Explorer, Beamer lives in a collapsible docked window, but Beamer is normally docked near the top of the StarOffice window between the Function toolbar and the Object toolbar. Figure 2-6 shows both the Explorer and Beamer windows open on the desktop — the Beamer window is the one on top. Expanding and hiding the Beamer window works just like expanding and hiding the Explorer window. And just as you can turn Explorer on and off, you also can turn Beamer on and off by choosing View⇨Beamer.

Beamer automatically displays the contents of whatever is selected in the Explorer window. When you select a directory or subdirectory in Explorer, Beamer displays a list of the files in the selected directory. When you select certain StarOffice resources in the Explorer window (such as the Address Book), Beamer displays the contents of the file (such as a list of Address Book entries).

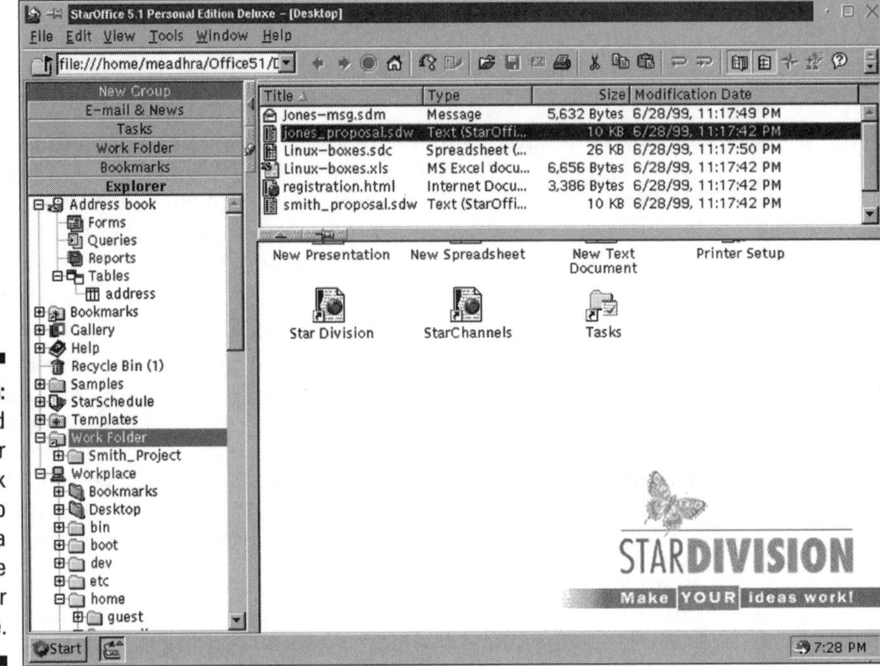

Figure 2-6: Beamer and Explorer work together to provide a complete file-browser feature.

Sometimes the Beamer window doesn't show the contents of the directory that is currently selected in Explorer. If you select a directory in Explorer that contains only subdirectories and no files, Beamer has nothing to display and doesn't update its list. The contents of the previously selected directory remain visible in the Beamer window until you select a directory or resource in Explorer that contains something that Beamer can display.

When Beamer displays a list of files, you can double-click a file to open that file for editing in a regular document window. You can also drag and drop items from Beamer onto your desktop or into a document. For example, you can drag a document file from Beamer to your desktop to move the file to the desktop directory.

If you drag an Address Book entry from Beamer and drop it into a document, StarOffice inserts the address book information into the document at the cursor position. Now that's a handy trick!

Customizing Your StarOffice Environment

Most people like to arrange their personal workspaces to suit their individual preferences and working styles. Some people like to keep their physical desktops completely clear of anything that doesn't pertain directly to the task at hand. (These people are sometimes called *neat freaks.*) Other people prefer to have numerous piles of papers covering their desks so that everything they may need is visible and within reach. (The neat freaks call these folks *slobs.*) But whether you're a neat freak, a slob, or something in between, you're probably more comfortable when your desk is arranged the way you like it.

The same thing applies to StarDesktop and the rest of the StarOffice program. Just as you can rearrange things on your physical desktop to suit your working style, you can rearrange things in StarDesktop and adjust some of the many StarOffice configuration options to customize the StarOffice environment the way you want it.

StarOffice is a highly customizable program with so many configuration options that I don't attempt to cover them all in detail in this book. I do show you how to use some of the more common options to personalize your StarOffice environment.

Working with document windows

When you open a document in StarOffice, the document appears in a separate window within the confines of the main StarOffice program window. Each document, file, Web page, and StarOffice tool appears in its own window, and you can have multiple documents open at one time. If you have six different documents or tools open at one time, then you have six different document windows within the StarOffice program window. The document windows stack on top of StarDesktop — which is really the background for the main StarOffice program window, rather than a separate document window.

A separate button on the StarOffice Task bar represents each document window. Clicking a document button on the Task bar brings that document window to the foreground, where you can work with it. Like shuffling a stack of cards, clicking a Task bar button pulls that document window out of the stack and moves it to the top.

By default, StarOffice opens document windows that are *maximized* to give you the maximum available space in the window's work area. When a document window is maximized, it doesn't have a separate title bar and border but is merged into the main StarOffice program window. As a result, you may not even realize that the document window is, indeed, a separate window — but it is.

Seeing that document windows are, in fact, separate windows is easier when they're floating instead of maximized (see Figure 2-7). A floating document window has its own title bar and border, and you can move and resize the document window independently of the main StarOffice program window. The available workspace in a floating document window isn't as large as in a maximized window, but floating windows enable you to see and compare the contents of two document windows side by side — something you can't do with maximized document windows.

One of the advantages of floating document windows is that you can use drag-and-drop techniques to copy and paste data from one document window to another. Just highlight a selection in one document window and then drag it over and drop it on another document window. StarOffice copies the selection from the first document and pastes it into the second document — provided the information that you're trying to insert is compatible with the second document.

Each document window has a set of buttons in its upper-right corner that control the size of the window. The buttons are easy to see at the right end of the title bar of a floating document window. (See Figure 2-7.) On the other hand, you can easily overlook the buttons in a maximized document window because the maximized document window has no title bar. In this case, the buttons appear at the right end of the StarOffice menu bar. The buttons appear from right to left as follows:

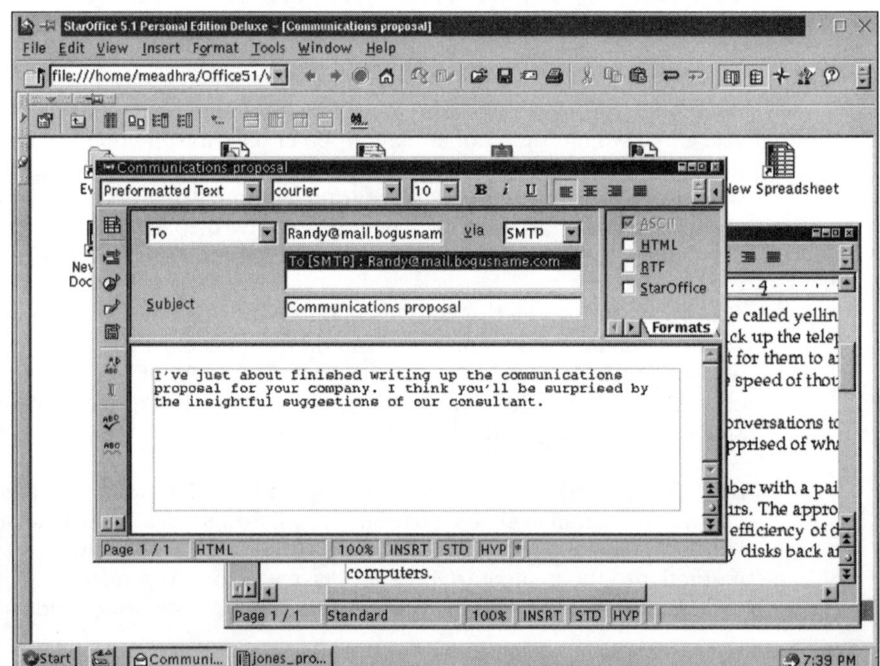

Figure 2-7: You can move and resize floating document windows.

- **Close:** Clicking the Close button closes the window and the document it contains. (If you've made any changes to the document since the last time you saved it, StarOffice prompts you to save the document before closing.)
- **Maximize/Restore:** Clicking the Maximize/Restore button on a floating document window maximizes the window. Clicking the same button on a maximized window restores it to a floating window.
- **Minimize:** Clicking the Minimize button hides the document window from view but doesn't close the document file. The document file remains open, and the document window is still represented by a button on the StarOffice Task bar. Clicking the document window's Task bar button restores the document window to its previous size.
- **Hide/Show:** Clicking the Hide button on a floating window hides the contents of the document window, leaving only the title bar visible. Clicking the button again shows the contents of the window. (Note: This button only appears on floating windows; it isn't available when the document window is maximized.)

Floating document windows have one additional button at the left end of the window's title bar — the Always Visible button, which is represented by a push pin. If you click this button, the window remains visible on top of any other windows, even when those windows are selected.

Docking and undocking windows

The Explorer and Beamer utilities normally appear as *docked* windows, which means that they're attached to the side of the main StarOffice window and you can show or hide their contents with the click of a button. (See the "Explorer" section earlier in this chapter for instructions on how to show or hide the Explorer window; the same technique works with other docked windows.) You can also use some other StarOffice utilities, such as the Stylist and Navigator utilities, as docked windows.

A docked window doesn't have to remain permanently attached to the side of the StarOffice program window. You can undock a docked window to make it a regular floating window with its own title bar and border. Then you can move or resize the floating window at your discretion. For example, Figure 2-8 shows the Explorer utility in a floating window.

To undock a docked window, follow these steps:

1. **If the docked window is not already open, click the Show button to open it. Otherwise, skip to Step 2.**
2. **Hold down Ctrl as you double-click the frame around the docked window.**

You must double-click one of the thin sides of the docked window's frame. Double-clicking the thick side of the window frame (the side that contains the Show/Hide button) doesn't work. When you double-click the right place, StarOffice converts the docked window into a standard floating window with its own title bar and border (refer to Figure 2-8).

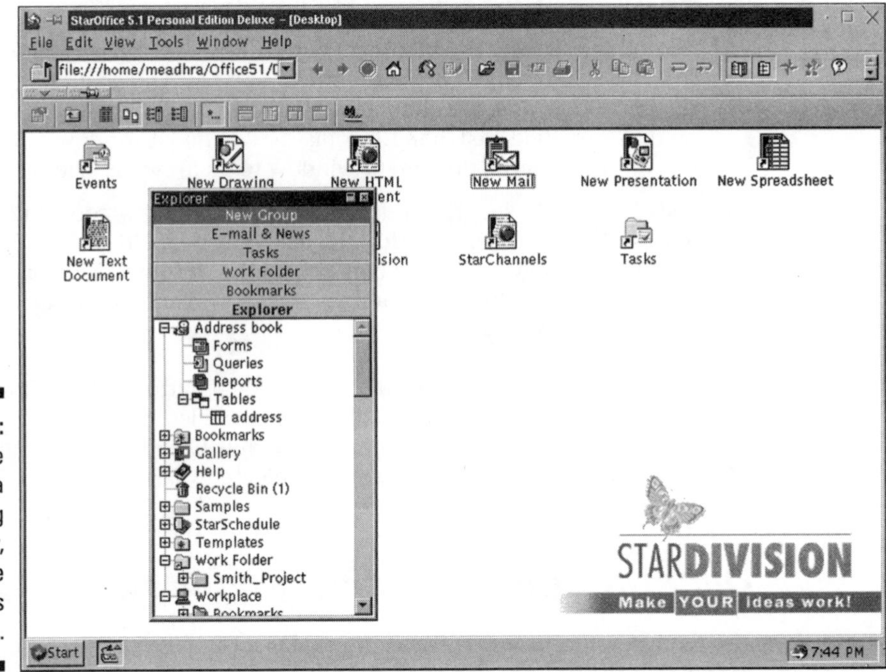

Figure 2-8: The Explore utility in a floating window, cut loose from its moorings.

When a dockable window is floating, you can still switch back and forth between showing and hiding the window's contents. Just double-click the open window's title bar to hide the window contents — only the window's title bar remains visible on-screen. Double-clicking the floating title bar expands the window to show its contents again.

To re-dock a floating dockable window, hold down Ctrl as you drag the window's title bar to the side of the StarOffice program window and then drop it. StarOffice reattaches the window to the side as a docked window.

Working with toolbars

StarOffice toolbars normally appear as a row of buttons attached to the edge of a window. But if you don't like the location of a toolbar, you can move it. To move a toolbar to another side of the window, hold down Ctrl as you click a vacant portion of the toolbar and drag it to the new location. (If you want to attach the toolbar to the side of the window, be sure to drop it on the window border.)

Actually, toolbars don't have to be attached to the side of a window; they can also appear in their own floating windows. To convert a toolbar to a floating window, just hold down Ctrl as you drag the toolbar and drop it somewhere in the middle of the document or program window to which it was attached. The toolbar appears in its own mini-window, complete with a title bar, as shown in Figure 2-9.

You can move a floating toolbar by dragging its title bar. You can also double-click the title bar to hide or show the toolbar buttons. To reattach the floating toolbar to the side of its parent window, hold down Ctrl as you drag the title bar and drop it on the window border.

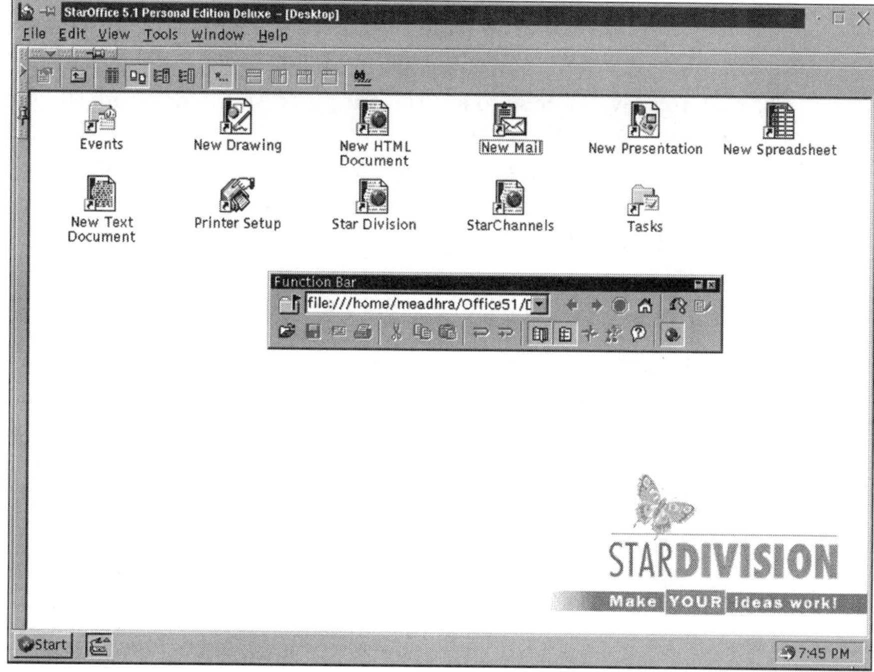

Figure 2-9: Toolbars can float in the middle of a window and be reduced to a simple title bar.

Moving or floating a toolbar in one document window affects the corresponding toolbar in other document windows. For example, if you move the Object toolbar to the right side of the document window while editing a text document in StarWriter, the Object toolbar appears on the right side of a spreadsheet document window as well. In fact, the Object toolbar attaches to the right side of all new and existing document windows in which it appears, until you move it to another location.

Arranging your StarDesktop

StarOffice gives you considerable flexibility in selecting what items appear on your StarDesktop and how they are displayed. The most obvious configuration that you can control is what icons appear on the desktop. StarOffice starts out with an assortment of default icons preinstalled on the desktop. To build an assortment of icons that suit your working style, you can remove, move, and add to these icons as follows:

- **To remove an icon from the desktop:** Right-click the icon and choose Delete from the pop-up menu that appears.
- **To move an icon to a different place on the desktop:** Drag the icon to the new location and drop it there.
- **To align all the icons on the desktop in neat rows:** Right-click the desktop background and choose Arrange Icons➪Align to Grid from the pop-up menu that appears.
- **To arrange all the icons on the desktop in alphabetical order:** Right-click the desktop background and choose Arrange Icons➪Title. (You can also arrange desktop icons by Type, Size, Marked, Read, and Modification Date file attributes.)
- **To add a folder icon to the desktop:** Right-click the desktop background and choose New➪Folder from the pop-up menu that appears; then enter a name for the folder and click OK. StarOffice creates a new subdirectory of the desktop directory and adds a link to the desktop.
- **To add a File Link icon to the desktop:** Right-click the desktop background and choose New➪Link from the pop-up menu that appears; then fill in the Properties of Link dialog box and click OK. StarOffice creates an icon on the desktop that is a link to the file or Internet address that you defined in the Link dialog box.
- **To create an icon on the desktop for an Internet e-mail account inbox:** Right-click the desktop background and choose New➪POP3 Account; then fill in the Properties of POP3 Account dialog box and click OK. (Filling in the dialog box for a POP3 Account is an involved process; see Chapter 21 for more information.) You can follow a similar procedure to create desktop icons for a database, IMAP e-mail account, Internet newsgroup account, e-mail outbox, VIM e-mail account, FTP account, search criteria, or Web subscription.

- **To move a document file icon to the desktop for easy access:** Use Explorer and Beamer to locate the file and display it in the Beamer window. Then drag the file icon from the Beamer window and drop it on the desktop. StarOffice moves the file from its previous location to the desktop directory and displays its icon in StarDesktop.

Getting the details

The default StarDesktop view shows the contents of the desktop folder as large icons arranged on the StarDesktop background. If you need to see more information about the items on the desktop, click the Details button in the StarDesktop Object toolbar. StarOffice displays the contents of the desktop as a list with columns for Title, Type, Size, and Modification Date, as shown in Figure 2-10.

The Details view isn't very useful for viewing the default desktop icons for creating new documents and so forth. (Who cares about the size or modification date of the icon that you click to create a new text document?) However, if you add document and folder icons to your desktop, the information in the Details view can be very helpful indeed.

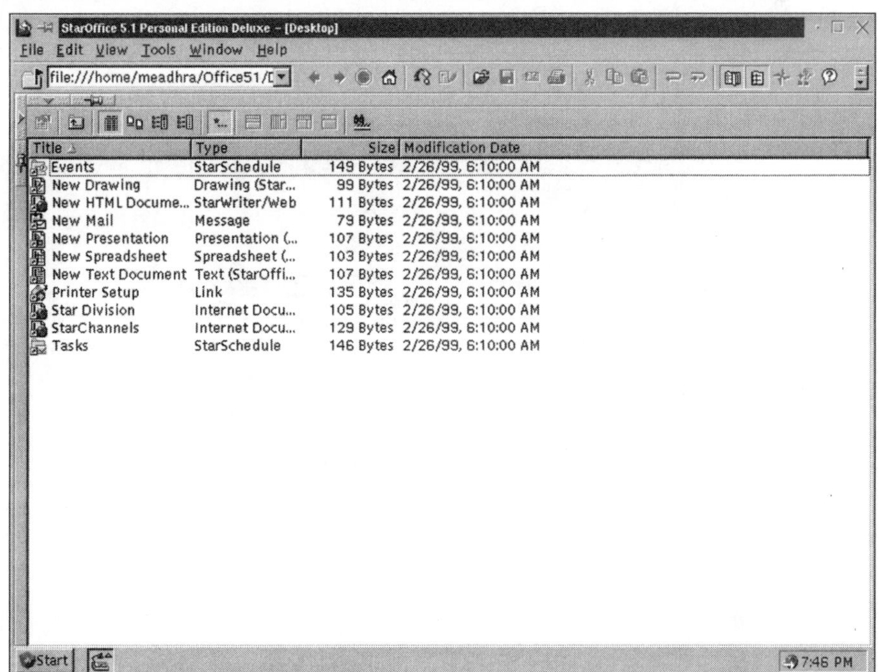

Figure 2-10: StarDesktop in Details view.

If you need access to even more information about a desktop item, select the desktop item that you're curious about and then click the Properties button in the StarOffice Object toolbar. StarOffice displays the Properties dialog box for the selected item. There you can view and edit the settings that define the desktop item.

Displaying the Description pane

Another way to show more information about a selected desktop icon is to display the Description pane of the StarDesktop window. To activate the Description pane, click the Description button in the StarDesktop Object toolbar. When you do, StarOffice splits the StarDesktop window into two sections (called *panes* — get it, window panes), one for desktop icons and one for detailed information about the selected icon. Figure 2-11 shows the Description pane to the right of the main desktop pane — just one of the layouts available for arranging the desktop panes.

Displaying the Preview pane

The Description pane provides some valuable information, but another desktop pane — the Preview pane — can be even more useful when you have document and folder icons on your desktop. The Preview pane automatically displays the contents of the selected desktop item without having to open the item in a separate document window. What a convenient way to peek inside the various folders and files on your desktop!

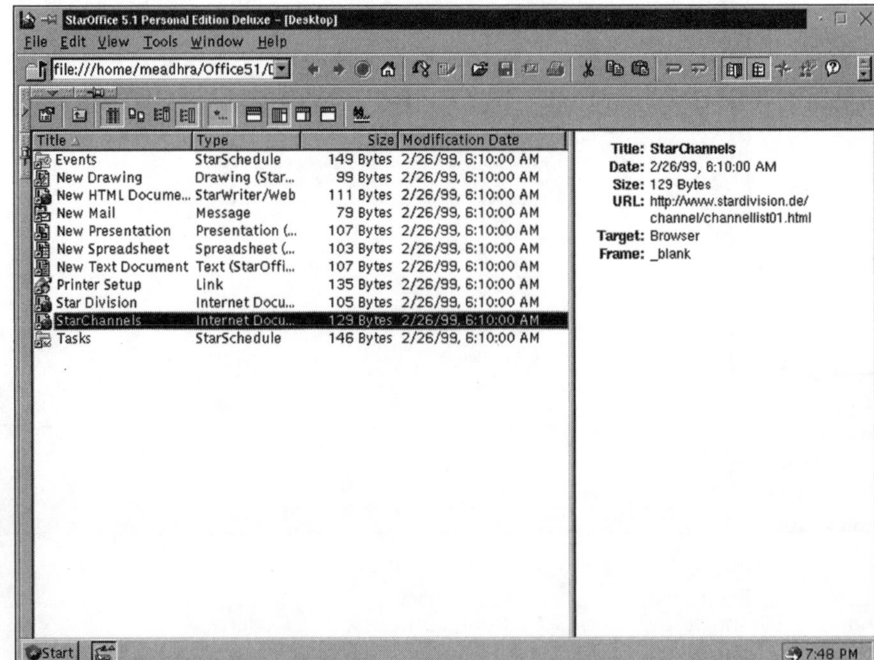

Figure 2-11: The Description pane shows details of the selected desktop icon.

To display the Preview pane, click the Preview button in the StarDesktop Object toolbar. StarOffice splits the desktop to add a separate pane, where the contents of the selected desktop item appear. In Figure 2-12, you can see the Preview pane in the lower-left section of the desktop.

Selecting desktop layouts

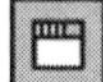

You can choose to display the Description pane, the Preview pane, both, or neither one by clicking the Description and Preview buttons. If either pane is active, you also can choose one of four desktop layouts that determine the relative positions of the desktop icons, the Description pane, and the Preview pane. You can select a desktop layout by clicking one of the Layout buttons in the StarDesktop Object toolbar. For example, Figure 2-11 shows the desktop with the desktop icons and the Description pane arranged using Layout 4. Figure 2-12 shows all three desktop panes active using Layout 3.

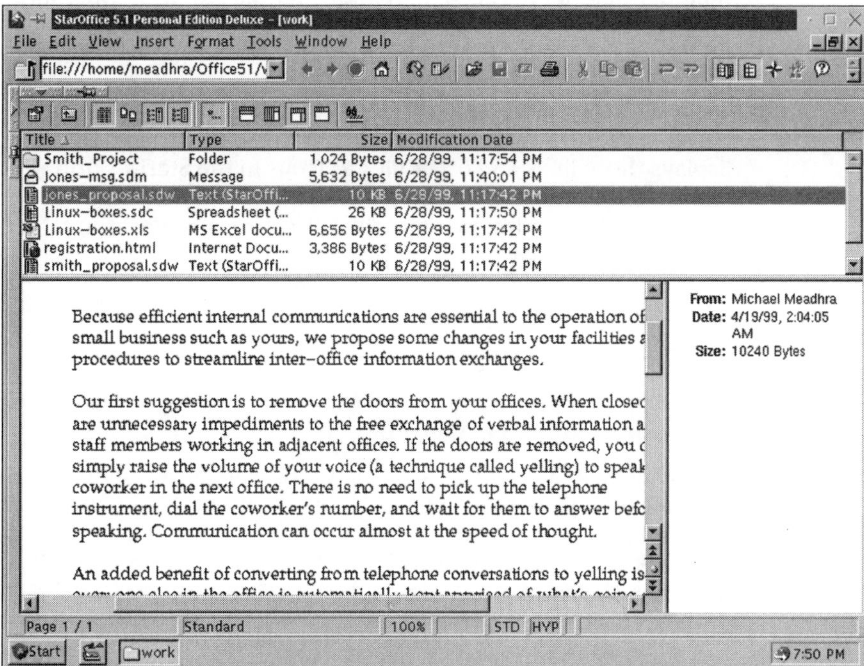

Figure 2-12: The desktop is broken into three panes.

Working with multiple desktops

Many people use more than one desk in the course of their work — or at least more than one work surface. Perhaps you have spread out materials for one project on your desk, for another project on a workbench or conference table, and for yet another on the countertop in a room across the hall. Spreading out your projects in this fashion has some obvious advantages: Everything you need for a particular project is in one place, and you can work on each project without the distraction of parts of other projects cluttering up your current workspace.

StarOffice enables you to create and use multiple virtual desktops so you can manage your computer projects in much the same way. You can have a different set of tools and documents on each of your StarOffice desktops. You can move and copy desktop icons by using Explorer and Beamer to locate files in an alternate desktop folder (or elsewhere) and drag the needed icons to your current desktop.

You can create a separate desktop for each of your projects and populate the desktop with icons for the templates that make creating the project's documents fast and easy. If you need to have the same document or resource available on more than one desktop, just create a link on each desktop and gain instant access to the original document or resource from multiple locations, without the hassle of updating multiple copies of the same file.

Creating a new desktop

StarDesktop is really just a directory containing files, folders, and links to other resources. If the directory is designated as the desktop directory, StarOffice displays those links and other files as icons in the StarDesktop window. By default, StarOffice has only one desktop. But you can create additional desktops as needed by designating other directories as desktop folders. To do so, follow these instructions:

1. **Choose Tools⇨Options.**

   The Options dialog box opens.

2. **Click the Paths entry under the General category in the list box at the left end of the dialog box.**

   By default, StarOffice displays the subcategories under the General category, expanded and ready for selection. If the General category isn't expanded, simply click the General category name in the list box, then click Paths. When you click the Paths subcategory, StarOffice displays a list of default paths in a list box on the right side of the dialog box, as shown in Figure 2-13.

3. **Select Desktop in the Default list box and then click Edit.**

   A Select Paths dialog box opens, showing the path to the current StarDesktop in the Paths list, as shown in Figure 2-14.

4. **Click Add.**

   This action opens a different Select Path dialog box.

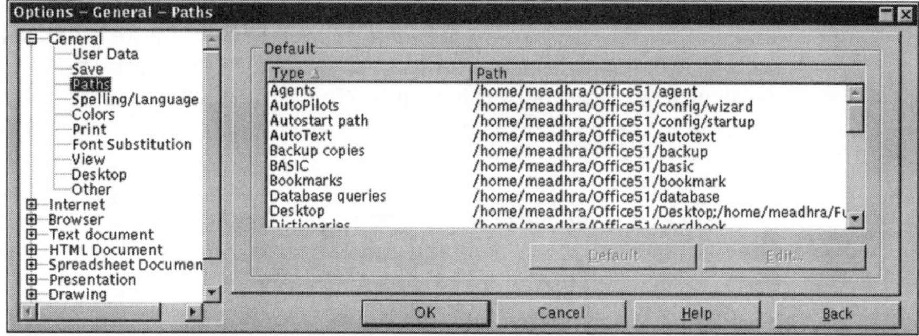

Figure 2-13: You can change the directories where StarOffice stores many files.

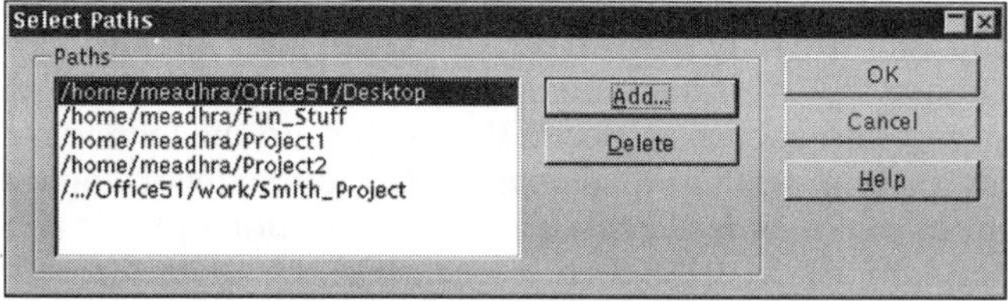

Figure 2-14: The list of available desktops has room for several paths.

5. **Select or type the path to the folder that you want to use for your new desktop.**

   If the folder you want to use doesn't exist, click the Create New Directory button to open yet another dialog box where you can enter a folder name and then click OK to create a new folder.

6. **Click Open.**

   The Select Path dialog box opens and adds the selected path to the Paths list in the Select Paths dialog box.

7. **Repeat Steps 4 through 6 to add more paths to the list as needed, and then click OK.**

8. **Click OK again to close the Options dialog box.**

   Although not immediately apparent, the new folders are available as alternate desktops.

Selecting a desktop to use

StarOffice can display only one desktop at a time. After you define alternate desktops, you must tell StarOffice which one you want to display in the StarDesktop window. To do that, you use a hidden feature of the Desktop button in the Task bar. The Desktop button reacts differently to a simple click, to a right-click, and to a prolonged click (in which you click and hold the left mouse button for a moment).

To select a desktop folder, right-click the Desktop button in the StarOffice Task bar. When the pop-up menu appears (refer to Figure 2-13), select the path to the desired desktop folder from the options on the menu. StarOffice displays the contents of the selected folder in the StarDesktop window. The selected folder remains the StarDesktop window until you select another folder.

By the way, a slow click on the Desktop button brings up a different menu — one that lists the icons available on the current desktop so you can select them, even when obscured by other windows. Handy, eh?

Changing the appearance of StarOffice

StarDesktop isn't the only part of the StarOffice environment that you can change. Choose Tools⇨Options to open the Options dialog box, click the various categories and subcategories in the list box on the left side of the dialog box, and peruse the settings available for each subcategory on the right side of the Options dialog box. Far too many configuration options are available for me to attempt to describe them all. If you're the adventurous type, you can try experimenting with some of the options.

One setting that you may want to try adjusting is located on the View subcategory under the General category. The Look & Feel drop-down list box gives you a choice of four different settings that control the appearance of things like menus, dialog box buttons, and title bars of document windows. StarOffice can emulate the appearance of programs in one of four different operating systems. You have a choice of OS/2, XWindows, Macintosh, or Star Division (which is similar to Windows 95 or 98). Make your selection and then click OK to test it. Try each of the settings to see which one you like the best.

If you're really brave, you can make even more substantive changes to the StarOffice user interface. Choose Tools⇨Configure to open the Configuration dialog box. There you can change the commands that appear on the StarOffice menus, assign commands to function keys, customize the status bar and toolbars, and link macros to various StarOffice events. I don't advise you to mess around with these settings, but I want you to know that you can do so.

Part II

Working with Words in StarWriter

"It's a ten-step word processing program. It comes with a spell-checker, grammar-checker, cliché-checker, whine-checker, passive/aggressive-checker, politically correct-checker, hissy-fit-checker, pretentious pontificating-checker, boring anecdote-checker, and a Freudian reference-checker."

In this part . . .

The word processing program is number one on nearly everyone's list of most used components in an office suite. StarWriter, the subject of this part of the book, is StarOffice's word processing tool. It delivers all the features you expect of a modern word processing program, from basic text editing to advanced formatting with styles, plus handy features, such as spell-checking, AutoCorrect, and AutoPilots and templates. The chapters in this part show you how to use all these tools and more.

Chapter 3

Writing Like a Star

In This Chapter

- Checking out StarWriter, the word processing tool
- Starting with a blank text document
- Entering and editing text
- Formatting text
- Saving your work
- Revising and editing documents
- Getting it down on paper — printing

Just about everyone needs to work with text documents sooner or later, and for many people, text documents make up the vast majority of their work. As a result, StarWriter, the StarOffice word processing tool, is probably the most frequently used tool in the StarOffice suite. Whether you're writing a simple letter or memo, or composing a more elaborate document such as a proposal, thesis, or research paper, StarWriter can handle the job.

This chapter introduces the StarWriter tool and covers basic text editing and formatting. I also show you how to save and print your documents and how to use StarWriter to open and edit text documents created in Microsoft Word.

Introducing StarWriter

StarWriter is the StarOffice word processing tool — the tool you use for creating and editing text documents. These text documents can be anything from a memo or shopping list to a fancy sales proposal or even the manuscript for a book. Text documents are composed primarily of, you guessed it, text, but StarOffice isn't restricted to working with text alone. You can also incorporate pictures, tables, and scientific formulas in your StarOffice documents.

StarWriter is *not* a separate word processing program. Instead, it is an integrated component of the StarOffice program. You can't separate StarWriter from StarOffice — it exists only in the context of the entire StarOffice program. In fact, StarWriter is really just a convenient label for the StarOffice built-in features for working with text documents. If you're accustomed to working with stand-alone word processing programs or other office suites that are really collections of separate programs, the tight integration of the StarOffice tools may take some getting used to.

Creating a New Text Document

The process for creating a new text document with StarOffice is probably a little different from what you're used to with other programs. When you work with text documents in StarOffice, you don't start by opening the word processing program that is part of the office suite before you create the document within that program. Instead, you simply create a text document from StarDesktop (or anywhere else in the program) and StarOffice automatically displays the new document in a StarWriter document window. In fact, you can't open the StarWriter word processing tool in StarOffice *except* by opening or creating a text (or HTML) document.

Starting a new document

You can find most of the StarOffice document creation tools in StarDesktop. (For more information on working with StarDesktop, see Chapter 2.) You can also create a new document using commands that are available from within StarWriter and other document windows. Because StarWriter is an integrated part of the StarOffice program — instead of being a separate, stand-alone program — you don't find any real difference between creating a new document when a StarWriter document window is open and creating a document from the desktop, except that the desktop icons aren't readily available.

To create a new text document, you can use any of the following techniques:

- Double-click the New Text Document icon in the StarDesktop work area.
- Choose File⇨New⇨Text Document from the StarOffice menu.
- Right-click the desktop background in StarDesktop and choose New⇨Documents⇨Text Document from the pop-up menu that appears.
- Click the Start button in the StarOffice Task bar and choose Text Document.

Regardless of the technique you use to tell StarOffice you want to create a new text document, the result is the same: StarOffice opens a document window (see Figure 3-1) containing a new blank text document and the StarWriter toolbars. Also, the StarOffice menu bar changes to display the StarWriter menus (Insert and Format menus) as well as some additional commands that appear on the standard menus. The new document doesn't replace the current document in the document window, although it may appear to do so because the new document window appears on top of other open document windows and obscures them from your view. The new document is labeled `Untitled` — at least until you save the document and give it a different name.

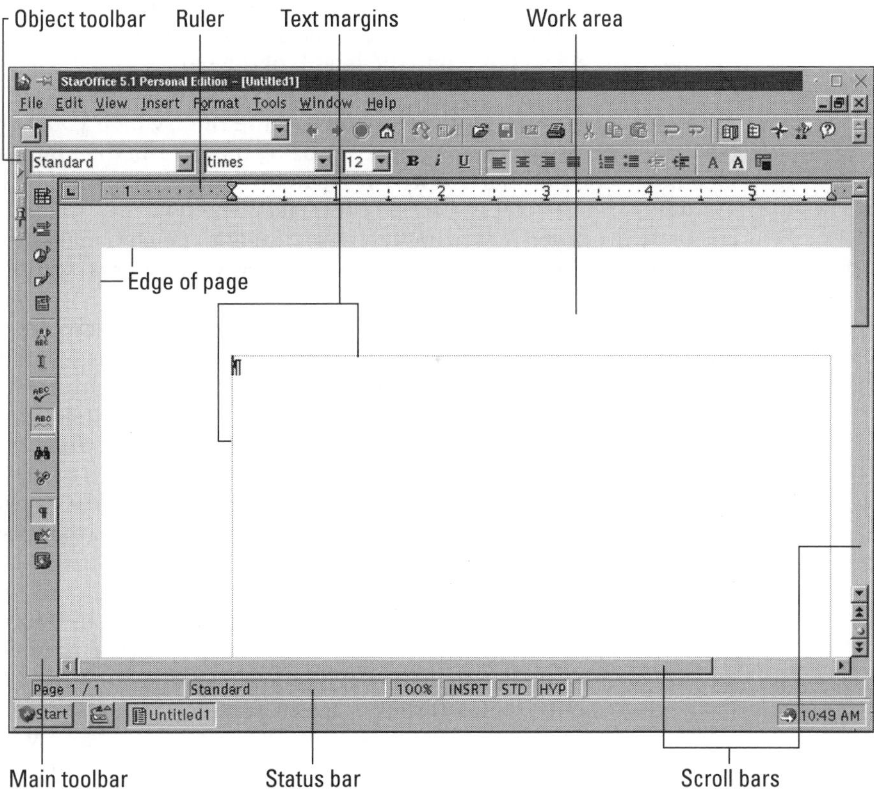

Figure 3-1: A new text document in a StarWriter document window.

Introducing the StarWriter document window

As you can see in Figure 3-1, the StarWriter document window doesn't have any distinctive markings identifying it as StarWriter. The work area in the center of the window emulates a blank piece of paper — nothing about it is very distinctive. The new document is, literally and figuratively, a blank page awaiting your input.

A white rectangle on a gray background represents the working page, although if you're using the default magnification setting, you probably won't see the entire page displayed within the StarWriter window. The gray lines visible within the page represent the edges of the text margins. The text insertion point cursor is a flashing vertical line that appears in the upper-left corner of the text area.

Scroll bars on the right and bottom edges of the work area enable you to view different parts of your document page. They work just like scroll bars in most other programs: You click the arrow buttons at either end of the scroll bar to scroll the window in that direction and bring a different portion of your document into view. For bigger moves, you can just drag the scroll button in the middle of the scroll bar along the length of the bar.

At the top edge of the work area, you find the ruler, which you can use to set tabs and indents for your text. I cover using the ruler in the "Tackling tabs and indents" section of this chapter. You can turn the ruler on and off by choosing View⇨Ruler. The ruler is a *toggle* command, which means that if the ruler is currently displayed, choosing the View⇨Ruler command makes it go away, and choosing the same command again causes the ruler to reappear.

The row of buttons immediately above the ruler is the StarWriter Object toolbar. (Anyway, that's where the StarWriter Object toolbar is located in Figure 3-1. You can move the toolbar to other locations if you want. See Chapter 2 for instructions on how to do it.) You can turn the StarWriter Object toolbar on or off by choosing View⇨Toolbars⇨Object Bar. The buttons and drop-down list boxes on the StarWriter Object toolbar provide a selection of the most commonly used text formatting tools. You can find instructions for using most of them in the "Making Your Text Look Pretty with Formatting" section of this chapter.

The toolbar that appears on the left side of the work area in Figure 3-1 is the StarWriter Main toolbar. (Again, this is the default position of the Main toolbar, but you can find instructions in Chapter 2 on how to move it to other locations.) Choose View⇨Toolbars⇨Main Toolbar to turn the toolbar on or off. The buttons in the Main toolbar give you access to a variety of major features of StarWriter such as the Insert Table dialog box, the AutoText feature, the spell checker, and the Direct Cursor feature.

The Status bar at the bottom of the StarWriter document window (just above the StarOffice Task bar) shows information about the current document and about the StarWriter operating mode. From left to right, the Status bar displays the current document page number, the page template in use, screen magnification, insert or overtype mode, selection mode, and edit or activate hyperlink mode. You can turn the Status bar on or off by choosing View⇨Status Bar.

Typing and Editing Text

Basic text entry and editing techniques in StarWriter follow the same conventions used in almost all word processing programs that employ a graphical user interface (where you interact with the program by clicking icons and making selections with a mouse). These conventions have evolved over time and have become a de facto standard whether you're working in Windows, Linux, or Mac OS. If you've ever used Microsoft Word, WordPerfect, Windows WordPad, or just about any other word processing software, then you already know how to enter and edit text in StarWriter. The following list gives you a quick overview of the basics:

- The flashing vertical bar cursor marks the insertion point where new text is added to the page. The cursor starts in the upper-left corner of the page and normally must remain within the confines of the text you have entered into your document — for example, you can't position the insertion point cursor at the bottom of the page until you've entered enough text to fill the page to that point. (The exception to this is when you're using the StarWriter Direct Cursor feature, which I explain in Chapter 6.)
- To add text to the page, just begin typing.
- Use the arrow keys to move the insertion point cursor around in your text. The left and right arrow keys move the insertion point one character left or right. The up and down arrow keys move the insertion point up or down one line.
- Use the Backspace and Delete keys to erase your typing mistakes. (The Backspace key erases the character to the left of the cursor, and the Delete key erases the character to the right of the cursor.)
- StarWriter automatically wraps text to fit within the page margins so that you don't have to press Enter at the end of each line. Use the Enter key only to mark the end of a paragraph.
- Use the I-beam pointer to position the insertion point cursor and to select text for editing.
    - To move the insertion point cursor to a new location, simply click the I-beam pointer at the desired location in your text.
    - To select a block of text for editing, drag the I-beam pointer across the text you want to select. After you release the mouse button, the text is highlighted and any editing commands you issue apply to the selected text.
    - To select a block of text that is inconvenient to select by dragging, click the I-beam pointer at the beginning of the text block you want to select and then hold down the Shift key as you click the I-beam pointer at the end of the text block. StarOffice highlights all the text in between.

  - To select an individual word, just double-click the word.
  - To quickly select a whole line of text, triple-click anywhere in the line.

- To delete the selected text, press the Backspace or Delete key.
- To replace the selected text, just start typing. The newly typed text automatically replaces the selection.
- To move a block of text, select the text you want to move and then drag and drop it to a new location within your document. (To drag and drop a selection, point to the selection, press and hold the main mouse button, and then drag the pointer to the new location and release the mouse button to drop the selection there.)
- To copy a block of text, select the text you want to copy and then press and hold the Ctrl key as you drag and drop the selected text to a new location within your document.
- You can also use the StarWriter built-in clipboard to cut, copy, and paste blocks of text.

- To cut text from your document and save it to the clipboard for later use, select the text you want to cut and then choose Edit➪Cut, press Ctrl+X, or click the Cut button in the Function toolbar.
- To copy text from your document and save it to the clipboard for later use, select the text you want to copy and then choose Edit➪Copy, press Ctrl+C, or click the Copy button in the Function toolbar.
- To paste text from the clipboard into your document, position the insertion point where you want to insert the text and then choose Edit➪Paste, or press Ctrl+V, or click the Paste button in the Function toolbar.

Making Your Text Look Pretty with Formatting

Plain, unadorned text is just plain boring. Plain text was the standard in the days of the typewriter (do you remember that antique apparatus?) and hung on into the early days of computers and dot matrix printers. But those days are over. Now that nearly everyone uses laser and inkjet printers, typeset-style fonts and formatting are almost universally available and easy to use. Taking advantage of them to make your documents more attractive and easier to read just makes sense.

Selecting fonts and text sizes

Perhaps the most basic formatting decision you need to make is font selection. Choosing the shape and size of the letters that make up your text profoundly affects both the aesthetics and the legibility of your document. Graphic artists sometimes spend years studying the subtleties of different typefaces and how to use them effectively. In the absence of that kind of background, you can choose the fonts you want to use for your documents by following your own good taste, combined with observations of the typefaces used in books, magazines, and documents that you consider attractive. StarWriter makes implementing your font choices easy.

The text you enter in a StarWriter document appears in a default font (usually Times, 12-point). If you like that font, you don't need to do anything. You can determine what font is currently in use by selecting some text. StarWriter displays the current font name in the Font box (second box from the left in the StarWriter Object toolbar) and the text size in the Size box just to the right of the Font box. Changing the font and size settings are easy, just use the appropriate technique from the following list:

- To change the font selection, first select the text you want to change and then select the new font name from the Font drop-down list box in the StarWriter Object toolbar.
- To change the text size of the selected text, choose a new text size from the Size drop-down list box.
- To change the font or size of new text that you insert into your document, position the insertion point cursor at the correct place in the document (or at the point were you want to insert new text), and make your selections from the Font and Size drop-down list boxes. Any new text that you enter into your document appears in the new font and size.

Technically, the terms *typeface, typestyle,* and *font* all have slightly different meanings. However, most people use the terms interchangeably to mean a set of type characters with a distinctive appearance. The term *style* refers to variations of the basic typeface such as bold or italic versions. *Size* refers to the size of the text measured from the top of the tallest letters to the bottom of the *descenders* (the tails of letters such as "g" and "y" that hang down below most other letters) and is expressed in *points* (a point is a printer's unit of measure and equals approximately 1/72 inch). Because different typefaces have different proportions, text set in one typeface may look larger or smaller and take up more or less horizontal space than the same text set in another typeface, even though they are both the same size, say 12-point.

Changing fonts and text sizes using the StarWriter Object toolbar is fast and easy. However, if you don't know what each of the fonts listed in the Font drop-down list box looks like, you may need to try a few different fonts before you find the one you want. StarWriter provides an alternative font selection technique that enables you to preview your font selection and gives you access to some additional formatting options that aren't available on the StarWriter Object toolbar. Here's the way the technique works:

1. **Select the text you want to format or position the insertion point cursor at the location where you want to insert text using the new format.**
2. **Choose Format⇨Character.**

   StarOffice opens the Character dialog box.
3. **Click the Font tab.**

   This action displays the font formatting options shown in Figure 3-2. StarOffice displays the current font settings in the Font, Style, and Size boxes. The Preview box in the lower-right corner of the dialog box gives you a brief sample of how your selected text looks using the current settings.

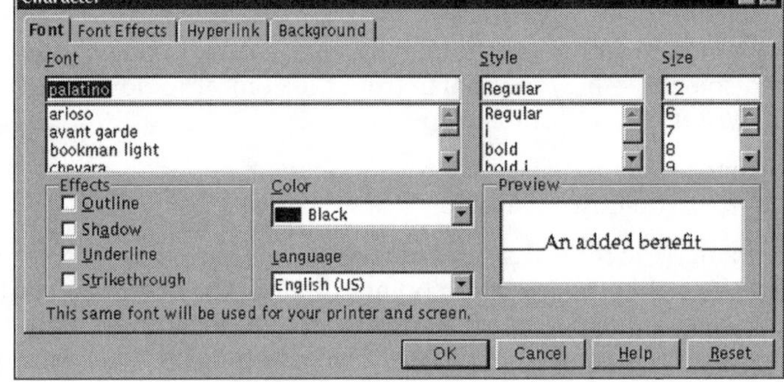

Figure 3-2: The Character dialog box gives you access to more font selection and formatting options.

4. **Change the settings by making new selections from the list boxes below the Font, Style, and Size boxes.**

   You may need to scroll through the list boxes in order to see all of the possible choices. You can also select one or more of the check boxes in the Effects box and choose a different text color from the Color drop-down list box. As you make your selections, the text in the Preview box changes to reflect the new settings.
5. **(Optional) Click the Font Effects tab and make additional formatting selections there.**

   The Font Effects tab is where you find More Effects (All caps, Lower case, Small caps, Title case, and Blinking), Position (Superscript, Normal, or Subscript), Spacing (Adjust the space between words and between letters), and options to customize underlining and strikethrough effects.

6. **If you're satisfied with the character formatting settings, click OK.**

   StarWriter closes the Character dialog box and applies the new character formatting settings to the selected text.

Quickly adding bold, italic, and underline

One way to select bold and italic text styles and the underline text effect is to do so by adjusting settings in the Character dialog box, as mentioned in the preceding section. That works great, but StarWriter provides a more convenient alternative — buttons on the StarWriter Object toolbar — for quickly applying the most frequently used formatting options.

- Click the Bold button or press Ctrl+B to add or remove the **bold** style in the selected text.
- Click the Italic button or press Ctrl+I to add or remove the *italic* style in the selected text.

- Click the Underline button or press Ctrl+U to add or remove the underline effect in the selected text.
- Click more than one button to create combination effects. For example, clicking both the Bold and the Italic buttons creates ***bold-italic*** text.

The Bold, Italic, and Underline buttons act as toggle switches. Clicking the button turns on the formatting attribute for the selected text and changes the appearance of the button slightly so that it looks depressed or engaged. If the selected text already has that formatting attribute applied, clicking the button turns it off and returns the button to its normal appearance.

Tackling tabs and indents

Another common formatting task is adjusting tabs and indents. Both are accomplished quickly and easily with the ruler. The ruler shows the tab and indent settings for the paragraph where the insertion point is located. Any changes you make to the ruler affect that paragraph.

Setting tabs

You can create new tab settings anywhere along the length of a line of text with just a couple of mouse clicks, and you can move and delete existing tab settings just as easily. Setting indents for a paragraph is simply a matter of dragging small buttons into position on the ruler.

By default, the ruler starts out with preset tabs at one-inch increments. (Refer to Figure 3-1 and examine the bottom edge of the ruler. Notice the markers under the inch numerals — the markers indicate tabs.)

- To move an existing tab to a new position on the ruler, use your mouse pointer to drag and drop the tab to the new location.
- To remove a tab from the ruler, just drag and drop the tab off the ruler.
- To create a new tab on the ruler, click the button at the left end of the ruler until it displays the symbol for the kind of tab you want to create and then click the ruler where you want to place the tab. The available tab symbols are as follows:
  - •Left tab
  - •Right tab
  - •Decimal tab
  - •Center tab

To use tabs in your text, just press the tab key to insert a tab character, which causes the following text to be aligned with the next tab. The text aligns flush left with a Left tab, flush right with a Right tab, or centered on a Center tab. Decimal tabs are a special case; they apply only to numbers and cause the decimals to be aligned on the tab, regardless of the number of digits to the right or left of the decimal.

Click the NonPrinting Characters On/Off button (the backward "P") in the StarWriter Main toolbar to display paragraph marks (¶), tabs (→), and spaces (·) in your document that wouldn't otherwise be visible on-screen. Displaying the nonprinting characters doesn't change the way your document prints; it only changes the appearance of the document on-screen in StarWriter. Having the nonprinting characters visible makes your document look a bit cluttered (see Figure 3-3) but enables you to see how tabs and other normally invisible characters affect your text. Most importantly, displaying nonprinting characters makes editing them much easier.

Adjusting indents

StarWriter enables you to separately adjust the left and right paragraph indents — the distance a paragraph is inset from the left or right page margins. You can also exercise independent control over the left indent of the first line of a paragraph.

You adjust paragraph indents using the three small arrow-shaped buttons on the ruler. The two lower buttons adjust the left and right indents. The top button adjusts the first-line indent. To increase the right indent of a paragraph, simply drag the right indent button to the left on the ruler. To increase the left indent, drag the left indent button to the right. If you move the left indent button, the first-line indent button moves along with it. If you want to change the first-line indent, simply drag the first-line indent button to a new location on the ruler after positioning the left indent button.

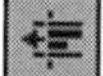 

The StarWriter Object toolbar provides two buttons — Decrease Indent and Increase Indent — that enable you to instantly change the left indent of a paragraph by 1 inch. To indent the paragraph one inch, just click the Increase Indent button. Clicking the Decrease Indent button moves the left indent back one inch to the left.

Figure 3-3 shows the ruler displaying settings for a paragraph that uses both tabs and indents. In this example, StarWriter is also set to display nonprinting characters such as tabs, spaces, and paragraph marks.

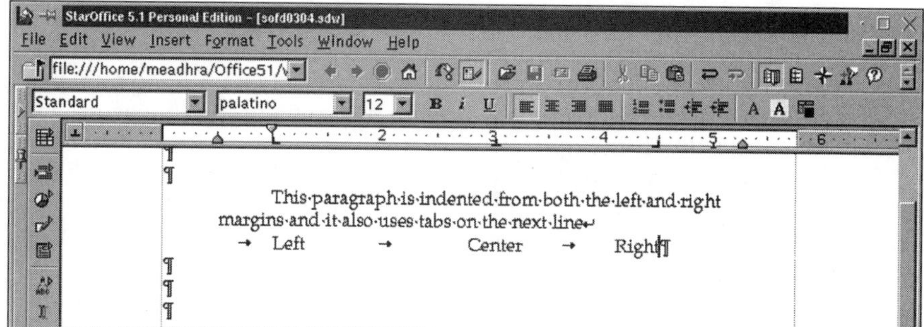

Figure 3-3: Using the ruler to set tabs and indents.

Despite what your typing teacher may have told you, using a tab (or several space characters) is *not* the proper way to indent the first line of a paragraph in a word processing program document. Virtually all modern word processing programs, including StarWriter, have a paragraph formatting feature to handle first-line indents. Using the indent feature instead of a tab or spaces makes your document easier to edit and much easier to translate into another file format for desktop publishing or publication on the Web.

Adjusting alignment and other paragraph formatting

Perhaps the most common paragraph formatting adjustment that you make is selecting text alignment. StarWriter lets you choose between Left, Right, Center, and Justify alignment. The default is Left alignment, which means the text is aligned with the left margin but not with the right margin (text lines break short of the right text margin). Right alignment aligns text with the right margin. Center alignment centers each line of text on the page. If you choose Justify alignment, StarWriter adjusts the spacing between words to force each line of a paragraph (except the last line) to fill the full width of the text margins, thus creating a block of text that's flush with both the left and right margins.

As with many other common formatting options, you can select paragraph alignment by clicking buttons on the StarWriter Object toolbar. Simply click on a paragraph to move the insertion point cursor into that paragraph and then click either the Left, Center, Right, or Justify button to set the paragraph alignment. You can also use shortcut keys to set paragraph alignment. Press Ctrl+L for left align, Ctrl+E for center align, Ctrl+R for right align, and Ctrl+J for justified.

If you want a little more control over the various aspects of paragraph formatting, you can find it in the Paragraph dialog box. You open the Paragraph dialog box by choosing Format⇨Paragraph or right-clicking the paragraph and choosing Paragraph from the pop-up menu that appears. With the Paragraph dialog box open, you can click on one of the tabs and adjust the settings you find there. For example, the Indents & Spacing tab shown in Figure 3-4 lets you control indents by typing precise measurements into the From Left, From Right, and First Line boxes. In addition, you can specify extra spacing to be added above and below the selected paragraph by entering values in the Top and Bottom boxes. You can also set the line spacing for the paragraph by making a selection from the Line Spacing drop-down list box. After adjusting the settings in the Paragraph dialog box, click OK to close the dialog box and apply the settings to the selected paragraphs.

Manipulating margins

StarWriter positions text on your document page within clearly defined text margins. You can change the text margins and a few other page layout options in the Page Style dialog box. To open the dialog box, choose Format⇨Page or right-click and then choose Page from the pop-up menu. After the Page Style dialog box appears, click the Page tab to display the options shown in Figure 3-5.

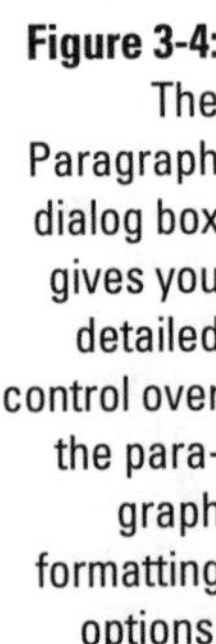

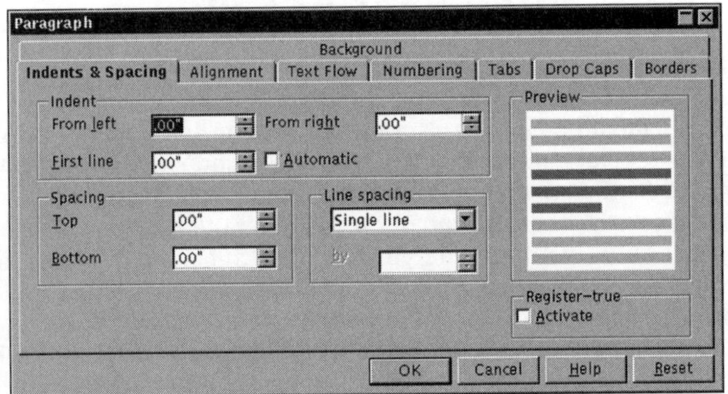

Figure 3-4: The Paragraph dialog box gives you detailed control over the paragraph formatting options.

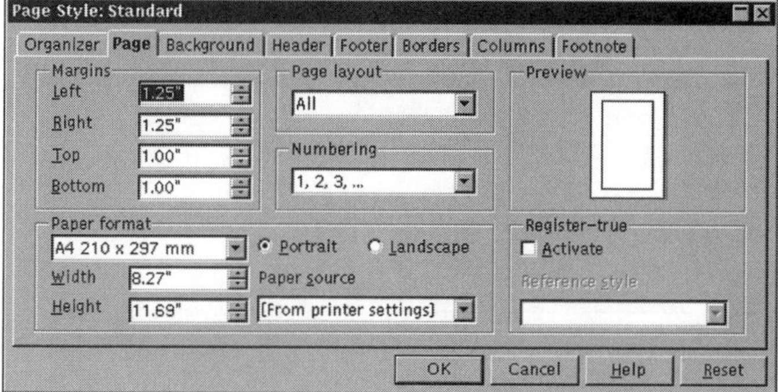

Figure 3-5: You can adjust margins and more in the Page Style dialog box.

The Left, Right, Top, and Bottom boxes in the Margins area let you adjust the distance between the text margins and the edges of the page. The selection you make in the Page Layout drop-down list box determines whether the margin settings apply to left pages, right pages, all pages, or mirrored pages (left and right page margins are mirror images of each other). As you make changes in the settings, the Preview box shows a thumbnail view of their effect. The Numbering drop-down list box in the middle of the Page tab allows you to select a numbering scheme for page numbers in your document. The settings in the Paper Format area in the lower left quadrant of the Page tab enable you to specify the paper size, the orientation (Portrait or Landscape), and which paper tray the printer uses. After adjusting the page settings to your satisfaction, click OK to close the Page Style dialog box and apply the settings to your document.

Saving Your Document

After you invest time and effort entering and editing text and formatting the text to create an attractive document, you undoubtedly want to save that document in a file so that you can reuse it in the future. You may even want to share the document with someone else by giving that person a copy of your document file.

To save your StarWriter document for the first time, follow these steps:

1. **Choose File⇨Save, press Ctrl+S, or click the Save button in the Function toolbar.**

   StarOffice opens the Save As dialog box shown in Figure 3-6. The dialog box shows the contents of your default WorkFolder.

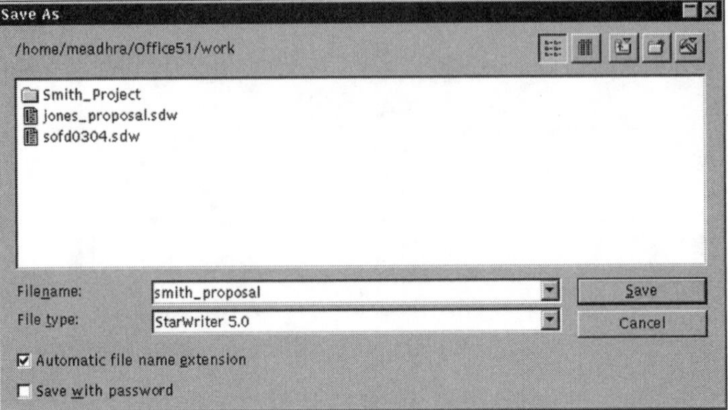

Figure 3-6: The Save As dialog box is where you name your document.

2. **Navigate to the directory where you want to save the file.**

   Double-click a folder icon in the central list box to open the directory. Click the Up One Level button (the left-most button of the three buttons in the upper-right corner of the dialog box) to move to a higher level in the directory tree on your system.

3. **Select a file type from the File Type drop-down list box.**

   The default setting — StarWriter 5.0 — is appropriate for text documents that you expect to reuse in StarOffice. You need to select a different file type if you must share the file with someone who needs to open it with a different program.

4. **Type a descriptive name for your file in the Filename box.**

   StarWriter supports long filenames that can include caps, lowercase, and spaces. However, you must make sure that the filename you enter is compatible with the file naming conventions of the computer system you are using. You don't have to manually add a filename extension in the Filename box. StarOffice automatically adds the appropriate extension to the filename as long as the Automatic File Name Extension option is checked.

5. **Click Save.**

   StarOffice closes the Save As dialog box and saves your document file in the specified location. The title bar changes to reflect the new name for your document.

After you save a text document the first time, you don't need to reopen the Save As dialog box and adjust its settings each time you save the file. If you simply want to update your document after adding some text or making some edits, you can choose File⇨Save, press Ctrl+S, or click the Save button in the Function toolbar. StarOffice skips the Save As dialog box and saves the file using its existing filename and location.

Saving a document you intend to share

By default, StarOffice saves text documents in its own StarWriter file format. You can open and edit these documents in StarOffice, but not in other programs. If you need to share a text document with a friend or coworker who uses a different word processing program, you need to save your text document in a file format that the other program can open. Fortunately, StarOffice can save text documents in the Microsoft Word 95 and Word 97 file formats and some other commonly used text file formats.

To save your text document in a file format suitable for use by another word processing program, choose File⇨Save As to open the Save As dialog box and fill in the information normally, except for the file type. In the File Type drop-down list box, select the appropriate file type for the word processing program that will be used to open the file. Choose a version of Microsoft Word or Rich Text Format if you plan to open the file in Word or in another word processing program that can read Word files.

If the other word processing program doesn't support one of these formats, StarOffice can also save your document as a plain text file. The text file will lack formatting information, but the plain text should survive the transition to any word processing or text editing program.

Saving a text document doesn't close the document window or remove it from your screen. The document remains open for further editing. That way you can save a work in progress quickly and easily and then continue working. You need to save your work any time you have more unsaved text than you are comfortable having to reenter if you were to lose that work to a power failure or other potential problem. If you are finally ready to close the document, choose File⇨Close or click the document window's Close button.

If you want to save your document under another filename or in another location, choose File⇨Save As (instead of File⇨Save) to reopen the Save As dialog box. Doing so allows you to enter a new filename or navigate to a different directory location before clicking Save to create another copy of your document.

Opening Existing Documents

Of course, StarOffice enables you to open existing text documents, not just create new text documents from scratch. To open an existing text document, follow these steps:

1. **Choose File⇨Open, press Ctrl+O, or click the Open button in the Function toolbar.**

   StarOffice responds by displaying the Open dialog box, as shown in Figure 3-7.

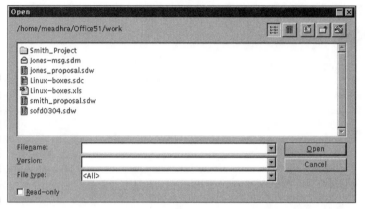

Figure 3-7: Use the Open dialog box to locate and open text documents.

2. **Navigate to the directory where the file is saved.**

   Double-click a folder icon in the central list box to open the directory. Click the Up One Level button (the left-most button of the three buttons in the upper-right corner of the dialog box) to move to a higher level in the directory tree on your system.

   By default, StarOffice lists all the files in the current directory in the Open list box. If you're looking for a particular kind of file, such as StarWriter text documents, you can make a selection from the File Type drop-down list box to display only the matching file types. Doing so can reduce the clutter in crowded directories and make finding the file you're looking for much easier.

3. **Select the file you want to open from the list box.**

   The default setting — StarWriter 5.0 — is appropriate for text documents that you expect to reuse in StarOffice. You need to select a different file type if you must share the file with someone who needs to open it in a different program.

4. **Click Open.**

   StarOffice closes the Open dialog box and displays the selected document in a new StarWriter document window.

You can use the Explorer and Beamer utilities to locate and open document files. Double-click a file icon in the Beamer window to open that document. You can also open documents by double-clicking their icons in the StarDesktop window. (See Chapter 2 for more information on the Explorer and Beamer utilities and on StarDesktop.)

If you attempt to open a document file for which you do not have write permission, StarOffice opens the file in read-only mode, so that you can view but not modify the file. You won't be able to edit the document while it's in read-only mode. However, you can use the file as a template to make a new document that you can edit. To do so, right-click the text, choose Edit from

Opening documents created by other programs

Just as StarOffice is capable of saving documents in file formats that can be read by other programs, StarOffice is also capable of reading files that were created by other programs and opening those documents in StarWriter for edition. You don't have to do anything special in order to open a document from a supported file format such as Microsoft Word. You just select the document in the Open dialog box and open it just as you would open a StarOffice document. StarOffice automatically recognizes the file formats it supports and uses the appropriate import filter to open the file — provided the filename includes the standard extension for the file type (such as .doc for Microsoft Word documents). Occasionally, you may need to help StarOffice identify a foreign file by selecting the file in the Open dialog box and then choosing the appropriate file format from the File Type drop-down list box before clicking Open to open the file. Importing foreign documents into StarOffice usually works pretty well. You may see some incompatibilities if you don't have the fonts on your system that are specified in the document or if the document incorporates some esoteric feature that isn't supported by StarOffice.

the pop-up menu that appears, and then click Yes after StarOffice asks whether you want to create a new document. After editing the document, you need to save the file using a different name. To avoid a problem with read-only files, make sure you have file ownership and permission settings that enable you to modify the files you need to edit. (Setting file ownership and permissions is something you need to do outside of StarOffice.)

Printing Your Documents

The paperless office is still a faraway dream for most people. Until the dream comes true, you need to convert many of your text documents from electronic documents on the computer screen to printed documents on paper.

Using Linux printers and fonts

Before you can print your documents from StarOffice, you must make sure that StarOffice can identify and communicate with the printer attached to your Linux system or with your network printer's print queue. StarOffice also needs information about your fonts in order to properly display and print the fonts used in your documents.

The Linux version of StarOffice includes a Printer Setup utility for configuring StarOffice to use your printer and fonts. Ordinarily, you only have to use the Printer Setup utility once, after you install StarOffice. You won't need to use the utility again unless you change your printer configuration or add new fonts. I cover the Printer Setup utility in the appendix as part of the StarOffice installation procedure.

Using Windows printers and fonts

Setting up a printer for use with the Windows version of StarOffice is a little easier than setting up a printer on a Linux-based system. StarOffice, like most Windows programs, can use any installed Windows printer. You simply install and configure your printer normally in Windows using the Add Printer Wizard in the Printers folder. (You can access the Printers folder by clicking the Start button on the Windows 98 taskbar and choosing Settings⇨Printers.) After you install the printer in Windows, the printer is available to any Windows application, including StarOffice. No further configuration is necessary to enable StarOffice to use your printer.

The same principle applies to using fonts under Windows. Windows comes with an assortment of preinstalled fonts (using the TrueType font technology). StarOffice, along with all other Windows programs, can use those fonts for both on-screen preview and for printing. If you install additional fonts in Windows, StarOffice can use them the next time you run the program. You don't need to go through any separate procedures in order to activate the Windows fonts or make them available to StarOffice. However, if you purchased the Deluxe StarOffice CD, you may want to install some of the fonts that came with the StarOffice program onto your Windows system.

If you need more information on installing printers in Windows, check out *Windows 98 For Dummies* by Andy Rathbone (IDG Books Worldwide). For information about installing fonts in Windows, see *More Windows 98 For Dummies* also by Andy Rathbone (IDG Books Worldwide).

Printing documents the quick way

If you're ready to print a text document, you can just click the Print button on the Function toolbar to send the current document on its way to your printer. Doing so is fast and easy — provided you want to print your document on the default printer using the default settings. After you click the Print button, StarOffice displays a status message while sending your document to the printer, which takes just a few seconds for the average document. In a few moments, the printer starts printing your document.

The StarWriter document window provides a pretty good simulation of what your document will look like when it's printed. However, you can choose File⇨Page View/Print Preview to display your document in another document window using print preview mode. Print preview mode is a handy way to get a quick overview of your document before printing. To print the document from the print preview view, click the Print button in the Function toolbar. To close the print preview view and return to the normal document window, click the Close button in the Object toolbar.

Clicking the Print button on the Function toolbar prints the current document using the default printer. If you have more than one printer and want to change which one is the default printer, choose File⇨Printer Setup to open the Printer Setup dialog box. Choose a new printer from the Name drop-down list box and then click OK to close the dialog box and set the selected printer as the new default printer. Henceforth, clicking the Print button sends your document to the new printer.

Selecting print options

Sometimes you may need a little more control over your document printing jobs than you get by just clicking the Print button. Perhaps you want to print only certain pages of a document or you want to make multiple copies. If you need that extra measure of control, you can choose File⇨Print (or press Ctrl+P) to open the Print dialog box shown in Figure 3-8. The Print dialog box enables you to control a number of factors affecting your print job, including the following:

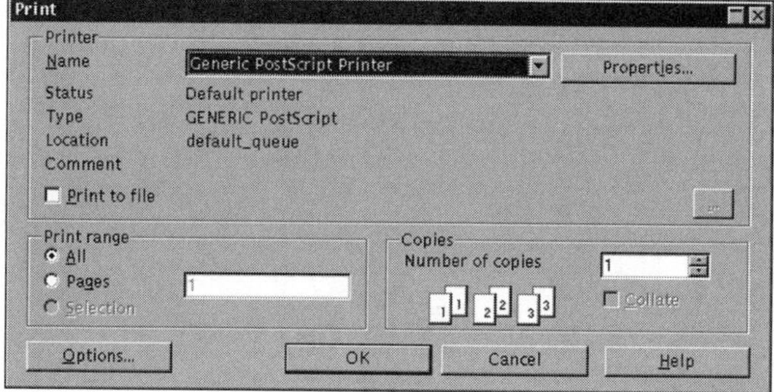

Figure 3-8: The Print dialog box.

- Select the printer by choosing it from the Name drop-down list box.
- To adjust the properties of the selected printer, click Properties to open a separate Printer Settings dialog box where you can adjust settings such as the paper size and orientation. Click OK to close the Printer Settings dialog box and return to the Print dialog box.
- To save the printer output in a file instead of sending it to the printer, check the Print To File option and enter a path and filename in the adjacent text box.

- In the Print Range area, select the pages of your document that you want to print. To print the entire document, select All. To print specific pages from the document, select Pages and list the page numbers in the adjacent text box. To print the currently selected text, select the Selection option. (How's that for a select selection of choices?)
- To print multiple copies of your document, specify the number of copies you want in the Number of Copies box. If you specify more than one copy, you can check the Collate option to print the documents in collated sets instead of multiple copies of each page.
- To adjust other printing options, click the Options button to open the Printer Options dialog box. In that dialog box, you can do things such as omit certain kinds of content (for example, graphics and tables), choose to print only left or right pages, and specify how footnotes print. Click OK to close the Printer Options dialog box and return to the Print dialog box.

After you adjust the settings in the Print dialog box, click OK to close the dialog box and begin printing your document using those settings.

Chapter 4

Adding Polish to Your Documents

In This Chapter

- Viewing your document different ways
- Moving around in your document
- Doing documents with style
- Getting fancy with effects
- Searching and replacing this for that
- Getting the words just right
- Magically correcting text and formatting

This chapter is about using some of the StarWriter editing and formatting tools to refine and enhance your documents. The techniques in this chapter go beyond basic text entry and simple stuff like centering a line of text and making it bold. This chapter is where you find out about using the StarWriter Navigator and Stylist features to move around your documents quickly and add sophisticated and consistent formatting to them. You also discover an assortment of built-in text effects that make short work of lists and other formatting challenges. Here, too, is information on editing tools that enable you to replace text, check spelling, and select synonyms from an online thesaurus.

Changing Your View of Your Document

The standard display in a StarWriter document window simulates the appearance of a printed document. The text appears on-screen at approximately the size it will be when printed, and StarWriter automatically arranges the text within the margins of a virtual on-screen page. As you scroll across or down through the document, StarWriter shows you the top, bottom, and edges of each page and simulates how the text breaks at the end of each line and at the top and bottom of each page. Of course, the text isn't as crisp as when you print the document with a good quality printer, and some of the line breaks and positioning may not be precisely accurate, but all in all the on-screen image is a pretty good simulation of a printed document.

The standard document view fills the bill most of the time, but StarWriter gives you some other viewing options for those times when the standard view isn't quite what you want to see.

- **Online Layout view** removes the page background and normal text margins from the screen and wraps your text to fit the document window. (See Figure 4-1.) Online Layout is designed for work on Web pages, rather than documents that you intend to print on paper, but it's useful any time that you're not concerned with page layout and just want to efficiently display your text content. To toggle between the standard document view and Online Layout view, choose View⇨Online Layout. You can also switch in and out of Online Layout view by clicking the Online Layout button at the bottom of the StarWriter Main toolbar.
- **Full Screen view** (shown in Figure 4-2) uses the entire screen area to display the contents of the StarWriter document window. The StarOffice title bar, menus, and toolbars disappear in Full Screen view — only the ruler, scroll bars, and StarOffice Task bar remain visible around the StarWriter window work area. To go into Full Screen view, choose View⇨Full Screen. If you are in Full Screen view, you won't be able to select menu commands to return to normal view. Instead, you click the Full Screen button in the small floating toolbar that appears in the upper-left corner of the screen.

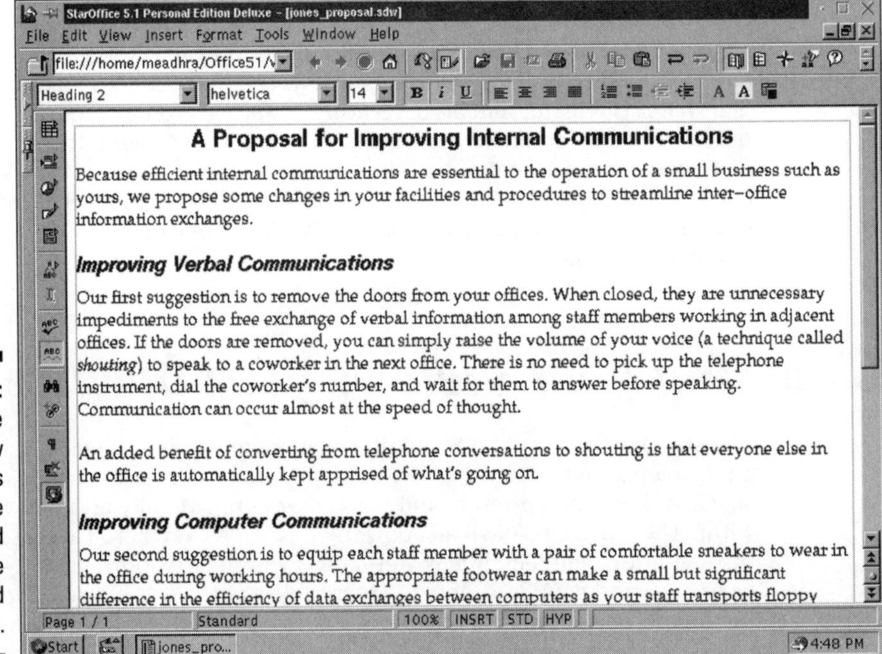

Figure 4-1: Online Layout view dispenses with the standard page margins and background.

- **Zoom** is the other viewing option you can adjust in the StarWriter document window. Increasing the Zoom magnification setting makes the text and other elements in the document window appear larger, which means that you can see a smaller portion of the page in the document window. Conversely, decreasing the magnification makes the text smaller (and harder to read) but enables StarWriter to display more of your page in the document window. To adjust the magnification setting, right-click the Zoom display in the status bar and choose a new magnification from the pop-up menu that appears. In standard view, the choices are 200%, 150%, 100%, 75%, 50%, Optimal, Page Width, and Entire Page. If you double-click the Zoom display, StarWriter opens the Zoom dialog box, in which you can choose Variable and enter a custom magnification in addition to choosing any of the standard magnifications. Click OK to close the Zoom dialog box and display your document at the selected setting.

Choose Optimal magnification to let StarWriter determine the best fit for the text area of your document within the width of the window. In addition, Optimal magnification often produces the best on-screen font rendering.

Click here to return to normal view.

A Proposal for Improving Internal Communications

Because efficient internal communications are essential to the operation of a small business such as yours, we propose some changes in your facilities and procedures to streamline inter-office information exchanges.

Improving Verbal Communications

Our first suggestion is to remove the doors from your offices. When closed, they are unnecessary impediments to the free exchange of verbal information among staff members working in adjacent offices. If the doors are removed, you can simply raise the volume of your voice (a technique called *shouting*) to speak to a coworker in the next office. There is no need to pick up the telephone instrument, dial the coworker's number, and wait for them to answer before speaking. Communication can occur almost at the speed of thought.

An added benefit of converting from telephone conversations to shouting is that everyone else in the office is automatically kept apprised of what's going on.

Improving Computer Communications

Our second suggestion is to equip each staff member with a pair of comfortable sneakers to wear in the office during working hours. The appropriate footwear can make a small but significant difference in the efficiency of data exchanges between computers as your staff transports floppy disks back and forth between computers.

The use of a "sneaker net" to effect file transfers between computers has several advantages over the hardwired computer network you're accustomed to using. The absence of wires running between computers means that you have more flexibility in the placement of the computers in your office and you can rearrange offices and computers more easily. Also, you and your employees will naturally have more

Figure 4-2: Full Screen view hides the StarOffice menus and toolbars.

Navigating Your Document with Navigator

If you're writing a short letter or a memo, moving around to various parts of your document isn't a problem. Most of the text of a letter to Aunt Jane probably fits within the StarWriter document window, and anything that isn't visible is easy to reach with just a couple of clicks on the scroll bar. However, the situation is different when you start working with longer, multi-page documents. Scrolling through page after page of text can be a real drag (pun intended). To work efficiently with a large document, you need a fast and flexible way to locate text and move to the different parts of the document.

The Navigator window (see Figure 4-3) is the StarOffice answer to the need for easy document navigation. To display the Navigator window, click the Navigator button on the Function toolbar, choose View➪Navigator, or press F5. Click the button again to close the Navigator window.

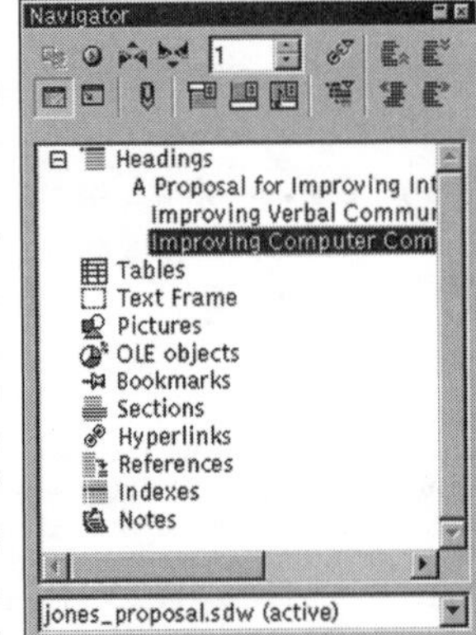

Figure 4-3: The Navigator makes moving around in even the largest of documents easy.

The Navigator window is a floating tool that remains visible on top of your document window, even when you open or select a different document. You can move the Navigator window to different locations within the StarOffice program window by dragging the Navigator window's title bar. You can also dock the Navigator at the side of the StarOffice window, just as you can the Explorer and Beamer windows. (See Chapter 2 for instructions on docking and undocking windows.)

The buttons across the top of the Navigator window perform an assortment of functions to help you navigate your document or control the Navigator window. Here's a brief summary of the main buttons and what they do:

- **Navigation.** Click this button to open a small toolbar with buttons for the various document elements (such as page, heading, table, selection, and picture) that StarWriter can identify and jump to. Select one of the buttons on that toolbar to designate the document element that the Previous and Next buttons (described next) can jump to.

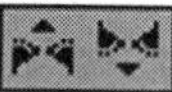

- **Previous/Next.** After you select the document element (such as page or header) to which you want to go using the Navigation button, click the Previous or the Next button to jump to the previous or next instance of that element in your document. You can continue to click the button to step through your document, going to each of the selected elements in sequence.

- **Page Number.** To go to a specific page in your document, simply type or select the page number in this box.

- **Drag Mode.** You can drag items from the Navigator window list box and drop them into your document. To determine whether StarWriter inserts an item as a hyperlink, a link, or simple text copy, click the Drag Mode button and make a selection from the pop-up menu that appears.

- **List Box On/Off.** Click this button to display or hide the list box below the buttons in the Navigator window.

- **Content View.** Click this button to toggle the view in the Navigator window list box between showing all the possible document elements or showing only those elements available for selection in the current document.

- **Header.** Click this button to jump to the page header area. (This button works only in regular page view, not in Online Layout view.)

- **Footer.** Click this button to jump to the page footer area. (This button works only in regular page view, not in Online Layout view.)

- **Outline Level.** To determine how many heading levels appear under Headings in the Navigator list box, click this button and make a selection from the pop-up menu that appears.

- **Promote/Demote Chapter.** Under Headings in the Navigator list box, select a heading and then click one of these buttons to move that heading up or down in the Headings list. StarWriter moves the corresponding heading *and text* in your document.

The Promote and Demote Chapter buttons in the Navigator window are very powerful tools that enable you to quickly and easily rearrange blocks of text in your document. All you have to do is rearrange the list of headings in the Navigator window list box. StarWriter automatically takes care of moving the text in your document to reflect the changes you make in the Headings list. The process is sure a lot easier than cutting and pasting large blocks of text.

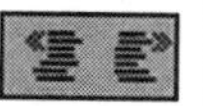

- **Promote/Demote Level.** Click one of these buttons to promote or demote (meaning to change the outline indent level for) the selected heading in the Navigator list box and in your document.

The Navigator window list box enables you to go directly to any identifiable element (such as a heading or picture) within your document, without stepping through intervening elements, as you must do with the Previous and Next buttons.

The drop-down list box at the bottom of the Navigator window lists all of the open StarWriter documents. If you select a different document from the drop-down list box, the Navigator window list box displays the document elements that are available for selection in that document. Click the plus (+) box beside an element name to expand the list so that it shows the individual items of that type. Double-click an item, such as a specific heading, in the list box to automatically move the insertion point cursor to that location in your document and display it in the active document window, ready for editing.

You see an extra copy of the Navigation button and the Previous/Next buttons at the bottom of the scroll bar on the right side of the StarWriter document window. These buttons work just as their counterparts do in the Navigator window. The advantage is that the buttons are available even when the Navigator window isn't open.

Adding Style to Your Document

Selecting a line of text that you want to format as a heading and then changing its font and type size, making it bold, centering it, and changing the paragraph spacing are relatively easy. (See Chapter 3 for more information about basic text selection and formatting techniques.) Each of these changes takes only a couple of mouse clicks. But when you need to make several formatting changes on several headings, you introduce the possibility of making a mistake on one of the settings, with the result that the heading isn't consistent with other headings in the document.

The process is easier when you use styles. A *style* is a predefined set of formatting information that is linked to a style name and saved in your document and/or document template. Styles can include character formatting such as fonts, paragraph formatting such as alignment and indents, page formatting such as text margins, and so on. You can select a paragraph or any block of text and apply a named style to automatically format that text with all the attributes defined in the style. For example, instead of individually making all the formatting changes to text that you want to become a heading, you simply apply a Heading style, which automatically formats the text to match the other headings in your document.

Styles save you even more time if you decide to change your document formatting. For example, if you want to change the font for all the headings in your document, you can simply change the definition of the Heading style, and StarWriter automatically changes all the headings in your document that use that style. You don't have to go through the document to change each heading individually.

Using styles to define document formatting is a proven concept. Even Web page documents employ styles. Consequently, StarWriter implements styles in much the same way as Microsoft Word and several other word processing and desktop publishing programs. StarWriter comes with an assortment of predefined styles included in the Standard document template on which most new text documents are based. These styles are available from the outset for use in formatting your documents. Later, you can change those style definitions to create new styles of your own as needed.

Applying predefined styles

To apply a style to some text in your document, just select the text and then select a style from the Applied Styles drop-down list box in the StarWriter Object toolbar (the drop-down list box at the left end of the toolbar). StarWriter automatically applies the formatting attributes associated with your chosen style to the selected text. If the style contains character-formatting information, StarWriter applies the formatting to the selected text only. If the style contains paragraph-formatting information, StarWriter applies the formatting to the entire paragraph.

Because paragraph formatting applies to the entire paragraph, regardless of how much text you select, you can simply click to place the insertion point cursor anywhere within the paragraph before applying a paragraph style. You don't have to select the entire paragraph.

The Applied Styles drop-down list box in the StarWriter Object toolbar is handy but lists only the styles currently in use in your document, rather than all the styles available. For a more complete selection of styles, you must refer to the Stylist, which I describe in the next section, or to the Style Catalog dialog box, which you can open by choosing Format➪Styles & Templates➪Catalog. To select a style using the Style Catalog dialog box, first select a style type (such as Paragraph Styles) from the drop-down list box at the top of the dialog box. Then select a style category (select All Styles to see all available styles) from the drop-down list box at the bottom of the dialog box. These selections control what styles appear in the list box in the middle of the Style Catalog dialog box. Select a style from the list and then click OK to close the dialog box and apply that style to the selected text.

Using the Stylist

The Stylist is a StarOffice formatting tool that displays a list of styles in a movable, floating window, much like the Navigator window. (The Stylist window shown in Figure 4-4 is labeled Paragraph Styles because those are the styles currently displayed.) Like the Navigator, Explorer, and Beamer windows, you can move and resize the Stylist window or dock it to the side of the StarOffice window. (See Chapter 2 for information on how to dock and undock windows.)

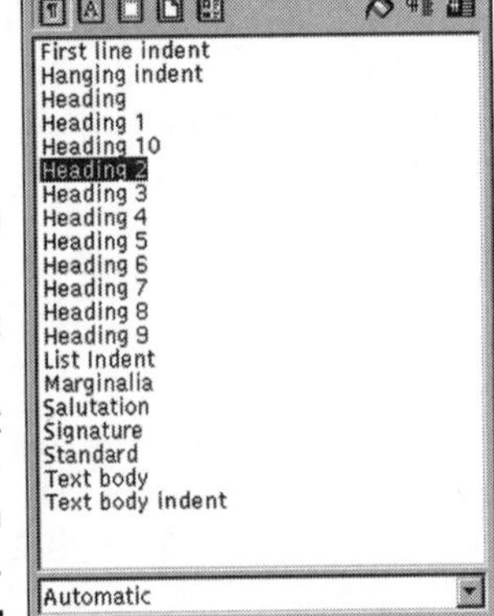

Figure 4-4: The Stylist displays an assortment of paragraph styles.

Applying styles to your text using the Stylist is a simple process. Just follow these steps:

1. **To open the Stylist window, click the Stylist button in the Function toolbar, choose Format⇨Stylist, or press F11.**
2. **To select the kind of styles that appear in the Stylist list box, click one of the Styles buttons at the top of the Stylist window.**

   The following style types are available:

   - **Paragraph Styles** contain paragraph formatting such as alignment, indents, and line spacing and also contain character formatting that applies to the entire paragraph.
   - **Text Styles** contain character formatting, such as font selection and bold or italic attributes, which apply to the selected text only.
   - **Frame Styles** apply to the frames, or borders, around text boxes, pictures, tables, and the like.
   - **Page Styles** contain page setup information such as text margins and headers and footers.
   - **Numbering Styles** contain number formatting for outlines and numbered lists.
3. **Select a style category from the drop-down list box at the bottom of the Stylist window.**

You have numerous selections available but you normally use Automatic (default styles), All Styles (all available styles), or Applied Styles (styles used in the current document).

4. **Double-click the desired style name in the Stylist list box.**

   StarWriter applies the selected style to the text in your document.

Unlike the Style Catalog dialog box, the Stylist doesn't close automatically when you apply a style. Instead, the Stylist stays open, ready to use again and again. That makes it a great tool to use when you need to scroll through your document applying and changing styles in numerous places. After you finish using the Stylist window, close it by clicking the Stylist button on the Function toolbar, by choosing Format➪Stylist, or by clicking the Close button in the Stylist window title bar.

Creating new styles of your own

The predefined styles that come with the StarWriter standard templates provide you with a good start, but you're not stuck with those styles alone. You can create and define your own custom styles to use in your documents.

You have two ways to create a new style. You can define a style from scratch by adjusting formatting settings in a dialog box, which is usually the quickest way if you know exactly what formatting you want for that style. You also can define a style by copying the formatting from a paragraph (or other document element) that's formatted to your liking. Defining a style by example may be the best approach in circumstances that require you to do a little trial and error experimentation in order to get the formatting right.

The following steps outline the procedure for creating a new paragraph style from scratch. You can easily modify the procedure to create other style types as well.

1. **Open the Stylist window or the Style Catalog dialog box and display Paragraph Styles.**

   Refer to the "Applying predefined styles" and "Using the Stylist" sections of this chapter for more information.

2. **Click the New button in the Style Catalog dialog box or right-click the list in the Stylist window and choose New from the pop-up menu that appears.**

   The Organizer tab on the Paragraph Style dialog box appears. (See Figure 4-5.)

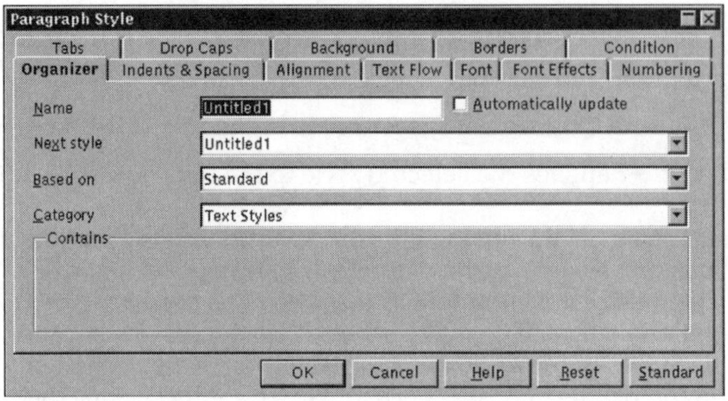

Figure 4-5: Defining a new paragraph style.

3. **Type a name for your style in the Name box.**

   The name needs to be short but descriptive or memorable — anything that enables you to identify the style and doesn't duplicate an existing style name.

4. **Select the appropriate companion styles from the Next Style and Based On drop-down list boxes.**

   The Next Style setting determines the following paragraph's default style. If you select a style in the Based On box, the style you are defining inherits the characteristics of that style.

5. **Select Custom in the Category drop-down list box.**

   This action categorizes the new style as a Custom style and keeps it separate from the list of predefined styles.

6. **Click the other tabs in the Paragraph Style dialog box in turn and adjust the settings as needed to define the characteristics of your new style.**

   You only need to adjust those settings that are different from the settings for the Based On style because the new style already includes a copy of the characteristics of the style you selected in the Based On box.

7. **After you finish defining the new style, click OK.**

   StarWriter closes the Paragraph Style dialog box and makes the new style available for your use by adding it to the lists in the Stylist window and the Style Catalog dialog box.

Sometimes it's easier to format a paragraph (or other document element) and then create a new style using that paragraph as an example. Just follow these steps:

1. **Open the Stylist window.**

   Refer to the "Using the Stylist" section in this chapter for instructions on opening the Stylist window.

2. **Format the paragraph that you want to use as an example and then select it (or just leave the cursor positioned in the paragraph).**

   You can format the example paragraph using any of the normal formatting controls. This process includes applying existing styles and then changing some of the formatting by using any combination of dialog box settings and toolbar buttons. You can try a number of different format settings until you achieve the effect you want.

3. **Click the New Style by Example button in the Stylist window.**

   The Create Style dialog box appears.

4. **Enter a name for your new style.**
5. **Click OK.**

   The Create Style dialog box closes, and StarWriter adds the new style name to the list in the Stylist window. The new style contains the formatting characteristics of the paragraph you selected as the example.

Redefining styles

The existing styles, whether predefined StarWriter styles or custom styles that you created, are not immutable. In fact, you can refine, update, or redefine styles as often as you want. Doing so is easy because the techniques mirror the techniques for defining new styles.

You can modify a style by adjusting settings in the same dialog box that you may have used to define the style in the first place. The steps are essentially the same as those I describe in the "Creating new styles of your own" section of this chapter. Just substitute the Modify button or menu item for the New button or menu item in Step 2 and skip Step 3 (because you don't need to change the style name). Change the definition of the style by changing the settings in the Paragraph Style dialog box.

To modify a style by example, follow these steps:

1. **Open the Stylist window.**

   Refer to the "Using the Stylist" section of this chapter for instructions on opening the Stylist window.

2. **Select a paragraph (or other document element) formatted with the style that you want to change.**

   Note that this action also selects the corresponding style name in the Stylist window list.

3. **Change the selected paragraph's formatting.**

Use any of the formatting commands at your disposal to format the paragraph. You can use menu commands, dialog box settings, or toolbar buttons. After the paragraph's formatting is revised to your satisfaction, proceed to the next step.

4. **Click the Update Style button in the Stylist window.**

   StarOffice immediately updates the style definition and automatically applies the changes throughout the document to any text using that style.

Creating Text Effects

Many documents are far more than pages of simple text. Documents may include features such as numbered lists and outlines, multiple columns, and headers and footers.

You can create most of these effects manually using formatting tools such as tabs and indents and careful text placement on each page — but doing so can be a difficult process. Fortunately, you don't have to work so hard to achieve the effects you want because StarWriter offers special tools and techniques to create such effects easily.

Creating bulleted and numbered lists

Making a bulleted list in a StarWriter document is easy. Just follow these steps:

1. **Enter the text for the first bulleted item as a separate paragraph and then select the paragraph.**

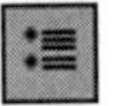

2. **Click the Bullets button on the StarWriter Object toolbar.**

   StarWriter indents the paragraph and adds a bullet in front of it.

3. **With the cursor at the end of the paragraph, press Enter to create a new paragraph and then type the text for the next bulleted item.**

   StarWriter automatically formats the paragraph as the next item in the bulleted list. Repeat this step to continue adding items to the list.

4. **After you reach the end of the bulleted list, create a new paragraph and click the Bullets button again.**

   This turns off the special Bullet formatting, so that you are once again working with normal paragraphs.

Making numbered lists is just as easy. Follow the same procedure but click the Numbering button on the StarWriter Object toolbar instead of the Bullets button. Instead of a bullet, StarWriter places a number in front of each paragraph and even assigns sequential numbers to the paragraphs automatically.

To revise the bullet/number style, select a bulleted paragraph and choose Format⇨Numbering/Bullets or right-click the selection and choose Numbering/Bullets from the pop-up menu that appears. After the Numbering/Bullets dialog box appears, click the Bullets tab or the Numbering Style tab and choose a bullet or number style by clicking one of the sample boxes. Click the Position tab and adjust the settings to control the paragraph indents and the position of the bullet or number in front of the paragraph. Click OK to close the dialog box and apply the new settings.

Numbering an outline

Creating a properly formatted outline, complete with different numbering schemes and indents for each outline level, can be a challenge if you try to do it manually. But outline numbering is easy with StarWriter because it treats an outline as a special kind of numbered list.

To format a series of paragraphs as an outline, follow these steps:

1. **Select a paragraph or series of paragraphs that you want to format as an outline.**
2. **Right-click the selection and choose Numbering/Bullets from the pop-up menu that appears or choose Format⇨Numbering/Bullets.**

   In response, StarWriter opens the Numbering/Bullets dialog box as shown in Figure 4-6.

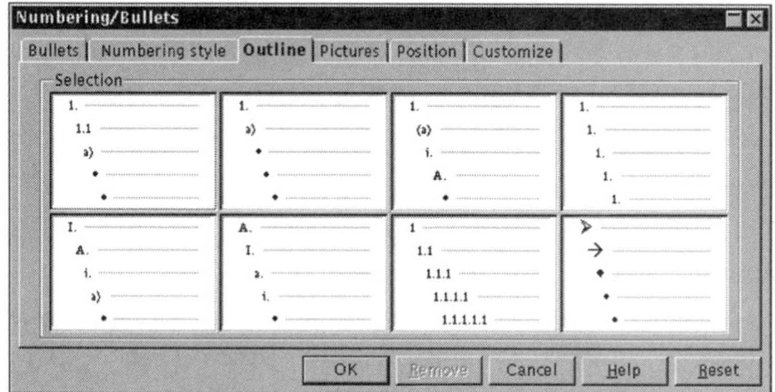

Figure 4-6: You can choose one of eight outline numbering styles.

3. **Click the Outline tab and select the outline numbering style by clicking one of the sample boxes.**

4. **Click the Position tab and adjust the settings to achieve the proper indents for each outline level.**

   The default settings are usually appropriate, but you can change them if necessary.

5. **Click OK.**

   StarWriter closes the Numbering/Bullets dialog box and applies the outline numbering and indent formatting to your paragraphs. Initially, all the paragraphs are the same outline level (no indents or different heading styles) and numbered sequentially.

6. **Adjust the outline levels for each paragraph as needed.**

   To change the outline level of a paragraph, position the cursor at the beginning of the paragraph and press Tab to indent the paragraph or press Shift+Tab to promote the paragraph to a higher outline level.

You can add more paragraphs to the end of an outline, just as you can add items to the end of a bulleted or numbered list. To end the outline, remove the outline formatting from the first non-outline paragraph by selecting the paragraph, opening the Numbering/Bullets dialog box, and clicking the Remove button.

Creating columns

In letters, reports, and similar documents, the text usually runs the full width of the page between the margins, making one column on the page. However, documents such as newsletters, flyers, and brochures often look best with multiple columns of text. If you need to create a document with multiple columns of text, follow these steps:

1. **Choose Format⇨Page or right-click the page background and choose Page from the pop-up menu that appears.**

   StarWriter opens the Page Style dialog box as shown in Figure 4-7.

2. **Click the Columns tab, if it isn't selected automatically.**

3. **Select one of the standard column layouts by clicking one of the thumbnails (miniature drawings) in the Columns area.**

   If you prefer to create a custom column layout, select or type the number of columns in the Amount box and then proceed to enter the column widths and intercolumn spacing in the Column Width area.

4. **If you want a separator line to appear between columns, select the line's thickness, height, and position in the Separator area.**

5. **After defining the column layout, click OK.**

   StarWriter closes the Page Style dialog box and reformats your document so that the text flows into the specified number of columns on each page.

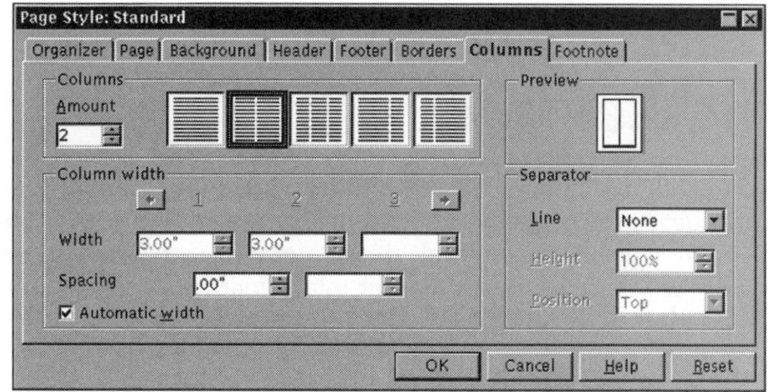

Figure 4-7: Defining columns in the Page Style dialog box.

Adding headers and footers

At the top or bottom of each page, documents often include a line or two of text that contains information such as the title of the document, the page number, or the date that the document was printed. This text is repeated from page to page throughout the document. If the repeated text appears at the top of the page, it's called a *header.* If it's at the bottom of the page, it's called a *footer.*

You can add a header (or footer) to your StarWriter document by choosing Insert➪Header➪Standard (or Insert➪Footer➪Standard). StarWriter adds a separate text block — defined by a gray outline like the text margins — to the top (or bottom) of each page and slightly reduces the size of the main text block to make room for the header or footer.

As soon as the header or footer exists, you can easily add text to it. Just click the I-beam pointer in the header or footer text block and enter or edit text as you do in the body of your document. The text you enter into the header or footer of one page is repeated automatically on the other pages in your document.

You can instruct StarWriter to automatically insert certain information into the text of a header or footer by using a feature called field codes. *Field codes* are placeholders that you insert into your text. StarWriter automatically replaces these placeholders with corresponding information when your document appears on-screen or is printed. For example, if you place a Page Numbers field in the footer, StarWriter replaces that field code with the current page number. To enter a field (such as Page Numbers) in your document, position the cursor on the spot where you want to insert the field and choose Insert➪Fields➪Page Numbers. By the way, StarWriter has many different fields available, and you can use them throughout your document, not just in headers and footers.

Making Changes with Search and Replace

Have you ever finished writing and editing a long document only to discover that a product name or some other term that appears in every other sentence is spelled wrong throughout the document? If so, you can really appreciate the StarWriter search and replace feature. It scans your document for the offending word, replaces it with anything you want, and does so automatically.

To use the search and replace feature, choose Edit⇨Search & Replace (or press Ctrl+F), which opens the Search & Replace dialog box shown in Figure 4-8. If you just want to find a word or phrase in your document, type the text you want to find in the Search For box and then click Search. StarWriter scans your document, starting at the current cursor location, and highlights each consecutive place where the search text appears in your document. After StarWriter finds the text for you, you can edit it or search for the next occurrence by pressing Search again.

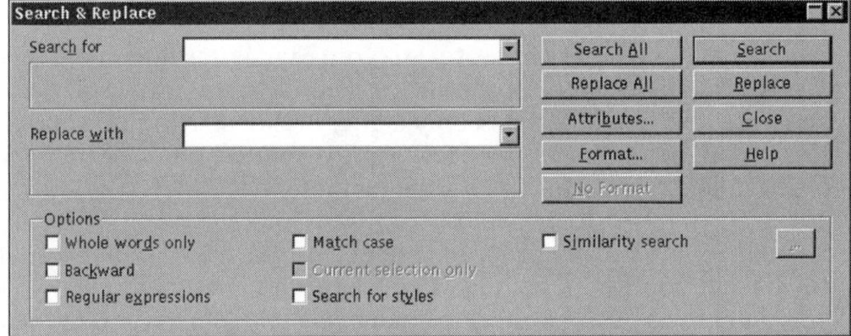

Figure 4-8: The Search & Replace dialog box.

StarWriter not only can find text in your document, it can automatically replace the text that it finds. To use the automatic replacement capability, start by opening the Search & Replace dialog box and entering the text you want to find in the Search For box. Next, enter the text you want to insert as a replacement into the Replace With box. Click Search to locate the first instance of the text you're searching for. As you cycle through the document, StarWriter automatically highlights each consecutive occurrence of the text in the Search For box. You decide in each case whether to replace that text with the text in the Replace With box. If so, click Replace. If StarWriter highlights some text that you don't want to replace, just click Search to go on to the next occurrence without replacing the highlighted text.

You can quickly move through your document in this fashion, retaining complete control over each replacement. On the other hand, if you're confident that you want to replace every occurrence of the search text in your document, you can click Replace All to let StarOffice proceed with the replacements automatically. After you're finished searching for and replacing text, click Close to close the Search & Replace dialog box.

The StarWriter Search & Replace feature is very powerful. The check boxes in the Options area enable you to modify the search in a variety of ways. Also, in addition to text searches, you can search for and replace attributes such as bold and formatting such as indents, using the Attributes and Format buttons.

Fixing Spelling Errors

Many people have trouble spelling some words, and even when you know the correct spelling, typing errors can show up in your documents with alarming frequency. It can be reallly embarasing when teh speling mistaks adn typin errrors lik these find thier way into yor finished docments. Fortunately, the StarWriter spelling tools can help you find and correct these errors before anyone else sees them.

The StarWriter Auto Spellcheck can monitor your text as you enter it and automatically alert you to any words for which it cannot find a match in the spelling dictionary. To turn the Auto Spellcheck feature on or off, choose Tools⇨Spelling⇨Auto Spellcheck or click the Auto Spellcheck button on the StarWriter Main toolbar. When Auto Spellcheck is active, StarWriter marks any unrecognized words with a red squiggly underline. Right-click an underlined word to bring up a pop-up menu that lists the program's best guesses about the correct spelling for the word and some other options.

- To replace the misspelled word with one of the suggested alternatives, just select the correct spelling from the pop-up menu.
- If the word is spelled correctly and you want to add it to the StarWriter dictionary, so the program does not mark the word as a misspelling in the future, choose Add and the dictionary filename from the pop-up menu. This method teaches StarWriter to recognize names and technical terms that repeatedly show up in your documents.
- Choose Ignore All from the pop-up menu to instruct StarWriter not to mark the word as misspelled in this document. Use this option for names and terms that are spelled correctly but that you don't want to add to the spelling dictionary.

In addition to Auto Spellcheck, StarWriter includes a spelling checker that you can start manually. Choose Tools⇨Spelling⇨Check, click the Spell Check button on the StarWriter Main toolbar, or press F7 to begin scanning your document for misspelled words. After StarWriter finds a word that isn't in its spelling dictionary, it highlights the word and opens the Spelling dialog box.

To replace the misspelled word, select a replacement from the Suggestions list box and then click Replace. Alternatively, you can click Replace All to automatically replace every occurrence of that word in your document. If the word is correctly spelled, click Ignore or Ignore All. To add the word to the spelling dictionary, click Add. After you deal with one misspelled word, StarWriter automatically advances to the next misspelled word in your document. When you finish checking the spelling in your document, click Close to dismiss the Spelling dialog box.

Finding Just the Right Word

Do you ever have trouble finding just the right word? Well, StarWriter can help by supplying from its online thesaurus a list of synonyms for any selected word in your document. Using the thesaurus is easy, just click a word and choose Tools⇨Thesaurus or press Ctrl+F7 to open the Thesaurus dialog box shown in Figure 4-9. The dialog box shows the selected word and below it, a list box of brief definitions. From the Synonym list box, select a word and then Click OK to close the Thesaurus dialog box and insert the synonym into your document in place of the original word. Say, wasn't that easy?

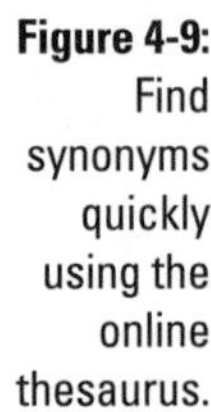

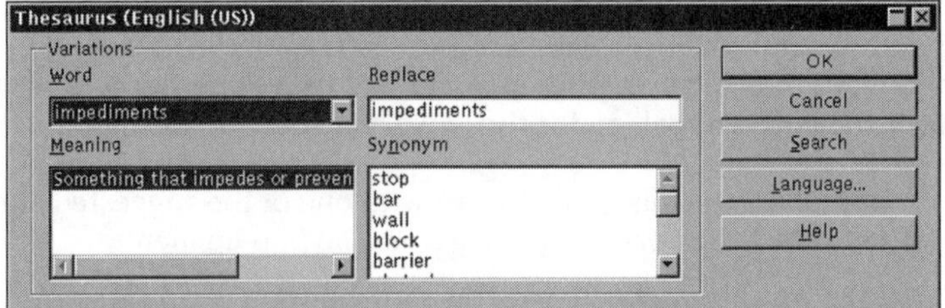

Figure 4-9: Find synonyms quickly using the online thesaurus.

Chapter 5

Automating Document Creation

In This Chapter

- Allowing the AutoPilot to lead the way
- Building documents with templates
- Letting StarWriter automatically correct errors and apply formatting
- Addressing envelopes and labels

Many of the documents you create with StarOffice are probably very similar to documents you have created in the past and will create in the future. Time and again, letters and memos follow the same format — only the content changes. Standard phrases and formatting show up repeatedly in many of your documents. Fortunately, computers and computer programs such as StarOffice are very good at handling repetitive tasks. In fact, computer programs can automate some of those repetitive tasks, thus freeing their human users for more important or pleasant activities. This chapter explores some of the StarWriter automation features that can help you with some common and repetitive document creation tasks.

Using AutoPilots to Automate Document Creation

AutoPilot is the StarOffice name for any of the program's built-in tools designed to automate document creation. AutoPilots ask you a series of questions and then create a document based on your answers. Similar features in Microsoft Office and other Windows programs are often called wizards.

AutoPilots don't create a finished document, but they can give you a good start by creating a document with the appropriate page formatting and some key elements of the finished document already in place. The AutoPilot takes care of the preliminary setup for your document — all that remains for you to do is to fill in the content of the rest of the document, such as the body text of a letter.

StarOffice includes AutoPilots to create the following kinds of StarWriter documents:

- Agenda
- Fax
- Letter
- Memo

In addition to the StarWriter documents that you can create with AutoPilots, StarOffice also includes AutoPilots for creating other document types:

- Web Page (using the StarWriter HTML editing capability)
- Presentation (using StarImpress)
- Table (using the StarBase database)
- Report (using the StarBase database)
- Form (using the StarBase database)
- Query (using the StarBase database)
- Microsoft Import (to import Microsoft Office documents)
- Internet Setup (to configure the StarOffice Internet access and e-mail settings)

To use an AutoPilot to create a new document such as a memo, follow these steps:

1. **Choose File⇨AutoPilot⇨Memo.**

   StarOffice opens the AutoPilot: Memo dialog box, as shown in Figure 5-1. The dialog boxes for each AutoPilot are different, depending on the information the AutoPilot needs in order to create the kind of document you selected. To create a different kind of document, select a different AutoPilot from the AutoPilot menu.

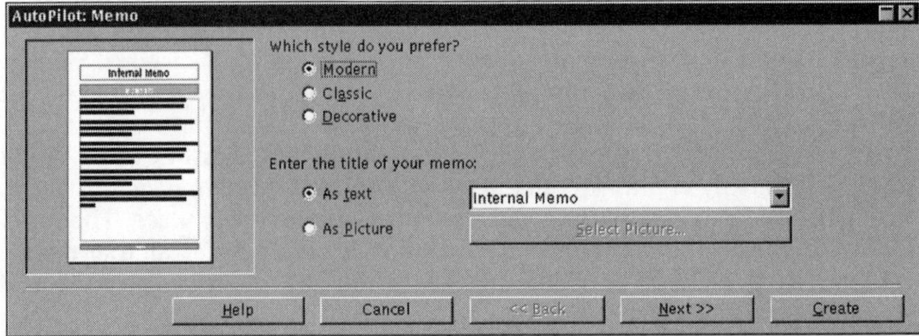

Figure 5-1: An AutoPilot dialog box for creating a memo.

2. **Make selections and enter information as prompted in the dialog box.**
3. **Click Next to proceed to the next AutoPilot dialog box.**
4. **Repeat Steps 2 and 3 until you reach the end of the AutoPilot.**
5. **Click Create.**

   StarOffice closes the AutoPilot dialog box, creates a new document based on one of its standard document templates, and incorporates the information and selections you entered in the AutoPilot. After a short wait, the new document appears, as shown in Figure 5-2.

After the AutoPilot does its thing, the skeleton document appears in a StarWriter document window. The document usually includes placeholders for the text that you need to enter to complete the document. To finish the job, just select the placeholder and start typing.

Using an AutoPilot creates not only a document, but also a document template customized with the key options and information that you entered in the AutoPilot. If you need to create a similar document in the future, you can run the AutoPilot again or just create a document based on the previously created template. See the next section of this chapter for information on creating documents based on templates.

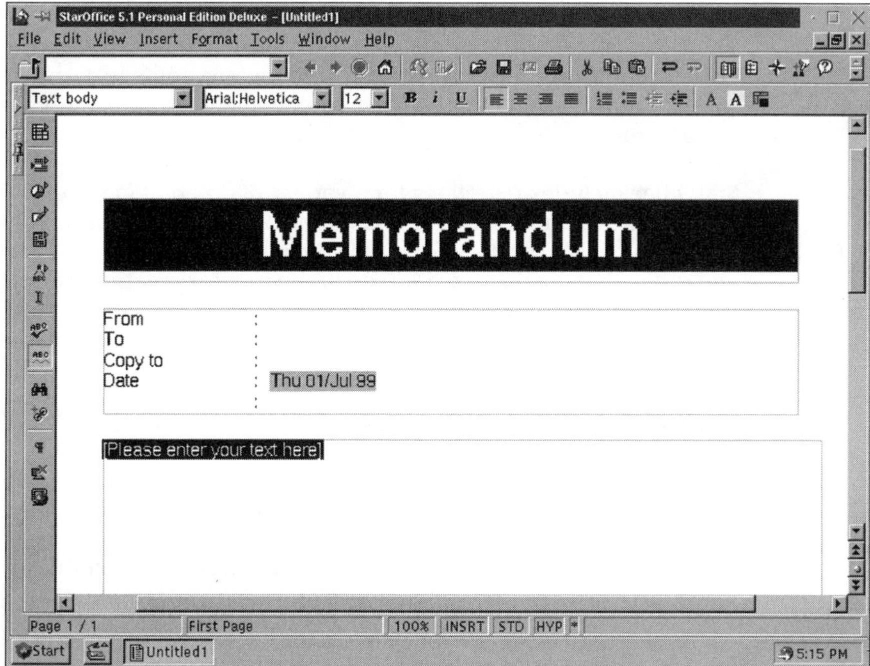

Figure 5-2: A memo created by the Memo AutoPilot.

Using Templates to Create Documents

Have you ever created a new document by copying an existing document and then editing the text to create a new version? If so, you've used a document template — or at least the idea of a document template. The old document served as the *template* or pattern on which the new document was based. The new document inherits contents and characteristics from the template, which means that you have less work remaining to do in order to finish the new document.

A StarOffice template is really a special kind of document that exists to be copied as a pattern for new documents. The new document then becomes available for editing, while the template stays safely tucked away — protected from accidental changes and ready to serve as a pattern for making other new documents.

One advantage of using a document template is obvious: You can reuse a significant portion of the existing document's text in your new document. But you can also benefit from a template by using only the document's structure, because modern word processing documents contain much more than just text. Each document contains information on page margins, default fonts, styles, tab settings, and so on. Without a template, you spend time adjusting and applying these settings for each new document. By using a template to configure these settings, you can reduce or eliminate that time. In fact, some templates contain little or no text — just page margins, styles, and other structural settings. Other templates also include some text and other elements that will be part of the finished document, but the text is almost a bonus.

StarOffice includes templates for a variety of different kinds of documents. Many of the templates are for StarWriter text documents, but you also can find templates to produce StarCalc spreadsheets, StarImpress presentations, and other kinds of documents. The procedure for creating a new document from a template is the same regardless of the kind of document you create.

Using the StarWriter document templates

StarOffice includes an assortment of predesigned templates. To create a new document based on one of the templates, follow these steps:

1. **Choose File⇨New⇨From Template or click the Start button on the StarOffice Task bar and choose More⇨From Template.**

   StarOffice opens the New dialog box, as shown in Figure 5-3. If the details in the lower half of the dialog box don't appear at first, click More to expand the dialog box.

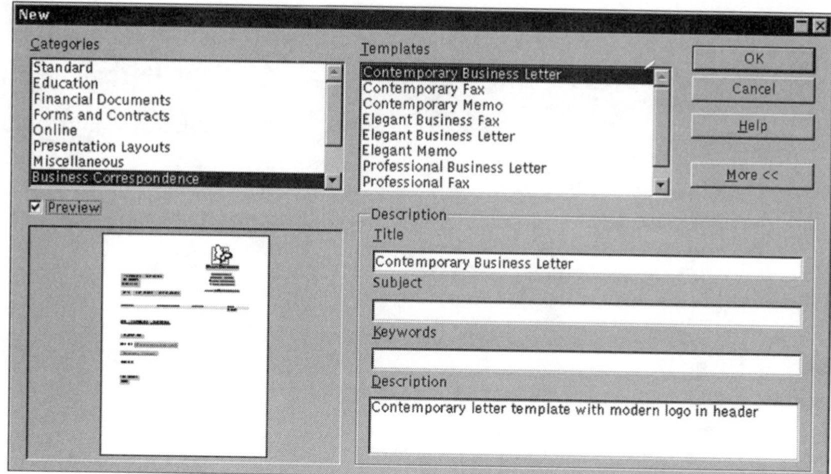

Figure 5-3: Selecting a template for a new document.

2. **Select a template category from the Categories list box.**

   The Templates list box appears, and StarOffice displays a list of templates in the selected category.

3. **Select a template from the Templates list box.**

   StarOffice loads information from the selected template, displays a thumbnail preview of the first page of the template in the Preview box (provided the Preview option is checked), and displays information about the template in the Description area. The loading process can take a moment or two, so be patient.

4. **Click OK.**

   StarOffice closes the New dialog box, creates a new document based on the selected template, and displays the new document in a separate document window.

When the new document appears, it already contains text, pictures, formatting, and other characteristics from the template. In some cases, the document may contain fields that automatically insert information, such as today's date, in the document. Some of the fields can automatically import data from a database — such as name and address information from selected entries in the StarOffice Address Book. Documents created from templates frequently contain placeholder text that provides instructions for how to complete the document. For example, Figure 5-4 contains database fields that StarOffice can automatically fill with information from the address database (the Address Book is open in the Beamer window so you can select whose address you want to use) as well as placeholder text that you select and replace by typing your own text into the document.

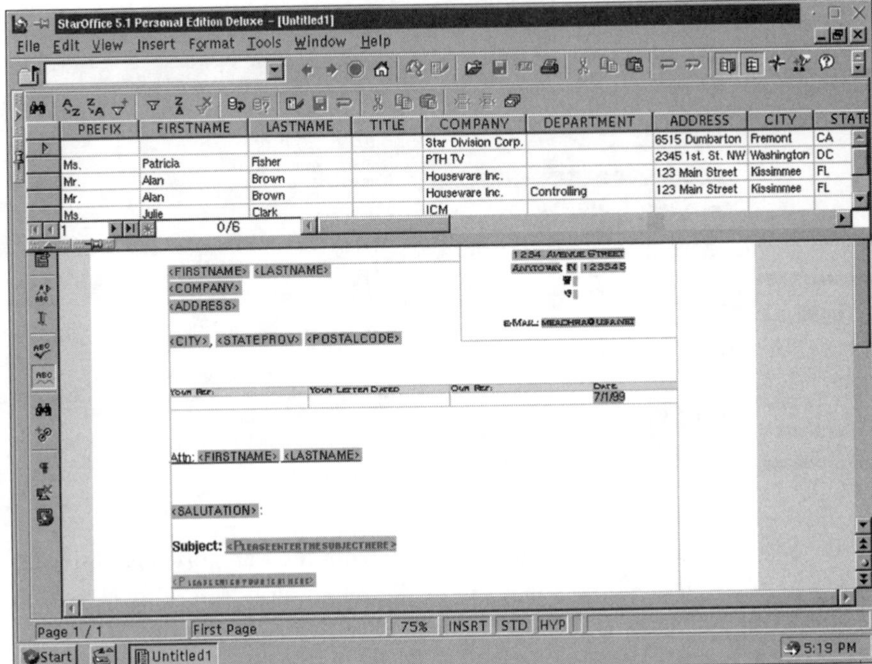

Figure 5-4: To finish creating your document, replace the placeholders with real text.

Creating your own templates

The predefined document templates that come with StarOffice are a good starting point for developing a set of templates to save you time. However, you can get even more benefit from custom templates that you design to automate the process of creating the documents you work with every day. You can create your own document templates and add them to the templates available in the New dialog box by following these steps:

1. **Create a document that contains all the common elements that you may want in any document you create using the new template.**

   The best way to get a good template is to start from a good finished document. Create a finished document and test, print, and proof it. After you're satisfied with the results, delete any text from the document that you don't want to include in the template.

   You can control the template's title and description that appears in the New dialog box by editing settings in the file's Properties dialog box. Choose File⇨Properties to open the Properties dialog box. Fill in the boxes on the Description tab and then click OK.

2. **Choose File⇨Save As.**

   StarOffice opens the Save As dialog box.

3. **Select StarWriter 5.0 Template from the File Type drop-down list box.**

   This action instructs StarOffice to save the document as a template instead of a document file. Make sure that the Automatic File Name Extension option is checked so StarOffice adds to the filename the appropriate extension (VOC), which identifies the file as a template.

4. **Change the Save As directory to ~/Office51/template/.**

   This directory is where StarOffice stores the templates accessed by the New dialog box. If you prefer, you can create a subdirectory under the template/ directory for your custom templates.

5. **Click Save.**

   StarOffice saves the document as a template and closes the Save As dialog box.

The next time you want to create a document based on a template (see the "Using the StarWriter document templates" section, earlier in this chapter), you find your new template available for selection in the New dialog box. If you saved the new template in the template/ directory, it appears in the Standard category list box in the New dialog box. If you saved the new template in a subdirectory of the template/ directory, it appears in a category with the same name as the subdirectory.

If you have a template you expect to use frequently, you can make it more accessible by adding it to the File/New submenu. That way, you can create a document based on the template by simply selecting the template name from the menu, instead of opening the New dialog box and selecting the template from the list box. To add a template to the New submenu, follow these steps:

1. **Use Explorer to locate and open the ~/Office51/config/new/ directory.**

   See Chapter 2 for information on using Explorer.

2. **Right-click the directory window and choose New⇨Link from the pop-up menu that appears.**

   This action opens the Properties of Link dialog box. Click the Bookmark tab if it isn't selected by default.

3. **Enter a name for the menu item in the Name box.**

4. **In the Target URL box, enter the path and filename for the template you want to add to the New submenu.**

   Instead of typing the path and filename, you can click the File button to open the Insert dialog box, which enables you to browse for the template file. After you locate the file, click Insert.

5. **Click the Open As Template check box.**
6. **Click OK.**

   StarOffice closes the Properties of Link dialog box and adds a link icon to the ~/Office51/config/new/ directory. The link is a very small file that simply points to the target file, in this case the template. Creating a link is better than making a copy of the template file because the link consumes less space on your hard drive and it doesn't get outdated when you make changes to the target file. For each link in the directory, you also have a menu item on the File/New submenu.

You can use this same procedure to add templates to the StarOffice Start menu. Simply substitute the ~/Office51/config/start/ directory for the ~/Office51/config/new/ directory in Step 1, and the template link appears on the Start menu in the StarOffice Task bar instead of in the File/New submenu.

This technique creates a link on a menu that instructs StarOffice to create a document using another document as a template. It doesn't create a separate template file in a directory devoted to storing templates. Instead, the link points to a regular document that is probably stored along with other documents. If you delete, move, or edit the document referred to in the link, the link may no longer work or may produce unexpected results. If you use this technique, I suggest that you make copies of the documents you plan to link to as templates and store them in a separate directory, away from other documents, where they are unlikely to be edited or deleted accidentally.

Automating Corrections and Formatting

StarOffice includes a couple of special features — called *AutoCorrect* and *AutoFormat* — that detect certain common spelling mistakes, typing errors, and formatting situations and correct them automatically as you type. You don't have to do anything special to use the AutoCorrect and AutoFormat features. They work (surprise!) automatically, all the time, unless you disable them. You simply type, and they fix your mistakes and format your text, almost like magic!

AutoCorrect monitors the text you type in your document, and if it detects a misspelled word (such as *teh*) that is on its list, AutoCorrect automatically substitutes the replacement word (such as *the*) from its replacement table. AutoFormat works the same way, replacing text strings with real symbols and properly formatted characters — for example, (C) becomes ©.

StarOffice comes with an impressive list of commonly misspelled or mistyped words and a reasonable assortment of symbols and formatting effects that it can correct automatically. As with most StarOffice features, you can customize the AutoCorrect/AutoFormat feature by adding and deleting words in the replacement list and by selecting the kinds of corrections the program makes automatically.

The AutoCorrect feature complements the spellcheck feature very nicely. AutoCorrect automatically corrects many typing errors and spelling mistakes before the spellchecker has a chance to flag them as misspellings. If the spellchecker finds a misspelled word in your document, you can add that word and its correction to the AutoCorrect replacement list. To do so, right-click a word that Auto Spellcheck identifies as misspelled and choose AutoCorrect⇨[Correct Spelling] from the pop-up menu that appears. If you make the same spelling or typing error again, AutoCorrect corrects it for you automatically.

If you need to exercise more detailed control over the AutoCorrect/AutoFormat feature, choose Tools⇨AutoCorrect/AutoFormat to open the AutoCorrect dialog box, as shown in Figure 5-5. The Replace tab enables you to edit the Replacement Table. On the Exceptions tab, you can edit a list of abbreviations that StarOffice will recognize as such instead of interpreting the period at the end of the abbreviation as the end of sentence and automatically capitalizing the next word. Also on the Exceptions tab, you can build a list of words that are supposed to begin with two capital letters. Otherwise, AutoCorrect assumes that two capital letters at the beginning of a word is the result of a heavy finger on the Shift key and automatically corrects the mistake. The Options tab enables you to individually activate or deactivate a list of AutoFormat options. The Custom Quotes tab is where you specify whether StarOffice is to replace the straight quotes you enter from the keyboard with the "curly," typographic-style quotes.

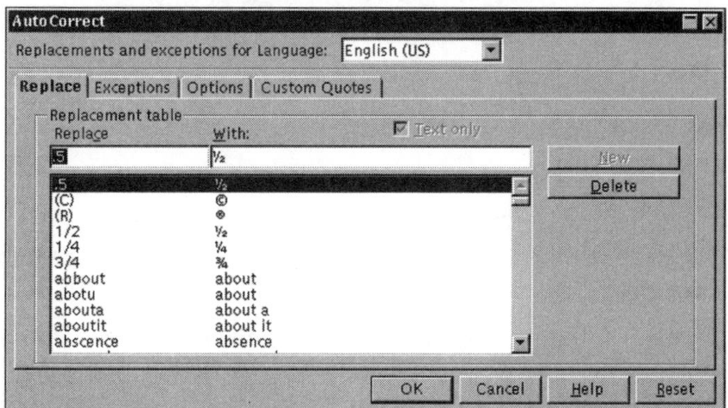

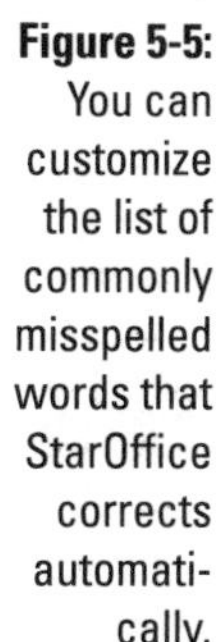
Figure 5-5: You can customize the list of commonly misspelled words that StarOffice corrects automatically.

Preparing Envelopes and Labels

Properly configuring the page margins and other settings to print an envelope or a page of labels can be a real pain. In fact, the hassle is so great with some word processing programs that many people resort to hand addressing their envelopes (or hauling out the old electric typewriter to get the job done). But StarOffice makes dealing with envelopes and labels easy. StarOffice does most of the tedious stuff automatically. All you do is fill in a simple dialog box.

To create an envelope, follow these steps:

1. **Select the recipient's address in your letter or document and copy the address to the clipboard by pressing Ctrl+C.**
2. **Choose Insert⇨Envelope.**

   StarOffice opens the Envelope dialog box, as shown in Figure 5-6.

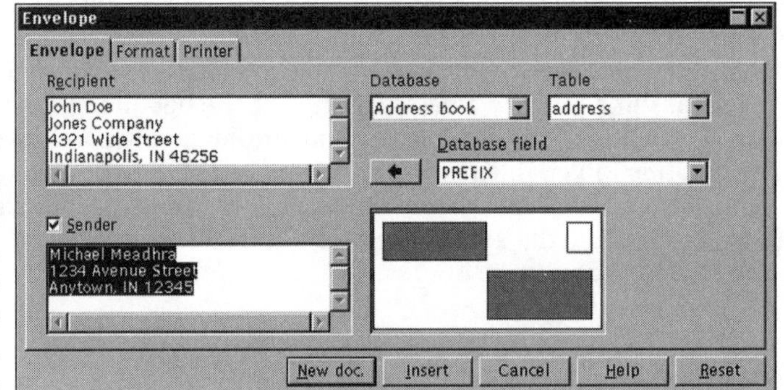

Figure 5-6: To create an envelope, just fill in the Envelope dialog box.

3. **Click the Recipient text box and press Ctrl+V.**

   This action inserts the address you copied from your document into the Envelope dialog box.

4. **Click the Sender check box and edit the return address information as necessary.**

   StarOffice automatically enters your name and address from the User Data you entered when you installed the program. You can edit the information as needed. If you're using envelopes with a preprinted return address, uncheck the Sender check box so that the program doesn't print the return address.

5. **Click the Format tab and adjust the settings as needed.**

   Select the envelope size and confirm the location of the recipient address and return address text blocks. Click the Edit buttons to change the character and paragraph formatting for the address blocks if necessary.

   The choices in the Format drop-down list box are European paper and envelope sizes. The DL size is close to the correct size for a standard business envelope. If the DL size isn't close enough, or if you need to use a different size envelope, you must select User Defined in the Format drop-down list box and then set the appropriate measurements in the Width and Height boxes.

6. **Click the Printer tab and select the appropriate envelope feed option for your printer.**
7. **Click New Doc.**

   StarOffice closes the Envelope dialog box and creates a new document with the page margins and addresses you defined in the dialog box.

8. **To print the envelope, insert an envelope into the printer and click the Print File button on the StarOffice Function toolbar.**

   StarOffice prints the envelope.

If you don't have an existing address in your document that you can copy and paste into the Envelope dialog box, don't worry. You can still create an envelope by manually typing the address into the Recipient box in the Envelope dialog box.

Printing labels is very similar to printing envelopes. You begin by choosing Insert⇨Labels to open the Labels dialog box. Then you enter the label text and make selections on the three tabs (Labels, Format, and Options) to define the sheet of labels you're printing. You can specify the brand and type of labels so that StarOffice configures the label page layout for you, or you can enter custom measurements for the page size and the sizes of the rows and columns. You can elect to print a single label or an entire page of labels. After completing the setup in the Labels dialog box, click New Document to create a new StarWriter document containing the properly laid out page of label text. Then just feed your labels into your printer and print that document.

Chapter 6

Working with More Than Just Words

In This Chapter

- Turning the tables on tabular text
- Adding pictures to your documents
- Stuffing text into a box
- Patrolling the borders
- Free-form text positioning

The text documents you create with StarWriter are, of course, mostly text. But StarWriter documents can also include tables, pictures, lines and borders, and text boxes. This chapter explores some of the StarWriter features that go beyond traditional text handling.

Tabulating Tables

Next to straight paragraphs of text, perhaps the most common text effect is creating tables to present information organized into rows and columns. Often tables include a combination of text and numbers such as you find in a budget proposal, a purchase order, or an invoice. However, a table can be anything arranged in columns and rows, such as a decision matrix, a feature checklist, or a calendar.

One way to create tabular material in a text document is to use tabs in a series of regular text paragraphs. Anyone who has suffered through a typing class is probably familiar with the basic technique, and you can refer to Chapter 3 for information on how to set and use tabs in StarWriter. But using tabs is the hard way to create rows and columns in your document. The StarWriter table feature is much more powerful, flexible, and easier to use.

Inserting a table

A table is a special kind of object that you can insert into your document and then edit to achieve a wide variety of effects. To insert a table into your document, follow these steps:

1. **Position the cursor at the place in your document where you want to insert the table.**

   Be sure to position the cursor between paragraphs. If you attempt to insert a table in the middle of a paragraph, StarWriter breaks your text into two separate paragraphs — one before and one after the table.

2. **Click and hold the main mouse button while pointing to the Insert button in the StarWriter Main toolbar.**

   The Insert button is at the top of the StarWriter Main toolbar. The button's appearance may differ depending on the kind of object you previously inserted using this tool. When you click and hold the Insert button, the Insert floating toolbar appears. After the floating toolbar appears, you can release the mouse button.

3. **Point to the Insert Table button in the Insert floating toolbar.**

   A small grid appears below the Insert Table button.

4. **Move the pointer down into the grid and drag down and to the right to select the number of rows and columns you want in your table.**

   The sizing grid expands automatically as you move the pointer down and to the right. If you know the exact number of columns and rows you need, select that size for your table in the sizing grid. If you're not sure about the size of your table, just select something close. You can edit the table later. In fact, adding rows to a table is particularly easy.

5. **Click the lower right corner of the selection.**

   StarWriter adds a table grid to your document, as shown in Figure 6-1. The table starts out as an empty grid. It's up to you to fill those boxes (called *table cells*) with text, numbers, or what have you. The "Editing a table" section of this chapter shows you how.

As an alternative to the preceding technique, you can insert a table into your document by choosing Insert⇨Table to open the Insert Table dialog box. Then you specify the number of columns and rows you want in the dialog box and click OK to close the dialog box and insert the table. You can open the same Insert Table dialog box by simply clicking the Insert button on the StarWriter Main toolbar — provided that the Insert button is in insert table mode instead of being set to insert a different kind of object. (If the insert button is set to insert another object type, simply click and hold on the button to display the Insert toolbar, and then click the table button on the toolbar.)

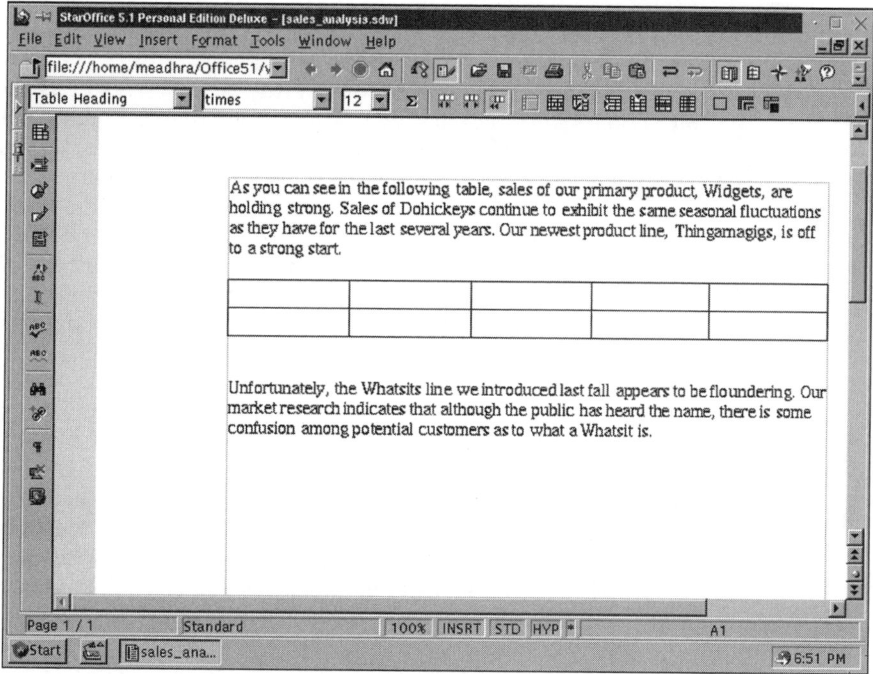

Figure 6-1: A newly created table is just an empty grid.

You can also insert a different kind of table by copying a portion of a StarCalc spreadsheet and pasting that information into your document using the Edit➪Paste or Edit➪Paste Special commands. Instead of a text table, you get a miniature spreadsheet embedded in your document. Flip to Chapter 22 for more information on inserting spreadsheet objects in other kinds of documents.

Star Division designed the StarWriter text tables to be compatible with the HTML tables used in Web page design. That may not seem like an important point when you're creating a document that you intend to print on paper. However, HTML compatibility is becoming increasingly important as more and more document publication moves to the Web. Not only does HTML table compatibility mean that converting your text documents into Web pages is easier, but it also means that your StarWriter document tables support a rich assortment of formatting options, such as using a picture as a background for the whole table or an individual table cell. These kinds of features enable Web page designers to use tables for far more than just presenting text and numbers in rows and columns. Tables are an important page layout tool for Web designers. Nothing prevents you from using tables the same way when you design your paper documents. You can find out more about the technique in a good Web design book such as *Creating Web Pages For Dummies,* 4th Edition, by Bud Smith and Arthur Bebak, or the Cliffs Notes *Creating Your First Web Page,* by Alan Simpson (both published by IDG Books Worldwide, Inc.).

Editing a table

If you insert a table into your document, the table starts out as just a bunch of empty boxes, all of equal size. If you activate the option to display nonprinting characters (choose View⇨Nonprinting Characters or press Ctrl+F10), you see a paragraph mark in each table cell.

To add text and numbers to your table, simply click a table cell and begin typing. If you enter more text than fits on a single line in the cell, the text automatically wraps to another line, keeping the text within the cell. The row height automatically expands to accommodate additional text in any of the row's cells.

You can move the text insertion point to another cell in the table by clicking the new cell or simply pressing the Tab key to move to the next cell in the row. After you get to the last cell in a row, pressing the Tab key moves the cursor to the first cell in the next row. After you reach the last cell in the table, pressing the Tab key adds a new row to the bottom of the table and moves the cursor to the first cell of the new row. This feature makes expanding a table with additional rows very easy as you continue to enter data into the table.

To change the table's column width, move the pointer over a column dividing line. When the pointer changes to a double-headed arrow, drag left or right to make the column wider or narrower. You can also resize columns by dragging the column divider lines in the ruler at the top of the StarWriter document window. As you resize the width of the table columns, StarWriter automatically reflows the text in those columns and adjusts the table's height accordingly.

In addition to changing the width of columns, you can manipulate the table's size and shape in several other ways. The following list summarizes the column editing options. In each case, a counterpart exists for manipulating rows.

- To select a column of cells, right-click any cell in the column and choose Column⇨Select.
- To add a column to the table, right-click a cell in an adjacent column and choose Column⇨Insert to open the Insert Column dialog box. Enter the number of columns to add and whether the new columns should be inserted before or after the selected column, and then click OK.
- To delete a column, right-click a cell in the column you want to get rid of and choose Column⇨Delete from the pop-up menu that appears.
- To automatically adjust the width of the columns in a table, select the columns you want to adjust and choose Column⇨Space Equally to make all the selected columns equal widths, or choose Column⇨Optimal Width to automatically size the columns to fit the text that they contain.

Besides manipulating whole rows and columns, you can also combine cells to create a larger cell that spans multiple rows or columns or split cells to create extra, smaller cells without inserting whole rows or columns.

- To merge two (or more) adjacent cells, select the cells you want to merge by dragging the pointer across the cells, right-click the selected cells, and then choose Cell⇨Merge.
- To split a single cell into two or more separate cells, right-click the cell you want to split and then choose Cell⇨Split to open the Split Cells dialog box. Select the number of cells you want to create within the single cell, choose whether to split the single cell horizontally or vertically, and then click OK. StarWriter divides the selected cell into two or more new cells that together occupy the space of the original cell.

Figure 6-2 shows a table after adjusting column widths and applying some formatting.

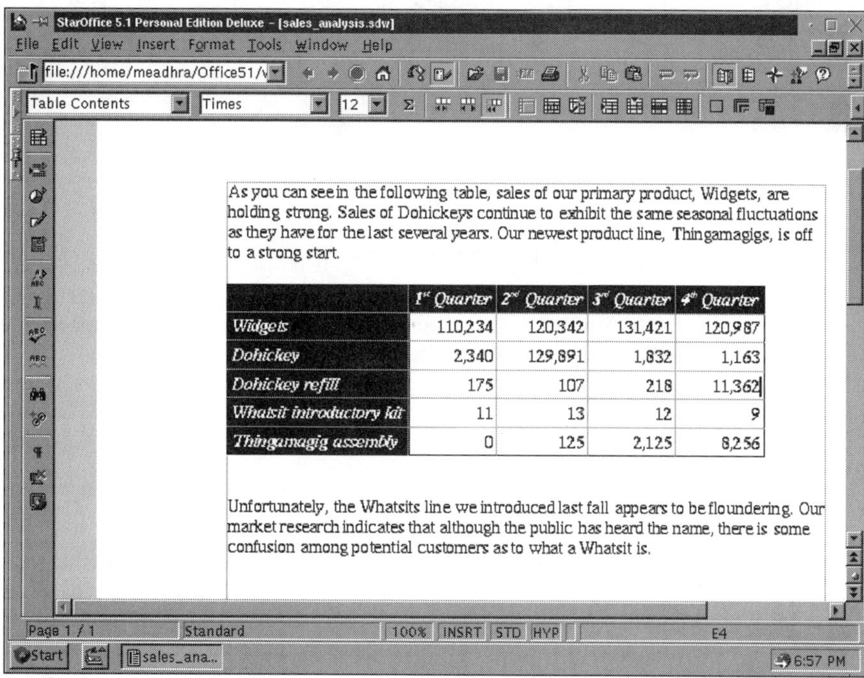

Figure 6-2: A few table adjustments help the text fit better in the table.

After you insert a table into your document, StarWriter automatically formats the top row of the table using the Table Heading style (bold, italic, and centered in each cell). The rest of the table cells are formatted with the Table Contents style. You can change the styles and other text and number formatting attributes applied to the contents of table cells by using the same techniques you use to format any other text in your document.

You can format your table manually and maintain total control over its appearance. However, if you want to take a shortcut to an attractive table, you can apply predefined formatting by taking advantage of the StarWriter AutoFormat feature. To use one of the AutoFormat table treatments, follow these steps:

1. **Select the table and choose Format➪AutoFormat.**

   StarWriter opens the AutoFormat dialog box, as shown in Figure 6-3. Click the More button if you want to display the Formatting options at the bottom of the dialog box.

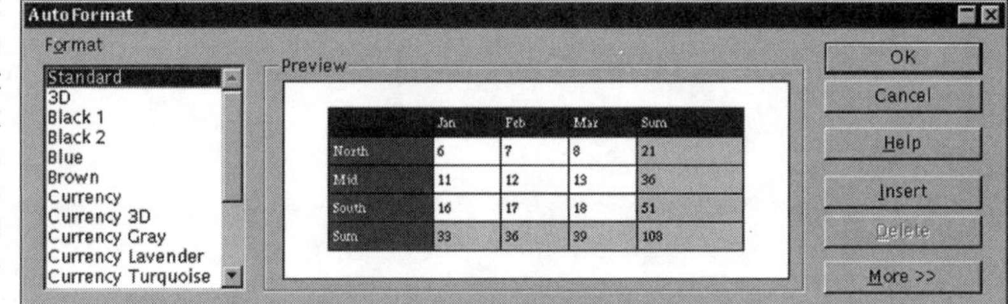

Figure 6-3: The AutoFormat dialog box gives you access to predesigned table formats.

2. **Select a format from the Format list box on the left.**

   A thumbnail preview of the selected format appears in the Preview box.

3. **If you want to selectively apply some format characteristics to your table, uncheck the check boxes in the Formatting area for those characteristics you don't want.**

4. **Click OK.**

   StarWriter closes the AutoFormat dialog box and applies the selected formatting to your table.

You can create a customized table with AutoFormat. Start by formatting a table with the characteristics you want to save as an AutoFormat. Then select the table and choose Format➪AutoFormat to open the AutoFormat dialog box. Click Insert to open the Add AutoFormat dialog box. Type in a name for your new format and click OK. StarWriter adds the new format to the Format list box in the AutoFormat dialog box. In the future, you can select and apply your format just as you do any of the predefined formats.

Inserting Pictures in Your Text

After straight text and tabular matter, the most common objects people add to their text documents are pictures. Whether they are pictures of the kids in a family newsletter or pictures of the product in a sales brochure, pictures can enhance all sorts of text documents.

You can insert a picture into a StarWriter text document several ways. The following list summarizes the most common techniques:

- **Copy a drawing from StarDraw or an image from StarImage and paste it into your document.** While in StarDraw or StarImage, select your drawing and use the Edit⇨Copy command to copy the drawing or image and then return to StarWriter and paste the drawing or image into your document using the Edit⇨Paste or Edit⇨Paste Special command. See Chapter 22 for more information on copying and pasting between StarOffice tools.
- **Create a StarImage object in your document.** Choose Insert⇨Picture⇨From Image Editor, define the size of the image in the New Image dialog box, and click Create to add the image object to your document. With the image open in your document, you have access to the StarImage menus and toolbars, which you can use to edit the image. After editing the image, click anywhere in your document that's outside the image to return to normal text editing.
- **Import an image from your scanner directly into your document.** Choose Insert⇨Picture⇨Scan⇨Acquire to open your scanner control dialog box. (You must have previously specified the scanner source.) After you scan the image, StarOffice automatically inserts the scanned image into your document.
- **Insert a picture file into your document.** This is the most common technique and the one covered in the most detail in the following steps:

  1. **Position the cursor at the point in your text where you want to insert the picture.**
  2. **Choose Insert⇨Picture⇨From File.**

     StarWriter opens the Insert Picture dialog box, as shown in Figure 6-4.
  3. **From the list box, select the picture file you want to insert.**

     The Insert Picture dialog box is essentially an Open File dialog box, and you use the same techniques to locate and select a picture file that you use to locate and select any other file you want to open in StarOffice. The nice feature of the Insert Picture dialog box is the preview box on the right (refer to Figure 6-4). If you check the Preview option at the bottom of the dialog box, StarOffice displays a low resolution rendition of the selected image in a large preview box.

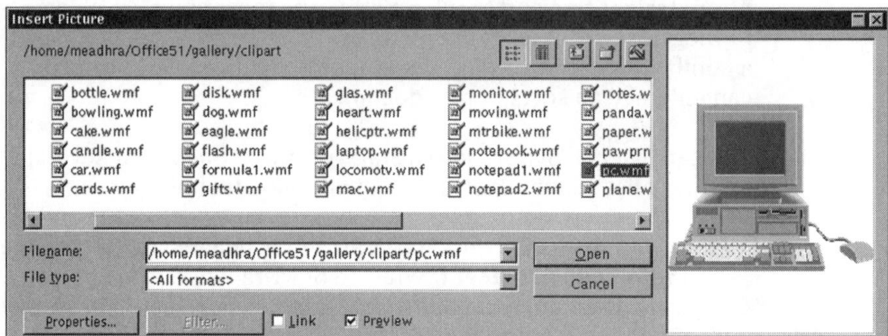

Figure 6-4: The Insert Picture dialog box enables you to preview an image before inserting it into your document.

The Deluxe CD version of StarOffice includes an assortment of picture files that you can add to your documents. You find them in the ~/Office51/gallery directory and its subdirectories. Check 'em out!

4. **After you select the desired image, click Open.**

   StarOffice closes the Insert Picture dialog box and inserts the selected picture into your text document, as shown in Figure 6-5. Notice the green control handles on the perimeter of the picture and the anchor button in the text. These on-screen tools enable you to move and resize the picture, but they won't show up in the finished document. Also notice that the Object toolbar changes after a picture is selected to give you an assortment of tools for formatting the picture and the box around it. You can find out what the buttons on the Object toolbar do by pointing to each button for a moment — StarOffice displays the button's descriptive name in a pop-up ToolTip.

5. **Move and resize the picture as needed.**

   To resize the picture, point to one of the green control handles on the perimeter of the picture. After the pointer changes to a double-headed arrow, drag the handle toward the center of the picture to make the picture smaller or drag the pointer away from the center to make the picture larger. As you drag, StarWriter displays an outline box to indicate the new size of the picture. When the box reaches the desired size, release the mouse button. Star Writer redraws the picture to the new size.

Press and hold the Shift key as you drag a control handle to resize the picture. Doing so forces StarWriter to maintain the aspect ratio (proper height to width proportions) of the image as you resize it. Resizing a picture without using the Shift key enables you to stretch or compress the picture.

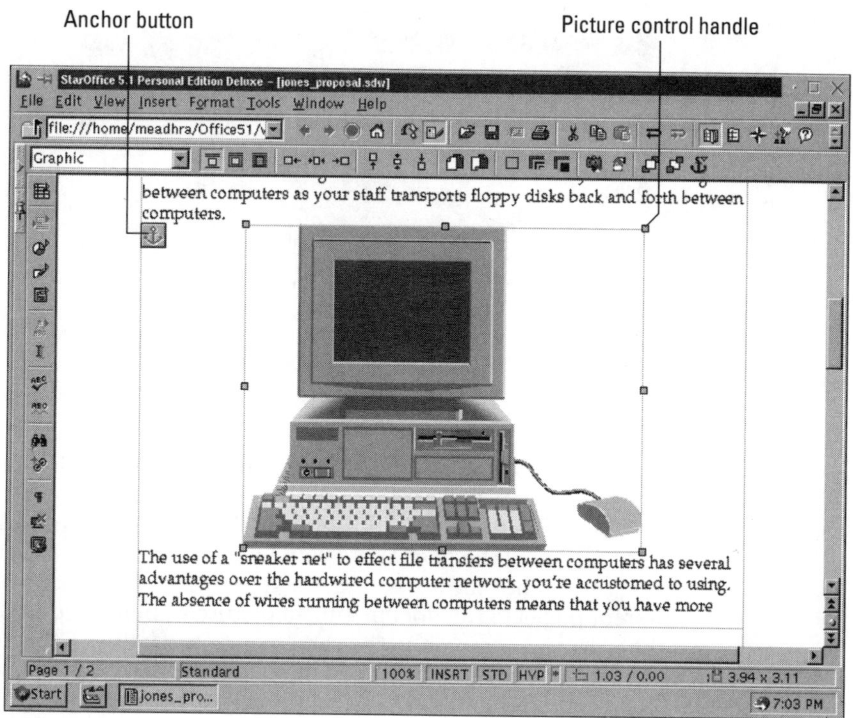

Figure 6-5: A picture inserted into a document.

To move the picture, just click and drag the picture itself. StarWriter displays an outline box as you drag. Release the mouse button to drop the picture in the new location. StarWriter redraws the picture in the new position and also moves text on the page to flow around the picture.

6. **Click anywhere in your document outside of the picture.**

   The picture control handles and anchor button disappear, and StarWriter displays the picture the way it will appear in your finished document.

After you place a picture into your document, you can go back and revise and reformat that picture at any time. Just click the picture to select it — the control handles and anchor button appear, to show that the picture is selected. Double-click the picture to open the Pictures dialog box, as shown in Figure 6-6. The various tabs in the Pictures dialog box contain settings that enable you to control almost every aspect of the picture's position and formatting. For example, the Wrap tab contains some of the settings that are most likely to need adjustment. Click one of the buttons across the top of the Wrap tab to select the way your document text flows around the picture. Adjust the settings in the Spacing area to control how much white space appears between the picture and the text. After adjusting the settings in the Pictures dialog box, click OK to close the dialog box and apply the formatting.

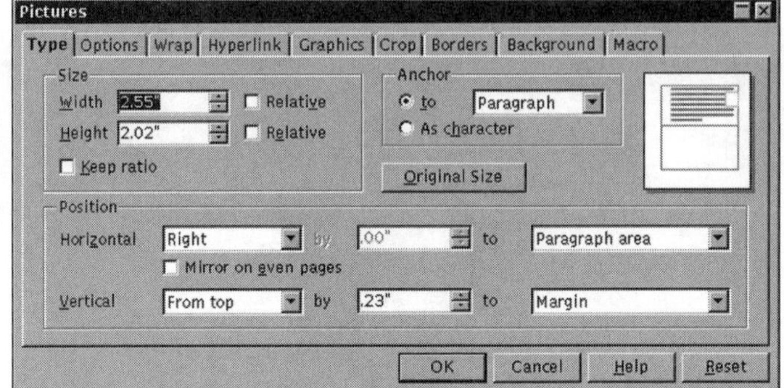

Figure 6-6: The Pictures dialog box provides many formatting options that you can apply to the selected picture.

The anchor button plays an important role in positioning a picture in your document. The anchor button indicates the picture's anchor point in the document text. StarWriter normally positions a picture relative to the text paragraph containing the anchor. As you add and delete text, before and after the anchor, the anchor moves with the text to different locations on the page or to different pages in the document. If a picture's anchor moves, StarWriter moves the picture, keeping it in the same position relative to the anchor. For example, a picture may be positioned immediately following the paragraph containing the anchor and flush left on the page. If you add two pages of text somewhere preceding the picture's anchor, StarWriter automatically moves the picture two pages so that it still appears immediately after the paragraph containing the anchor and flush left on the page.

To control the way StarWriter keeps track of a picture's anchor relative to the surrounding text, click the Anchor button on the Picture Object toolbar. (The picture must be selected in order to display the Picture Object toolbar.) You can choose one of the following options:

- **Paragraph.** This option positions the picture relative to the paragraph containing the anchor. This is the default setting.
- **Page.** This option anchors the picture to a page in your document, not to a specific text paragraph.
- **At Character.** This option positions the picture relative to the exact location of the anchor within the text, not just relative to the whole paragraph. This is mostly useful for smaller pictures that may fit within a paragraph.
- **As Character.** This option inserts the picture into the text at the anchor point. This option is useful for very small pictures that you may use as symbols in your text.
- **Text Box.** This option is available only if the picture anchor is inside a text box. Naturally enough, this option causes the picture to move relative to the position of the text box containing the anchor.

Boxing Text in Text Boxes

One of the great things about adding pictures to your documents is the flexibility to resize the picture and move it around on the page. StarWriter lets you do the same thing with a text box. You can use text boxes to create blocks of text that you can move around and freely position in your document. Text boxes work great for those enlarged quotes (called *pull quotes*) that you often see in newsletters and articles, and they're terrific for creating coupons and all sorts of other text effects in flyers and brochures.

To create a text box, follow these steps:

1. **Position the cursor at the point where you want to insert the text box.**
2. **Choose Insert⇨Text Box.**

   StarWriter opens the Text Box dialog box, which looks very similar to the Pictures dialog box (refer to Figure 6-6).
3. **Enter the desired size of the text box in the Width and Height boxes.**

   You can create the text box to your exact specifications by adjusting the size and other settings, or you can just accept the defaults and resize the text box later.
4. **Adjust other settings as needed and then click OK.**

   StarOffice closes the Text Box dialog box and inserts an empty box into your document. Notice on your screen the green control handles on the perimeter of the box and the anchor button in the text — just like those that appear with a newly inserted picture. Also notice that the Object toolbar changes to provide tools for formatting the text box.
5. **Move and resize the text box as needed.**

   Moving and resizing a text box require the same procedures as moving and resizing a picture. For more information, see the "Inserting Pictures in Your Text" section, earlier in this chapter.
6. **Click anywhere in your document outside of the text box.**

   The picture control handles and anchor button disappear, and StarWriter displays the text box as a gray outline (unless you previously defined a border or background for the text box).
7. **Click anywhere in the text box to place the cursor inside.**
8. **Type the text you want to appear inside the text box.**

   Use normal text entry and editing techniques to add text in the text box. You can also format the text using the same text styles and formatting attributes you use on other text. Paragraph alignment and indents are applied relative to the text box margins, rather than the page margins.

9. **After entering text into the text box, click anywhere in your document outside the text box.**

   StarWriter returns to normal editing mode. The text box containing your newly entered text appears in the document page, and the regular text flows around the text box according to the wrap settings for the text box. See Figure 6-7.

When you click anywhere in a text box, StarWriter assumes that you want to edit the text in the text box and moves the cursor to the spot you click. That feature makes editing the text in a text box the same as editing the rest of the text in your document. If you want to select the text box itself — for instance, you want to move or resize the box — you must click the edge of the text box to select it. When you do so, the control handles and anchor button appear, to show that the text box is selected. The buttons on the Object toolbar change to give you access to formatting options appropriate for manipulating text boxes. You can also double-click the text box to open the Text Box dialog box, which enables you to exercise even more precise control over the various text box formatting options.

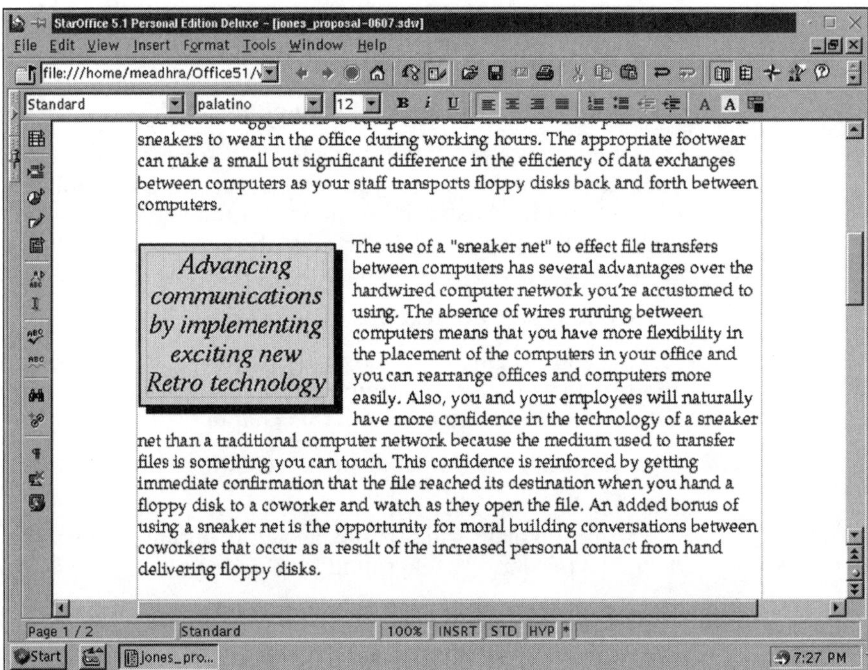

Figure 6-7: The finished text box inserted in a document.

Adding Lines and Borders

A very effective technique for adding emphasis to a paragraph of text is to draw a border around the paragraph, or create a colored background box for the paragraph, or use a combination of the two. StarWriter makes creating text borders and backgrounds easy — simply follow these steps:

1. **Select a paragraph to which you want to add a border or background.**
2. **Right-click the paragraph and choose Paragraph from the pop-up menu that appears, or choose Format➪Paragraph from the menu.**

   StarWriter opens the Paragraph dialog box.

3. **Click the Borders tab.**

   StarWriter displays the options shown in Figure 6-8.

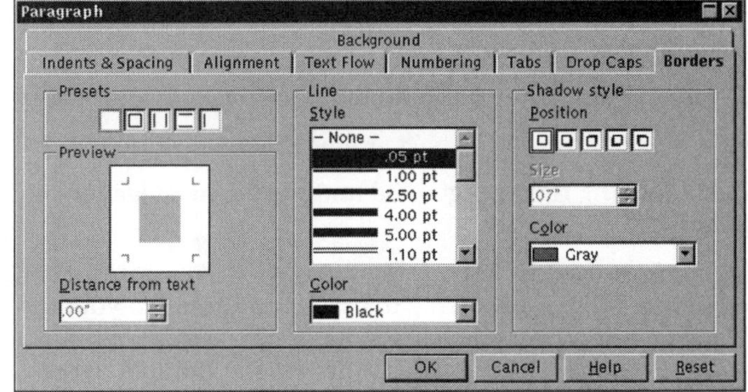

Figure 6-8: Defining the border for a paragraph.

4. **Select a line style and thickness from the Style list box.**
5. **Click one of the buttons in the Presets area.**

   StarWriter previews the selected effect in the Preview area. In addition to using the presets, you can manually select the sides of the paragraph on which you want the border to appear by clicking that side of the gray box in the Preview area. Click once to turn the border on and click again to turn it off.

6. **If desired, you can also add a shadow to the paragraph border by clicking one of the Position buttons in the Shadow Style area. Then select the Size and Color of the Shadow in the respective boxes.**
7. **Click the Background tab.**

   StarWriter displays the options shown in Figure 6-9.

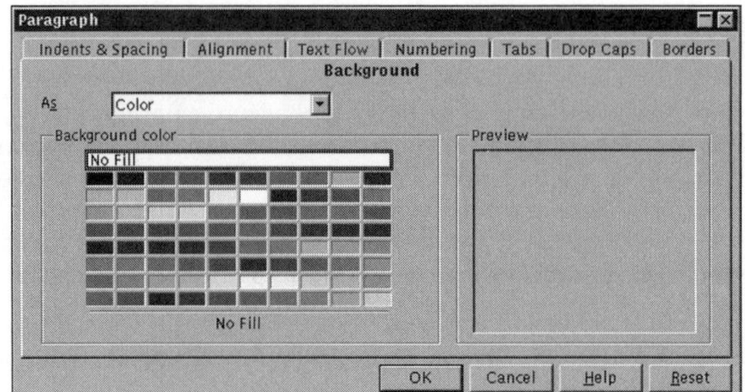

Figure 6-9: Pick a color for the paragraph background.

8. **Select Color in the As drop-down list box.**

   Your other option is to select Graphic, which causes StarWriter to replace the Background Color palette with a Browse button and options that enable you to select a picture file to use as the paragraph background.

9. **Click one of the color boxes in the Background Color palette.**

   StarWriter previews your background color selection in the Preview box.

10. **After adjusting the background and border settings to your liking, click OK.**

    StarWriter closes the Paragraph dialog box and creates a background and border for the selected paragraph, according to your specifications.

You can also create a background and border for multiple paragraphs. Just select several adjacent paragraphs, open the Paragraph dialog box, and define the border and background treatment. StarWriter draws the border around all the selected paragraphs as if they were a single unit and then adds a background.

Border and background treatments aren't confined to paragraphs. You can also add borders and backgrounds to an entire page by using the settings on the Borders and Background tabs of the Page Style dialog box (right-click the page and from the pop-up menu choose Page to open the Page Style dialog box).

Borders and backgrounds can also apply to tables. The Borders and Background tabs in the Tables dialog box are similar to their counterparts in the Paragraph dialog box. The biggest difference is that you have the option of applying borders and backgrounds to individual table cells, to rows of cells, or to the entire table.

Positioning Text with Direct Cursor

Normally, you can only enter text starting at the top of a document. If you want to position text somewhere down the page, you must first enter empty paragraphs to move the insertion point down, away from its starting point in the upper-left corner of the page.

The StarWriter Direct Cursor feature doesn't really change that situation, but it does make positioning text on a blank area of the page a little easier by automating the process of entering the multiple paragraph marks, tabs, and spaces needed to position the insertion point at a given location on the page. To use Direct Cursor, follow these simple steps:

1. **Click the Direct Cursor button on the StarWriter Main toolbar.**
2. **Click anywhere you want to enter text, within the text boundaries of your document page.**

   StarWriter automatically inserts enough blank paragraphs, tabs, and spaces to move the insertion point to the selected location on your page.
3. **Enter, edit, and format text normally.**
4. **Click the Direct Cursor button again to turn off the feature.**

   StarWriter returns the I-beam pointer to normal operation.

Part III

Calculating with StarCalc

"MY GIRLFRIEND RAN A SPREADSHEET OF MY LIFE, AND GENERATED THIS CHART. MY BEST HOPE IS THAT SHE'LL CHANGE HER MAJOR FROM 'COMPUTER SCIENCES' TO 'REHABILITATIVE SERVICES.'"

In this part . . .

If you deal with numbers all day long, the chapters in this part of the book are for you. They cover StarCalc, the StarOffice spreadsheet tool. StarCalc enables you to do more than just create simple spreadsheets that perform basic math operations — StarCalc also supports sophisticated functions for statistical and financial calculations and lets you create multiple spreadsheets in the same spreadsheet file. Also in this part is coverage of StarChart, StarOffice's charting tool that converts raw numbers into bars and pies and lines that help you discover and illustrate trends in the data.

Chapter 7

Basic Number Crunching

In This Chapter

- Getting to know StarCalc
- Spreading out your spreadsheet
- Using the proper form for cell addresses
- Entering data into your spreadsheet
- Performing basic math calculations
- Saving and sharing spreadsheets

Budgets, invoices, sales projections, job cost estimates, and loan comparisons all have something in common — they involve numbers and calculations. They have another thing in common, too — they're the kind of things that spreadsheet programs are designed to handle quickly and easily. But that's probably no big surprise. Spreadsheets have been a mainstay of computer applications since the days of the original VisiCalc and Lotus 1-2-3 spreadsheets. In fact, for many people, the ability to create electronic spreadsheets and use them for many things are the main reasons they use computers in the first place.

This chapter introduces StarCalc, the StarOffice spreadsheet tool. It covers basic spreadsheet operations, such as creating spreadsheet documents, entering text and numbers, performing calculations, and saving your spreadsheet files. You also find out how to exchange spreadsheets with colleagues who use Microsoft Excel. The other chapters in this part show you how to create more sophisticated spreadsheets and how to use StarChart to create charts. But StarCalc and StarChart can do more than I have room to cover in these pages. For information on any of the StarOffice features not covered in this book, check out the *StarOffice Bible* by Jacek Artymiak, Katherine Wrightson, and Joseph Merlino (published by IDG Books Worldwide, Inc.).

Introducing StarCalc

StarCalc is the StarOffice spreadsheet tool — the tool for creating documents composed of text and numbers arranged in rows and columns. That description of a spreadsheet may sound like a description of a table, and in a way, a spreadsheet is just a big table. But a spreadsheet is also much more. A StarCalc spreadsheet can contain multiple sheets, perform sophisticated calculations on the data in those sheets, and display the results.

StarCalc is a very powerful tool for performing calculations and analyzing data. Despite its power, though, StarCalc is easy to use. You can quickly figure out how to enter text and numbers into a spreadsheet and perform basic math operations, even if you've never used a spreadsheet before. On the other hand, if you're familiar with Microsoft Excel, then you already know a lot about how to use StarCalc, because StarCalc is very similar to its counterpart from the big Microsoft Office suite. If you're a math whiz who enjoys creating and editing long formulas, StarCalc can accommodate you.

StarCalc is *not* a separate spreadsheet program. Unlike Microsoft Excel, which is a stand-alone program that is bundled with other programs to form the Microsoft Office suite, StarCalc is an integrated and inseparable component of the StarOffice program. In fact, StarCalc is really just a convenient label for StarOffice's built-in features for working with spreadsheet documents. If you're accustomed to working with separate stand-alone programs in other office suites, the tight integration of the StarOffice tools may take some getting used to.

Creating a New Spreadsheet

Because StarCalc is an integrated component of the StarOffice program, you can create a new StarCalc spreadsheet document from just about anywhere in StarOffice. You don't need to launch a separate spreadsheet program and then create or open a file in that program as you do with some other office suites. In StarOffice, you simply click an icon in StarDesktop (see Chapter 2 for more information on working with StarDesktop) or choose a command while you're editing another spreadsheet in a StarCalc document, working on a StarWriter document, or working in some other window. StarOffice pops open a new StarCalc document window for you. In fact, the *only* way to get the StarCalc menus and toolbars on-screen is to have a spreadsheet document open for editing. Here's a summary of the techniques you can use to create a new StarCalc spreadsheet:

- Double-click the New Spreadsheet icon in the StarDesktop work area.
- Choose File⇨New⇨Spreadsheet from the StarOffice menu.
- Right-click the desktop background in StarDesktop and choose New⇨Documents⇨Spreadsheet from the pop-up menu that appears.
- Click the Start button in the StarOffice Task bar and choose Spreadsheet.

Regardless of the technique you use to create a new spreadsheet, the result is the same: StarOffice opens a new document window (see Figure 7-1) containing a new blank spreadsheet, and the StarCalc menus and toolbars replace the menus and toolbars previously displayed. The new spreadsheet is creatively labeled "Untitled" until you give it a name the first time you save the spreadsheet file.

Formula toolbar
StarCalc Object toolbar
Active cell
Row buttons
Column buttons
Sheet tabs
Status bar
Work area
Scroll bars
StarCalc Main toolbar

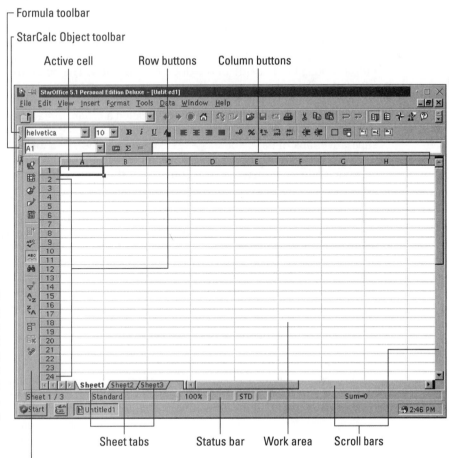

Figure 7-1: A new spreadsheet document in a StarCalc document window.

Although the new spreadsheet appears to replace whatever you were working on before, it's really just a new document window sitting on top of the StarDesktop window and any other document windows you may have open. The other documents, and their accompanying menus and toolbars, aren't gone — they're just hidden temporarily. StarOffice always displays the menus and toolbars that provide the appropriate context for the contents of the active document window — in this case, your new StarCalc spreadsheet.

Understanding the Anatomy of a Spreadsheet

The StarCalc document window doesn't sport a separate title bar labeling it as a StarCalc spreadsheet. But that won't keep you from identifying a StarCalc document at first glance. Notice that the work area of the document window is filled with a grid delineating the rows and columns characteristic of spreadsheets in any program. The rows are labeled with numbers that appear on buttons along the left side of the document window. The columns are labeled with letters on buttons across the top of the work area.

The intersection of a row and a column is called a *cell* in spreadsheet parlance. A cell is the basic building block of a spreadsheet. Each cell can contain a separate chunk of data, such as a text label, a number, or a formula that performs calculations and displays the result. What's more, those formulas can reference other cells and use the contents of those cells in the formula's calculations.

Each spreadsheet can stretch to hundreds of columns and thousands of rows. (If you're getting picky about the exact numbers, there are 256 columns and 32,000 rows, for a total of over 8 million cells.) Naturally, StarOffice can never squeeze that many cells into the confines of the StarCalc document window. Instead, the scroll bars on the right and bottom edges of the work area enable you to view different portions of the spreadsheet. You're probably already familiar with scroll bars from other programs, and the StarCalc scroll bars don't harbor any surprises. Just click the arrow buttons at either end of a scroll bar to move the spreadsheet view in that direction.

One thing you may notice about the bottom horizontal scroll bar is that it doesn't extend all the way across the bottom of the spreadsheet. Instead, three tabs and some more buttons occupy the left end of the space. Each StarCalc spreadsheet file can contain multiple spreadsheet pages, and the tabs represent the three sheets that the program creates by default. You simply click a tab to display the corresponding spreadsheet page. I show you how to work with multiple spreadsheet pages in Chapter 8.

Notice that when a StarCalc document is open, the StarOffice menu bar changes to include the Insert, Format, and Data menus. The standard StarOffice Function toolbar appears just below the menu bar in Figure 7-1. As with all the StarOffice toolbars, you can move the Function toolbar to another location if you want (see the instructions in Chapter 2). Figure 7-1 shows the toolbar in its default location.

The StarCalc Object toolbar sits just below the Function toolbar in Figure 7-1. Like its counterpart in StarWriter, the StarCalc Object toolbar contains an assortment of buttons that give you easy access to StarCalc's formatting tools. I cover how to use most of them in Chapter 9. You can turn the StarCalc Object toolbar on or off by choosing View⇨Toolbars⇨Object Bar.

Just below the StarCalc Object toolbar is another toolbar — the Formula toolbar. You use this toolbar as you enter and edit text, numbers, and formulas in your spreadsheet's cells. As with the other toolbars, you can turn this one on and off by choosing View⇨Toolbars⇨Formula Bar, but you don't want to do that. Entering and editing formulas without access to the Input line (the large text box that occupies most of the Formula toolbar) can be difficult.

The StarCalc Main toolbar sits on the left side of the document window in Figure 7-1. The buttons on this toolbar are typical of what you find on the Main toolbar in other StarOffice tools. Some of the buttons, such as the ones that control spellchecking, are common to most StarOffice tools, whereas the buttons to insert cells and sort lists are specific to StarCalc. To turn the Main toolbar on or off, choose View⇨Toolbars⇨Main Toolbar.

The status bar at the bottom of the StarCalc document window rounds out the inventory of standard window parts. From left to right, the status bar displays the current sheet (page) number, the page template in use, the screen magnification, the selection mode (more on selection modes in the Selecting cells section of this chapter), and either the date and time or the sum (or one of five other functions) of the numbers in the selected cells. You can turn the status bar on or off by choosing View⇨Status Bar.

Addressing Cells

Each individual cell in a spreadsheet has a unique address that allows you to refer to that cell and no other. You can use cell addresses to navigate to specific locations in your spreadsheet.

However, cell addresses are even more important when they're used in formulas. You can use a cell address in place of a number or variable in a mathematical formula to instruct StarCalc to use the contents of that cell in its calculations. This feature is the real power of a spreadsheet program. The ability to use cell addresses in formulas enables you to enter a value in one cell of your spreadsheet and have numerous formulas in various locations throughout the spreadsheet reference that cell and use its value in calculations. Furthermore, other formulas can use the results of those calculations by referencing the cells where the formulas are stored. That means you can change one number in one cell, and StarCalc automatically updates the results of calculations throughout the spreadsheet.

The format for cell addresses in StarCalc is very simple and mimics the cell addressing system in other popular spreadsheets, such as Lotus 1-2-3 and Microsoft Excel. Each cell is formed by the intersection of a column and a row in the spreadsheet grid. Therefore, the cell address is derived from a combination of the column and row identifiers. A cell address is composed of a letter (representing the column) and a number (representing the row). For example, the address of the cell that lies at the intersection of column C and row 15 is C15.

Moving Around in Your Spreadsheet

As you work in a spreadsheet document, you frequently move around to various cells, entering data here, building a formula there, and checking a result somewhere else. So being able to move to a given cell location quickly and easily is important.

Selecting cells

The simplest way to select a spreadsheet cell for editing is to simply click the cell. StarCalc marks the selected cell with a bold outline, and the selected cell's address appears in the Sheet Area box at the left end of the Formula toolbar. (Refer back to Figure 7-1, in which cell C15 is selected.)

As long as the cell you want is displayed in the StarCalc document window, clicking the cell is the fastest way to select it. Even if you need to scroll the document window a little to bring a cell into view, the process is still fast and easy. However, some spreadsheets get quite large, and scrolling long distances can be tedious. So StarCalc gives you some alternate methods for selecting cells.

One way to select an individual cell is to use the Sheet Area box in the Formula toolbar. Instead of clicking a cell to select it (so that StarCalc displays the cell address in the Sheet Area box), you can type a cell address into the Sheet Area box and press Enter. StarCalc instantly selects that cell and brings it into view in the StarCalc document window.

You can also select a whole range of cells for use in a Sum calculation or to apply formatting attributes. To select a range of contiguous cells, just click and drag the pointer down the row or column, over the cells you want to select. Release the mouse button when you have selected all the cells you want.

Another way to select a range of cells is to select an entire row or an entire column. To do so, simply click the row or column button along the left side or top of the document window. StarCalc automatically selects all the cells in the corresponding row or column.

To select a rectangular area of cells, click a cell in one corner and drag diagonally to the opposite corner of the area you want to select. When you release the mouse button, StarCalc selects all the cells within the area you defined.

Sometimes selecting a range of cells by clicking and dragging is cumbersome, particularly if you need to scroll the spreadsheet to move from the beginning to the end of the selection. Fortunately, StarCalc offers some alternative selection techniques. You can select a range of cells by clicking the cell at one corner of the range and then pressing and holding the Shift key as you click the cell at the opposite corner of the range. StarCalc selects the cells you clicked and all the cells in between. You can accomplish the same thing by clicking the first cell, then clicking the selection mode display in the status bar until it reads `EXT` (for *extend selection*), and then clicking the cell at the opposite corner of the selection. Just as it does when you select an individual cell, the Sheet Area box in the Formula toolbar displays the address of the selected range of cells by listing the first cell address and the last cell address separated by a colon — A5:D8. You can also type a cell range address in the Sheet Area box to select that cell range and bring it into view in the StarCalc document window.

You don't have to select only a contiguous group of cells, such as a row, column, or rectangular range. You also can select disconnected cells, such as a row across the top of the spreadsheet plus three additional cells in a column on the left side. To do so, make your first selection, click the selection status display in the status bar until it reads `ADD` (for *add to selection*), and then click (or click and drag) to select additional cells. StarOffice selects the additional cells without deselecting the previously selected cells. (After using the ADD selection mode, don't forget to click the selection mode display in the status bar until it reads `STD` (for *standard selection*) to return the selection mode to normal operation.

Navigating your spreadsheet with Navigator

StarCalc provides another set of spreadsheet navigation tools in the Navigator window (see Figure 7-2). The Navigator in StarCalc is similar to the Navigator in StarWriter (see Chapter 4 for more information on Navigator in StarWriter). In fact, you see the same Navigator window, but the buttons and the items in the list box change to present options appropriate for navigating in a spreadsheet instead of a text document.

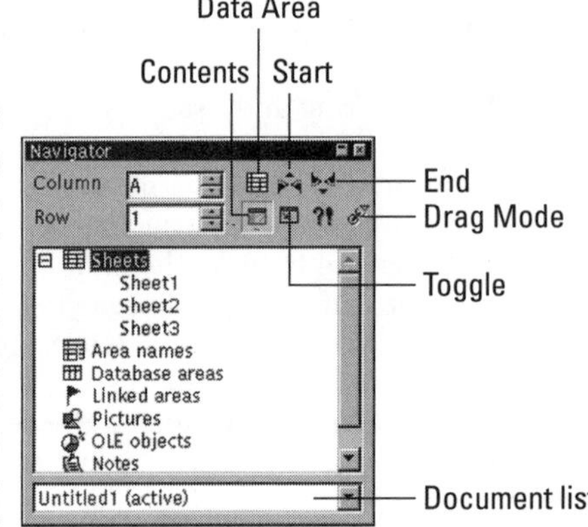

Figure 7-2: The Navigator adapts to show spreadsheet navigation options in StarCalc.

To display the Navigator window, click the Navigator button on the Function toolbar, or choose Edit⇨Navigator, or press F5. Click the button again to close the Navigator window. The Navigator window is a floating tool that remains visible on top of your document window, even when you open or select a different document. You can move the Navigator window to different locations within the StarOffice program window by dragging its title bar. You can also dock the Navigator window to the side of the StarOffice window, as you can the Explorer and Beamer windows (see Chapter 2 for instructions on docking and undocking windows).

Here's a list of the main StarCalc Navigator boxes and buttons and what they do:

- **Column and Row boxes.** Adjust the column and row settings to create a cell address and press Enter to select that cell.
- **Start/End.** Use these buttons to select the start or end of the current data area (range).

- **Content.** Click this button to display or hide the list box below the buttons in the Navigator window. You can double-click items (such as sheets or named database areas) in the list box to go to those items.

- **Toggle.** Click this button to cause the list box in the Navigator window to toggle between showing all the possible document elements or only those elements that are available for selection in the current document.

- **Drag Mode.** Drag items from the Navigator window list box and drop them into your document. Click the Drag Mode button and make a selection from the pop-up menu that appears, to determine whether StarWriter inserts those items as hyperlinks, links, or simple text copy.

The Navigator window list box enables you to go directly to any identifiable element (such as a sheet, named range [data area], or picture) within your spreadsheet without having to know the exact cell address.

The drop-down list box at the bottom of the Navigator window lists all the open StarWriter documents. When you select a different document from the drop-down list box, the Navigator window list box displays the document elements that are available for selection in that document. Click the plus (+) box beside an element name to expand the list so that it shows the individual items of that type. Double-click an item, such as a specific area name, in the list box to automatically select the cell at that location in your spreadsheet and display it in the active document window, ready for editing.

Changing your view of your spreadsheet

The standard StarCalc document window displays about eight columns and about two-dozen rows, more or less, depending on your system's screen resolution and other factors such as the text sizes in your spreadsheet. However, you can change the view of your spreadsheet to show more or less information in the StarCalc document window. Your viewing options include the following:

- **Full Screen** hides the StarOffice title bar, menus, and most toolbars in order to maximize the space available for spreadsheet cells. To go into Full Screen view, choose View⇨Full Screen. When you are in Full Screen view, you can't select menu commands to return to normal view. Instead, you click the Full Screen button in the small floating toolbar that appears in the upper-left corner of the screen.
- **Zoom** enables you to adjust the magnification of the StarCalc document window's contents. Choose View⇨Zoom to open the Zoom dialog box, in which you can select a magnification level. Click OK to apply the magnification level to your spreadsheet window. Right-clicking the Zoom display in the status bar at the bottom of the StarCalc window brings up a pop-up menu from which you can quickly select most of the standard zoom settings.

These viewing options are essentially the same as those available for StarWriter documents. See Chapter 4 for a more complete explanation of the Full Screen and Zoom options.

Entering Text and Numbers

If you've ever used another spreadsheet program, such as Microsoft Excel or Lotus 1-2-3, you already know the basics of entering text and numbers into StarCalc spreadsheet cells. StarCalc uses the same standard text entry and editing techniques as the other popular spreadsheets. Even if you've never used a spreadsheet before, doing so is pretty easy to figure out. The following list gives you a quick overview of the basics:

- The bold rectangle around a cell marks the selected cell in which you can add new text and numbers.
- To add text or numbers to a cell, just select the cell and begin typing. The text you enter appears in the selected cell and in the Input line on the Formula toolbar.
- Text in a cell automatically appears aligned flush left; numbers automatically appear aligned flush right.
- You can enter longer strings of text or numbers than seem to fit in a cell. The cell's contents scroll automatically to accept longer entries. The entry may appear truncated on-screen, but all the information is stored in the spreadsheet at the cell address.
- To complete an entry in one cell and move to the next cell, you can press one of the arrow keys, the Tab key, or the Enter key; or you can click another cell.
- To edit a cell entry, select the cell and then double-click it to get a flashing vertical bar cursor inside the cell. Use the normal text editing keys to edit the text within the cell.
- You can also edit text in the Input line on the Formula toolbar. Select a cell to display its contents in the Input line and then click the Input line to place an insertion point cursor. After the cursor appears in the text, you can use the normal text editing keys to edit the text.
- To delete the contents of the selected cell, right-click the cell and choose Delete Contents from the pop-up menu that appears. StarCalc opens the Delete Contents dialog box. Select the kind of information you want to delete from the cell and then click OK to close the dialog box and get rid of the unwanted data or formatting.
- To copy the contents of a cell to adjacent cells, select the cell you want to copy and then click and drag the small box on the lower-right corner of the selection box to copy the selection to the other cell or cells. After you release the mouse button, StarCalc fills the selected cells with copies of the information from that original cell. Note that this is a special, intelligent copy process in which StarCalc automatically adjusts cell references in copied formulas and performs other neat tricks.

- You can use the built-in StarOffice clipboard to cut, copy, and paste the contents of a cell.
- To cut the cell's contents from your spreadsheet and save the contents to the clipboard for later use, select the cell and then choose Edit⇨Cut, or press Ctrl+X, or click the Cut button in the Function toolbar.

- To copy a spreadsheet cell's contents and save the contents to the clipboard for later use, select the text you want to copy and then choose Edit⇨Copy, press Ctrl+C, or click the Copy button in the Function toolbar.
- To paste a cell's contents from the clipboard into your spreadsheet, position the insertion point where you want to insert the text and then choose Edit⇨Paste, press Ctrl+V, or click the Paste button in the Function toolbar.

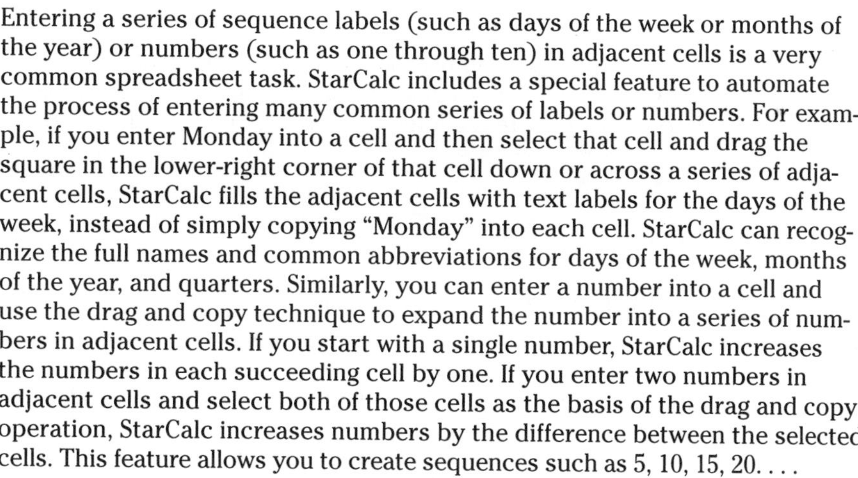

Entering a series of sequence labels (such as days of the week or months of the year) or numbers (such as one through ten) in adjacent cells is a very common spreadsheet task. StarCalc includes a special feature to automate the process of entering many common series of labels or numbers. For example, if you enter Monday into a cell and then select that cell and drag the square in the lower-right corner of that cell down or across a series of adjacent cells, StarCalc fills the adjacent cells with text labels for the days of the week, instead of simply copying "Monday" into each cell. StarCalc can recognize the full names and common abbreviations for days of the week, months of the year, and quarters. Similarly, you can enter a number into a cell and use the drag and copy technique to expand the number into a series of numbers in adjacent cells. If you start with a single number, StarCalc increases the numbers in each succeeding cell by one. If you enter two numbers in adjacent cells and select both of those cells as the basis of the drag and copy operation, StarCalc increases numbers by the difference between the selected cells. This feature allows you to create sequences such as 5, 10, 15, 20. . . .

Arranging Rows and Columns

In addition to editing the text and numbers in a spreadsheet, you can edit the structure of the spreadsheet itself by inserting and deleting rows and columns and changing their height and width. Here's how:

- To insert a column, select a column to the right of where you want to insert the new column, and then right-click the column header and choose Insert Columns from the pop-up menu that appears. StarCalc inserts a new column at that location and moves the existing columns to the right to make room.

- To insert a row, select a row below where you want to insert the new row, and then right-click the row header and choose Insert Rows from the pop-up menu that appears. StarCalc inserts a new row at that location and moves the existing rows down to make room.
- To delete a column or row, select the column or row you want to delete, and then right-click it and choose Delete Columns (or Delete Rows) from the pop-up menu that appears. StarCalc deletes the selected column or row and moves the remaining columns or rows in the spreadsheet to fill in the space.
- To adjust the width of a column, drag the right edge of the column's header button left or right and release the mouse button when the column reaches the desired width.
- To adjust the height of a row, drag the bottom edge of the row's header button up or down and release the mouse button when the row reaches the desired height.
- To automatically adjust the width of a column, double-click the right edge of the column's header button. StarCalc adjusts the column width to accommodate the longest data entry in any cell in that column.

Doing the Math

The whole point of a spreadsheet is to be able to do mathematical calculations using the data you enter into the spreadsheet cells. Otherwise, you just have a big table. The StarCalc spreadsheet can tap into the power of your computer to serve as a very sophisticated and powerful calculator.

In addition to text labels and numeric values, you can enter a third kind of information into a spreadsheet cell — a mathematical formula.

The simplest formulas to understand are the ones that involve the standard arithmetic operations: addition, subtraction, multiplication, and division. These operations alone are enough to enable you to build spreadsheets that do things like create invoices and purchase orders, balance checkbooks, and develop budgets. StarCalc also supports more sophisticated mathematical formulas and functions to support financial and statistical analyses and many other kinds of calculations. See Chapter 8 for more information on how to use some of those functions.

StarCalc follows the same conventions for entering and editing mathematical formulas as Microsoft Excel. So, if you're familiar with Excel, you already know how to do basic math calculations in StarCalc. If you haven't used an Excel-style spreadsheet before, check out the following list to get up to speed on how to perform basic arithmetic operations in StarCalc:

- Start each formula with an equal sign (=) to differentiate a formula from a text label or numeric value. If the contents of a cell start with the equal sign (=), StarCalc treats the rest of the cell's text and numbers as a formula and attempts to solve the formula and display the results of its calculations rather than the formula used to perform the calculations.
- The simplest formula is just a reference to another spreadsheet cell. For example, you can enter **=E6** in cell C10 to display the contents of cell E6 in cell C10. If you type your name in cell E6, it appears in cell C10 also. If you enter a complicated formula in cell E6, the results of the calculation appear in cell E6 and also in cell C10.
- To enter a mathematical calculation formula in a cell, start with the equal sign (=), followed by a number, followed by the symbol for a mathematical operation — such as the plus sign (+) — followed by another number, and so on. StarCalc calculates the results and displays them in the cell in place of the formula. For example, if you enter **=6+5+3** in a cell, StarCalc displays the results — 14 — in that cell. You can use the following symbols for the standard arithmetic operations:
  - + for addition
  - - for subtraction
  - * for multiplication
  - / for division
- You can use the address of a spreadsheet cell containing a number (or a formula producing a numeric result) in place of a number in a mathematical formula. For example, if cell A4 contains the number 5, then the formula =6+A4+3 returns the result 14.
- When calculating the results of a formula, StarCalc follows the same standard order of operations that you learned in math class. You can use parentheses around portions of a formula to control the order of operations and thereby achieve the results you want. For example, =(2*4)/(2+2) yields a different result than =2*4/2+2.
- When you enter a formula into a spreadsheet cell, StarCalc displays the results of the calculation in that cell. However, if you select a cell containing a formula, StarCalc displays the formula in the Input line box in the Formula toolbar. To edit the formula, click the Input line box where the formula appears or double-click the cell containing the formula.

Saving Your Spreadsheet

After you build your spreadsheet by entering text, numbers, and formulas into the spreadsheet cells, you want to save the spreadsheet document in a file in order to protect your work and make sure it's available for editing and updating later.

To save your StarCalc spreadsheet document, follow these steps:

1. **Choose File⇨Save As.**

   StarOffice opens the Save As dialog box. The dialog box shows the contents of your default WorkFolder (or the last folder you accessed in StarOffice).

2. **Navigate to the directory in which you want to save the file.**

   Double-click a folder icon in the central list box to open the directory. Click the Up One Level button (the left-most button of the three buttons in the upper-right corner of the dialog box) to move to a higher level in the directory tree on your system.

3. **Select the StarCalc 5.0 format from the File Type drop-down list box.**

   The default setting — StarCalc 5.0 — is appropriate for spreadsheets that you expect to reuse in StarOffice. You need to select a different file type if you must share the file with someone who needs to open it with a different program.

4. **Type a descriptive name for your file in the Filename box.**

   StarOffice supports long filenames that can include caps, lowercase, and spaces. However, you must make sure that the filename you enter is compatible with the file naming conventions of the computer system you're using. You don't need to manually add a filename extension in the Filename box. StarOffice automatically adds the appropriate extension if you have the Automatic File Name Extension option checked.

5. **Click Save.**

   StarOffice closes the Save As dialog box and saves your document file in the specified location. The title bar changes to reflect the new name of your document.

After you save a text document the first time, you don't need to reopen the Save As dialog box and adjust its settings each time you save the file. If you simply want to update your document after adding some text or making some edits, you can choose File⇨Save, or click the Save button in the Function toolbar, or press Ctrl+S. StarOffice skips the Save As dialog box and saves the file using its current filename and location.

To save your StarCalc spreadsheet in a file format that you can share with friends and colleagues who use Microsoft Excel, follow the preceding steps but choose MS Excel 97 (or MS Excel 95 or MS Excel 5.0) from the File Type drop-down list box mentioned in Step 3. This instructs StarOffice to use the appropriate file format and extension (XLS) for Excel to recognize and open the spreadsheet file.

Opening Existing Spreadsheets

Spreadsheets tend to be living documents that undergo frequent changes and updates. When you need to open an existing spreadsheet to work on it, just follow these steps:

1. **Choose File⇨Open, or click the Open button in the Function toolbar, or press Ctrl+O.**

   The Open dialog box appears.

2. **Navigate to the directory in which the file is saved.**

   Double-click a folder icon in the central list box to open the directory. Click the Up One Level button (the left-most button of the three buttons in the upper-right corner of the dialog box) to move to a higher level in the directory tree on your system.

3. **(Optional) Select StarCalc 5.0 from the File Type drop-down list box.**

   This step reduces the clutter in the list box by restricting the display to only StarCalc spreadsheet documents.

   TIP

   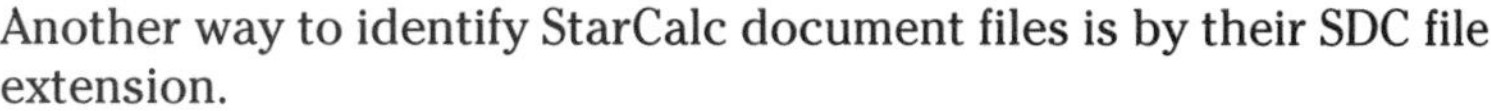

   Another way to identify StarCalc document files is by their SDC file extension.

4. **Select the file you want to open from the list box.**

5. **Click Open.**

   StarOffice closes the Open dialog box and displays the selected spreadsheet document in a new StarCalc document window.

Not only can StarOffice open and edit StarCalc spreadsheet documents, but the program can also open spreadsheet files created by Microsoft Excel. To open an Excel file, follow the same steps you use to open a StarCalc spreadsheet, but select one of the MS Excel entries from the File Type drop-down list box in Step 3. StarCalc can open and edit the Excel spreadsheet, and it supports almost all the Excel features.

Chapter 8

Crunching More and Bigger Numbers

In This Chapter

- Naming that data
- Factoring functions and formulas
- Working with multiple spreadsheets
- Getting a head start with spreadsheet templates

Simple spreadsheets, which contain only text, numbers, and a few formulas that perform basic mathematical operations, are adequate for many projects. But StarCalc is capable of far more. StarCalc functions and formulas enable you to do sophisticated calculations and financial modeling. Multisheet spreadsheets enable you to do things such as create a series of departmental sales reports and a consolidated, company-wide summary — all within the same StarCalc spreadsheet file. This chapter shows you how to take StarCalc beyond simple tables and basic math.

Addressing Data Areas by Name

The standard way to address a cell in a spreadsheet is to use a cell address, such as *C15,* which is composed of the column letter (C) and row number that describes the location of the cell (15). Similarly, you can address a rectangular block of cells by specifying the cell addresses of the cells and opposite corners of the block, such as C15:E18. Computers are really good at keeping track of data stuffed into little numbered pigeonholes called cells. But human beings don't naturally relate to data that way. Instead of thinking that cell D16 shows the result of multiplying the contents of cell D15 and the contents of cell C15, humans think about the same operation as: The *sales tax* box shows the result of multiplying the *subtotal* times the *tax rate.*

StarCalc includes a feature that enables you to address spreadsheet cells and cell ranges by name rather than by number. You select a cell (or cell range) and assign it a name, a process called *defining a database area*. After you define a database area, you can refer to that area in your spreadsheet formulas by name rather than by cell address. You can also use named database areas to navigate to different spreadsheet locations by selecting the database area in the Navigator window or the Select Database Area dialog box. (Choose Data⇨Select Area to open this dialog box.)

To define a database area, follow these steps:

1. **Select the cell or cell range to which you want to assign a name.**
2. **Choose Data⇨Define Area.**

   StarCalc displays the Define Database Area dialog box, as shown in Figure 8-1. The address of the cell or cell range that you select appears in the Area box at the bottom of the dialog box. The names of any previously defined database areas in the current spreadsheet appear in the Name list box.

Figure 8-1: Defining a more meaningful name for a spreadsheet cell.

3. **Type a name for the selected cell (or cells) in the Name text box at the top of the dialog box.**

   The name must not include any numbers, spaces, or punctuation characters. It's not case sensitive (uppercase and lowercase letters are all the same). Try to keep the name short, but meaningful, so that you can more easily use it in formulas.

4. **Click Add.**

   StarCalc adds the new database area name to the Name list box.

5. **Click OK.**

   StarOffice closes the Define Database Area dialog box and stores the newly defined database area name in your spreadsheet. You can now refer to the selected cells using the name rather than the cell address. Of course, the cell address still works, too.

To use database area names, just substitute a previously defined name for its cell address when you enter a formula into a spreadsheet cell. For example, if you named cell D15 *subtotal* and cell C16 *taxrate,* you can create a formula to calculate sales tax by entering **=D15*C16** or by entering **=subtotal*taxrate**. (Remember: = signifies a formula and * is the symbol for multiplication.) Both formulas produce exactly the same results, but the second version is much easier for us humans to understand.

Using Common Functions

You can easily put together simple spreadsheet formulas by using numbers and cell addresses combined with symbols for standard arithmetic operations (+, -, *, /). Add a few parentheses, and you can create some pretty sophisticated formulas using just those elements. However, even formulas for basic operations, such as adding a column of numbers, can quickly get long and cumbersome to deal with. For example, suppose that you need to add a column of numbers in rows 3 through 13 in column C of your spreadsheet. The formula can look something like this:

```
=C3+C4+C5+C6+C7+C8+C9+C10+C11+C12+C13
```

As columns of numbers go, this formula is an easy one. Imagine what the formula looks like if you need to add a column of numbers with more than 50 entries. Then try to perform some more sophisticated operations, such as calculating the average or mean value, and the formula gets ugly. If you paid attention in algebra class, the logic isn't too hard to follow, but entering long formulas without making a typing error is a real challenge.

Functions are StarCalc's answer to dealing with long complex formulas. Basically, functions are pre-programmed formulas that are built into StarCalc. Instead of entering a long formula manually, you just tell StarCalc what function to use and then define the input that function requires. StarCalc uses its built-in formula to perform the calculation for you.

A StarCalc function takes the form of the function name, followed by a set of input data or *arguments* (values, cell addresses, limit settings, and such) enclosed in parentheses. For example, `SQRT(E24)` returns the square root of the number in cell E24.

You can use functions as stand-alone formulas or as part of a larger formula. Sometimes the arguments for a function are a formula or calculation instead of a simple cell reference, such as in the formula `=SQRT((A1^2)+(B1^2))`, which is the StarCalc version of the classic formula for calculating the length of the hypotenuse of a right triangle.

Perhaps the most-used and easiest-to-understand function in StarCalc's arsenal is the SUM( ) function, which I describe in the next section.

Using some SUM

One of the most common spreadsheet operations is adding up a column (or row) of numbers — in other words, finding the mathematical sum of a series of numbers. You see this operation all the time. Totaling the line item amounts on an invoice is just one example.

Of course, you can create a formula that simply adds all the individual cells in the column of numbers you want to total. (See the example in the preceding section.) Such formulas are simple, but long.

Using StarCalc's SUM function is a much easier way to total the numbers in a column or row. Instead of the preceding formula, you just enter **=SUM(C3:C13)** into the cell where you want the total to appear.

The SUM function is a kind of formula, so it starts with the equals sign (=), just like other formulas in StarCalc spreadsheet cells. Next comes the name of the function — SUM. Then you list the cells that you want to add up in the parentheses. In the preceding example, the cells are addressed as a range — C3:C13 — which means rows 3 through 13 in column C.

You can enter the SUM function (and any other StarCalc function) simply by typing it into a spreadsheet cell in place of (or in addition to) a regular formula that uses ordinary mathematical symbols and operations. But you can also use the SUM function in an easier way.

Because people use the SUM function so frequently in StarCalc, the program developers created a special toolbar button for it. And as an additional feature, when you use the SUM button, StarCalc doesn't just stick the SUM function to the current spreadsheet cell. The program makes an educated guess about the range of cells that you want to total with the SUM function and automatically fills in those cells for you. You can easily edit the range, but often you don't need to.

Suppose that you have a column of numbers in rows 3 through 13 in column C of your spreadsheet. The logical place for a total is at the bottom of the list, in cell C14, right? Here's how you create the appropriate formula to total a column of numbers using the SUM button:

1. **Click the empty cell at the bottom of a list of numbers.**

   In this example, you click cell C14. The cell that you select can be at the bottom of a column of numbers or at the right end of a row of numbers. Actually, you can select any cell in which to enter the SUM function, but the automatic range detection only works up or to the left of the selected cell.

2. **Click the SUM button on the Formula bar.**

   StarCalc inserts the SUM function in the selected cell and in the Input line on the Formula bar. StarCalc also automatically inserts the range address of the list of cells above the selected cell (C3:C13) into the parentheses following SUM. The range address is highlighted in the cell and in the Input line for editing. A blue rectangle surrounds the target range of cells.

3. **Adjust the target range of cells, if necessary.**

   Often, you don't need to adjust the range of cells that StarCalc automatically selects as the target of the SUM function. If you do, you can do so by typing your changes in the formula cell or Input line or by dragging the blue selection rectangle around the desired cells.

4. **When the target range is correct, press Enter or click the Accept button on the Formula bar.**

   StarCalc enters the finished formula/function into the selected cell and displays the result.

That's all you need to do. You can total a column of numbers using the SUM function with just three quick mouse clicks: Click the cell at the bottom of the column of numbers, click the SUM button, and then click the Accept button.

Entering functions using the Function AutoPilot

StarCalc supports a large number of functions that you can use in your spreadsheet, but only the SUM function has an easy-to-use dedicated button on the Formula bar. You have to work a little harder to use the other functions, but not too much harder, because StarCalc includes an AutoPilot to help you build formulas containing functions.

To use the Function AutoPilot to insert a function into your spreadsheet, follow these steps:

1. **Select the spreadsheet cell where you want to insert the function.**

2. **Click the Function AutoPilot button on the Formula bar.**

   StarCalc opens the Function AutoPilot dialog box shown in Figure 8-2.

3. **Select the kind of function that you want from the Category drop-down list box.**

   The list of StarCalc functions is a long one. So to help you find the function that you're looking for, StarCalc groups the functions into categories such as Financial and Statistical. To browse through the entire list of available functions, select All.

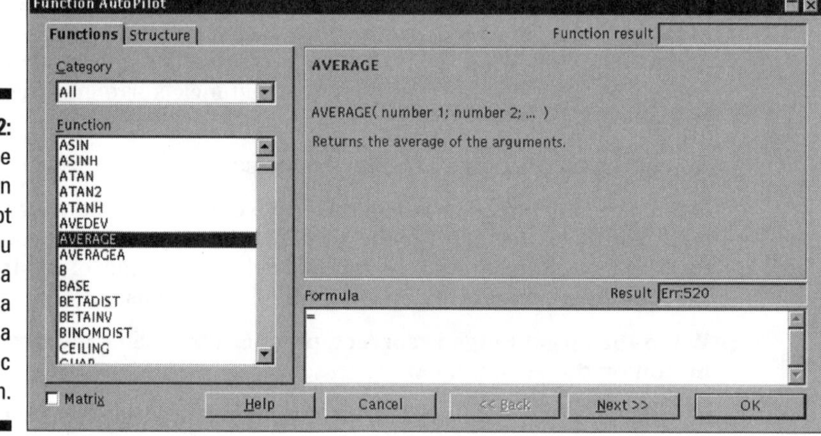

Figure 8-2: The Function AutoPilot helps you build a formula containing a StarCalc function.

4. **Select a function from the Function list box.**

   StarCalc displays a description of the function and its *syntax* (the arguments or parameters the function needs to have enclosed in parentheses in order to complete its calculation) in the box to the right of the Function list.

5. **Click Next.**

   StarCalc displays instructions and a series of data-entry text boxes (labeled Number 1, Number 2, and so on in the example) in the large box to the right of the Function list. The contents of this box vary depending on the function that you choose in Step 4. Figure 8-3 shows the instructions for the AVERAGE function. The Formula text box at the bottom of the Function AutoPilot dialog box shows the formula that you're building with the AutoPilot.

6. **Enter the data needed for the function's arguments.**

   You can enter data by typing it into the text boxes or by typing it into the Formula text box. If you want to enter a cell address, you can type it in or click the button on the right side of the data-entry text box. If you choose the latter, StarCalc reduces the Function AutoPilot to a title bar, so you can access your spreadsheet and select the cell address by clicking it; then press Enter to restore the Function AutoPilot to its normal size, but with the cell address entered. If you want to enter another function as an argument, click the fx button at the left end of the data-entry text box to proceed to another page of the Function AutoPilot where you can define that function and its arguments.

   The Function AutoPilot also shows the result of the calculation using the current function and arguments in the Result box.

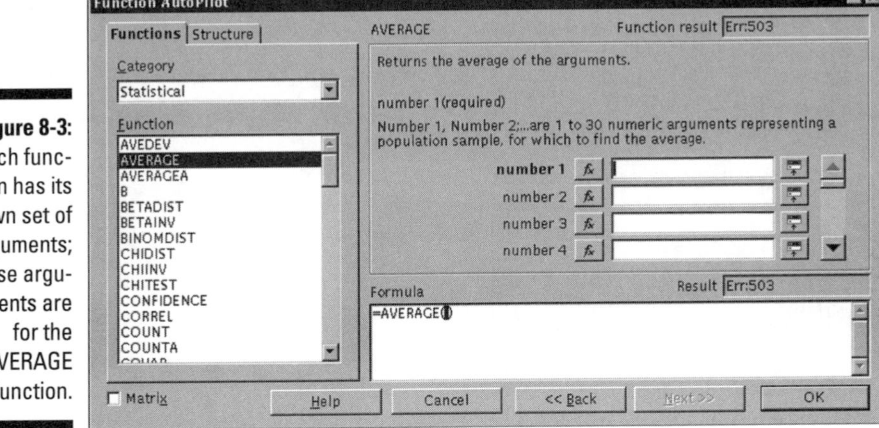

Figure 8-3: Each function has its own set of arguments; these arguments are for the AVERAGE function.

7. **After entering the arguments, click OK.**

   StarCalc closes the Function AutoPilot dialog box and enters the formula containing the function that you just defined into the desired spreadsheet cell.

Entering functions from the Function List

After you get the hang of working with functions, you may find going through the Function AutoPilot every time a little cumbersome. Fortunately, StarCalc gives you another alternative for entering functions, without having to resort to typing a formula containing a function directly into a spreadsheet cell. It's called the Function List.

The Function List window, shown in Figure 8-4, is another of the StarOffice dockable windows like Explorer, Beamer, and Stylist. By default, this window appears docked to the right side of the StarOffice program window, but you can move it, show or hide it, or make it a floating window. Choose Insert⇨Function List to display this window.

To use the Function List to enter a function, just follow these steps:

1. **Select the cell in which you want to insert a function.**
2. **Choose Insert⇨Function List to open the Function List window if it's not already open.**

   Click the Show/Hide button to show the contents of the Function List window if it's open but hidden.

3. **Select a function category from the drop-down list box at the top of the Function List window.**

   StarCalc displays the functions available in that category in the list box and in the middle of the Function List window.

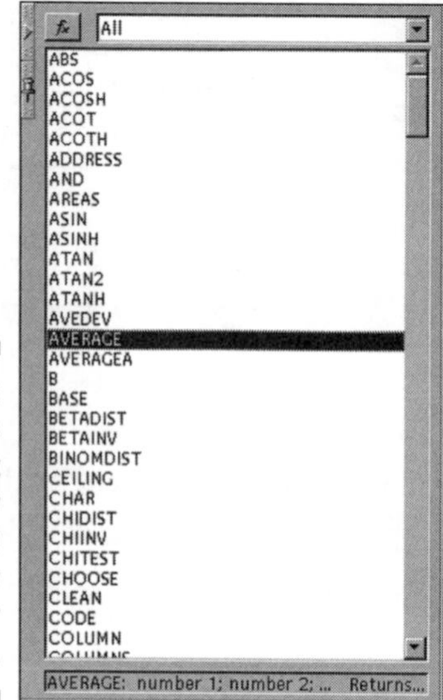

Figure 8-4: The Function List window gives you another way to enter functions.

4. **Select a function from the list box.**

5. **Click the fx button in the upper-left corner of the Function List window.**

   StarCalc inserts the selected function into the selected cell in your spreadsheet and into the Input Line on the Formula bar. StarCalc also highlights the arguments portion of the formula/function.

6. **Enter the arguments necessary to complete the formula.**

   You can type in the numbers or cell addresses, or you can select a cell or range of cells by using the mouse.

7. **Press Enter.**

   StarCalc completes the formula and displays the result in the selected spreadsheet cell.

Working with Multiple Sheets

StarCalc supports multiple *sheets,* or spreadsheet pages, in one spreadsheet file. You can easily access the individual sheets by using the tabs in the lower-left corner of the StarCalc spreadsheet window. Furthermore, you can reference cells and data areas on other sheets that are in the same file and use them in formulas that you build in the current sheet.

This handy multiple-sheet feature provides you with more options for organizing your spreadsheet data. For example, suppose that you need to create a set of spreadsheets to track and analyze quarterly sales of your products and to generate a year-to-date summary. One option is to create separate spreadsheet files for each quarter and manually transfer information to a fifth spreadsheet file for the year-to-date summary. Or you can put all the information into one big spreadsheet and scroll around to different parts of the spreadsheet for each quarter and for the yearly summary. Although both of these scenarios work, they're cumbersome and inconvenient compared to what you can do with multiple sheets.

By using multiple sheets, you can create a separate sheet for each quarter's sales and a fifth sheet for the year-end summary. Your data is all together in one file but neatly compartmentalized for easy access. You can easily flip to the proper sheet for the quarter that you need to work on. And because StarCalc enables you to reference cells on other sheets in the same file, pulling together a year-end summary sheet is a snap.

The applications for StarCalc's multiple-sheet feature are limited only by your imagination. Any time that you have multiple blocks of similar information (such as sales reports for multiple months, or departments, or regions), arranging them on multiple sheets in a spreadsheet file makes sense. And multiple sheets are an ideal solution when you need to create a summary or consolidate information that can be stored on multiple sheets in the same file.

Shuffling sheets

Each StarCalc spreadsheet file starts out with three defined sheets. These sheets are rather unimaginatively named: Sheet 1, Sheet 2, and Sheet 3. (There's a Dr. Seuss rhyme in there somewhere.) The sheets are represented by tabs, which are visible in the lower-left corner of the StarCalc window. The buttons to the left of the sheet tabs enable you to scroll through the available tabs when your spreadsheet file grows to the point that the tabs don't all fit in the allotted space.

When you first start working in your spreadsheet file, Sheet 1 is active. If you need only a single spreadsheet page, you can just work in Sheet 1 and ignore the other sheets. When you're ready to use multiple sheets in your spreadsheet file, the other sheets are readily accessible. To select another sheet, simply click the corresponding tab. StarCalc brings that sheet to the foreground so you can work on it. The other sheets, with all their cells and formulas, are hidden from view, but they're still part of the spreadsheet file.

You can move from sheet to sheet in your spreadsheet file by pressing Ctrl+PgUp or Ctrl+PgDn to go to the previous or next sheet.

Addressing cells on different sheets

One of the most useful aspects of StarCalc's multiple-sheet feature is the ability to use data from one sheet in formulas and calculations in another sheet in the spreadsheet file. Using data from another sheet is as simple as referencing another cell on the same sheet. The only difference is that the cell address for a cell on another sheet is a little longer because it includes the name of the sheet in addition to the usual cell address. For example, if you want to use the contents of cell C15 on Sheet 1 in a formula in a cell on Sheet 2, you enter the cell address **Sheet1.C15**. (Note the period separating the sheet name from the cell address.)

You can address ranges of cells on another sheet in the same way. For example, you can create a formula in a cell on Sheet 2 to calculate the sum of a column of numbers on Sheet 1 like so: `=SUM(Sheet1.C3:C13)`.

Entering cell addresses into formulas for cells on other sheets is just like entering cell addresses for cells on the same sheet. You start entering the formula, and when you need to enter the cell address, you can either type the cell address or click the target cell to show StarCalc what cell you want to use in the formula. When you're building a formula, StarCalc allows you to click sheet tabs, scroll bars, and the like to move around your spreadsheet file to locate and select the target cell(s) you want to use in the formula. StarCalc doesn't record the cell or cell range address until you press Enter or a mathematical operation key.

You don't need to add a sheet name in front of a database area name in order to use the contents of the cell(s) in the database area in a formula — even if the database area is on a different sheet. That feature is one of the advantages of using database area names! Of course, each database area name in your spreadsheet file must be unique. You can't assign the same name to database areas on different sheets in your spreadsheet file.

Adding sheets to a spreadsheet

You aren't restricted to just the three default sheets that StarCalc creates when you create a new spreadsheet file. You can add one or more sheets to a spreadsheet file any time that you want by following these steps:

1. **Right-click a sheet tab and choose Insert from the pop-up menu that appears.**

   StarCalc displays the Insert Sheet dialog box, as shown in Figure 8-5.

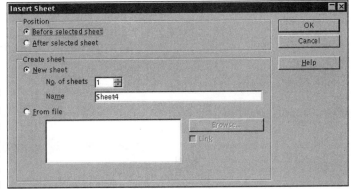

Figure 8-5: Adding sheets to a spreadsheet file.

2. **Select Before Selected Sheet or After Selected Sheet in the Position area.**

   StarCalc lets you insert the new sheets before or after the sheet that you clicked to open the dialog box.

3. **Select New Sheet in the Create Sheet area.**

   Selecting New Sheet tells StarCalc that you want to create a new, blank sheet and insert it into the current spreadsheet file. Alternatively, you can select the From File option and then click the Browse button to locate and select another spreadsheet file from which to copy the sheet and then add it to the current spreadsheet file.

4. **Enter a number in the No. of Sheets box.**

   Normally, you want to insert only one sheet at a time, but you can insert dozens of sheets at once if you want to. If you're inserting only one new sheet, you can type a name for the sheet in the Name text box. If you're inserting multiple sheets, StarCalc names them automatically.

5. **Click OK.**

   StarCalc closes the Insert Sheet dialog box and inserts a new sheet into the spreadsheet file in the location that you specified. StarCalc automatically selects the new sheet and brings it to the foreground for editing. Notice that the new sheet has its own tab.

After you add a few sheets to your spreadsheet file, you may notice that all the tabs no longer fit in the allotted space in the lower-left corner of the StarCalc window. This situation brings into play the set of four buttons to the left of the sheet tabs. The buttons enable you to scroll through the list of available sheet tabs in much the same way that the buttons at the ends of scroll bars enable you to scroll through the columns and rows of your spreadsheet. The left- and right-arrow buttons scroll the tabs one sheet at a time. The buttons with an arrowhead and a vertical bar jump to the beginning and end of the list of sheet tabs.

Deleting an unwanted sheet from your spreadsheet file is even easier than adding a sheet. Simply right-click the tab for the sheet that you want to delete and choose Delete from the pop-up menu that appears. Click Yes to confirm the action, and (poof!) the sheet and all its contents disappear.

Naming sheets

Sheet names such as Sheet 1, Sheet 2, and Sheet 3 are not only boring but also confusing. Let's see, does Sheet 2 contain the East Region figures and Sheet 3 the South Region, or the other way around? Don't worry — StarCalc lets you change those boring names to almost anything you want. To change a sheet name, just follow these easy steps:

1. **Right-click the sheet tab for the sheet that you want to change.**

   A pop-up menu appears.

2. **Choose Rename from the pop-up menu.**

   The Rename Sheet dialog box appears.

3. **Type a new name in the Name text box and click OK.**

   StarCalc closes the Rename Sheet dialog box and changes the name of the sheet that appears on the sheet tab. In addition, StarCalc automatically changes the name of the sheet in any cell references to the renamed sheet.

Sheet names cannot include punctuation characters and symbols that may be confused with any punctuation and symbols used in a formula. StarCalc refuses to accept sheet names containing any of these characters. Although StarCalc accepts space characters in a sheet name, try to avoid them, because extra spaces within a name can make your formulas harder to read.

Using Templates to Create Spreadsheets

You don't have to start every new spreadsheet with a completely blank spreadsheet file and build all the formulas from scratch. StarOffice's predefined templates can help you get a head start on creating some spreadsheet documents. Instead of creating a new spreadsheet by choosing File⇨New⇨Spreadsheet, you can choose File⇨New⇨From Template to open the

New dialog box. Then you select an appropriate template and click OK. *Voilà* — you get a new spreadsheet file with some of the text and formatting and most of the formulas already in place. Just enter your data, and you have a finished spreadsheet document.

I explain how to create a new document based on a StarOffice template in more detail in Chapter 5. In that chapter, I use StarWriter text documents as examples, but the process is nearly the same with StarCalc spreadsheets. The only difference is the kind of document template that you select in the New dialog box. If you select a template for a document such as a memo or letter, you get a StarWriter text document. If, on the other hand, you select a template for something like a Personal Budget, you get a StarCalc spreadsheet.

You can also create your own spreadsheet templates, just as you can create your own templates from your word processing documents. You can create templates for invoices, purchase orders, monthly budgets, and anything else you use repeatedly. Then you can create a new spreadsheet based on the template any time you need one.

Again, the procedure for creating a spreadsheet template is almost exactly the same as the one described in detail in Chapter 5 for creating a text document template. The only difference is that you start with a spreadsheet instead of a text document, and you choose StarCalc 5.1 Template instead of StarWriter 5.1 Template as the file type in the Save As dialog box.

Chapter 9

Making Your Numbers Look Good

In This Chapter

- Dressing up your spreadsheets with formatting
- Adding borders and backgrounds
- Playing hide-and-seek with columns and rows
- Printing spreadsheets

Spreadsheets aren't just about getting the numbers right. After you enter all the text and data and do all the calculations, you usually need to share your information with others, so your numbers need to look good, too. This chapter explores some of StarCalc's formatting and printing capabilities — the tools that you use to jazz up your spreadsheets.

Formatting Your Spreadsheet

In the past, getting the numbers right in a spreadsheet used to be the main focus. When you were ready to print your spreadsheet and show the results of your calculations to someone else, all that mattered was that the numbers were legible. (Of course, glazed eyes and a faraway stare used to be the typical reaction to a page of numbers, too.) But times have changed and now appearances matter as much for spreadsheets as they do for word processing documents.

StarCalc gives you a full set of formatting features that enable you to manipulate the way text and numbers appear on your spreadsheets. You can control fonts and text sizes, bold and italic attributes, alignment, borders and backgrounds, headers and footers, and the like to create attractive documents that present your numbers in the best way.

Selecting fonts and adding text attributes

Spreadsheets may seem fundamentally different from the text documents that you create with the StarWriter word processing tool, but actually a great many similarities exist. You use the same text and number characters in text documents and spreadsheets. You display them both on the same kind of screen, and you print them on the same printer.

So you can also use many of the same formatting tools to format text and numbers in word processing documents and spreadsheets. For example, you can change the font and text size, make the text bold or italic, and change the alignment by making selections and clicking buttons on the StarCalc Object toolbar. Normally, you select a cell and apply the formatting to the contents of that cell. However, you can also select a single word or number within a cell and format it differently from the rest of the cell's contents.

The following is a summary of the spreadsheet formatting options that you probably need most often:

helvetica

- **Font name:** Select a font from the Font Name drop-down list box to change the selected cell's text and numbers to that font.

10

- **Font size:** Select a size from the Font Size drop-down list box to change the selected cell's text size.

B

- **Bold:** Click the Bold button to add or remove the **bold** style in the selected cell.

i

- **Italic:** Click the Italic button to add or remove the *italic* style in the selected cell.

U

- **Underline:** Click the Underline button to add or remove the underline in the selected cell.
- **Font color:** Click the Font Color button to display a pop-up color palette and then click a color box to change the selected cell's text and numbers to that color.
- **Left align:** Click the Align Left button to align the selected cell's contents to the left edge of the cell.
- **Center align:** Click the Align Center button to horizontally center the selected cell's contents within the cell.
- **Right align:** Click the Align Right button to align the selected cell's contents to the right edge of the cell.
- **Top align:** Click the Align Top button to align the selected cell's contents to the top edge of the cell.

- **Vertical center align:** Click the Align Vertical Center button to vertically center the selected cell's contents within the cell.

- **Bottom align:** Click the Align Bottom button to align the selected cell's contents to the bottom edge of the cell.

I explain how to use toolbar buttons to apply formatting to text in more detail in Chapter 3. Although the examples in Chapter 3 relate to formatting text in StarWriter text documents, the formatting buttons work essentially the same way in StarCalc spreadsheets. Of course, some differences do exist.

For example, when you use the alignment buttons in a text document, you align text paragraphs relative to the page margins. When you use the corresponding alignment buttons to format your StarCalc spreadsheets, you align text or numbers within a cell relative to the edges of the cell. Also, you won't find the vertical alignment buttons in Chapter 3 because you can't vertically align text paragraphs. However, those buttons work basically the same way as the horizontal alignment buttons.

Formatting numbers as percents and currency

Not all the formatting options in StarCalc spreadsheets are the same as the text formatting options in StarWriter text documents. One group of formatting options is unique to spreadsheets — the number formats that enable you to specify how StarCalc displays numeric values. For example, you can display a number formatted as currency or as a percent. The same number can take on a very different meaning when you change its number format.

StarCalc gives you easy access to the most frequently used number formats via the toolbar buttons on the StarCalc Object toolbar. These format options are as follows:

- **Currency:** Click the Number Format: Currency button to format the selected cell's contents as currency. By default, choosing the currency format means displaying the number with two decimal places and adding a U.S. dollar sign ($) currency symbol in front of the number.

- **Percent:** Click the Number Format: Percent button to format the selected cell's contents as a percent. StarCalc moves the decimal point two places to the right and adds the percent sign (%) to the number.

- **Standard number:** Click the Number Format: Standard button to format the selected cell's contents as a standard number. You use this button to reverse the effects of the Currency or Percent buttons.

- **Add decimal:** Click the Number Format: Add Decimal button to display the selected cell's number with one more decimal place.

- **Delete decimal:** Click the Number Format: Delete Decimal button to display the selected cell's number with one less decimal place.

Many other number format options exist in StarCalc. You can access all of them on the Numbers tab of the Cell Attributes dialog box. (Choose Format⇨Cells or right-click a cell and choose Format Cells from the pop-up menu that appears.) However, the Number Format toolbar buttons can handle your most common number formatting needs.

Adding borders and backgrounds — the quick way

You probably add a lot of borders and backgrounds to your spreadsheet's cells. Adding background color to the cells in a row or column is perhaps the best way to highlight that information in your spreadsheet. Putting a border around a cell or group of cells is another good way to make information stand out. In addition, you can use a border on the bottom edge of a cell as the total line, separating a column of numbers from the total or sum of those numbers.

To add a border to a cell or group of cells, follow these steps:

1. **Select the cell or group of cells to which you want to add a border.**

   If you select a group of cells, you have the option of applying a border to the perimeter of the group or to all the individual cells within the group.

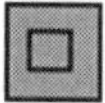

2. **Click the Borders button on the StarCalc Object toolbar.**

   StarCalc displays a pop-up menu showing thumbnail representations of standard border options.

3. **Select a border by clicking one of the thumbnail buttons in the pop-up Border menu.**

   StarCalc applies the border to the selected cell or cells.

If you need more control over the border around a spreadsheet cell, select the cell and then choose Format⇨Cells to open the Cell Attributes dialog box and adjust the settings on the Borders tab. In addition to selecting which side of the cell gets a border, you can also specify the line thickness and style, the line color, and whether to add a shadow effect to the cell.

To add a background color to a cell or cells, you use the same basic technique that you use for adding a border:

1. **Select the cell or cells to which you want to add the background color.**

2. **Click the Background Color button on the StarCalc Object toolbar.**

   StarCalc opens a pop-up color palette.

3. **Click a color box in that color palette to apply that color to the selected cells as a background.**

Adding style to your document with styles

If you find yourself making the same formatting changes over and over to different cells in your spreadsheet, you can save some time by using styles to apply multiple formatting attributes all at once. Yes, you can apply styles to cells in a spreadsheet just as you can apply styles to paragraphs in a text document. Although StarCalc doesn't come with a large assortment of predefined cell styles, you can create your own styles and apply them as needed.

The process of creating cell styles for use in StarCalc is the same as the process for creating paragraph styles for use in StarWriter; refer to Chapter 4 for details. After you create your cell styles, you can apply them using the Style Catalog dialog box or the Stylist window, which I also cover in Chapter 4. Just remember that in StarCalc, you apply styles to cells instead of paragraphs. Everything else works the same. (Can you say déjà vu?)

Using Conditional Formatting

Have you ever wanted to highlight all the negative numbers on a spreadsheet? StarCalc has a slick trick that does just that. This feature, Conditional Formatting, enables you to instruct StarCalc to automatically apply specific formatting to a cell if the cell's contents meet certain conditions that you specify. So, you can make every negative number in your budget projection bright red if you want to.

Before you set up conditional formatting, you need to define a cell style for formatting the cells that meet your criteria. Then you define the conditions in which StarCalc should apply that style by following these steps:

1. **Choose Format⇨Conditional Formatting.**

   The Conditional Formatting dialog box opens, as shown in Figure 9-1.

2. **Set the conditions and formatting by making selections and entering values or cell addresses.**

   For example, to apply the Negative style to all negative numbers, select Cell Value Is in the first drop-down list box and Less Than in the second box. Then enter **0** in the third box and select Negative in the Cell Style box.

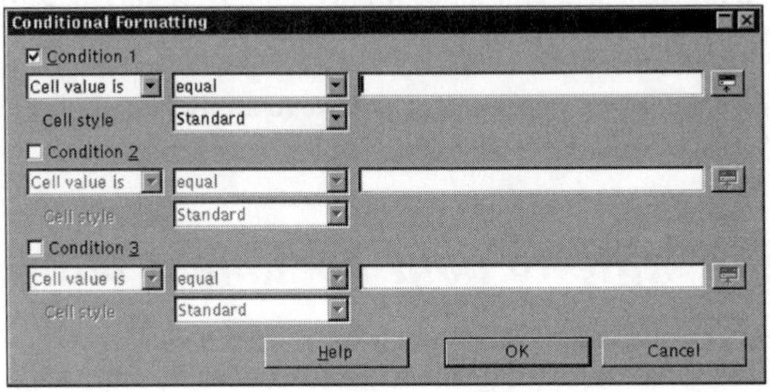

Figure 9-1: StarCalc automatically formats cells according to the criteria you establish.

3. **Click OK.**

   StarCalc closes the Conditional Formatting dialog box and applies the Negative cell style to all the cells in your spreadsheet that contain numbers less than 0.

Hiding Rows and Columns from View

Sometimes, you don't want others to see everything in your spreadsheet. Sometimes, you don't even want to see everything yourself. Occasionally, you may have some sensitive information in your spreadsheet that is used in calculations, and you want to show the results of the calculations without revealing all the factors you used to do the calculations. More often though, you just want to clean up the clutter of a busy spreadsheet by hiding your suppositions and intermediate working calculations from view. For those times, StarCalc gives you the ability to hide selected columns or rows. The hidden columns and rows aren't deleted from your spreadsheet; they're just temporarily hidden from view.

To hide a column or row of cells in your spreadsheet, follow these steps:

1. **Select the entire column or row (click the column or row selector button at the top or left edge of the work area).**
2. **Right-click the selected column or row and choose Hide from the pop-up menu that appears.**

   StarCalc removes the selected column or row of cells from the display and moves the other columns or rows to fill in the vacant space.

Notice that although StarCalc closes up the vacant space previously occupied by the hidden column or row, the program doesn't change the column or row letters or numbers. So, if you hide column D, the remaining columns are labeled A, B, C, E, F, G, and so on. If you had deleted the column instead of hiding it, StarCalc would have relabeled the remaining columns. The missing D column is your tip off that the column still exists — it just isn't currently visible. One more indication of a hidden column is a slightly heavier line separating the columns that surround the hidden column.

To make the hidden column reappear, follow these steps:

1. **Select a column range that spans the hidden column.**

   For example, to unhide column D, select columns C and E.

2. **Right-click the selected columns and choose Show from the pop-up menu that appears.**

   StarCalc returns the hidden column to the display and pushes the other columns over to make room.

Printing Your Spreadsheet

When you're ready to print your spreadsheet, StarCalc gives you the options that you need to print an impressive report. Many of the printing options are the standard fare that you deal with when printing any StarOffice document. However, a few printing issues are specific to spreadsheets.

Defining what to print

The first thing that you need to do when you want to print a spreadsheet is to define what portion of the spreadsheet you want to print. Remember that a StarCalc spreadsheet contains millions of cells, and you probably don't want to print them all. By default, StarCalc selects a rectangular area that encompasses all the active cells that contain data or formulas and defines that area as the print area. When you print your spreadsheet, StarCalc ignores the cells outside this print area.

Most of the time, the default print area works just fine. However, you may want to place data-entry cells and intermediate calculations and such below or to the right of the portion of the spreadsheet that you want to print and then exclude those cells from printing by defining a smaller print area.

To define a print area, follow these steps:

1. **Select the area that you want to print (it must be a rectangular area).**
2. **Choose Format⇨Print Range⇨Set.**

   StarCalc records the selected cell range as the print range and ignores cells outside that block when you print.

   You can define an additional print range by selecting another cell range and choosing Format⇨Print Range⇨Add. StarCalc prints the contents of both ranges.

Printing spreadsheets the quick way

The fastest and simplest way to print your spreadsheet after defining the print range is to simply click the Print button on the Function toolbar. StarCalc prints your spreadsheet to the default printer using the default printer settings. If you want to get an on-screen preview of your spreadsheet before printing it, choose File⇨Page View to display a preview image in a separate document window. After viewing the preview image, click Close Window on the Object toolbar to close the page preview window and return to your spreadsheet.

Setting Page Style options

If you need to exercise more control over the way that your spreadsheet looks when it is printed, you can probably find the options that you need in the Page Style dialog box. To open the Page Style dialog box (shown in Figure 9-2), choose Format⇨Page. The tabs in this dialog box give you access to options that control numerous aspects of the printed spreadsheet page. The following list provides a brief summary of the main features:

- The **Sheet** tab settings enable you to select what elements print as well as the page order.
- The **Footer** tab enables you to define the size of the footer that StarCalc usually adds to each printed page. Click the Edit button to open a separate Footer dialog box in which you can determine what information appears in the footer.
- The **Header** tab settings enable you to define the size of the header on each spreadsheet page. Click the Edit button to open a separate Header dialog box in which you can determine what information appears in the header.

- The **Background** tab is where you select the background color for the spreadsheet pages.
- The **Borders** tab settings enable you to add a border around each spreadsheet page.
- The **Page** tab enables you to set page margins, paper size, numbering, and related settings.

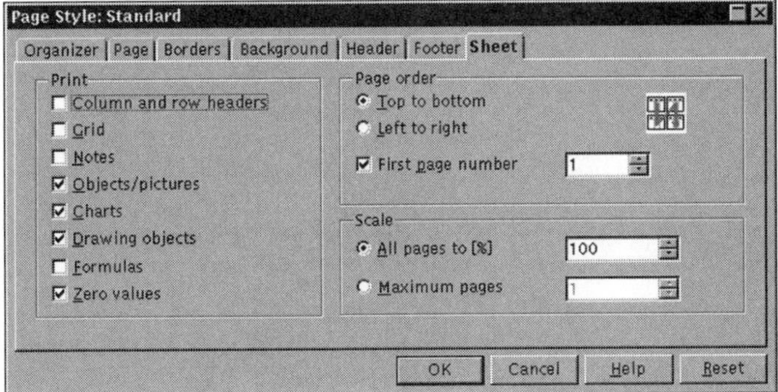

Figure 9-2: The Page Style dialog box is home to many useful document formatting options.

Chapter 10

Creating Charts

In This Chapter

- Charting your numbers
- Doing the data entry thing
- Choosing pictures to represent your data
- Formatting your chart
- Coloring within the lines
- Traveling to the third dimension

Even the most impressively formatted spreadsheets can't match the impact of a chart. Charts give form to abstract numbers, making them easier to understand and remember. So after you use a StarCalc spreadsheet to calculate your numbers, you may want to transform some of those numbers into charts to analyze them or present them to others. The StarOffice StarChart is a powerful charting tool for preparing a variety of two- and three-dimensional chart types. This chapter shows you how remarkably easy this tool is to use.

Creating a New Chart

Like other StarOffice document types, you can create a new StarChart chart in several different ways. Here's a summary of those ways:

- Choose File⇨New⇨Chart from the StarOffice menu.
- Right-click the desktop background in StarDesktop and choose New⇨Documents⇨Chart from the pop-up menu that appears.
- Click the Start button in the StarOffice Task bar and choose More⇨Chart.

Regardless of what technique you use to create a new chart, StarOffice opens a new StarChart document window, which is standard operating procedure for creating most StarOffice document types. But the contents of the initial StarChart window are a little different.

Instead of starting out with a blank document, StarChart displays a dummy chart in the StarChart window, as shown in Figure 10-1. As a result, you don't create a chart by defining it from scratch; instead, you edit the default chart and change it to meet your needs. The new chart window is labeled *Untitled* until you give it another name by saving the file with the File⇨Save As command.

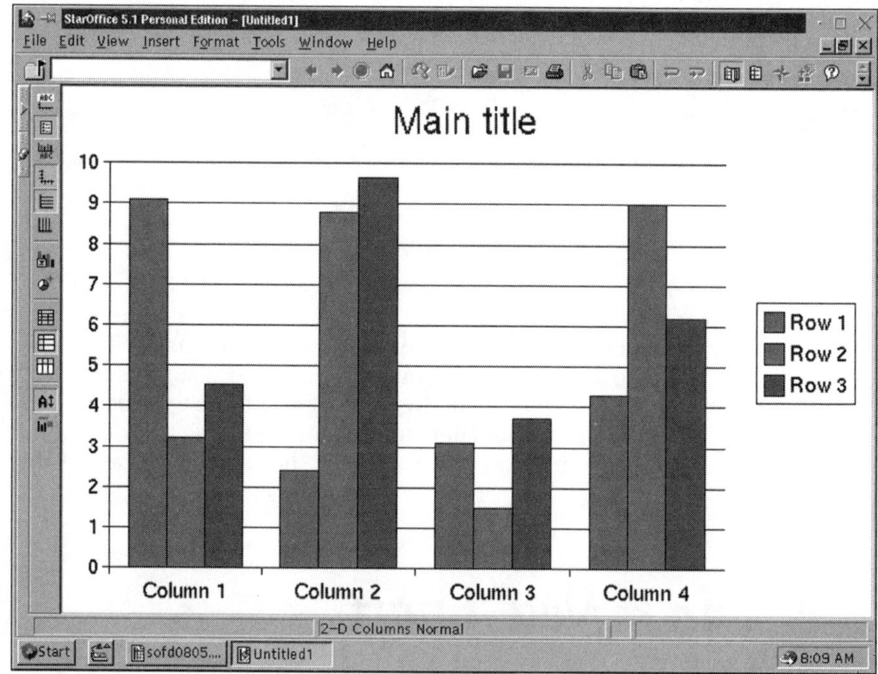

Figure 10-1: StarChart launches with a dummy chart in the document window.

Entering Chart Data

A StarChart chart is a graphical representation of numeric data. To change the main components of the chart, such as the number and height of the bars, you must change the underlying data on which the chart is based. Think of the chart as a picture of a data set. Changing the data changes the picture.

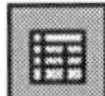

A new StarChart document starts out with some arbitrary, sample data entered into the default chart that you first see in the StarChart window. The chart data resides in a separate data table that isn't normally visible in the StarChart window. To display the chart data table, choose View⇨Chart Data or click the Chart Data button on the StarChart Main toolbar. The Chart Data window appears, as shown in Figure 10-2.

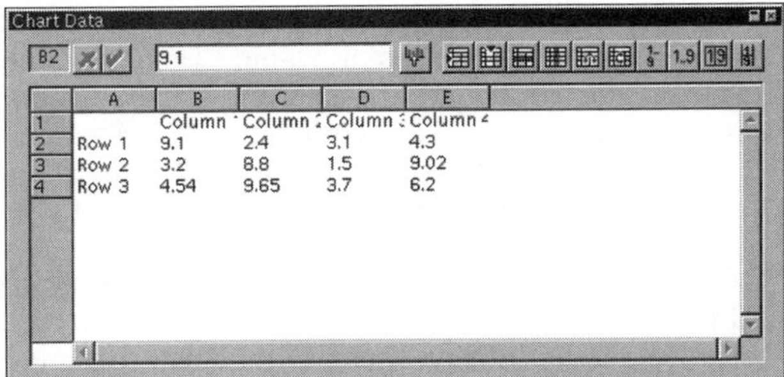

Figure 10-2: The Chart Data window holds the data that serves as the basis for the chart.

Although the Chart Data window resembles a miniature StarCalc spreadsheet, it's really just a very simple table. The spreadsheet editing and navigational tools are *not* present. You can't enter formulas or cell references into the cells. You can't even directly edit the cell's contents.

Naturally, you want to replace the sample data with your own data in order to create your own chart. To edit the contents of a cell in the Chart Data window, follow these steps:

1. **Select a cell to edit by clicking it.**
2. **Edit the contents of the selected cell in the Input Field.**
3. **After editing the contents of the Input Field box, click the Accept button or press Enter.**

StarCalc records the change and enters it into the corresponding cell in the Chart Data table.

If you need to change the number of rows or columns in the table, you can use the buttons in the toolbar at the top of the Chart Data window to do so. To delete a row or column from the table, select a cell in the row or column that you want to remove and then click the Delete Row or the Delete Column button. StarChart immediately removes the row or column from the Chart Data table.

If you click the Insert Row or Insert Column buttons, StarChart inserts a new row of cells above the currently selected cell or inserts a new column of cells to the left of the selected cell. The new column or row is filled with zeros, except for the cell in the first column or the first row. That's the column or row label, and it's blank.

After editing the Chart Data table so that it contains your data, click the Transfer Data button to transfer the revised data from the Chart Data table to the chart in the main StarChart window. StarChart redraws the chart to reflect the new data. If you deleted rows or columns from the table, the chart contains fewer bars. If you added rows to the Chart Data table, the chart contains more bars. The data scale changes automatically to accommodate the range of data that you entered into the Chart Data table. Any changes that you made in the row and column labels appear in the legend and the axis labels.

As long as the Chart Data window is open, you can continue to make changes to the data and then click the Transfer Data button to redraw the chart so you can see the effect of your changes. When you finish entering data into the Chart Data window, choose View⇨Chart Data or click the Chart Data button on the StarChart Main toolbar to close the Chart Data window.

Rearranging chart data

Sometimes when you enter data into the Chart Data table and then generate a chart based on that data, you may find that StarChart doesn't create the chart that you expected — the relationship between the columns and rows of data and the bars on the chart are reversed. That's a common problem that's easy to fix. The Data in Rows and the Data in Columns buttons on the StarChart Main toolbar enable you to swap the row/column orientation of the chart to the table. The default arrangement is Data in Rows. Simply click the Data in Columns button to instantly rearrange the chart. Click the Data in Rows button to redraw the chart using rows as the primary data category.

Using chart data from a spreadsheet

Entering data into the Chart Data window is a fairly straightforward process, and for the typical chart, you can enter the data quickly and easily. The best charts are usually simple, so you don't have to enter many data points.

However, if you've already set up a StarCalc data table that you want to use as the basis for a chart, you may as well use that data instead of manually reentering the data into the StarChart Chart Data window. You can't move the data from your StarCalc spreadsheet into the StarChart Chart Data table, but you can do the next best thing, which is to add a StarChart chart to the StarCalc spreadsheet. To do so, follow these steps:

1. **Open your StarCalc spreadsheet and select the data that you want to use as the basis for your chart.**

   The data must be in one contiguous block of cells and arranged similarly to the Chart Data window, with labels in the top row and the left column.

2. **Choose Insert⇨Chart.**

   StarOffice opens the AutoFormat Chart dialog box, as shown in Figure 10-3. The selected spreadsheet area's cell addresses are already entered in the Area box.

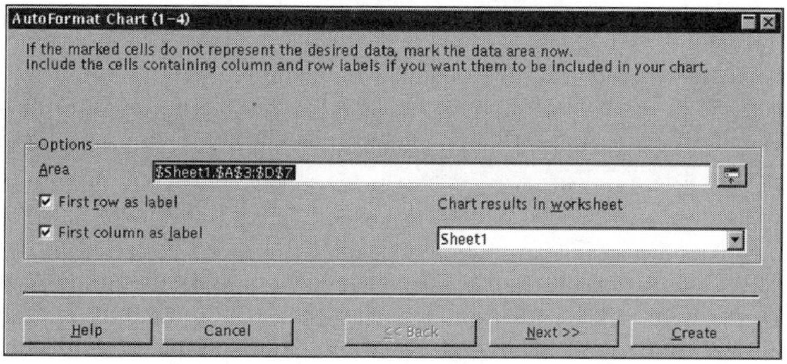

Figure 10-3: The AutoFormat Chart dialog box enables you to define a chart to add to a StarCalc spreadsheet.

3. **Select a sheet in the Chart Results in Worksheet drop-down list box.**

   Creating the chart on a separate sheet in the spreadsheet file usually works best.

4. **Click Create.**

   StarOffice creates a chart based on the selected data from your spreadsheet and inserts the chart as an object in the designated sheet of your spreadsheet file. See Figure 10-4.

The chart appears as a selectable object in your spreadsheet. When the chart is selected for editing (as it is by default when you first create it), the StarChart menus and toolbars replace the standard StarCalc menus and toolbars, and you can edit the chart just as if it were in its own StarChart window. You can select different chart types, edit the title, and do anything else that you can normally do to a chart.

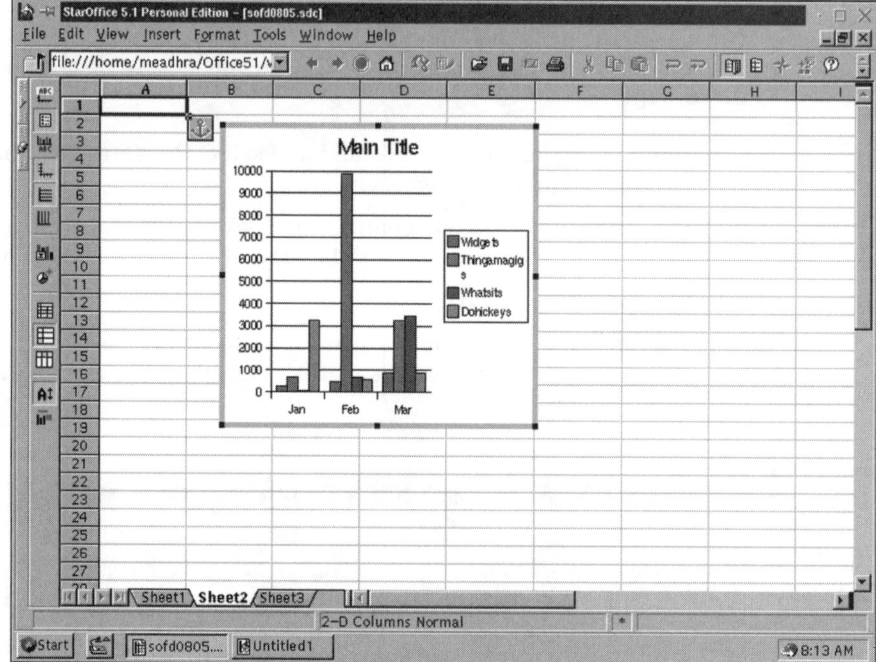

Figure 10-4: A StarChart chart object in a StarCalc spreadsheet.

When you're finished editing the chart, click anywhere on the spreadsheet page outside the chart to deselect it and return to the normal StarCalc editing mode. Click the chart once to select the chart object and move or resize it on the spreadsheet page. Double-click the chart object to reenter StarChart editing mode.

Selecting a Chart Type

The standard chart that StarChart draws is a column chart (sometimes called a vertical bar chart). A column chart is a good choice for a default because it's by far the most common chart type. But StarChart can produce lots of other chart types as well. The StarChart inventory includes eight main chart types with multiple variants of each type, for a total of more than 75 chart types. You can choose the chart type and variant that presents the best picture of your data. Doing so is quick and easy.

To select a different chart type, follow these steps:

1. **Choose Format⇨Chart Type or click the Edit Chart Type button on the StarChart Main toolbar.**

   StarChart displays the Chart Type dialog box, as shown in Figure 10-5.

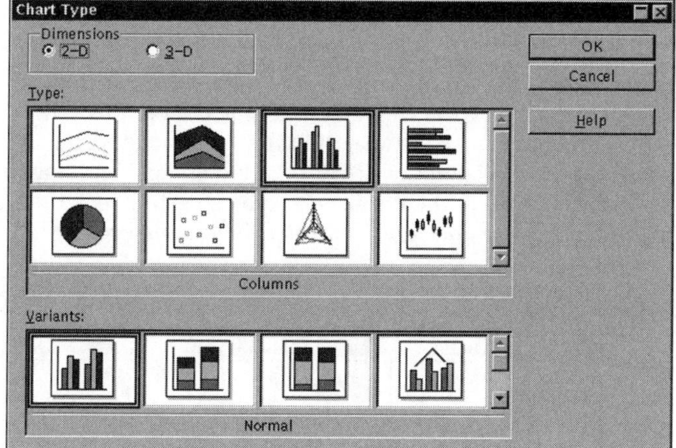

Figure 10-5: Select from one of StarChart's many chart types.

2. **Select 2-D or 3-D in the Dimensions area.**

   Select 2-D for standard, flat, two-dimensional charts. Select 3-D for charts with simulated three-dimensional effects.

3. **Select a main chart type by clicking a thumbnail in the Type list box.**

   StarChart displays the available variations for the selected chart type in the Variants list box at the bottom of the dialog box.

4. **Select a chart subtype from the Variants list box.**

5. **Click OK.**

   StarChart closes the Chart Type dialog box and redraws the chart using the selected chart type.

You can repeat the Chart Type selection process as often as you like, selecting different chart types until you find the one that works best for your data.

Controlling Chart Features with AutoFormat

StarChart's AutoFormat feature enables you to change chart types and also manipulate grid lines and titles, all from within the same dialog box. With AutoFormat, you can take care of most of your chart formatting chores in one quick pass. To use AutoFormat on your chart, follow these steps:

1. **Choose Format⇨AutoFormat or click the AutoFormat button on the StarChart Main toolbar.**

   StarChart opens the AutoFormat Chart dialog box, as shown in Figure 10-6. Notice the Preview box at the left end of the dialog box. The Preview box previews the effects of each selection that you make within the AutoFormat Chart dialog box. To get the full effect, including titles and other text elements, in the Preview box, be sure to check the Show Text Elements in Preview check box (located below the Preview box).

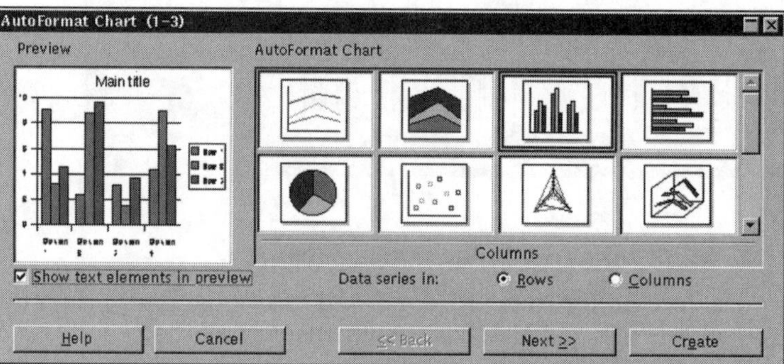

Figure 10-6: Selecting a chart type using the AutoFormat Chart dialog box.

2. **Select a chart type from the AutoFormat Chart list box and click Next.**

   StarChart displays Page 2 of the AutoFormat Chart dialog box. The selections in the Choose a Variant list box differ depending on the chart type that you selected in the previous page.

3. **Select a variant of your chosen chart type by clicking a thumbnail in the Choose a Variant list box.**

   As always in the AutoFormat dialog box, StarChart updates the Preview box to reflect your choice.

4. **Check or uncheck options in the Grid Lines area as desired and then click Next.**

   The third and final page of the AutoFormat dialog box appears, as shown in Figure 10-7.

5. **Adjust the settings as needed to add, remove, and edit the titles on your chart.**

   Check or uncheck check boxes to turn titles on or off. Type the titles in the corresponding text boxes.

6. **Click Create.**

   StarChart closes the AutoFormat Chart dialog box and redraws the chart using the new settings.

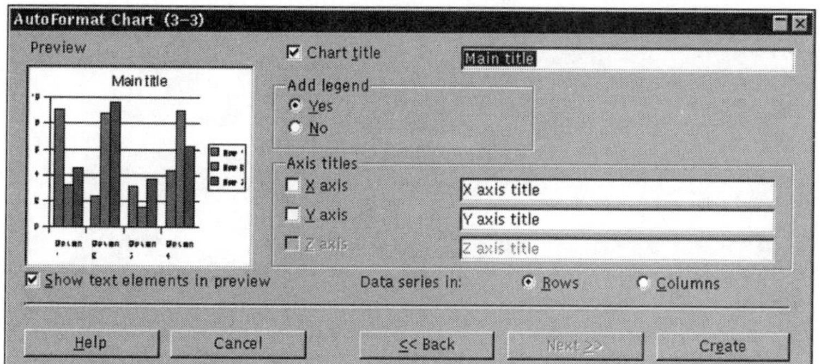

Figure 10-7: Labeling your chart.

Filling Your Chart with Color

One important aspect of your chart's format that is not addressed in the AutoFormat Chart dialog box is the color of the different chart segments. StarChart uses a default color scheme to assign colors to the chart elements. You can use these colors or change them at your discretion.

To change the color of a data element, follow these steps:

1. **Click the data element to select it. (You may need to click more than once.)**

   A small, square selection handle appears in the center of each data element in the series to indicate that the data element is selected.

2. **Right-click the selected element and choose Object Properties from the pop-up menu that appears.**

   StarChart opens the Data Row dialog box, as shown in Figure 10-8.

3. **Click the Area tab if it isn't already selected.**

   The tabs available in the Data Row dialog box vary depending on the chart type and the data element you select. For example, line charts have a Line tab instead of the more common Area tab.

4. **Click the Color radio button and then select a color from the list box below it.**

   The Preview box shows a sample of your color selection.

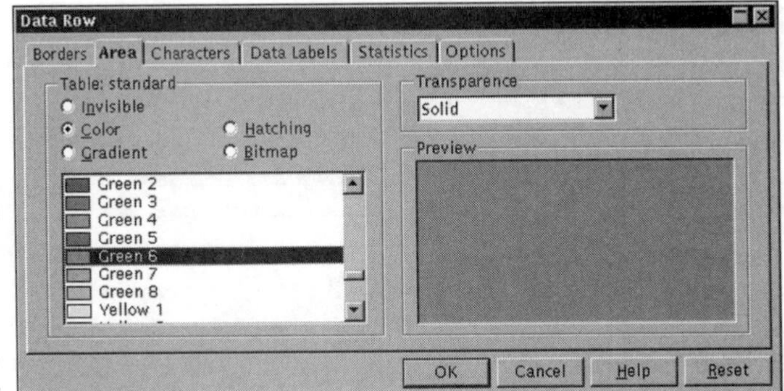

Figure 10-8: Selecting a color for the data bars.

(Optional) While the Data Row dialog box is open, you may want to check out some of the other color effects available on the Area tab and also some of the settings available on the other tabs in the dialog box.

5. **After adjusting the settings, click OK.**

   StarChart closes the Data Row dialog box and applies the new color to your chart.

Adding 3-D Effects

In addition to the standard two-dimensional charts, StarChart can produce an assortment of three-dimensional charts. Creating a 3-D chart is as simple as selecting one of the 3-D chart types in AutoFormat or choosing 3-D in the Chart Type dialog box. After you select the appropriate chart type, StarChart creates charts such as the one shown in Figure 10-9.

When you create a 3-D chart, you have the opportunity to adjust some chart characteristics that simply do not exist in a simpler 2-D chart, such as the chart perspective, or angle of view.

To adjust the chart perspective, follow these steps:

1. **Click the chart background (but not on a data element or grid line).**

   A set of small black selection boxes appears around the chart. Unlike the selection boxes that appear around a two-dimensional object, the selection boxes have small arrows beside them.

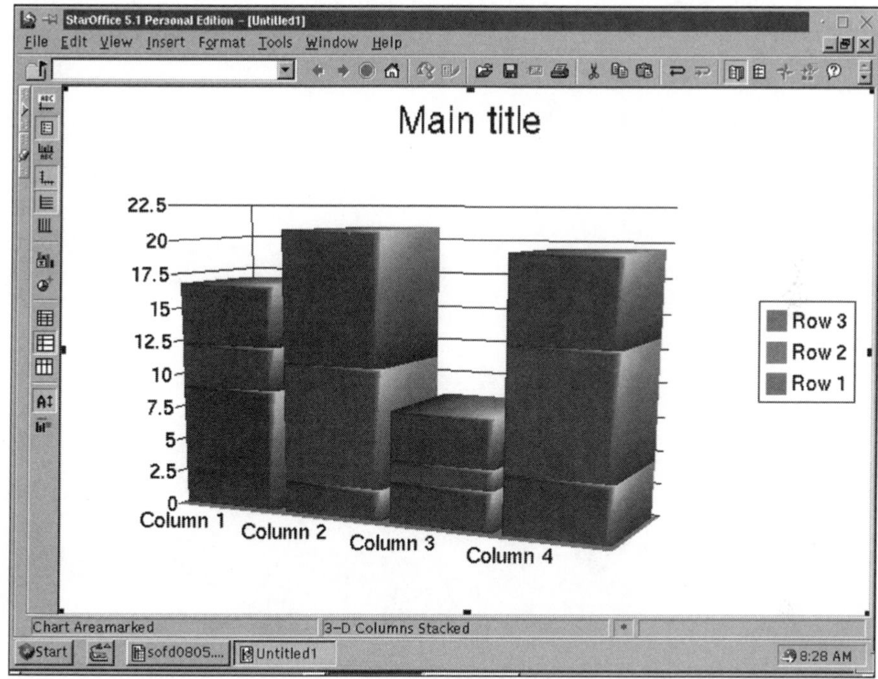

Figure 10-9: StarChart can create sophisticated 3-D effects.

2. **Click and drag one of the selection boxes and observe the changes in the wireframe box surrounding the chart.**

   After you release the mouse button, StarChart redraws the chart using the new perspective setting. Notice that dragging the corner selection boxes produces a very different effect than dragging the side, top, or bottom selection boxes. The effects are hard to describe but easy to see when you try them for yourself.

Part IV

Impressing an Audience with Graphics and Presentations

"Of course graphics are important to your project, Eddy, but I think it would've been better to scan a picture of your worm collection."

In this part . . .

You don't have to get butterflies in your stomach when you make your next presentation. With the graphics and presentation tools in StarOffice at your disposal, you're sure to impress your audience. StarDraw gives you the tools you need to create flow-charts, diagrams, and the like. StarImage gives you control over scanned photographs and clip art images. And StarImpress lets you assemble a presentation that pulls these elements together with text, tables, and charts and then present them in a slick, on-screen slide show.

Chapter 11

Creating Drawings

In This Chapter

- Introducing StarDraw
- Playing with basic drawing tools
- Rearranging objects on the page
- Creating 3-D objects
- Saving your drawing

Whoever said a picture is worth a thousand words was right. Whether you're arranging the floor plan of your house, presenting next quarter's sales projections, or e-mailing mom to tell her little Billy's latest exploits, pictures can help you say it better.

StarOffice comes with several tools to help you create a variety of pictures. StarDraw, the subject of this chapter, is the tool that you use to produce charts and diagrams (flowcharts, organizational charts, floor plans, and so on). StarImage, which I cover in Chapter 12, is for playing with images, such as that photograph of little Billy wrestling with the cat (and losing). With StarImpress (Chapters 13 and 14), you can present your new works of art in a slideshow presentation.

Introducing StarDraw

StarDraw is a *vector drawing* tool, which means that StarDraw stores your drawing as a bunch of commands (such as "draw a circle here") and the program executes those instructions in order to display the drawing on-screen or print it. StarDraw is fundamentally different from other drawing programs you may be familiar with, in which you grab a paintbrush and start playing Picasso with the mouse. Instead, think of placing objects (lines, squares, circles, and so on) onto the page. StarDraw remembers where you put them, and you can move or change them later. Because StarDraw provides the drawing tools that enable you to draw and manipulate basic shapes, you can use those shapes as building blocks to create anything from a simple organizational chart or floor plan to a complex map, diagram, or technical illustration.

One of the first things you may notice about StarDraw is that you won't find an eraser tool. You don't need one. Instead of erasing the digital paint you deposit on-screen, you select an object and delete it by pressing the Delete key — just as you delete text from a word processing document.

Creating a New Drawing

As with all the StarOffice document types, you can create a new drawing in any one of several ways:

- Double-click the New Drawing icon in the StarDesktop window.
- Right-click the StarDesktop background and choose New⇨Documents⇨Drawing from the pop-up menu that appears.
- Choose File⇨New⇨Drawing from the StarOffice menu in any document window.
- Click the Start button in the StarOffice Task bar and choose New Drawing.

Which technique you use to create a drawing document doesn't make any difference. StarOffice displays a blank StarDraw document window similar to Figure 11-1. The StarDraw menus and toolbars replace the menus and toolbars of whatever document window you were previously working in.

The StarDraw Main toolbar on the left side of the window contains buttons for selecting the StarDraw drawing tools. The StarDraw Object toolbar contains buttons for formatting and editing the objects (boxes, circles, and text) in your drawing. The selection of buttons on the StarDraw Object toolbar varies dramatically, depending on what drawing tool or object you select. The Object toolbar's changing button selection happens throughout StarOffice, but the changes that occur when you select different objects and drawing tools in StarDraw are more pronounced.

Drawing Basic Shapes

You can put many different objects into a StarDraw drawing — simple ones such as boxes, lines, and circles; 3-D objects such as cones and spheres; objects from other programs, such as charts; and even "widgets," which you may see on a Web page (text input boxes, push buttons, and so on).

Many of the drawing tools use the same basic technique for drawing objects. First, you select the kind of object you want to draw by clicking the corresponding tool button in the StarDraw Main toolbar. Then you specify the location and size of the object by dragging the mouse pointer on the drawing

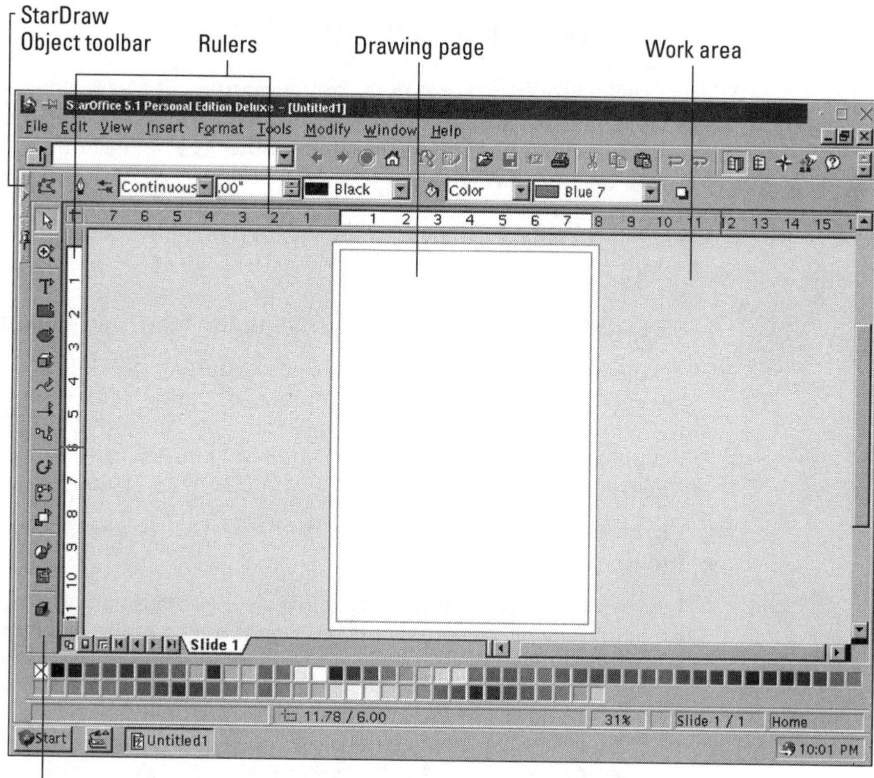

Figure 11-1: Welcome to StarDraw.

page to define a bounding box — a box that sets the limits or bounds of the object. You define a bounding box by defining two opposite corners. Click to define the first corner, and then drag to the location of the opposite corner of the bounding box and release the mouse button. An object such as a rectangle completely fills its bounding box, while an ellipse just touches the sides of the bounding box but doesn't fill the corners. StarDraw draws the largest object of the selected type that fits within the bounding box.

The basic drawing technique varies, depending on the object you're drawing. For some of the objects, you must make a few extra mouse clicks beyond dragging the bounding box in order to define the object. Some objects, such as lines, don't use a bounding box. All the drawing tools offer options and variations on the basic object type as well. For example, rectangles can be elongated rectangles or squares, with square corners or rounded, filled shapes or outlines. To use one of the other object subtypes, instead of the default, select the subtype before you begin drawing with that tool. (I explain how to do so in the next section of this chapter.)

Using drawing tool buttons

All the drawing tools can create several variations of the basic object type. Notice the small arrowhead or triangle in the corner of the buttons on the Main toolbar, which indicates that the tool has a set of options available. Before you begin drawing with a tool, you need to select which of those options you want to use. The process is the same for all the drawing tools. For example, to select which subtype of the rectangle you want to use, follow these steps:

1. **Slow-click the Rectangle tool button in the StarDraw Main toolbar.**

   A *slow-click* means pressing the mouse button and holding it down for a second or so. The technique resembles dragging, only you don't move the mouse. After a moment, a small toolbar attached to the Rectangle button appears (see Figure 11-2), and you can release the mouse button. The toolbar stays visible.

2. **Click one of the option buttons in the toolbar to select a variation of the Rectangle tool.**

   If the icon on the button doesn't give you enough information about the object type that it represents, you can point to a button and let the pointer hover on it for a moment to display a pop-up box with the name of the button.

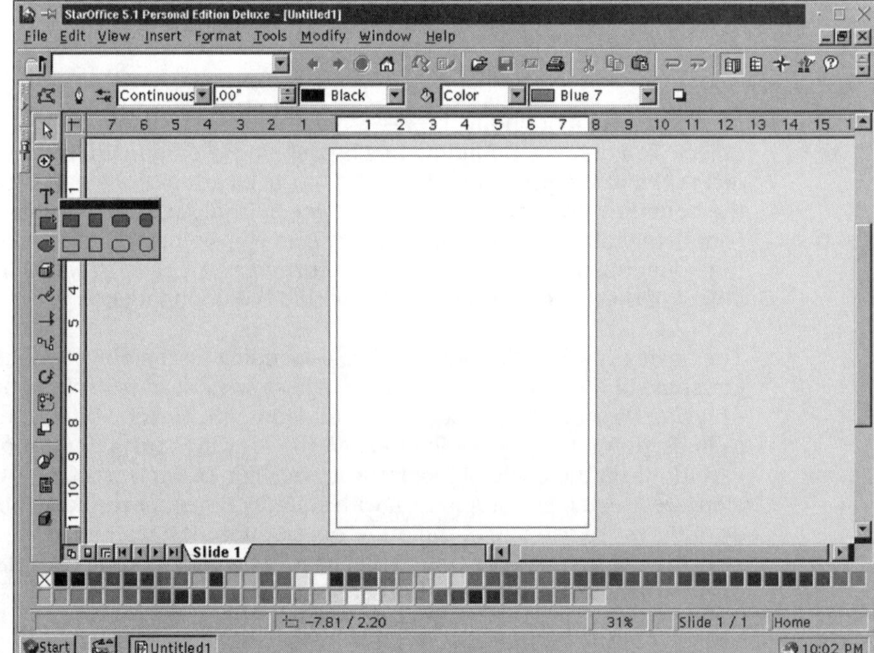

Figure 11-2: A small blue triangle on a tool button indicates that a toolbar of variations is available.

When you click a button in the Rectangle tool's option toolbar, the toolbar disappears and the Rectangle button on the Main toolbar changes to reflect the option you selected. When you use the Rectangle tool, it draws that kind of rectangular object. The rectangle option you select remains available for further use until you reopen the Rectangle tool's option toolbar and select a different option.

After opening a toolbar attached to a drawing tool button, you can drag the title bar to move the toolbar away from the drawing tool button from whence it came. This action is called *tearing off* a toolbar. When you make a selection from a tear-off toolbar, the toolbar doesn't disappear, and you can begin using that variation of the drawing tool without clicking the main drawing tool button. So, you can leave the option toolbar open and select different tools from it without having to constantly call it back. As you work on your drawing, you can tear off several option toolbars to keep them all open and available for quick access to all the tools they contain.

Drawing boxes

You can draw several variations of the basic rectangular object with StarDraw's Rectangle tool. The default rectangular object is a filled rectangle with sharp corners. If you want to draw one of the other variations on the basic shape, you must select that option from the Rectangle tool's options toolbar before clicking the Rectangle drawing tool. See the previous section for instructions on using the options toolbars.

You may think having different tools for, say, a rectangle and a square is redundant, because a square is just a rectangle with sides of equal length — but after you see how easy drawing a perfect square is with the appropriate option selected, you'll understand the intent of the program's designers.

To actually draw any rectangular shape on your active drawing page, follow these steps:

1. **Click the Rectangle drawing tool button in the Main toolbar.**

   When you move the pointer into the drawing area, the pointer changes to a small crosshair (or + sign) with a small rectangle next to it to reflect the current drawing mode.

2. **Move your cursor to the spot in your drawing where you want to place one corner of the rectangle.**

   Rectangles are often drawn from the upper-left corner to the lower right, but no rule says you must do it that way.

3. **Click and drag the mouse to the opposite corner of the rectangle.**

   A *rubber-band* rectangle follows the cursor, drawing a constantly resizing rectangle as you go. The rubber-band rectangle follows in any direction, even if you go backward. You can drag the rubber band over your other shapes, and it won't disturb them.

If you selected a square, you notice that the rubber band's movement is choppy as you draw the bounding box for the object. StarDraw doesn't move the square exactly to follow your cursor. Instead, the program always keeps the dimensions equal, so that you still have a square. This is called a *constrained* tool.

4. **Release the mouse button.**

   The rubber band becomes a solid shape. You just drew your first rectangle! If you chose one of the filled options, StarDraw fills your rectangle with the current color, which you can see in the Object bar. (See Figure 11-3.) Your cursor becomes a black arrow, representing the Select tool, again. The small green squares on your new rectangle's perimeter indicate that the rectangle is selected for further editing.

After drawing the rectangle, you can move and edit it if you want. To move it, just point to the middle of the rectangle and drag it to another location. To resize it, click and drag one of the small green selection handles on the perimeter of the rectangle. Drag a handle toward the center of the object to make it smaller, away from the center to make it larger. This technique works with all the objects you draw in StarDraw, not just rectangles.

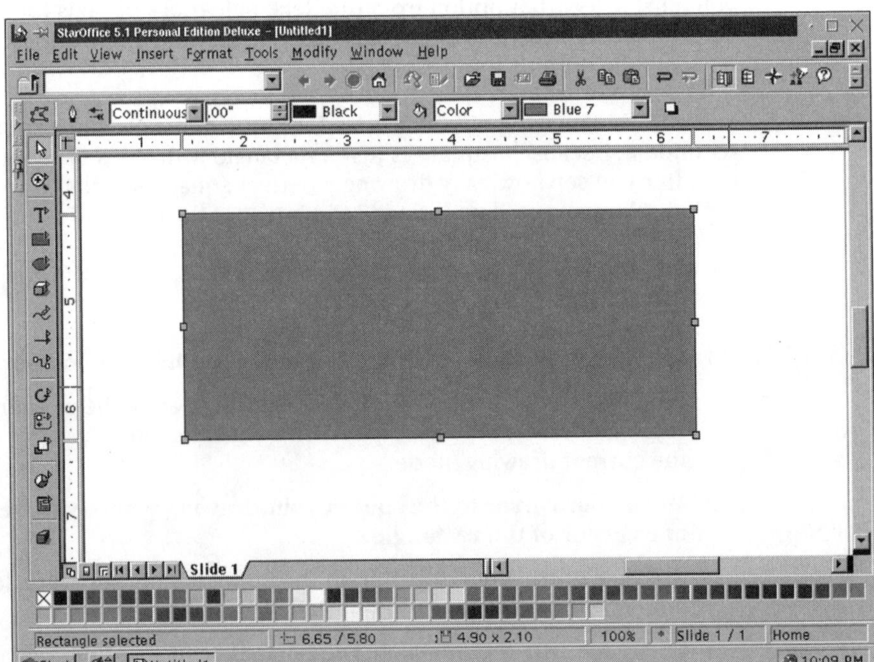

Figure 11-3: The finished rectangle is selected for further editing.

Normally, every time you use a tool such as the Rectangle tool, the cursor returns to the Select tool after you place one shape. So if you want to continue drawing multiple objects of the same kind, select your drawing tool by double-clicking it. That way, after drawing one object, you can draw another without clicking the drawing tool again. The drawing mode stays active until you choose a different tool. To stop drawing, choose the Select tool.

Drawing ellipses

The Ellipse tool works in much the same way as the Rectangle tool described in the previous section. One difference is that the Ellipse tool offers more options than the Rectangle tool. So, in addition to circles and ellipses, you can draw pie slices and arcs or segments using this tool.

Drawing a plain circle or ellipse is almost the same process as drawing a rectangle. First, you select the ellipse or circle option you want, then you click the Ellipse drawing tool button in the Main toolbar and drag the pointer in the drawing area to define a bounding box for the ellipse. You still drag the mouse from one corner to the opposite one, only this time the rubber band that follows you is an ellipse. When you release the mouse button, StarDraw draws the ellipse and shows it selected, with green selection handles on the sides and corners of the invisible bounding box that surrounds and defines the ellipse. (See Figure 11-4.)

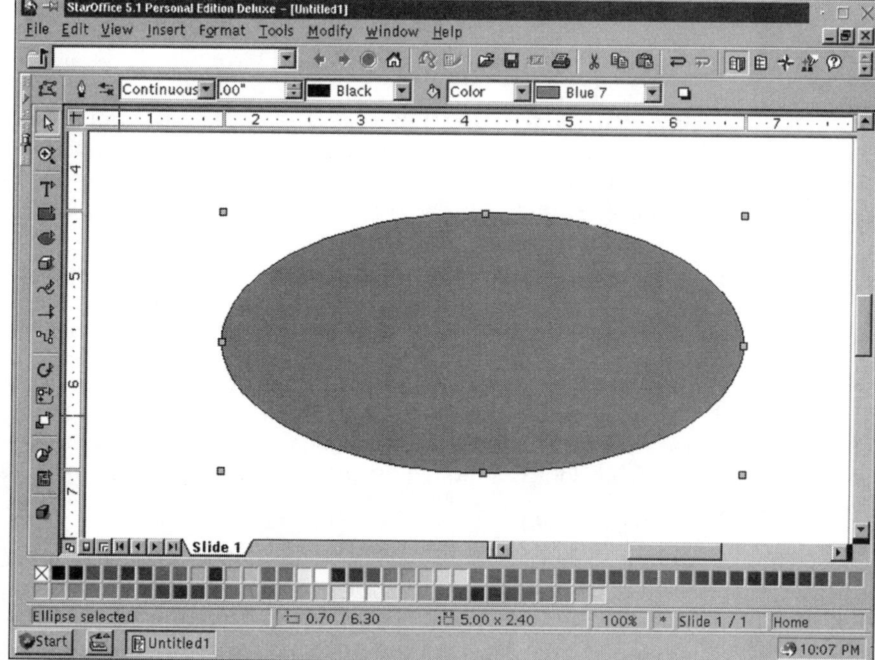

Figure 11-4: An ellipse's selection handles mark the edges and corners of an invisible bounding box that surrounds the ellipse.

When drawing ellipses, think of drawing a box that just barely contains and confines the ellipse inside. Drawing a rounded shape by defining corners may seem a little strange at first because there really are no corners (obviously!) on the object you're actually drawing. In school, you may have learned to draw circles by starting at the center and going out to the radius. Even some drawing tools make circles that way, but it's not as common as the bounding box method that StarDraw uses.

The Ellipse drawing tool also enables you to draw pie slices, arcs, and segments — all of which are portions of ellipses or circles. Drawing these shapes is just a bit more complicated than drawing a simple ellipse. Basically, you start by defining an ellipse and then make an extra mouse click or two in order to define the portion of the ellipse that you want to draw. The process is similar for drawing a pie slice, segment, or arc. Here are the steps for drawing a pie slice:

1. **Select the Ellipse Pie option from the options toolbar for the Ellipse tool.**

   See the "Using drawing tool buttons" section earlier in this chapter for instructions.

2. **Click the Ellipse drawing tool button on the Main toolbar.**

   Note that the icon on the Ellipse drawing tool button indicates the Ellipse Pie is selected.

3. **Drag the pointer in your drawing to define the ellipse's bounding box.**

   As you drag the pointer, the rubber band ellipse shape follows your moves.

4. **Release the mouse button.**

   StarDraw anchors the rubber band ellipse in place but doesn't fill in the shape or add selection handles around it. The pointer still has the crosshair shape that indicates you're still in ellipse drawing mode. A radius line appears in the rubber band ellipse pointing from the center of the ellipse to the pointer.

5. **Click to place one edge of the slice.**

   As you move the pointer around the ellipse, the radius line follows the pointer. When the radius line is correctly positioned, click to place it as one edge of your pie slice. When you do, another radius line appears. As you move the second radius line around, your ellipse begins to look like a pie with a slice removed. If you spin more than halfway around the circle, it actually looks as though the pie is gone and you have only a slice.

6. **Click again to place the other edge of the slice.**

   Your pie slice is complete. (See Figure 11-5.) If you chose a filled pie shape, the pie slice fills with the current color. The selection handles surround the finished pie slice to denote a bounding box just big enough to contain the pie slice, not the whole ellipse that you drew in Steps 3 and 4.

The procedure for drawing an arc is the same as that for drawing a pie slice. The difference is that you end up with just a portion of an ellipse — a curved line. You define the arc by using the same kind of radius lines you use to define the sides of a pie slice, but they disappear when you are finished, leaving only the arc.

You can use the Segment tool to add a line segment (defined by two endpoints that touch the circle) and then split the circle into two uneven pieces. The resulting shape looks as though you started with a circle and then took scissors and snipped off a piece.

The Segment tool works exactly as the pie slice tool does, requiring three separate mouse actions to complete the shape. However, the rubber band draws itself differently after the first line segment is placed.

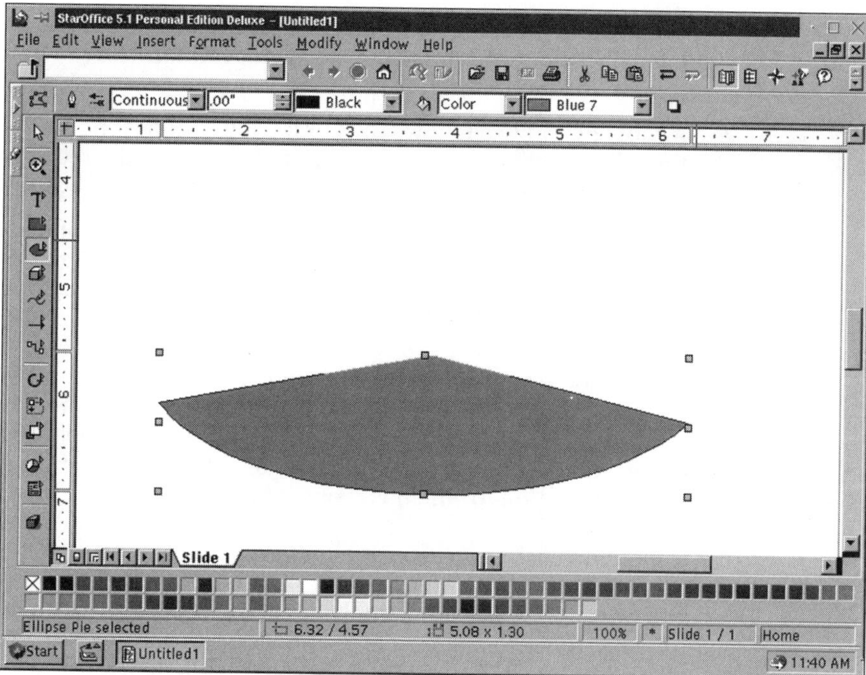

Figure 11-5: A completed pie slice.

For each of the modified ellipse options (arc, slice, segment), you may notice that the ellipse disappears after you click the first line segment. That just means, based on where the cursor is currently sitting, that the resulting shape may be invisible. Imagine if you made one cut into a pie, made the second cut in the same spot, and took away the pie. You'd be left with a slice so thin it's nonexistent. (That's one way to go on a diet.) Just move the pointer to define a larger slice of the pie (forget the diet), and your ellipse reappears.

Drawing lines and arrows

Sometimes you just need a plain line, or an arrow. And every once in a blue moon you need a dotted line or a dimension line. You can handle all those things with the Lines and Arrows tool.

1. **Click the Lines and Arrows drawing tool button on the Main toolbar.**

   The pointer changes to a crosshair with a diagonal line beside it. As always with the StarDraw drawing tools, if you want to use one of the tool's other options instead of the default option, you can select the desired option from the tool's option toolbar before you click the tool to begin drawing. For instructions, see the "Using drawing tool buttons" section earlier in this chapter.

2. **Position the pointer in your drawing page at the spot where you want the line to start.**

3. **Drag the pointer to the spot where you want the line to end and release the mouse button.**

   A rubber band line follows the cursor. If you chose the Line (45-degree) tool, the rubber band snaps back and forth on 45-degree lines only, trying to follow the cursor as best it can.

   When you release the mouse button, the rubber-band line becomes permanent. The endpoints of the line are marked with light blue control squares. No bounding box exists for a simple line because a line has no width beyond the thickness of the line itself.

When you draw a simple line, the direction in which you draw the line makes no difference. You can start at either endpoint and drag to the other. However, when you draw arrows, the starting and ending points do make a difference because of the arrowhead on one end. When you're drawing arrows, pay attention to which end of the line you click first.

The Dimension Line option is a little different from the other options. Instead of a single line or a line with an arrowhead on one end, a dimension line is actually two short lines with a double-ended arrow between them. When you start drawing a dimension line, it resembles a football goalpost. You draw the dimension line much the same way as you do other lines, but you drag along the line that the dimension line is measuring (the side of a rectangle, for instance). StarDraw creates the dimension line above, below, or to the side of the line you drag. StarDraw not only draws the dimension line's end lines and dimension arrows, it also automatically measures the length of the line and labels it accordingly. (See Figure 11-6.)

Making connections

You probably recognize that the arrows you draw with the Lines and Arrows tool can be used to point from one shape to another in a flowchart. One problem exists, though. What happens if you move some of the shapes in the flowchart? Of course, the arrow stays where you first placed the objects. Maybe that's okay with you; you just move the arrows. But you don't have to. The Connector tool makes this happen automatically.

A connector is a smart line. You attach each end point (as if with glue) to a connection point on a shape. The connector then knows how to redraw itself if you ever move one of the shapes it's attached to.

To draw a connector line between objects, have the objects you want to connect already in place on your drawing page. Then you follow these steps to connect them.

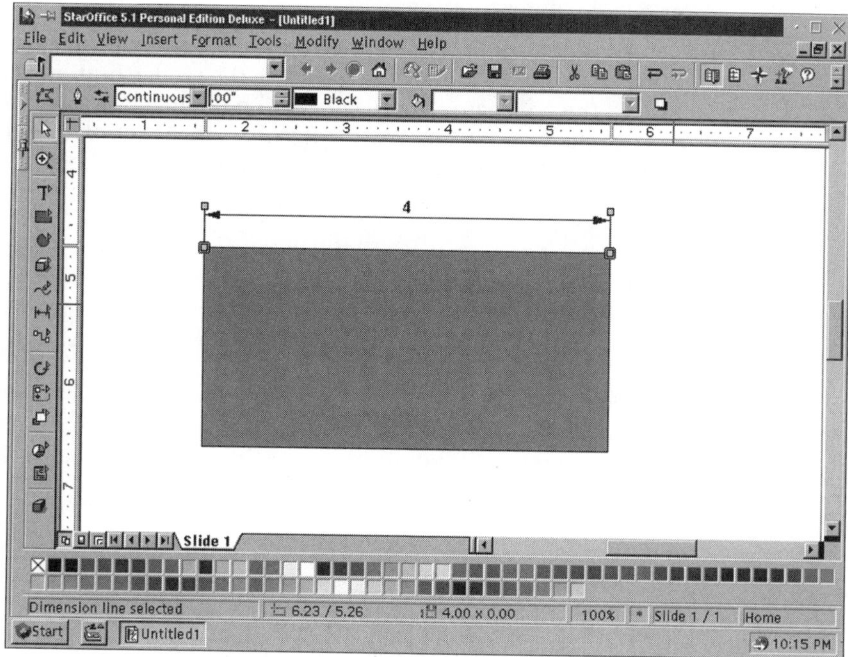

Figure 11-6: The dimension line automatically determines the distance between two markers and uses that value to label itself.

1. **Click the Connectors drawing tool button in the Main toolbar.**

   The default connector is a simple line, but you have many connectors to choose from. If you want to draw one of the other connectors, you must select that option from the Connectors tool's options toolbar before you click the Connectors drawing tool. For instructions, see the "Using drawing tool buttons" section earlier in this chapter.

2. **Move the cursor over an existing shape.**

   StarDraw surrounds the shape with a dotted line and small boxes representing available connection points on the edges. All shapes have connection points (even lines). If you move the cursor onto another shape, the first dotted line disappears, and the new shape is surrounded.

3. **Move the cursor near one of the connection points.**

   The connection point itself is surrounded by its own dotted box. This is StarDraw's way of saying "If you press now, the connector attaches here." You can only attach a connector at the specified connection points.

4. **Click the control point and drag to another object.**

   You've glued one end of the line to the first object. As you drag, you see a smart rubber band following the cursor, repositioning itself to show you as you go where StarDraw can draw the connector.

5. **Position the pointer over another object's connection point and release the mouse button.**

   You can see the dotted lines again as you move over the new shape (as shown in Figure 11-7). After you release the mouse button, StarDraw anchors the connector to the connection point and draws the connector between the two objects. While the connector is selected, red boxes at both ends of the line verify the connection points to the attached objects.

If you move one of the objects, StarDraw redraws the connector line automatically and is actually very smart at figuring out where and when to bend the connector. With the connector selected, you can see the red boxes at the endpoints. If you want, you can select one of the boxes to break the connection.

If you're not sure where to put the connector, you don't have to attach it right away. Just go ahead and draw it somewhere. When you know where you want it, you can click on the endpoints and drag them onto the shapes you want to attach.

Controlling Lines and Fill Colors

By default, StarDraw draws objects with thin black lines and fills all the filled shapes with a light blue color. When you want to add a little more color and variety to your drawings, you can play with those line and fill colors by manipulating object properties.

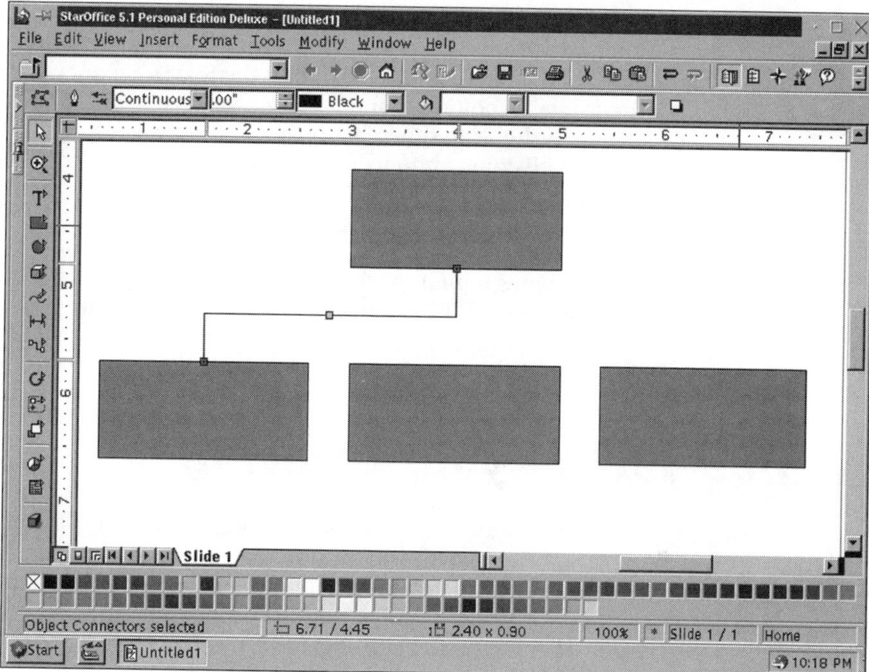

Figure 11-7: A connector attached to two objects.

To edit an object's properties, first select an object by clicking it. Selection handles (small green boxes) surround the object, and the buttons and drop-down list boxes on the StarDraw Object toolbar give you easy access to properties such as color and line thickness. Simply make your choice from the appropriate button or drop-down list box on the Object toolbar. For example, to change the color of a line (or the outline around a filled shape), just select a color from the Line Color drop-down list box.

You can also use the StarDraw Object toolbar to change an object's properties while you're drawing it. After you click a drawing tool in the Main toolbar, go to the Object toolbar and change the settings before you begin drawing the object. StarDraw creates the object using the color and line settings you choose in the Object toolbar.

If you need even more control over the properties of an object, you can right-click the object and choose Line or Area from the pop-up menu that appears. Depending on your choice, StarDraw opens the Line dialog box or the Area dialog box. The various tabs and settings in these boxes enable you to change the basic properties of the selected object, as you can with the Object toolbar, and much more. For example, settings on the Gradients tab of the Area dialog box enable you to define a custom gradient fill instead of just selecting one of the predefined gradients.

For quick color selections, you can't beat the Color bar. You can elect to display this separate toolbar by choosing View⇨Toolbars⇨Color Bar. The Color bar normally appears across the bottom of the StarDraw document window, displays the available colors as small color swatch buttons, and is faster and easier to use than the drop-down list boxes in the Object toolbar. To change a selected object's fill color, simply click the desired color button. To change the color of a line or the outline around a filled shape, right-click a color button. You can also click and drag a color button in the Color bar and drop it on an object to fill the object with the color. The object doesn't have to be selected. This technique comes in handy when you want to change the color of several objects, because you don't have to select each object before changing its color.

Adding Text to Your Drawing

My pictures don't always say a thousand words. Sometimes I have to help them along by adding text. StarDraw offers a variety of ways to put text on a drawing page — either as an object of its own or a property of another object.

To create a stand-alone text object, follow these steps:

1. **Click the Text drawing tool in the Main toolbar.**

   The pointer becomes a text cursor, which looks like a crosshair with an I-beam beside it.

2. **Click in your drawing at the spot where you want to place some text.**

   A thin group of green selection handles appears where you click. This item is a text box with a width of 0. As you type, it grows.

3. **Type your text.**

   Your text appears inside the box. The more you type, the bigger the box grows. And you can use the normal text editing and formatting techniques. The buttons and drop-down list boxes of the Object toolbar enable you to do things such as select fonts and text sizes and apply bold and italic attributes.

4. **Click outside the text box when you finish entering text.**

   Pressing the Enter key doesn't get you out of text mode; it just creates a new line. When you exit the text box, the text box and the selection handles go away, leaving just your text.

If you want to edit the text object later, you can click once to select the text object to resize, move, copy, or delete it. To re-enter the text box and edit the text itself, double-click the text. You get a flashing vertical bar cursor that enables you to select and edit text.

A different way to place text into your drawing is to actually make the text part of an object, such as a rectangle or ellipse.

1. **Double-click the object into which you want to insert text.**

   A blinking cursor appears in the middle of the shape.

2. **Type something.**

   Your text appears at the center of the shape and moves outward as you type. Press Enter to break the line of text if necessary. While you're entering text, you can use the normal text editing and formatting tools, including the Object toolbar's buttons.

3. **Click the mouse somewhere outside the object.**

Drawing Curves and Shapes

Rectangles and ellipses are fine for flowcharts, but for more sophisticated drawings, you need to be able to draw more complex shapes. The Line drawing tool is the answer to that need. Although the tool is named Line, you can think of it as the curve and polygon drawing tool. With the Line tool, you can create lines and shapes composed of multiple straight or curved segments. Using polygons and curves, you can draw the outline of a state for a map or trace the route of a river or road.

As with the Rectangle and Ellipse tools, the Line tool enables you to create objects in two flavors — filled or not filled. The easiest object to draw with the Line tool is a polygon, because the segments are clearly defined. To draw a polygon, follow these steps:

1. **Select the Polygon option from the Line tool's option toolbar.**

   For information on selecting drawing options, see the "Using drawing tool buttons" section earlier in this chapter.

   The pointer changes to a crosshair with a multi-segment line (it looks like a check mark) beside it.

2. **Click and drag in your drawing to define the first line segment of the polygon.**

   A rubber band line appears, as if you were drawing a plain straight line.

3. **Release the mouse button.**

   StarDraw freezes the first line segment, but instead of drawing the line in its finished color and adding selection handles, StarDraw stays in drawing mode. The drawing cursor is still active, and a new rubber-band line appears between the end of the first line segment and the pointer.

4. **Move the pointer somewhere else and click.**

StarDraw adds another segment to the line each time you click. You're drawing a polygon.

5. **Repeat Step 4 until you have a polygon you like.**
6. **Double-click to complete the polygon.**

   If you previously selected one of the filled polygons, you see StarDraw close your polygon by adding one more line back to the original point. This is so that it can *flood* your shape with color without it leaking all over the rest of the drawing. If you selected an unfilled polygon, then your shape remains exactly as you drew it.

The other polygon option available is a constrained version that only allows you to draw 45-degree lines.

The polygon is the simplest of the Line tools because it does exactly what you expect. You see the lines as you draw them, and the endpoints stay where you put them. That situation isn't always the case with the other curves. The Freeform Line and Freeform Curve options aren't too hard to use, but the Curve option is difficult. Drawing curves with alternating nodes and control vectors is *not* for the uninitiated and should only be attempted by those experienced at drawing Bezier curves.

To draw a freeform shape, follow these steps:

1. **Select the Freeform Line option from the Line tool's options toolbar.**

   Your cursor changes to look like a crosshair with a speck of thread beside it. You may expect this tool to simply draw a line wherever the mouse goes. Not quite.

2. **Click and drag in your drawing, moving the pointer around the perimeter of a curved shape.**

   The rubber band line that appears as you draw with the Freeform tool looks like a piece of string following you. Notice that it moves around behind you, it doesn't just lie there. The line keeps redrawing itself in an attempt to smooth out what you're doing.

3. **Release the mouse button when you finish the shape.**

   StarDraw closes any gap between the pointer location and the starting point of the freeform line and fills the resulting shape with color. The finished shape displays selection handles on the perimeter of an invisible rectangular bounding box surrounding the shape, as shown in Figure 11-8.

   If you attempt a jagged line with the Freeform drawing tool, you may be able to create it, but your corners won't be as sharp as you expect. The Freeform tool isn't very good at precision drawing in which you want your line to remain exactly where you put it. However, this tool is excellent for "clean" freehand lines.

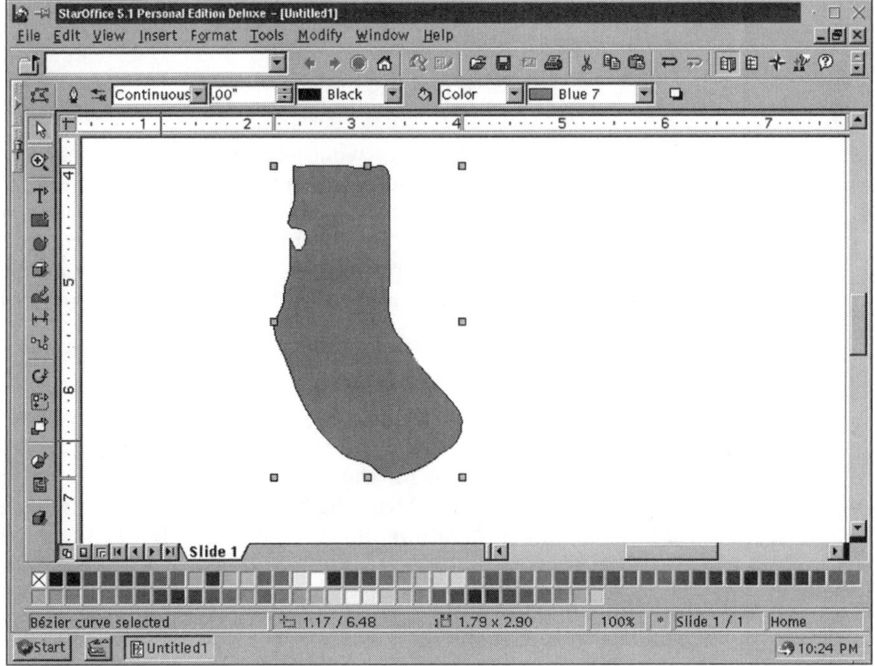

Figure 11-8: Freeform shapes are fast to draw but not very precise.

Drawing with Precision — Using Grids

The first time you tried to draw a square freehand, you probably found out that doing so isn't easy. Moving the cursor only one point at a time is tricky. This process can be very frustrating, especially when you're trying to draw several shapes of the same size or align them along a common border.

StarDraw provides some help for you with Grid mode. Like some of the other constrained tools, Grid mode makes sure that your cursor only sits on coordinates that are located a fixed distance apart. So, instead of having to move one point at a time in order to get a shape just right, Grid mode enables you to work in steps of 5 or even 10 points at a time.

1. **Choose Tools⇨Options.**

   You see the Drawing Options dialog box.

2. **Double-click Drawing and then click Grid in the list box at the left end of the Options dialog box.**

   StarOffice displays the options shown in Figure 11-9.

3. **Select Visible Grid.**

Little dots appear all over your drawing. Don't worry, they don't show up on the final version. They're just there to help you line up your shapes.

4. **Select Snap to Grid.**

   Snapping is another term for what happens when you use a constrained tool. Imagine that each grid point has its own gravity force. When the cursor is near a point on the grid, the cursor "snaps" over to that point. If you move the cursor out far enough and get outside the point's gravity, you move closer to another point and snap to that one. You won't see the cursor between points; it's either on one point or another.

5. **(Optional) Choose a resolution by typing a measurement into the X Axis and Y Axis boxes.**

   These settings control the spacing between rows and columns of grid dots on the drawing area in the StarDraw window. You can also change the Subdivision settings for the X axis and Y axis. The subdivisions control the spacing of the intermediate grid points. If you use one grid setting to draw or position objects and decide later to change the settings, the objects that you've already placed won't move.

   You don't need to set the other options in this dialog box, but you may want to explore them:

   - **Synchronize Axes.** If this box is checked, any change you make to the X axis is also made to the Y axis. This option is useful if you want a square grid.
   - **Size to Grid.** Two grids actually exist: the *main* grid and the *snap* grid. When you set the resolution, you set it for the main grid. The Size to Grid option sets the snap grid to the same size as the main grid. If this option is unchecked, you can set a different resolution for the snap grid.

6. **Click OK.**

   StarDraw closes the Drawing Options dialog box and applies your settings. With the grid displayed and the Snap to Grid option activated, anything you draw and any object you move automatically snaps to the nearest grid point. Actually, you don't have to display the grid in order to snap to it (and all the grid points may not show up on your screen even when it's visible). Making the grid visible just serves as a reminder that it's there.

Arranging Objects in Your Drawing

The advantage to a vector drawing tool such as StarDraw is that at any time you can pick up a bunch of objects and put them somewhere else on your drawing. This feature is very handy for doing things like tossing half a dozen

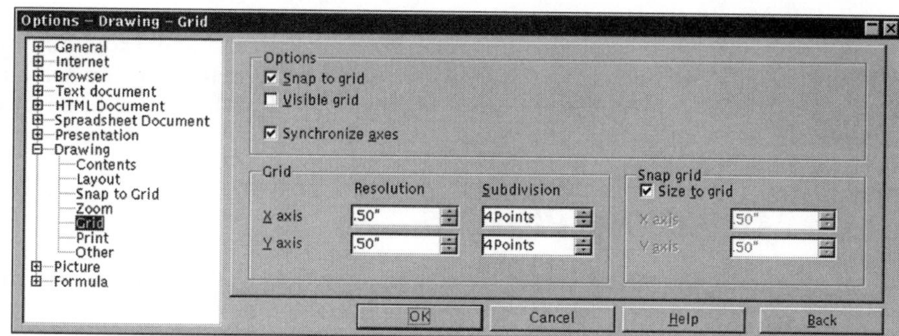

Figure 11-9: Adjust these options to control the drawing grid.

rectangles onto your drawing and then aligning them all against a left border. Or putting one object on top of another.

Aligning objects

After you place most of your objects in your drawing, you want to go in and clean up the drawing's appearance. One of the first things you do is make sure that the edges of objects are lined up, where appropriate. For example, if you're drawing a flowchart, you probably want all the boxes to share a common left border. To align multiple objects, follow these steps:

1. **Select several objects by holding down the Shift key as you click each object in succession.**

   Selection handles appear around each object.

   Another quick way to select several objects is to click and drag in the drawing page with the selection tool pointer, so that you draw a box around all the objects that you want to select. This selection box is called a *marquee selection* because it reminded someone of a theatre marquee. When you release the mouse button, StarDraw selects everything contained within the marquee selection box.

   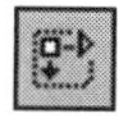

2. **Slow-click the Alignment tool on the StarDraw Main toolbar.**

   This action displays the options available in the Alignment tool's option toolbar.

3. **Select the Left option from the Alignment options toolbar.**

   The selected shapes move to the left to align with the left-most object of the bunch.

You can also align your shapes to the right, top, bottom, or middle.

If you select just one object and then click an alignment tool button, StarDraw aligns that object to the drawing page instead of to the other selected objects. This feature makes it easy to align an object to the center or edge of the page.

Grouping objects

Grouping allows you to treat several objects as if they were one, so that you can perform a variety of tasks, such as aligning objects and arranging them on the page. Grouping is different from just selecting multiple objects and then moving or aligning them or something of that sort. When you perform some action on a multiple object selection, StarDraw performs the action on each selected object individually. But when you perform operations on grouped objects, the objects retain their relationships to other objects in the group. So if you select two groups and left align them, the groups as a whole are left aligned but all the individual objects within each group aren't forced into left alignment.

Grouping objects is easy to do, although seeing the grouping may be somewhat difficult or confusing. To group several objects, follow these steps:

1. **Select the objects you want to group together.**

   You can select multiple objects by holding down the Shift key as you click each object in turn. StarDraw surrounds each object with its own selection handles. You can also marquee select objects by dragging a selection box around them.

2. **With a group of objects selected, choose Modify⇨Group.**

   The individual selection handles disappear and are replaced by selection handles for a bounding box that extends around the entire group.

Now you can select and manipulate the group as if it were one object. If you want to break up the group into individual objects again, select it and choose Modify⇨Ungroup. StarDraw dissolves the glue binding the group together and selects the individual objects.

To select an individual object within a group for editing or other manipulation, without dissolving the group, first deselect the group and then hold down the Ctrl key as you click the object. StarDraw displays selection handles for the individual object. After completing your edits, you can deselect the object and reselect the group.

Arranging overlapping objects

Handling overlapping objects is one thing that vector drawing programs do very well. As you add new objects to your drawing, StarDraw keeps track of them in order. You can create new objects in front of older existing objects, and you can draw objects that overlap other objects. When you do, the object in front may obscure another object from view, but the object in back remains intact — no part of it is erased or changed because another object overlaps it. If you move or delete the overlapping object, the object previously hidden from view reappears. These objects resemble cards in a deck. The top card obscures other cards from view, but the other cards are still there.

The Position tool lets you shuffle the deck and rearrange the order of the objects on your drawing page. Having the ability to rearrange objects means you don't have to draw every object in sequence in order to have them appear, overlapping properly, in your drawing. The Position tool is easy to use. Just follow these steps:

1. **Select the object you want to move.**

   You see a square of green control boxes around the selected shape (even if your shape is not a box).

2. **Slow-click the Position tool button on the Main toolbar.**

   Clicking and holding momentarily on the Arrange button causes the Arrange tool's options toolbar to appear.

3. **Choose one of the following Arrange options from the Arrange options toolbar:**

   - **Bring to Front** brings your selected object in front of all others.
   - **Bring Forward** brings your selected object forward one layer at a time.
   - **Send Backward** sends your selected object backward one layer at a time.
   - **Send to Back** sends your selected object all the way to the bottom layer.
   - **In Front of Object** brings your selected object in front of the object you click next (the cursor changes to a pointing hand awaiting your selection of the second object).
   - **Behind Object** sends your selected object behind the object you click next (the cursor changes to a pointing hand awaiting your selection of the second object).
   - **Reverse** swaps the order of *two* selected objects (select two objects in Step 1 if you plan to use this tool).

StarDraw changes the order of the selected object relative to the other objects in your drawing, moving each object in front of or behind other objects depending on the Position option you selected.

Copying objects

If you put a shape someplace you don't like, you can change it. (That's the beauty of vector programs such as this.) Think of the shapes as jigsaw puzzle pieces. You place them where you want, and if you change your mind later, you pick them up and move them (or toss them away altogether). Something StarDraw can do that a jigsaw puzzle can't is change the size of your shapes, or even make exact copies.

Copying an object is somewhat more complex. StarDraw has two ways for you to do it, depending on the number of copies you want.

To make a quick copy of an object, follow these steps:

1. **Select the object you want to copy.**

   The familiar selection handles appear.

2. **Choose Edit⇨Copy or press Ctrl+C.**

   Your shape is copied to the clipboard. The *clipboard* is a place in your computer's memory that StarOffice uses to keep temporary copies of things, such as StarDraw objects, StarWriter pieces of text, and so on. After you place something on the clipboard, you can change to a different application, and the item stays on the clipboard.

3. **Choose Edit⇨Paste or press Ctrl+V.**

   StarDraw adds a copy of your object to the drawing in exactly the same spot, so you won't be able to see it.

4. **Drag the selected object to another location.**

   When you move the shape, you notice another copy immediately behind it.

To create multiple copies of an object, follow these steps:

1. **Select the object you want to copy.**

   StarDraw highlights the object with selection handles.

2. **Choose Edit⇨Duplicate.**

   The Duplicate dialog box appears.

3. **Select the number of copies.**

   Unlike the previous method, this method doesn't stack all the copies in one place. Adjust some or all of the following settings as needed:

- **Placement:** These settings determine the placement of the copies across the page.
- **Angle:** This rotates every copy of the shape.
- **Enlargement/Width:** This option changes the width of each copy. Choose a negative number to make the copies smaller.
- **Enlargement/Height:** This option changes the height of each copy. Choose a negative number to make the copies smaller.
- **Colors Start/End:** Use these fields to make your object slowly change color as it moves from one copy to the next.

4. **Click OK.**

   StarDraw closes the Duplicate dialog box and draws the specified number of copies (in accordance with any other specified settings) and distributes the copies across the page, based on the values of the X axis and Y axis settings.

Saving Your Drawing

Your drawing is beautiful! Time to save it. You should get in the habit of saving your work frequently, no matter which tool you're using. Doing so only takes a few seconds but is guaranteed to save you hours of work after the first power failure or system crash.

1. **Choose File⇨Save As.**

   StarOffice opens the Save As dialog box. You probably recognize this box, because all StarOffice tools use it for saving files to disk. The major difference for each tool is that you need to specify a format that makes sense to that tool.

2. **Choose a directory in which to save your file.**

   This box provides three buttons for navigating the directories. You can choose to create a new directory, go back to the default directory, or go up one directory level. As you use these buttons, the list of files refreshes itself.

3. **Enter the filename you want to use.**

   Keep the filename simple. Try to avoid using any symbols other than letters and numbers, because some operating systems can't handle them. If you have the Automatic File Name Extension option checked, you don't have to add an extension.

4. **Click OK.**

   You should see the Save icon in the toolbar become disabled. This action is StarOffice's way of saying, "The current file is up-to-date. It doesn't need to be saved."

Windows Explorer uses a file extension to associate a file, such as a StarDraw file, with a program. This feature lets you double-click a filename so Windows automatically launches StarDraw for you. If you prefer to use this feature, you should leave the automatic extensions on, so that Windows knows what sort of files you're saving.

In addition to saving your drawing in a file that you can open and edit at a later time, you can also export your drawing to a variety of file formats that you can then insert into other documents and import into other programs. Choose File⇨Export to open the Export dialog box, which is very similar to the Save As dialog box. The biggest difference in the dialog boxes is the selections available in the File Type drop-down list box. The Export dialog box includes a larger range of file format options, including bitmap image formats such as JPG, GIF, or BMP (your drawing is converted to a bitmap image) and vector drawing file formats, such as Encapsulated PostScript and Windows Metafile. For the complete list of export file formats, see Chapter 23.

Chapter 12

Creating and Editing Images

In This Chapter

- Creating an image
- Scanning your photos
- Manipulating an image
- Drawing on your image

With the popularity of digital cameras and image scanners, you're no longer limited to words to describe via e-mail that great sunset you saw or the funny face little Billy made at his first birthday party. You can even add images to your Web site. And regardless of where and how you use them, you can edit your images to enhance their impact. StarImage, the StarOffice painting program, helps you do this and more.

Unlike StarDraw (see Chapter 11), StarImage is a bitmapped graphics program. *Bitmaps,* no matter what they eventually look like, are made up of rows and columns of tiny colored dots called *picture elements* or *pixels.* The only thing a bitmap knows is what color to make each pixel, which means that if you erase something or put one thing on top of another, your change becomes permanent — just as if you took a paintbrush to a canvas. Of course, the program does have an Undo feature that can help if you make a mistake. But unlike StarDraw, which lets you toss objects into your picture and move them around later, whatever you put into a StarImage picture stays there.

In this chapter, you find out how to use StarImage, the StarOffice painting program, to create new images or load existing ones from disk. You discover how to scan images and touch them up with a number of filter tools. Of course, you also explore how to directly draw an image, just in case you're in the mood to play Picasso.

Creating a New Image

StarImage is one StarOffice tool in which you probably won't need to create new documents very often. Creating a new image from scratch is sufficiently difficult (for non-artists) that most people just don't do it. And you rarely need to do so, because you have an ample supply of scanned photographs and ready-made images that you can adapt to your needs.

Still, if you need to create a new, blank image document, you can create one in any of the following ways:

- Right-click the StarDesktop background and choose New⇨Documents⇨Image from the pop-up menu that appears.
- Choose File⇨New⇨Image from the StarOffice menu in any document window.
- Click the Start button in the StarOffice Task bar and choose More⇨Image.

StarOffice opens a StarImage document window and also opens the New Image dialog box shown in Figure 12-1. Before you can begin working in the new image document, you need to supply the image size (width and height) and the number of colors. The default size of 256 pixels high by 256 pixels wide is about a three-inch square image on most computer screens, which is fine to start with. You don't have to specify the image format — that comes later, when you save your masterpiece.

Click Create to close the New Image dialog box and begin drawing. A small white square appears in the center of the StarImage window. The white area is the 256-pixel square image defined in the New Image dialog box. Most of the other features of the StarImage document window are fairly standard.

The StarImage Main toolbar on the left side of the window contains buttons for selecting the StarImage drawing tools. The StarImage Object toolbar contains buttons for setting the attributes of the drawing tools you use to create your image. The Color bar near the bottom of the document window facilitates quick color changes as you work with the painting tools. The StarImage Status bar at the very bottom of the document window displays an assortment of information about the current image, including the amount of memory it takes.

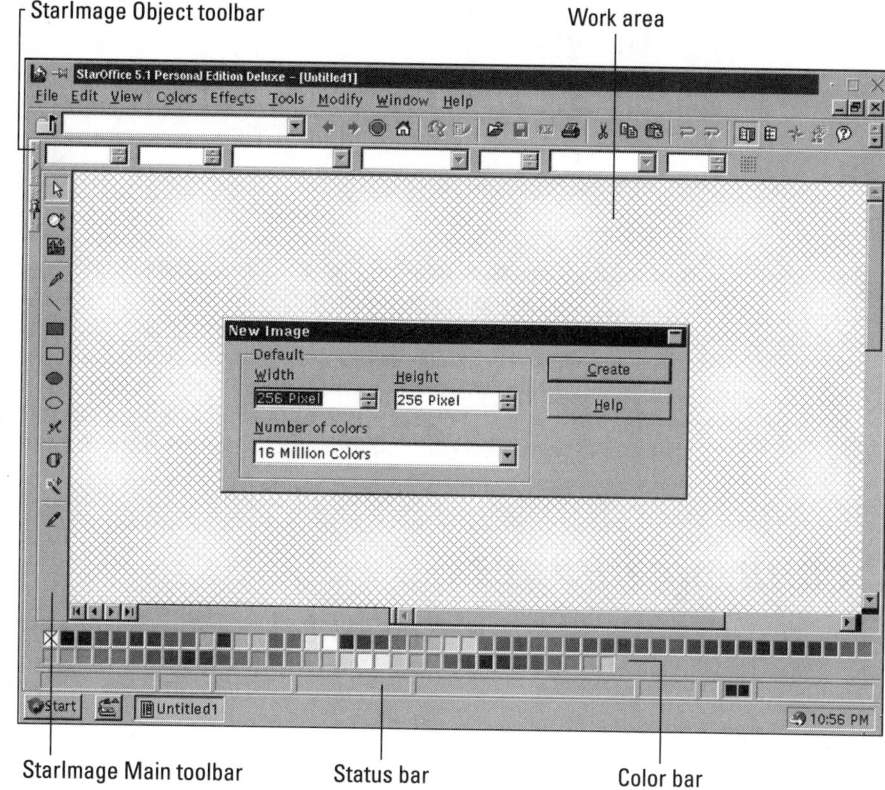

Figure 12-1: To create a new image, specify the width, height, and number of colors you want.

Opening Existing Images

StarImage is really more of an image-editing tool than an image-creation tool. So you probably already have an image that you want to edit. StarImage can open image files in a variety of different file formats. To open an image file for editing, follow these steps:

1. **Select File⇨Open.**

   The File Open dialog box appears. This is the same dialog box used to open files throughout StarOffice.

2. **Navigate to the directory in which your file resides.**

   Click a folder icon in the list box to display the contents of that directory. Use the Up One Level button to move up your system's directory tree.

3. **If you know the format of the file you want to open, select it from the File Type drop-down list box.**

   This action reduces the clutter in the file list by displaying only those files that match the File Type selection. Some of the more common image file types are BMP, GIF, JPG, and TIF.

4. **Select your file from the list.**

5. **Click Open.**

   StarOffice closes the Open dialog box, opens the selected file, and displays it in a new StarImage document window.

If the Main and Object toolbars disappear from the StarImage window when you open an image file, the file is probably read-only. In Linux, that means that the file is in a directory that you have permission to read but don't have permission to modify. You can still look at the picture, but you can't change it.

Scanning Images

Scanners are very popular these days. By scanning a photograph, you can quickly send it to all your friends and relatives. Using StarImage, you can also touch up those "red eyes" or just pluck yourself out of the living room and put yourself in front of the Eiffel Tower, if you like.

If you have a scanner, you need to install the proper drivers for StarOffice to recognize it. These drivers are called *TWAIN* drivers, so if you haven't installed them yet, you may want to search for the word *TWAIN* in your scanner's manual.

You have two ways to get scanned images into StarImage for editing. You can use your scanner software to scan the image and save it as a file on your hard disk. Then you can open the file and edit it in StarImage. This is the most common way to work with scanned images and works even if StarOffice can't recognize and interact with your scanner.

On the other hand, if you've installed your scanner so StarOffice can access it via TWAIN drivers, you can bypass the step of saving a scanned image as a file before opening it in StarImage. Instead, you can choose File⇨Scan⇨Acquire to start the process of scanning an image and bringing it directly into StarImage for editing. StarOffice actually doesn't have anything to do with the scanning process — your scanner software does everything. So if you want to manipulate certain scanning options to get a particular effect, you need to read the documentation that came with your scanner and do some experimenting. After the scanner software does its thing, the image appears in a StarImage document window.

Whichever process you follow to obtain a scanned image, you can manipulate the image as though you created it from scratch. But the first thing you want to do is save it, just in case you make a mistake and need to start over.

Zooming In for a Closer Look

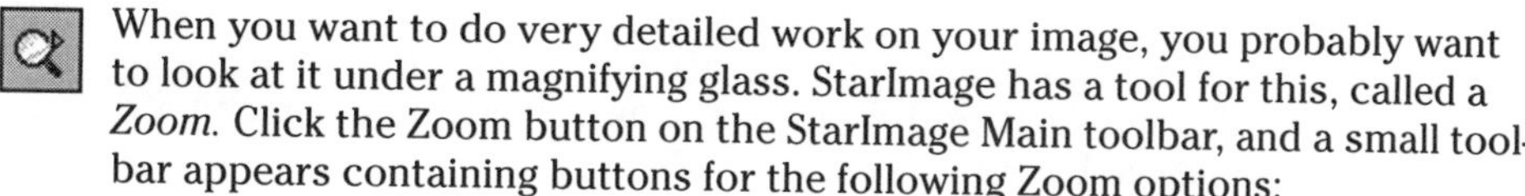

When you want to do very detailed work on your image, you probably want to look at it under a magnifying glass. StarImage has a tool for this, called a *Zoom.* Click the Zoom button on the StarImage Main toolbar, and a small toolbar appears containing buttons for the following Zoom options:

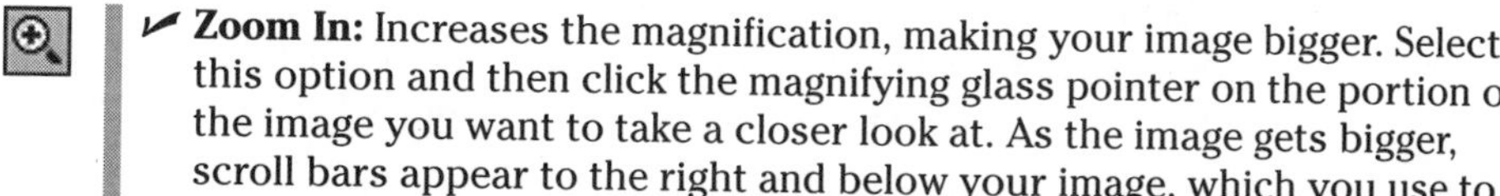

- **Zoom In:** Increases the magnification, making your image bigger. Select this option and then click the magnifying glass pointer on the portion of the image you want to take a closer look at. As the image gets bigger, scroll bars appear to the right and below your image, which you use to see the whole image.
- **Zoom Out:** Decreases the magnification, making your image smaller. You can make your image look smaller than it actually is if you want. This feature is useful for big pictures that don't fit entirely on the screen.
- **Zoom 100%:** Resets the magnification so that you see the "normal" size of your image.
- **Zoom Page:** Shows your entire image sized to fit within the StarImage window.
- **Optimal:** Sizes the image for optimum quality display. (This option is usually grayed out and unavailable when working with scanned photos and similar images.)

The Zoom tool doesn't actually change your image, just the way you see it. You can play with this tool all you like without concern for your picture.

Manipulating Images

You don't have to edit your images — perhaps you just loaded them into the computer so that you can e-mail them to someone. But before you send anything off, why not touch it up a little bit? You have the tools right in front of you.

If you modify your image and don't like the result, you can restore the version that's saved to disk by clicking the Reload button in the toolbar. This method is shorter than using the File⇨Open method every time.

Adjusting brightness, contrast, and color

One of the easiest and most useful things you can do to an image is to manipulate the brightness, contrast, and color. These options aren't new — old television sets used to have three dials on them to modify the same values.

1. **Choose Colors⇨Brightness/Contrast.**

   The Brightness & Contrast dialog box appears. The box contains two sliders, one for each value (brightness and contrast). The values start in the middle at zero, and you can move both sliders in either the positive or negative direction.

2. **Change one value at a time by moving the slider button.**

   Changes don't take effect until you close the box. Change only one thing at a time, so that you can see how each slider affects your picture.

3. **Click OK to see your changes.**

   StarImage closes the Brightness & Contrast dialog box and implements the changes you specified. You may not notice any change if you only moved the slider a little. To see what this tool really does, set one of the values to the maximum and watch what happens to your picture. Even though the dialog box displays the options ranging from –100% to 100%, you can actually perform these functions many times.

You can also modify the individual color levels in your picture if you wish. If you've ever taken a picture at sunset and thought "too much red," StarImage can fix it for you.

1. **Choose Colors⇨RGB Colors.**

   The RGB Values dialog box appears. RGB stands for Red, Green, and Blue. You can change these primary colors, and by combining the changes, you can produce different colors.

2. **Move the sliders to change values of Red, Green, and Blue.**

   As with the Brightness & Contrast box, your changes only take effect after you click OK. Practice with one slider at a time until you get a good feel for the difference it makes.

3. **Click OK to see your changes.**

   StarImage closes the RGB Values dialog box and applies the color balance changes you specified.

If you don't like what you see after applying a color change, choose Edit⇨Undo before you make any other changes. StarImage returns your image to its previous condition, before the unwanted color change. You can use this same command to reverse the effects of just about any action or command in StarOffice.

Applying filter effects

StarImage comes with a number of special effects filters you can apply to create a variety of changes to your picture. To get at them, click the Effects button or choose Effects from the menu and then choose one of the following effects:

- **Charcoal sketch:** This effect produces a very attractive, almost hand-drawn-looking version of your picture in black and white.
- **Mosaic:** This effect makes your image blocky and fuzzy by reducing the resolution and creating bigger pixels. It simulates the old pre-Renaissance wall mosaics (or the effect used on TV to censor things).
- **Relief:** Imagine that your entire image is made from one sheet of metal, and the shapes on it are simply indentations. Very cool looking.
- **Poster:** This effect drastically reduces the number of colors in your picture, as if it were printed on a poster.
- **Pop-art:** You need to see this effect to believe it.
- **Aging:** This effect adds yellowish-brown to your image, making it look much older than it is. The effect is fun when you're sending photographs to your friends.
- **Solarization:** Your image ends up looking like a photo negative.
- **Tile:** This effect is very similar to Mosaic but produces subtly different results.
- **Definition:** This effect makes the objects in your image much more pronounced, making the distinction between overlapping objects clearer.
- **Smoothing:** The opposite of definition, this effect adds a slight blur to your picture to help cover up lines you may not want.
- **Remove noise:** Noise refers to small spots of color in the image that the scanner may have introduced but that are probably not part of the original picture. This effect attempts to remove those spots. The effect may end up removing something that is actually supposed to be there, though.

Some of these effects may sound obvious, some not. The best way to discover what each does is to try it. (Remember to save your work first!) If you don't like what happens, you can always use the Edit⇨Undo or Reload option to remove the filter effects.

Rotating and scaling images

StarImage can turn your picture on its side or change its size (permanently, unlike Zoom). You can also flip an image so that it comes out backward or upside-down. You can perform any of these manipulations using the Image tool. The options for this tool include the following:

1. **Click the Picture Toolbar button on the StarImage Main toolbar.**

   An options toolbar appears, giving you the following rotation choices:

   • **Horizontal:** Flips the image left-to-right

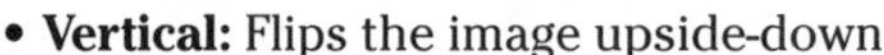

   • **Vertical:** Flips the image upside-down

   • **Rotation Left:** Rotates the image a quarter-turn counter-clockwise

   • **Rotation Right:** Rotates the image a quarter-turn clockwise

   • **Free Rotation:** Rotates the image to the specified angle

2. **Click the button for the option you want.**

   All these Image options take effect immediately.

You also have the option of resizing your image using the Image tool.

1. **Click the Picture Toolbar button on the StarImage Main toolbar.**

   The options toolbar appears.

2. **Click the Size button on the Picture Toolbar's options toolbar.**

   The Modify Size dialog box appears.

3. **Adjust the Width and Height settings.**

   You may change the settings for width and height of your image as measured by pixels, inches, or percent of current size. A change in one of the settings is automatically mirrored in the others. Uncheck the Scale option if you want to adjust the height and width independently (and therefore distort the proportions of the image).

4. **Click OK.**

   StarImage closes the Modify Size dialog box and redraws your image at its new size. The size change is a permanent change in the image, not a temporary display change like the change you get when you alter the Zoom setting.

The Picture toolbar also includes a tool that enables you to crop your image. But before you can use it, you must select the portion of the image that you want to crop by clicking the Select tool and then dragging your image to select a rectangular area with the rubber-band box. After you make the selection, click the Picture Toolbar button and then click Crop on the Options toolbar. StarImage keeps the selected portion of your image and deletes the rest.

Drawing on an Image

StarImage provides a set of tools that enable you to draw on your image. Theoretically, you can use these tools to build an image from scratch, but almost nobody really does that. You're more likely to use the drawing tools to retouch and modify existing images. Putting in thought balloons saying "Ugh, strained peas again?" on those new baby pictures is always fun.

Drawing rectangles and ellipses

StarImage provides tools for drawing rectangles and ellipses on your picture. However, these shapes aren't like the moveable jigsaw puzzle pieces that you can draw in the vector based StarDraw tools (see Chapter 11). The StarImage tools more closely resemble specialized paintbrushes that only draw one particular shape.

Separate tools exist to create filled rectangles, outlined rectangles, filled ellipses, and outlined ellipses. The following steps demonstrate how to draw a filled rectangle, but the other rectangle and ellipse tools work the same way.

1. **Click the Rectangle tool on the StarImage Main toolbar.**
2. **Select the properties of the rectangle from the drop-down list boxes on the Object toolbar.**

   You can adjust any of the following properties for the rectangle you're about to draw:

   - **Line Width:** Sets the thickness of the outline or edge around the object.
   - **Radius:** Sets the radius of rounded corners. Leave this set to 0 Pixel for sharp corners. This setting is only available for the rectangle tools, not the ellipse tools.
   - **Foreground Color:** Controls the color of the outline or edge around the object.
   - **Background Color:** Selects the color of the fill or area inside the rectangle. This property has no effect with the Rectangle Frame or Ellipse Frame tools.
3. **Position the pointer where you want to place one corner of the rectangle.**

Position the pointer carefully. Remember, you can't move the rectangle after you draw it.

4. **Click and drag toward the opposite corner of the rectangle.**

   The rectangle shape follows along behind you as you drag. When you draw an ellipse instead of a rectangle, you still drag to define a rectangular area (called a *bounding box)* on the image. You click and drag to define opposite corners of a bounding box, and StarImage draws an ellipse to fit within it.

5. **Release the mouse button.**

   StarImage finalizes the rectangle and makes it a permanent part of your image. You can't move or erase it, although you can choose Edit⇨Undo to cancel the drawing action if you do so before you issue any other commands.

Drawing lines

If you're drawing on your image, you may want to make some straight lines. Doing so is easy with StarImage. Here are the steps:

1. **Click the Line tool on the Main toolbar.**

   Only one line style exists; you don't have any options for making it dotted or an arrow.

2. **In the Object toolbar, choose the width of the line and its color.**

   A 1-pixel line is not very visible on your image. You probably want to increase that value.

3. **Move the cursor over your image and press the mouse button.**

   Press the left mouse button to produce a line in the foreground color. Press the right button for a line in the background color.

4. **Drag the mouse.**

   A straight line in the chosen color follows you.

5. **Release the mouse.**

   Your line is now permanent.

Drawing with pens

The pen may be the most useful tool. You can scribble on your image with it.

1. **Click the Pen tool on the StarImage Main toolbar.**

   The Pen options fly-out toolbar appears.

2. **Click a button on the Pen options toolbar to select a pen shape.**

   In addition to round or square dots, you can choose one of four straight-line calligraphy pens. Using the calligraphy pens produces a line that varies in thickness, depending on the direction you drag.

3. **Select the pen size in the Object toolbar.**

   The larger the pen size you select, the thicker the line you draw.

4. **Hold down the mouse button and start moving the cursor over your image.**

   A trail of color follows your cursor wherever it goes. Use the left button to draw in the foreground color, the right to use the background color. Unlike the freeform tool that comes with StarDraw (see Chapter 11), the trail goes exactly where the cursor does, as if you were using a magic marker.

Figure 12-2 shows an image that has been touched up with some lines, ellipses, and freehand pen drawing.

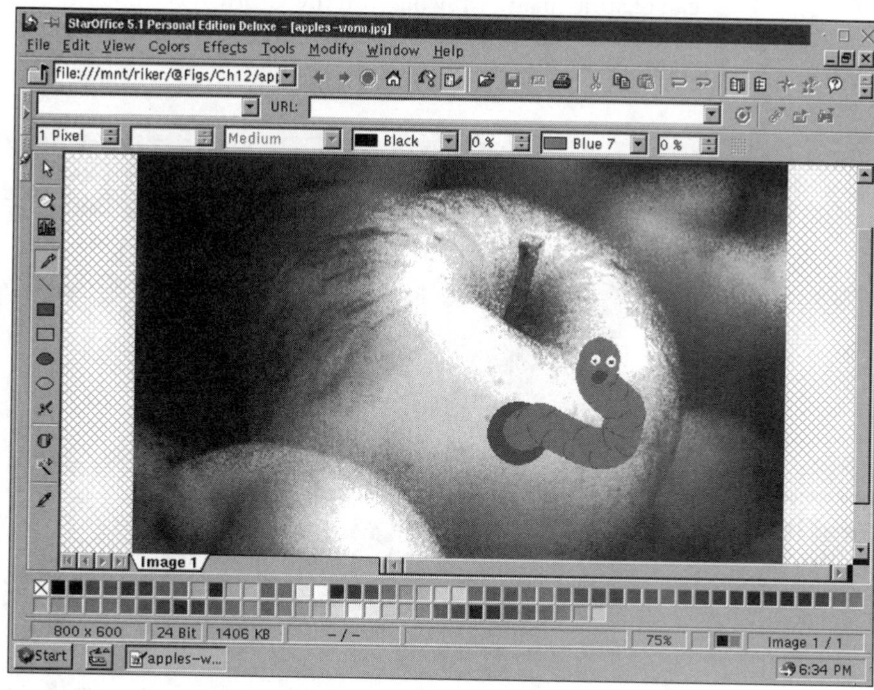

Figure 12-2: The StarImage drawing tools help you make your pictures say another thousand words.

Drawing with the Airbrush

The Airbrush tool simulates a can of spray paint, blasting random dots of color onto your image. You can use this tool when you want to deposit large areas of color, but you don't want them to be hard-edged and one solid color.

1. **Click the Airbrush tool button on the StarImage Main toolbar.**
2. **Select the size of the airbrush in the Object toolbar.**

   The larger the number you use, the wider the circle of paint.
3. **Select the density of the spray from the Airbrush Intensity list box on the Object toolbar.**

   Low sprays only a few dots, and High sprays almost a solid color.
4. **Click and drag the mouse on your image.**

   Use the left button to spray with the foreground color, and the right button to spray with the background color. This tool supposedly simulates painting with an airbrush, but the effect is really more like using a can of spray paint. Drawing with the airbrush is similar to using a wide pen except the trail doesn't appear to be a solid color (as shown in Figure 12-3).

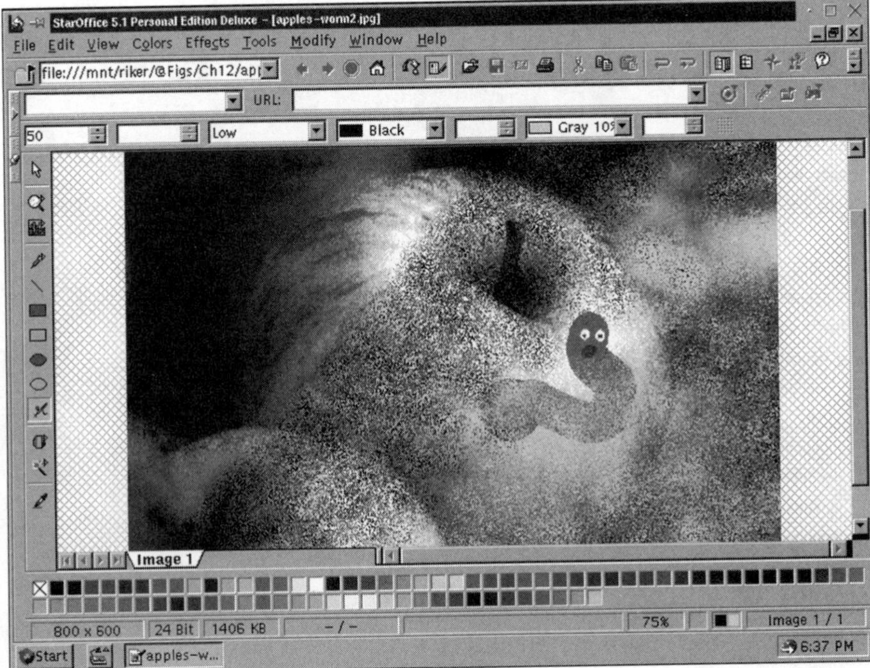

Figure 12-3: When the intensity of the Airbrush is set low, a little more of the image shows through.

Manipulating Colors with the Eyedropper

The Eyedropper is a very specialized tool (officially called the Masking tool). Use it to change all occurrences of one color in your picture to another color. For example, you can make the sky pink if you want. Here's how:

1. **Click the Masking tool on the StarImage Main toolbar.**

   The Eyedropper dialog box shown in Figure 12-4 appears. You need to move it away from your image so that you can grab colors.

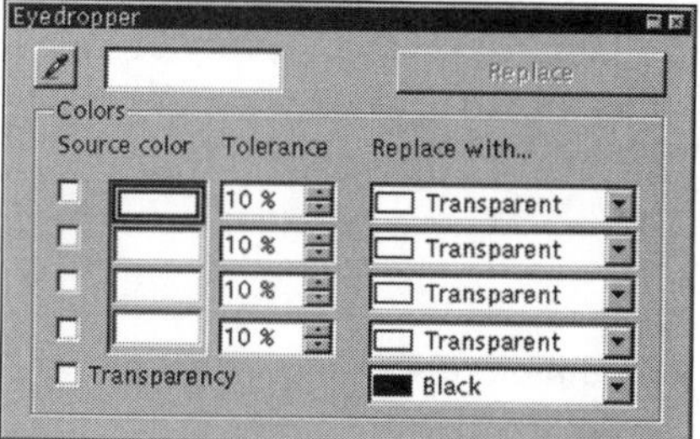

Figure 12-4: The Eyedropper is a fancy way to replace the colors in your picture.

2. **Click the Eyedropper button.**

   This action activates the eyedropper, which grabs the color underneath the cursor. As you move the pointer over areas in your image, the preview field in the dialog box shows that color.

3. **Click the color you wish to replace.**

   This action promotes the current color to the *Source color.* Source colors are the ones that StarImage replaces when you say so.

4. **Repeat Steps 2 and 3 if you want to replace more colors.**

   You can modify only four colors at a time. Transparency is considered a color and has its own box (since you can't point your cursor to a transparent area).

5. **For each source color, select a tolerance.**

   Most images have hundreds or even thousands of colors, and you can't expect to individually select them all. Instead, you can select a single example color and use the Tolerance field to tell StarImage to automatically select similar colors. To replace only the exact color you selected, reduce the Tolerance setting to 0%. The default setting of 10% selects only colors that are a reasonably close match for the Source Color. Increasing the setting to 50% selects anything that is even remotely similar to the Source Color.

6. **For each source color, select a Replace With color in the other drop-down list box in the same row.**
7. **Click Replace.**

   Your changes appear immediately. The Eyedropper dialog box remains active so that you can repeat the process. To close the dialog box, click the Close button in the dialog box's title bar.

Saving Your Image

Unlike some of the other tools in StarOffice, StarImage doesn't have its own format for saving files. No need really — you have plenty of excellent, very popular graphic formats to choose from. By using one of these standard formats, you can share your pictures with others who may not use StarOffice. Here's how to save your image:

1. **Choose File⇨Save As.**

   StarOffice opens the Save As dialog box.
2. **Choose where to save your file.**

   If you know the name of the directory you want to use, you can type it in as part of the filename. Otherwise, you can navigate through the directories by clicking the folder icons.
3. **Name your file by typing the name in the Filename box.**
4. **Select a file format from the File Type drop-down list box.**

   The default is BMP, which is very common, although the files end up pretty big. GIF files are compressed, and therefore smaller, but can only hold pictures with 256 colors. JPG is a good format that can hold lots of colors, with a good file size. However, JPG is *lossy,* meaning that it loses some detail in order to achieve a small file size (very often you can't even tell). TIF is the standard format used by many scanners and desktop publishing programs, so it's often a good choice.
5. **Click Save.**

   StarOffice closes the Save As dialog box and saves your file in the location and format you specified. Depending on the file format you chose, you may see a dialog box presenting options for various compression levels and so forth. Don't worry about these options; your image is saved just fine if you use the default values and simply click OK.

Chapter 13

Creating a Slide Show

In This Chapter

- Impress your friends with StarImpress
- Creating slides for your presentation
- Working with an outline
- Getting your thoughts (and slides) in order
- Changing all slides at once
- Saving your work

Surveys show that many people rate public speaking as one of their greatest fears. The surveys don't always show that those people are often the ones who use hastily scribbled note cards and hand-drawn slides and who didn't rehearse their timing. The StarOffice presentation tool, aptly called StarImpress, helps you overcome all these hurdles. After you dazzle your boss with a spectacular presentation, you may find yourself volunteering to get up in front of the stockholders next time.

In this chapter (and the following one), you find out how to create a presentation composed of several kinds of slides, including text, graphics, and tables. You also discover how to organize your slides into the best order and change them all at once to help you develop a theme.

Introducing StarImpress

StarImpress makes preparing for any presentation easy. StarImpress helps you create text slides, add drawings and images that you create in StarDraw and StarImage (see Chapters 11 and 12, respectively), and then arrange your slides into an effective presentation. Whether you're presenting to a group of friends gathered around your computer at home or to an audience of 50 vice presidents in the company boardroom, StarImpress can help you get your thoughts (and your slides) in order.

StarImpress is roughly comparable to Microsoft PowerPoint from the Microsoft Office suite or Freelance Graphics from the Lotus SmartSuite office suite. StarImpress offers similar features for doing the same kinds of things — creating a series of *slides,* or screens, for presentation on-screen or as printed pages or handouts. StarImpress can even open PowerPoint 97 presentation files and save StarImpress presentations in the PowerPoint 97 file format.

Creating a New Presentation

Creating a new presentation is just like creating any other document in StarOffice. Just think of the slides in the presentation as analogous to the pages in a report or proposal. You can create a new presentation by using any of the following techniques:

- Double-click the New Presentation icon in the StarDesktop window.
- Right-click the StarDesktop background and choose New⇨Documents⇨Presentation.
- Choose File⇨New⇨Presentation from the menu.
- Click the Start button in the StarOffice Task bar and choose Presentation.

When you create a new presentation, the StarImpress document window doesn't appear immediately. Instead, StarOffice runs the Presentation AutoPilot to lead you through the process of selecting a slide background, presentation template, default timings, and so on. If you elect to use a template, the AutoPilot even creates many of the individual slide pages for you — all that remains for you to finish your presentation is to add your text and graphics. After you complete the AutoPilot, the StarImpress window appears and you can proceed to build your new presentation by adding and editing slide pages.

The paragraph above gives you a brief overview of what the Presentation AutoPilot does. The following steps fill in the details:

1. **Start the Presentation AutoPilot by using one of the techniques listed above for creating a new presentation, or by choosing File⇨AutoPilot⇨Presentation.**

   The AutoPilot Presentation dialog box appears, as shown in Figure 13-1.

2. **Select the type of presentation you want to open and then click Next.**

   You can select one of the following options:

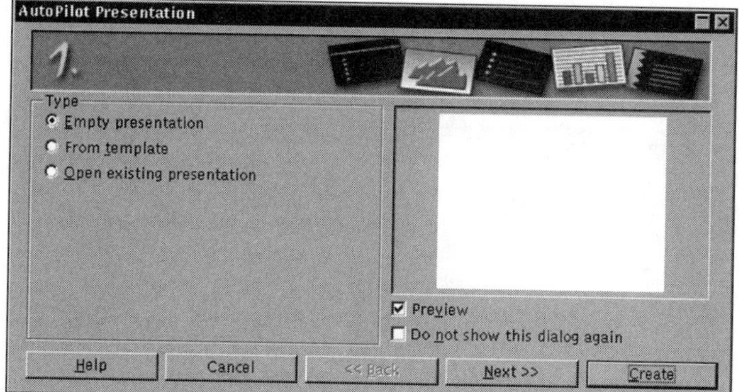

Figure 13-1: Select the type of presentation you want to create.

- **Empty Presentation.** Selecting this option instructs StarOffice to create a new presentation containing a single blank slide. Then you can build your own custom presentation manually. This is the default option.
- **From Template.** If you select this option, a drop-down list box of template groups and a list box showing the templates available in the selected group appear in the AutoPilot Presentation dialog box. A small preview of the selected template appears in the box on the right side of the dialog box. Select the template you want to use as the basis for your new presentation by clicking the template name in the list box. (If you want to use a template that includes an assortment of predefined slides as well as a background treatment and font selections, be sure to select one from the Presentations group.)
- **Open Existing Presentation.** If you select this option, a list box appears in the AutoPilot Presentation dialog box listing the presentation files in your default work folder (usually ~/Office51/Work). Select a presentation from the list and click Create to close the AutoPilot Presentation dialog box and open the presentation file in StarImpress.

If you want to make a quick exit from the Presentation AutoPilot, you can select Empty Presentation and click Create to skip the rest of the AutoPilot pages and go directly to the StarImpress window where you can build your presentation totally manually.

If you don't want to go through the Presentation AutoPilot in order to create new presentations in the future, check the Do Not Show This Dialog Again option before proceeding. The next time you create a new presentation, the StarImpress window will open immediately and display a blank slide for you to begin editing.

When you click Next, Page 2 of the AutoPilot Presentation dialog box appears, as shown in Figure 13-2.

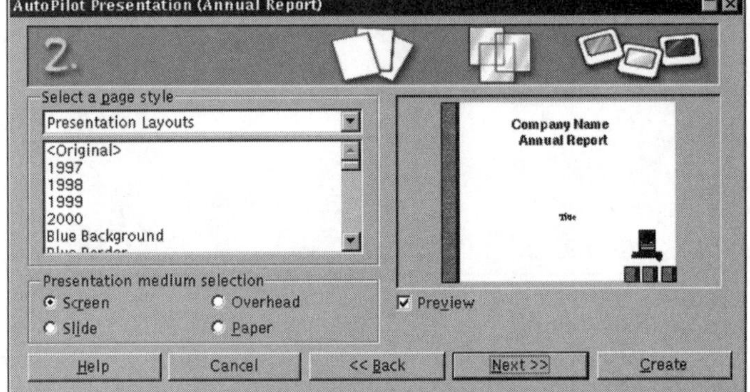

Figure 13-2: Select a page style for your presentation.

3. **Select a page style and presentation medium, and click Next.**

   Select a page style (background treatment) for the slides in your presentation by first selecting a group name from the Select a Page Style drop-down list box and then selecting one of the styles that appear in the list box. (If you selected a presentation template in the previous step, selecting the <Original> style in the Presentation Layouts group allows StarImpress to use the default page style included in the template.)

   Select one of the four options (Screen, Slide, Overhead, Paper) in the Presentation Medium Selection area to match the medium you plan to use to present your presentation.

   When you click Next, Page 3 of the AutoPilot appears, as shown in Figure 13-3.

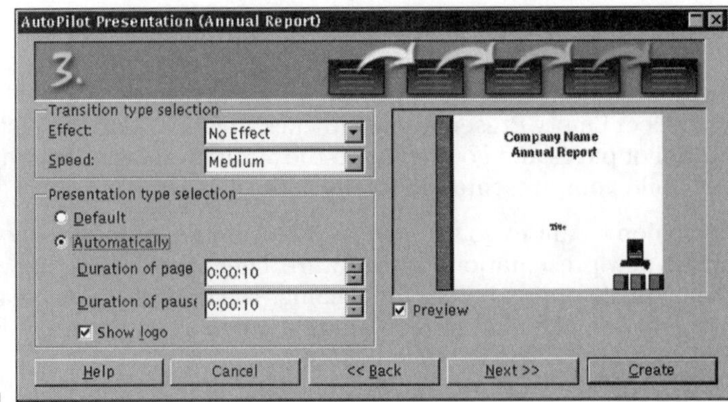

Figure 13-3: Select the default transition effects for your slides.

4. **Select a default transition effect and timing, and then click Next.**

   Make selections from the Effect and Speed drop-down list boxes to control the default transition effect when you change slides in an on-screen slide show. If you want StarImpress to automatically advance to the next slide during an on-screen presentation, set the appropriate values in the Duration of Page and the Duration of Pause boxes. Otherwise, select Default.

   When you click Next, Page 4 of the AutoPilot appears.

5. **(Optional) Type your name or company name, a description of your presentation, and the main ideas you plan to cover into the text boxes provided; then click Next.**

   This page of the Presentation AutoPilot only appears if you elected to create your presentation based on a template. The AutoPilot automatically inserts the information you enter here into the appropriate places on some of the template slides. However, if you skip this step (just leave the text boxes empty), it's just as easy to enter the information directly onto the slides when you work with the presentation in StarImpress.

   When you click Next, Page 5 of the AutoPilot appears, as shown in Figure 13-4.

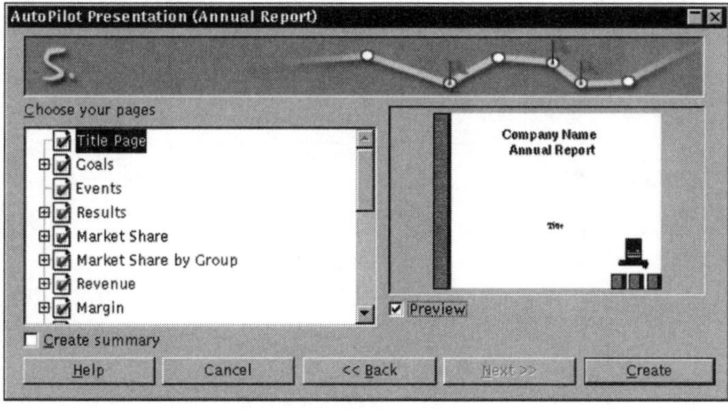

Figure 13-4: Select which template pages you want in your presentation.

6. **(Optional) Select the template pages you want to include in your presentation.**

   This is another page of the Presentation AutoPilot that only appears if you base your presentation on a template. The list box on the left side of the dialog box contains a list of the predefined slides available in the selected template. Click a slide name in the list box to view a preview of that slide on the right. Click the page icon beside a slide name to toggle the check mark on or off. The Presentation AutoPilot includes all the slides with check marks beside them when it creates your presentation.

7. **Click Create.**

   The AutoPilot Presentation dialog box disappears, and after a few moments, a StarImpress window opens displaying your new presentation, ready for you to begin adding and editing your text graphics and other elements.

When the StarImpress document window appears, as shown in Figure 13-5, you may notice that StarImpress starts with the StarDraw tool set, plus a few additional tools. If you create an empty presentation, it doesn't start out truly empty — StarImpress creates the first slide for you and immediately asks you to choose a name and layout for your first slide (more on that in a moment).

StarImpress includes an optional toolbar — the Presentation toolbar — that isn't available in the other StarOffice tools. To display the Presentation toolbar, choose View⇨Toolbars⇨Presentation. The Presentation toolbar normally appears as a floating toolbar, and is populated with buttons that have text labels, such as `Insert Slide`. The Presentation toolbar may look

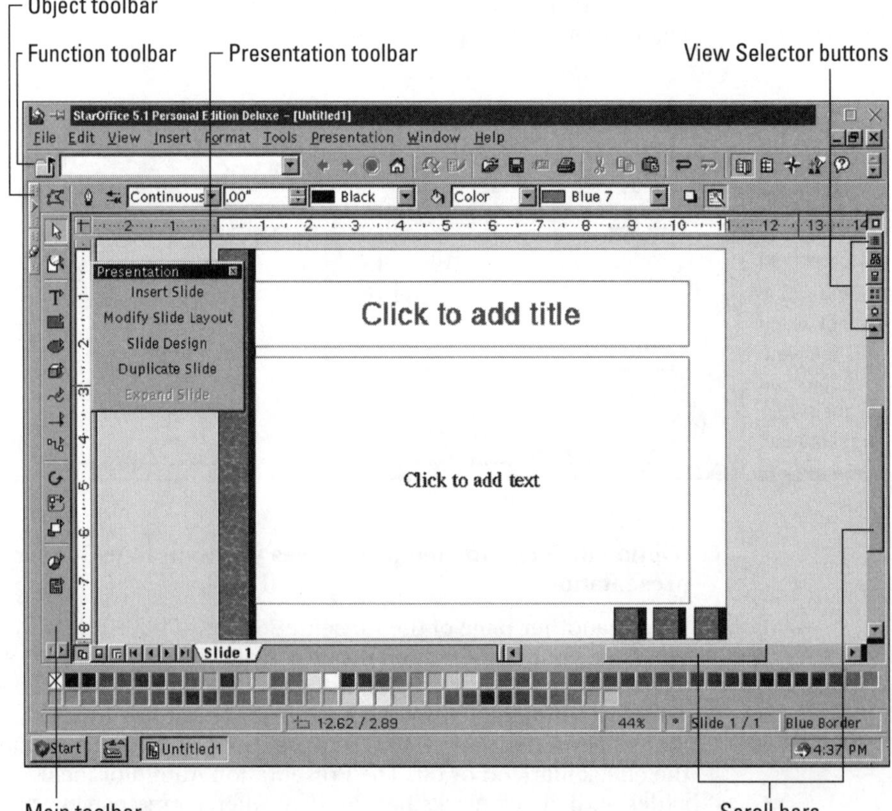

Figure 13-5: StarImpress uses the StarDraw tools plus a few more for adding special effects and animations.

different from the typical toolbar — which is docked to the side of the document window and contains buttons labeled with icons — but it works the same way. The Presentation toolbar gives you quick access to useful functions, such as adding a new slide. If you prefer to attach the toolbar to the side of the StarImpress window, see Chapter 2 for instructions.

Creating Slides for a Presentation

When you start a new presentation, StarImpress automatically creates at least the first slide for you. If you create a presentation based on a template, StarImpress creates multiple slides with slide names, layouts, backgrounds, and so on, as determined by the template.

If, on the other hand, you create an empty presentation, StarImpress starts by creating just one slide and brings up the Modify Slide dialog box shown in Figure 13-6. In this dialog box, you assign a name to your slide and select one of the standard slide layouts. The name simply helps you organize your presentation — it doesn't show up on the actual slide. It appears on a small tab at the bottom of the window, which you can click to go immediately to that slide. The layout describes the structure of the slide: what goes on it and where you plan to put it. Don't overlook the scroll bar down the right side of the layout window. You have many layouts to choose from. Select the layout you want by clicking its thumbnail representation. Then click OK to close the Modify Slide dialog box and begin building your presentation.

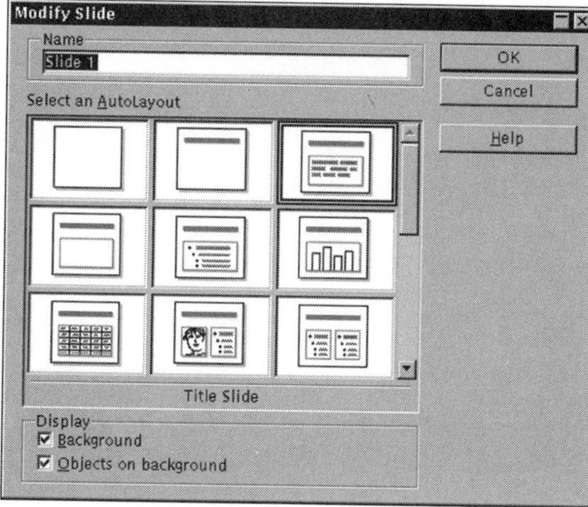

Figure 13-6: The dialog boxes for Modify and Insert Slide are the same, except for the title.

Adding a slide to a presentation

You can add slides to your presentation whenever you like. You have several ways to do so:

- Click Insert Slide in the floating Presentation toolbar.
- Choose Insert⇨Slide from the menu.
- Right-click the tab at the bottom of the slide window and then choose Insert Slide from the pop-up menu that appears.

All these techniques have the same effect: StarImpress creates a new blank slide immediately after the current slide. The Modify Slide dialog box appears, just as when you started creating the presentation, except the title of the dialog box is *Insert Slide* instead of *Modify Slide.*

If you prefer to start a new slide using a copy of the current slide as a guide, you can click Duplicate Slide in the Presentation toolbar or choose Insert⇨Duplicate Slide from the menu. Oddly, you can't choose the Duplicate Slide option by right-clicking the slide name tab. When you use the Duplicate Slide option, StarImpress skips the Insert Slide dialog box and inserts a copy of the existing slide.

Selecting a slide layout

The layout of a slide dictates what objects go on it and where they are placed. The most common layouts are as follows:

- Title Slide
- Title, Object
- Title, Text (Bullet list)
- Title, Chart
- Title, Spreadsheet
- Title, Clipart, Text

Most of the other layouts are variations and combinations of the preceding items (such as a title, text, and a chart or a title, two objects, and text). You can alter the layouts if you like, but that takes some practice to get right.

You can also use the drawing tools to add objects, such as text boxes and shapes, to any of the standard layouts, or you can select a blank slide layout and use the drawing tools to create your own layout.

You don't have to follow any firm rules for what layouts to use for your slides. Common sense and good taste are the best guidelines. Figure out what you want to say, and find the layout that helps you say it. Usually, you want to keep your slides simple, so that you keep your audience's attention. If you really need to enhance a layout by using the extra tools, you certainly can, but make such additions judiciously.

Entering text into a slide

A prominent feature of many standard slide layouts is a text box — the most common are for titles, headers, and bullet lists. StarImpress shows you which boxes expect text by inserting a placeholder such as `Click to add title.` To add your own text, simply click the placeholder text. The placeholder disappears, the text box appears surrounded by a heavy outline and selection handles, and a flashing vertical bar (or insertion point) appears in the text box. Type the text for the title of the slide. When you're finished, click anywhere outside the title text box.

To add bullet items, click the `Click to add an outline` placeholder and type the first bullet item. Press Enter to start a new line. Press the Tab key to indent bullets (move text to the right) or Shift + Tab to *outdent* your bullets (move text to the left).

You can also add your own text boxes to your slides. The procedure for doing so is exactly the same as adding text to a StarDraw drawing. See Chapter 11 for instructions.

Adding other elements to a slide

Bulleted lists are great for getting your point across. That's why they are a staple of most presentations. However, a presentation composed only of bulleted lists and a few titles looks pretty boring. Adding other elements — such as clip art, charts, and tables — can go a long way toward making your presentation look more interesting.

Adding a table

Presentations often involve numbers arranged in rows and columns: sales figures, research results, and budgets are just a few examples that show up frequently. You may call these arrangements of rows and columns *tables,* but StarImpress calls them *spreadsheets.* In fact, these tables are actually miniature StarCalc spreadsheets. As you work on the spreadsheet, it looks like a StarCalc spreadsheet — complete with row and column buttons and other StarCalc tools — but only the result appears in your slide.

Don't get carried away by having all the power of the StarCalc spreadsheet tool available within your presentation slide. You don't want to make your presentation spreadsheets too big or complex. In any presentation, you need just enough data to make your point; and you need to keep the table simple, clean, and big, so that your audience can read it from a distance.

To create a slide containing a spreadsheet, follow these steps:

1. **Click Insert Slide in the Presentation floating toolbar.**

   StarImpress opens the Insert Slide dialog box.

2. **Select the Title, Spreadsheet layout, and click OK.**

   The Insert Slide dialog box disappears, and your new slide appears in the editing window. The slide contains placeholders for a title and a spreadsheet.

3. **Double-click anywhere within the spreadsheet placeholder box to add a spreadsheet.**

   A spreadsheet appears in place of the placeholder box (see Figure 13-7). Notice that the spreadsheet, like the StarCalc document window, is a grid of cells surrounded by column and row buttons and scroll bars. Also notice that the StarCalc menus and toolbars have replaced the StarImpress menus and toolbars.

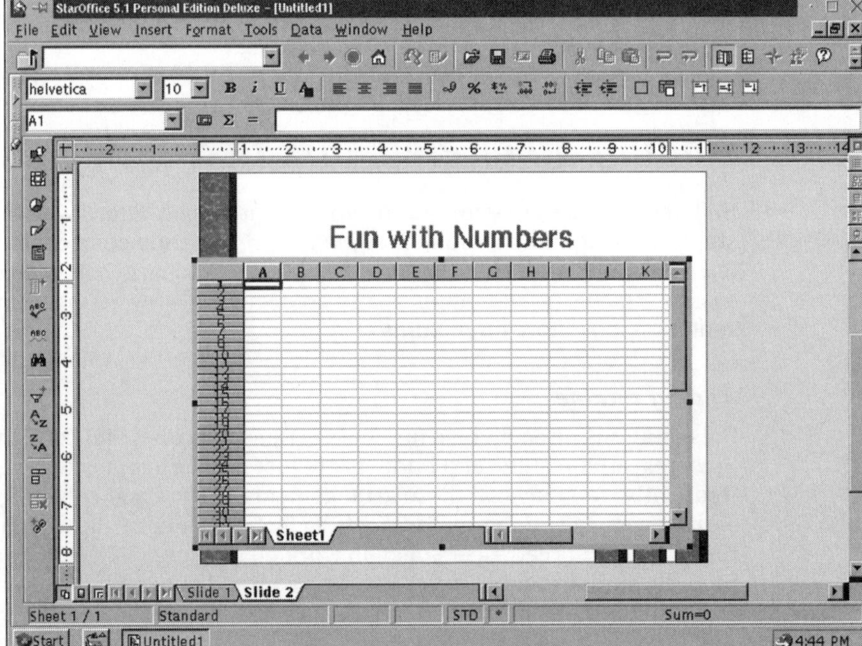

Figure 13-7: Your slide contains a minispreadsheet, complete with StarCalc menus and toolbars.

4. **Enter your text, numbers, and formulas into the spreadsheet.**

   As you fill in the figures that you want to appear in your slide, you can use any of the StarCalc tools and techniques that you use in a full-sized StarCalc spreadsheet. Refer to Chapters 7, 8, and 9 in Part III for information on using StarCalc.

5. **After you finish editing the spreadsheet, click anywhere in the slide background outside the spreadsheet.**

   The trappings of a StarCalc spreadsheet disappear from your slide, leaving only the result — text and numbers arranged in rows and columns (see Figure 13-8). The StarCalc menus and toolbars disappear, and the StarImpress menus and toolbars resume their place.

To edit or add to your spreadsheet at any time, simply double-click anywhere in the spreadsheet to re-enter the StarCalc editing mode. If you click just once on the spreadsheet, green selection handles appear around the spreadsheet, enabling you to move or resize the spreadsheet box in your slide.

Adding a picture

The simplest way to add a picture to a slide is to create the slide using a layout with predefined space for a picture (or *clipart,* as it's called). The slide includes a placeholder that says `Double click to add`

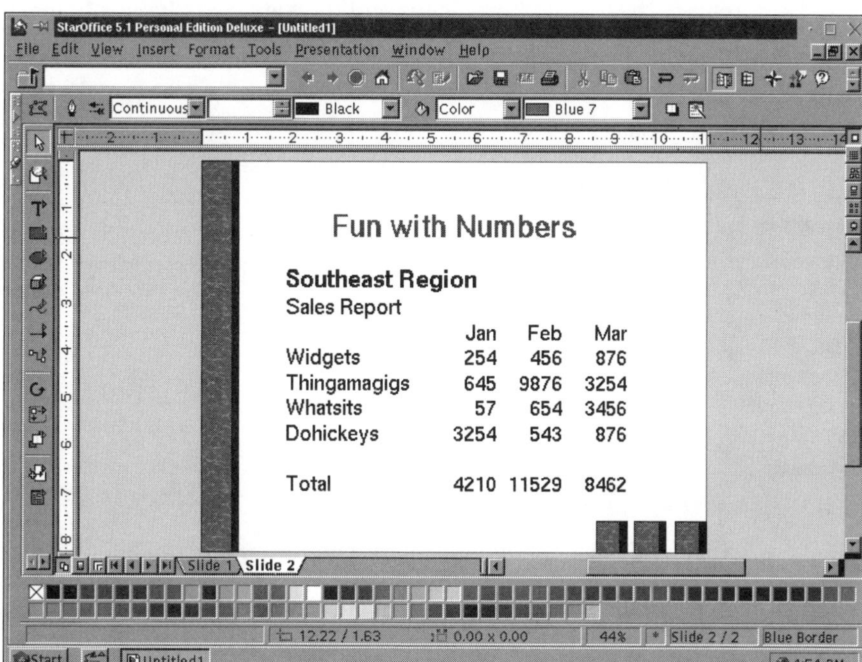

Figure 13-8: A finished spreadsheet table in a slide.

a picture. When you double-click anywhere within the placeholder box, StarImage opens the Insert Picture dialog box. Using this dialog box, you can preview the images you have available and select the picture you want to add to your slide. The default directory is the StarOffice gallery. If you want to use one of your own pictures, you need to navigate through the folders until the contents of the proper directory appear in the list box. When you find the picture you want, select it and click Open to close the Insert Picture dialog box and add the selected picture to the current slide.

You can also add pictures to slides that don't have predefined picture placeholders. The procedure is the same as for adding pictures to a text document. See Chapter 6 for detailed instructions.

Adding a chart

Charts are an excellent way to display results that you otherwise put in a table. A pie or bar chart can sometimes illustrate your point better than columns of numbers.

Although you can use the Insert⇨Chart command to add a chart to any slide, creating a new slide using a layout that includes a chart placeholder is much simpler. When you double-click anywhere within the placeholder box labeled `Double click to add a chart`, StarImpress places a sample chart on your slide (see Figure 13-9). This is a miniature version of a StarChart document. In fact, when the chart is selected for editing, StarChart menus and toolbars replace the StarImpress menus and toolbars. See Chapter 10 for detailed instructions on how to edit charts in StarChart.

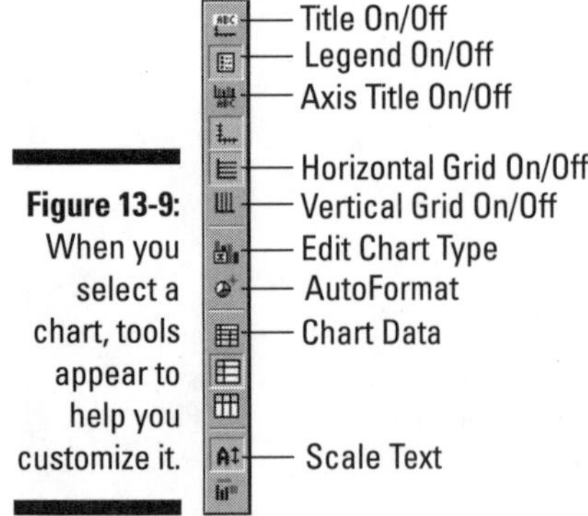

Figure 13-9: When you select a chart, tools appear to help you customize it.

When you finish editing the chart, click anywhere outside the chart area to deselect the chart. When you do, the StarChart menus and toolbars disappear and the StarImpress menus and toolbars resume their place.

A chart, like a table, reverts to display-only mode when not in edit mode in order to save screen space. If you're looking for a chart option and can't find one, you may not have activated edit mode for the chart by double-clicking it.

Creating text effects with FontWork

If you discover that you have a slide with only a little bit of text, but you don't really want to add unnecessary graphics, you can still make the slide interesting. StarImpress lets you turn the text itself into a graphic and do interesting things by using a tool called FontWork (see Figure 13-10).

1. **Select one of the text boxes on your slide.**

   You want to select a title or other simple, one- or two-line blocks of text. The FontWork effects aren't really appropriate for larger blocks of text, such as a bullet list.

2. **Select Format⇨FontWork.**

   The FontWork dialog box appears, as shown in Figure 13-11.

3. **Click one of the text guides.**

   Most are circle related, so you can picture your text lying on top of a circle, below it, and so forth. As you make selections in the FontWork dialog box, StarImpress immediately redraws the slide to display the

Figure 13-10: The FontWork tool enables you to transform plain text into eye-catching graphics.

selected effect. You can work interactively with the text object on your slide and the settings in the FontWork dialog box.

If the text guide doesn't stay selected, the window that contains your text probably isn't big enough. After you use FontWork, your text appears very different from when you started and takes up much more space. Since the text box is selected, grab one of the green control handles and make the text box bigger, and then try clicking the text guide again.

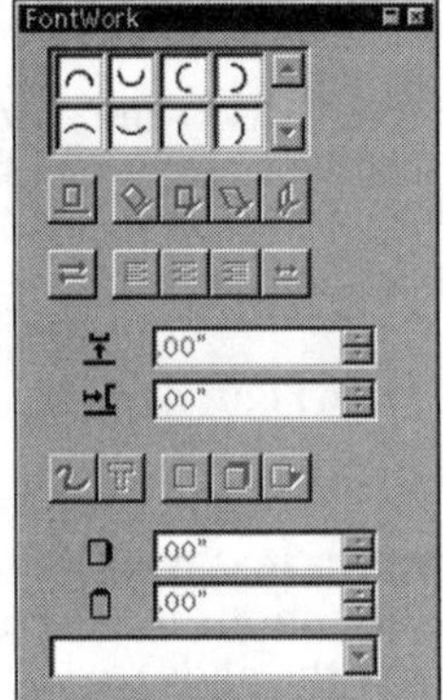

Figure 13-11: The FontWork tool offers a variety of options for spicing up plain old left-to-right horizontal text.

4. **Click one of the text rotation options.**

   As your text curves around, this option specifies what the letters should do. They can stand straight up or curve along with the guideline (called *tangential*).

   You can experiment with several other options in FontWork as well, including the following:

   - **Alignment:** You can specify where to place the text relative to the beginning, middle, and end of the guideline.
   - **Orientation:** You can make your image go right to left, if you prefer.
   - **Distance:** You can determine the amount of space between the text and the guideline.
   - **Indent:** Only active when you choose an alignment. You can determine the distance between the specified alignment guidepoint and the beginning (or end) of the text.
   - **Shadow:** You can add a shadow to your text. If you do, you can also specify the size, location, and color of the shadow.

5. **When you achieve the effect you want, close the FontWork dialog box by clicking the Close button in its title bar.**

Drawing on a slide

All the StarDraw tools are available to you in StarImpress. As a result, you can do anything to a slide that you can do to a drawing. See Chapter 11 for instructions on how to use the StarDraw drawing tools. Remember, though, that the goal of your presentation is to present your information to your audience in an easy-to-understand manner. Some special effects may wow them, but too many will lose them.

Working in Outline View

Because you're probably going to work with titles and bullets a great deal, StarImpress provides a great shortcut called Outline View. To use this mode, follow these steps:

1. **Click the Outline Mode button on the right side of the window or press F12.**

   The Outline View, shown in Figure 13-12, becomes active. In this view, you see the titles and bullet lists from your slides, but no graphics, charts, or other objects.

   The F12 key may not activate the StarImpress Outline Mode as expected if your window manager uses that key to activate one of its functions. You may run into the same problem with some of the function keys as well. StarOffice can't respond to a function key if the window manager usurps it.

2. **Type your slide's title next to the first slide icon and press Enter.**

   The Insertion Point Cursor moves to the next slide icon.

3. **Press the Tab key.**

   StarImpress inserts a bulleted line, indented under the previous slide title.

4. **Type the text for the bullet item and press Enter.**

   Repeat as needed to enter additional bullet items.

5. **Press Shift+Tab.**

   StarImpress removes the last bullet and positions the insertion point cursor beside the next slide icon.

6. **Repeat Steps 2 through 5 as needed to define additional slides for your presentation.**

7. **Click the Drawing View button on the right side of the window or press Ctrl+F12.**

   StarImpress returns to Drawing View.

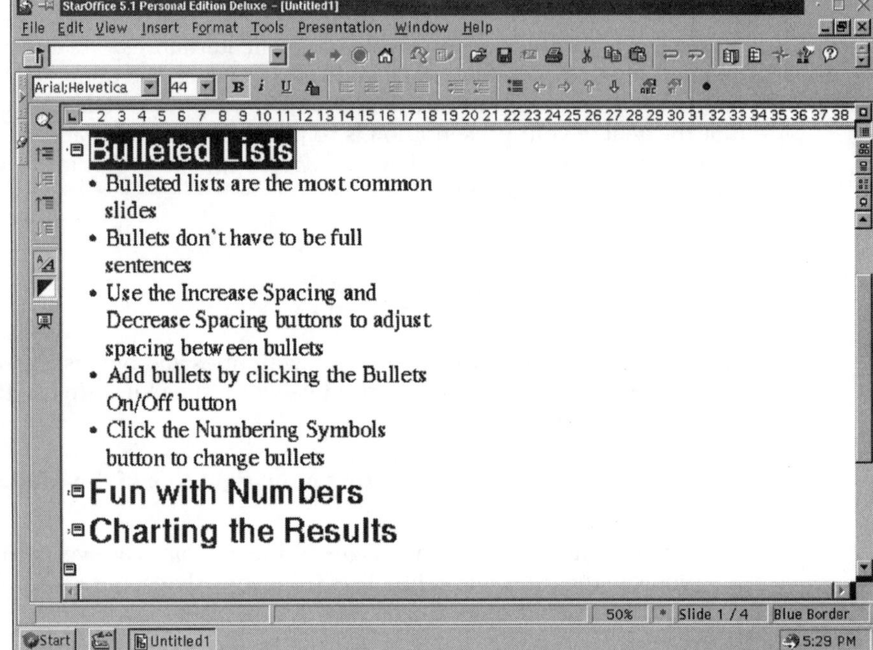

Figure 13-12: Outline View allows you to quickly create slides with titles and bullet items.

When you leave Outline View and return to Drawing View, StarImpress converts your outline into a series of basic title and bullet list slides. The Outline View is a great way to quickly enter the key text slides for a presentation. Then you can go back and spruce up the presentation by adding slides with charts, tables, and other graphics.

Rearranging slides in Slide Sorter View

As you prepare a presentation, you may find helpful the ability to step back for an overview that encompasses several slides at a time. In the old days, I used to spread out 35mm slides on a light table, so I could see the sequence of slides for a presentation and experiment with rearranging them in different orders. StarImpress gives you the same capability with its Slide Sorter View. (And you don't have to worry about accidentally bumping the light table and knocking everything out of order.) Slide Sorter View shows you thumbnail-sized versions of your slides and enables you to shuffle and rearrange them with simple drag-and-drop moves.

To select Slide Sorter View, click the Slide Sorter View button on the right side of the StarImpress window. StarImpress displays thumbnails of the slides in your presentation, arranged in order from left to right, as shown in Figure 13-13. The current slide is highlighted with a box around the slide.

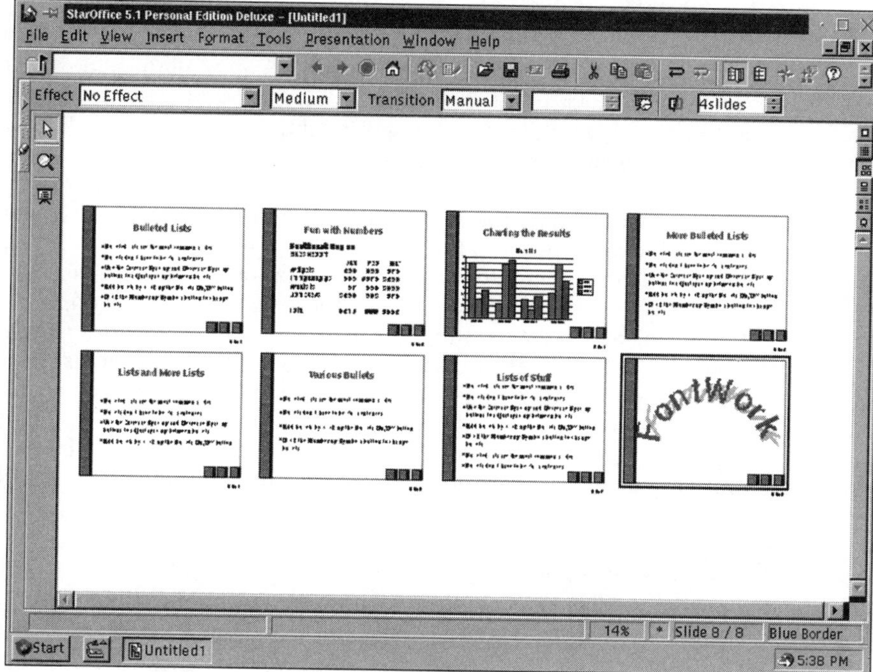

Figure 13-13: The Slide Sorter View simulates viewing slides on a light table.

Rearranging slides in Slide Sorter View is easy and intuitive. Simply click a slide to select it, and then drag the slide to a new location and drop it. StarImpress moves the selected slide to the new location and rearranges the other slides to fill the gap.

The Slide Sorter View is also a great navigational tool. If you need to locate and edit a certain slide in a large presentation, switch to Slide Sorter View and scan the thumbnails for the slide you need to edit. Double-click that slide to select it and return to Drawing View with the selected slide displayed for editing.

Changing colors and backgrounds for the whole presentation

One difference between a professional-looking presentation and a random collection of slides and images is the consistent use of colors and text styles on all the slides in the presentation. To help maintain consistency in all the slides of your presentation, StarImpress uses a master background slide to hold formatting information for those slides. When you create a new slide, it inherits background color and text formatting from the master background slide.

If you decide that you want to change the color scheme for your presentation or select a different font for the titles, you don't have to go through all your slides, making the changes on each one. Because all the slides are based on the master background slide, you can simply edit that slide and StarImpress automatically implements changes in all the presentation's slides that are based on the master background slide.

To display the master background slide, choose View⇨Background⇨Drawing. The slide that appears in the drawing area (see Figure 13-14) is the template on which the other slides in your presentation are based. The sample text on the master background slide is only there so that you can apply styles and formatting and see what they look like. The actual text doesn't appear on your slides, though the color, size, and style does. You can use all the normal formatting tools to change the text on the master background slide.

Changing text formatting on the master background slide is fairly straightforward. Changing the background color is a little more involved. Here are the steps you need to follow:

1. **Choose Format⇨Styles & Templates⇨Catalog.**

   StarImage opens the Style Catalog dialog box.

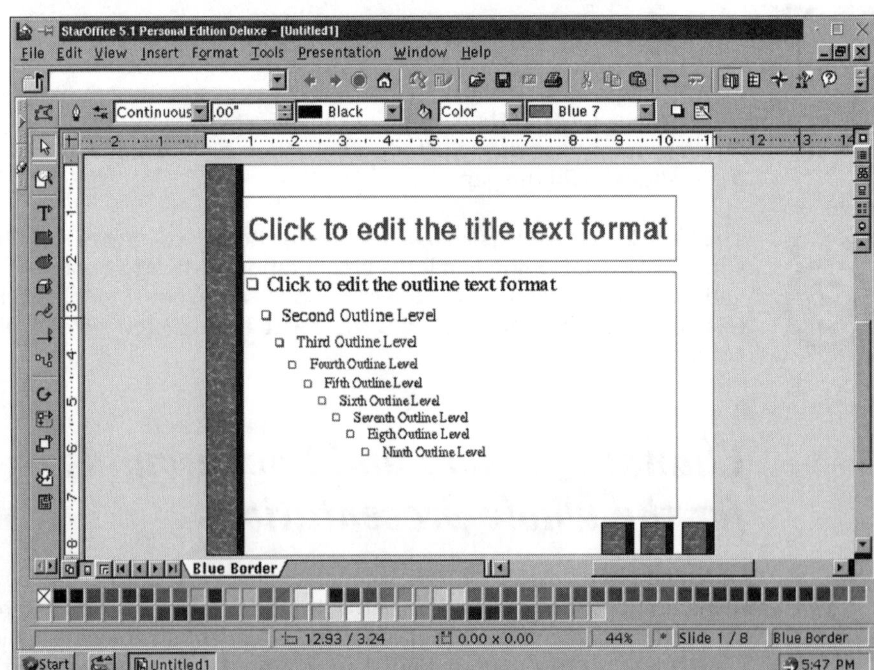

Figure 13-14: The master background slide contains sample text you can use to preview formatting changes.

2. **Select Presentation Styles from the drop-down list box at the top of the Style Catalog dialog box.**

   StarImpress updates the large list box to display the available presentation styles.

3. **Select Background from the large list box.**
4. **Click Modify.**

   StarImpress opens the Background dialog box, as shown in Figure 13-15.

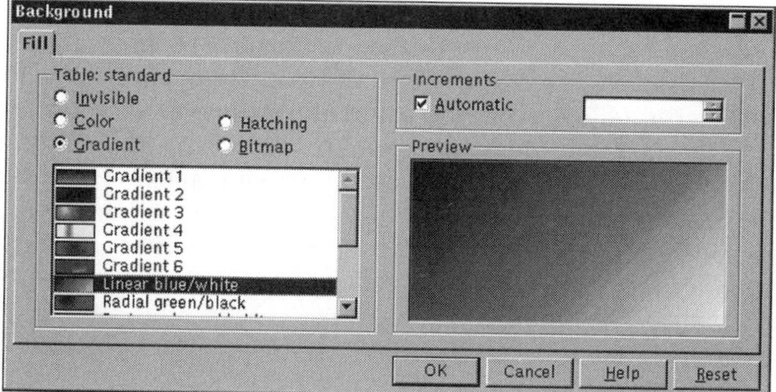

Figure 13-15: Selecting a background for the entire presentation.

5. **Adjust the settings to specify the desired background treatment and color.**

   Click one of the radio buttons (Invisible, Color, Gradient, Hatching, or Bitmap) to select a general background treatment, and then select a more specific example from the list box below. The Preview box lets you sample the selected effect.

6. **Click OK to close the Background dialog box.**

   StarImpress applies the selected background treatment to the master background slide.

7. **Click OK to close the Style Catalog dialog box.**

When you're through making changes to the master background slide, choose View⇨Slide to return to normal slide editing mode. The changes you made to the master background slide are reflected in all the slides of your presentation that are based on the master background slide.

If you make manual formatting changes to some text on an individual slide, that action breaks the link between that text and the master background slide. Changes to the master background slide no longer affect any text where you have overridden the default formatting.

Use Background mode to make important changes in only one place and thereby maintain consistency across your slides. If you decide that the text in the heading isn't big enough, try to remember to change its style in the background rather than just the current slide. Otherwise, you have to make the same change on every slide, and inevitably you forget one.

Saving your presentation

Be sure to save your presentation often. You probably put much more effort into your presentation than you do into any single image or drawing. To save a presentation, follow the same procedure you use to save any other document in StarOffice. Choose File⇨Save As to open the Save As dialog box. Give your presentation file a name and select the folder where you want to store the file. In the File Type drop-down list box, select the file format to use for saving the file. Select the StarImpress file type if you expect to always edit your presentation with StarOffice. Select the MS PowerPoint 97 file type if you need to share the presentation with a friend or coworker who needs to open the presentation file in PowerPoint. Click Save to close the Save As dialog box and save your presentation file.

Chapter 14

Printing and Presenting Your Presentation

In This Chapter

- Moving from slide to slide
- Getting the timing right
- Showtime!
- Printing for posterity's sake

You have a dazzling presentation set to go, and you're ready to show it to the world. After all, a presentation isn't very useful until you present it to somebody. This chapter describes several ways to impress the world with what you have to say. You discover how to run a slide show right from StarImpress — complete with animations and sound effects — or print slides, notes, and handouts for when you don't have your computer available.

Adding Transitions Between Slides

If you plan to show your presentation live, you can fancy it up by adding transitions between slides. Why just pop from one slide to the next, when you can have slides swoop in from all directions, fade in or out, or engage in a whole bunch of other animations? You can even attach sound effects to your slides.

Try switching to the Slide Sorter View before you attempt to add transition effects to your slides. Working in Slide Sorter View helps you select slides for transitions and visualize which slide you're coming from and going to. Follow these steps to add transitions:

1. **Choose Presentation⇨Slide Transition.**

   The Slide Transition dialog box appears, as shown in Figure 14-1, from which you can select a variety of transitions. This box stays active as you move between slides.

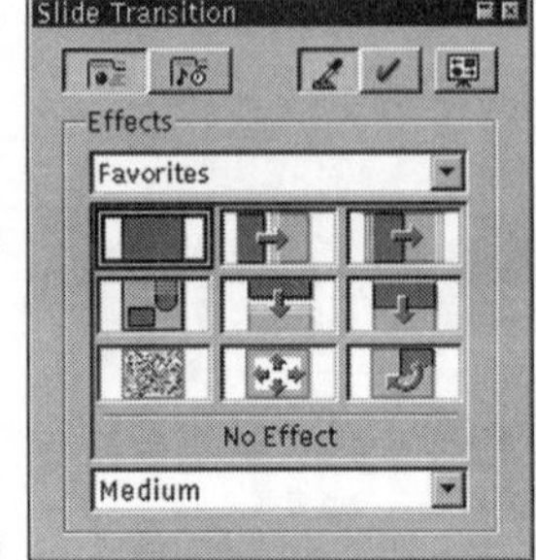

Figure 14-1: StarImpress offers a variety of transition effects to choose from.

2. **Click the Preview button.**

   A small window opens and displays a copy of your slide. You may need to drag the Slide Transition dialog box to one side so that you can see the slide preview and still have access to the buttons and settings in the dialog box.

3. **Choose a transition, such as Uncover From Left.**

   The transitions are organized into categories that you pick from. If you double-click the transition, you see an example in the Preview window. You need an active, selected slide for this feature to work. If you try it with a blank slide, you won't see the transition.

4. **Click the Apply button.**

   The Apply button makes the transition permanent. The Slide Transition dialog box remains active. If you change your mind, simply select and apply No Effect.

5. **Select another slide.**

   The currently applied transition applies to the currently selected slide. Specifically, the transition applies to getting *to* the current slide, not exiting *from* it. Select the next slide, and the Slide Transition dialog box and Preview window remain active. Now you can set the transition for this slide.

6. **Repeat Steps 3 through 5 to apply transitions to additional slides.**

If you're going to have a sound source available, you can attach sounds to your transitions as well. This option is a good way to keep your audience awake. Here's how to attach sounds:

1. **In the Slide Transition box, click the Extras button.**

   StarImpress replaces the transition options with clocks and musical notes, as shown in Figure 14-2.

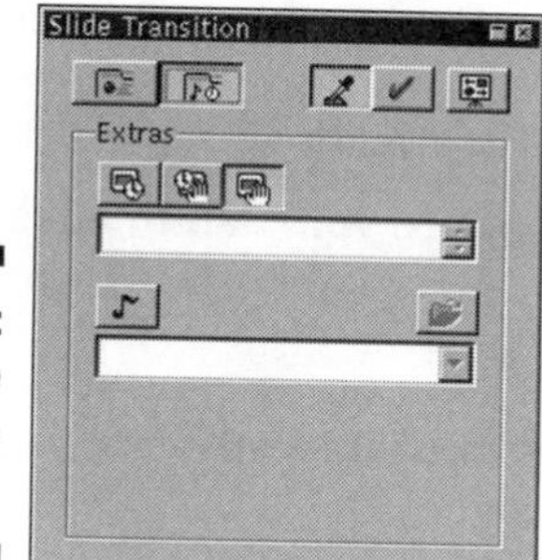

Figure 14-2: The Slide Transition extras.

2. **Click the musical note to attach a sound to this transition.**

   The drop-down list box below the musical note button becomes available (if it was grayed out before).

3. **Select a sound from the drop-down list box.**

   The drop-down list box normally displays the assortment of sounds that come with StarOffice. However, you can click the Browse button to display an Open dialog box that you use to browse to other directories on your system. Select a file in the Open dialog box and then click Open to close the dialog box and display the sound files from the directory in the drop-down list box.

4. **Click the Apply button.**

   StarImpress adds the selected sound to the transition effect that your audience experiences when you advance to this particular slide.

Timing Your Presentation

StarImpress offers several options to help you practice your presentation. As you rehearse what you're going to say, you can add a stopwatch to tell you how much time you're spending on each slide. After you have the presentation down and you're confident of your pacing and delivery, you can even choose for your slides to transition automatically. Your audience may look under the podium for your hidden assistant!

To rehearse your presentation, follow these steps:

1. **Choose Presentation⇨Rehearse Timings.**

StarImpress begins displaying your presentation as a full-screen slide show. You may notice a small stopwatch displayed in the lower left corner of the screen. Don't pay too much attention to it — yet.

2. **Practice your speech up to the point where you plan to advance to the next slide.**
3. **Note the time display on the stopwatch.**
4. **Click the mouse button or press the spacebar to advance to the next slide.**

   The stopwatch starts again at 00:00.
5. **Repeat Steps 2 through 4 until you complete your speech.**

You can rehearse your presentation as much as you like. Not only does the rehearsal option help you practice your pacing, but it also gives you a good idea of how long your presentation runs. If you have only ten minutes allotted, and you spend five on your first slide, you probably need to trim your presentation.

You can add a little dazzle to your presentation by creating automatic transitions. When these transitions are turned on, you can walk around the room as you speak without needing a pointer. This option is also useful if the audio portion of your presentation has been prerecorded. If you are presenting live, however, you probably want to limit your use of this trick to a few special occasions. Otherwise, one mistake in timing can throw off your entire presentation.

To create automatic transitions, follow these steps:

1. **Choose Presentation⇨Slide Transition (if the Slide Transition dialog box is not already active).**

   The Slide Transition dialog box appears (refer to Figure 14-2).

2. **Click the Extras button.**

   StarImage displays the Extras options in the Slide Transition dialog box.
3. **Click the Automatic Transition button.**

   This action selects the automatic slide timing option, but no change is visible.
4. **Enter the amount of time you expect to spend on this slide into the box below the Automatic Transition button.**

   You can type in the time in H:mm:ss format (0 hours, 2 minutes, 30 seconds would be 0:02:30) or click the small arrow buttons at the right end of the box to increase or decrease the time setting.

5. **Click Apply.**

   StarImpress records the timing settings for the current slide.

6. **Select the next slide you want to automatically transition.**
7. **Repeat Steps 3 through 6 until you finish your slides.**

After you create some automatic transitions, go back to rehearsing your presentation. Pay attention to how the presentation feels. If you feel rushed as you go through your slides, go back and add some time to your transitions.

Showing Your Presentation On-Screen

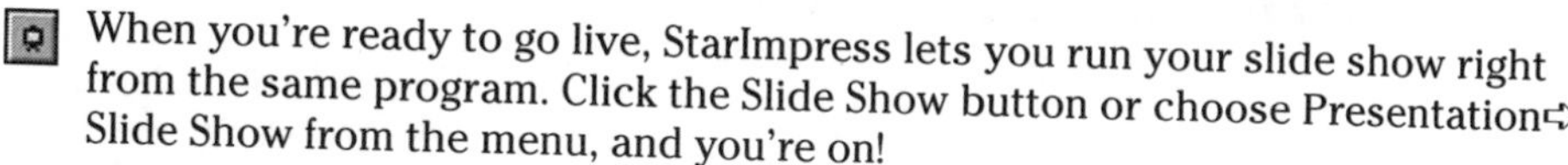

When you're ready to go live, StarImpress lets you run your slide show right from the same program. Click the Slide Show button or choose Presentation⇨Slide Show from the menu, and you're on!

You can choose one of the following ways to move through your presentation:

- Click the mouse to move to the next slide.
- Use the right or left arrows to move forward or backward one slide. You may find yourself using this process if someone in the audience asks you to go back to a slide.
- Create automatic transitions between slides.
- Press the Escape key to end the show early.

StarImpress attempts to load your slides into memory when you start the slide show. If you're running on a slower machine, this process may take a little while. So plan to bring up your title slide as quickly as possible and leave it on-screen while your audience gets settled. Do not automatically transition off the title. The more time you allow StarImpress to load your slides in the background, the smoother your transitions.

You may find that using a *splash* slide as your first slide works well. Splash slides don't convey any important information about your presentation, they simply capture your audience's attention. Your second slide can be the title of your presentation and your name.

Printing Your Presentation

On-screen presentations are impressive, with their colorful slides and slick transition effects. But sometimes you also need to deliver your presentation on paper. Furnishing your audience with a printed copy of your slides gives the audience the opportunity to follow along with your presentation, take notes, and have a permanent reference. Sometimes the printed version of your slides takes the place of a live presentation when circumstances make it impractical for someone to attend.

When you can't deliver your presentation on a computer screen, you can print your slides on transparent sheets and then show them with an overhead projector. You can also make good use of slides that are printed in note form by using them to practice and deliver your presentation.

StarImpress meets your presentation needs by letting you print your presentation in three formats: slides, handouts (for the audience), or notes (for you).

Printing slides

Turning your presentation slides into real 35mm slides to use in a slide projector requires special equipment and techniques. You can't do it yourself, but an imaging center or service bureau (businesses that specialize in transferring computer images to film) can. Look in your phone book under *slides* or *multimedia* for local imaging centers. Many centers may not know how to deal with StarOffice presentation files, but most of them can create slides from Microsoft PowerPoint files. Simply save your presentation as a PowerPoint file and then take your file to the imaging center to get your slides made.

Unlike 35mm slides, overhead transparencies are something you can do yourself — provided you have access to a color printer (you do want your overheads in color, don't you?). You can buy overhead transparency stock at your local office supply store and then load the transparencies rather than paper into your printer.

To print overhead transparencies (or full-page prints in black and white or color), just follow these steps:

1. **Open your presentation in StarImpress and choose File⇨Print from the menu.**

   The Print dialog box appears.

2. **Select the correct printer and the pages and number of copies you want to print.**

   Select the printer from the Name drop-down list box. Of course, the printer must already be installed and properly configured for your system. If you're printing overhead transparencies, you may need to click Properties to open the Printer Settings dialog box in which you can adjust the settings to accommodate the transparency stock; then click OK to return to the Print dialog box.

   To specify what pages (slides) to print, select one of the options (All, Pages, Selection) in the Print Range area. If you need more than one copy of each slide, enter the appropriate number in the Number of Copies box.

3. **Click Options.**

   The Printer Options dialog box appears, as shown in Figure 14-3.

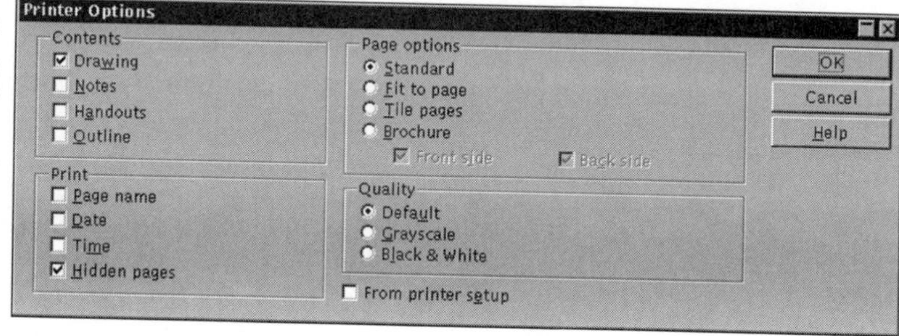

Figure 14-3: Many options are available for printing presentations.

4. **Adjust the print options settings as needed and click OK.**

   You can choose from a number of printing options. Here's a rundown on what they mean:

   - **Drawing:** Prints your slides as they appear in the Drawing View. (Select this option to print your slides as overheads.)
   - **Notes:** Prints your notes pages (see the "Printing notes" section of this chapter).
   - **Handouts:** Prints your handouts (see the "Printing handouts" section of this chapter).
   - **Outline:** Prints the outline view of your presentation.
   - **Page Name:** Adds the page (slide) name to each slide.
   - **Date:** Adds the current date to each slide.
   - **Time:** Adds the time to each slide as it's printed.
   - **Hidden Pages:** Prints hidden pages. Uncheck this option to exclude hidden pages from printing.
   - **Standard:** Prints slides at the standard (printer default) size.
   - **Fit to Page:** Resizes slides to fit the paper stock.
   - **Tile Pages:** Prints oversized slides by printing portions of the slides on separate sheets of paper, which you can then assemble as tiles to produce composite images.
   - **Brochure:** Prints your presentation as a brochure. You can select Front Side, Back Side, or both. This is a strange one. You need to experiment some if you plan to use this option.
   - **Default:** Prints your presentation in the printer's default mode (presumably color).

- **Grayscale:** Prints your presentation in grayscale (converts colors to shades of gray).
- **Black & White:** Prints your presentation in black and white.

To print overhead transparencies on a color printer, select Drawing, Standard, and Default, and leave the other options off.

After you adjust the settings, click OK to close the Print Options dialog box and return you to the Print dialog box.

5. **Click OK.**

   StarOffice closes the Print dialog box and begins printing your presentation (or the selected slides from your presentation).

Printing handouts

If you plan to provide handouts to your audience, you can print them in one of two ways. If you have only a few slides, you can simply use the process for printing slides (except, of course, onto paper, not transparencies) to produce a handout. But if you have a long presentation, you may fare better by using the StarImpress handouts feature to put multiple slides on a single page. You can print from one to six slides on a single page. Doing so not only gives your audience less paperwork to carry away, but also saves paper, which saves you time and money and spares the environment.

To print a handout as multiple slides on a page, follow these steps:

1. **Open your presentation in StarImpress and choose View⇨Master View⇨Handout or click the Handout View button.**

   StarImpress displays the master layout for handout pages, as shown in Figure 14-4. You see only one sample page, and you cannot flip through all your slides in this view.

2. **Right-click the tab near the bottom of the screen (the Home tab in Figure 14-4, but the name may change) and select Modify Slide from the pop-up menu that appears.**

   StarImpress displays the Modify Slide dialog box giving you a choice of five different layouts that accommodate one, two, three, four, or six slides per page. No five-slide-per-page layout option is given.

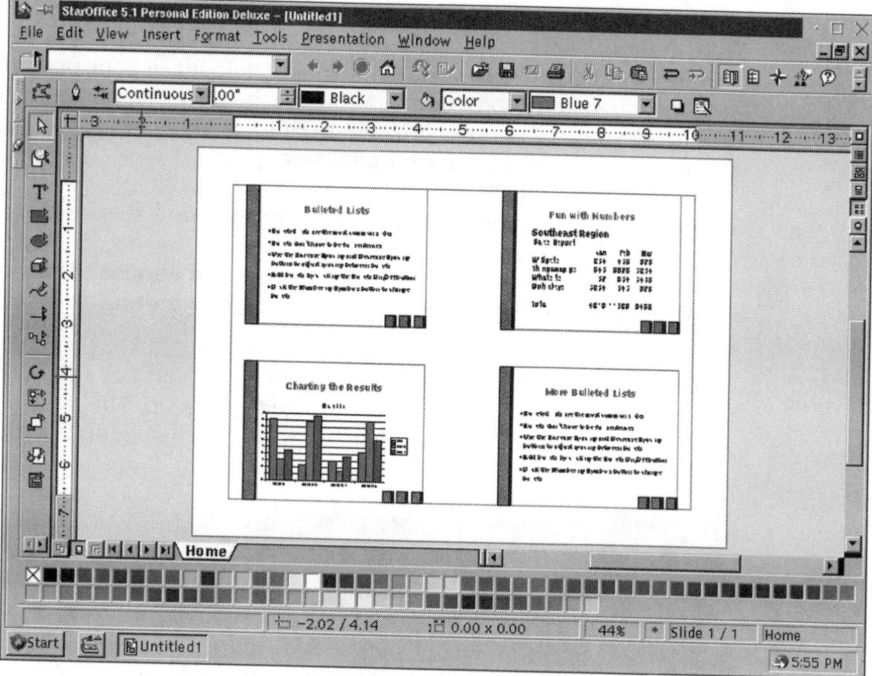

Figure 14-4: In Handout view, you don't actually see your slides, just a model you use to place your slides on the printed page.

3. **Select a layout for your handouts and then click OK.**

   StarImpress closes the Modify Slide dialog box and updates the display in the Handout view to show the new arrangement of slides on the handout page.

4. **Choose File⇨Print from the menu.**

   The Print dialog box appears.

5. **See the "Printing slides" section, earlier in this chapter. Follow Steps 2 through 5 of the procedure for printing slides, except be sure to check the Handouts option rather than the Drawing option in Step 4.**

   StarImpress closes the Print dialog box and prints your handout pages. Because StarImpress places several slides on a page, the last page of your handouts may contain an odd number of slides.

Printing notes

A stack of index cards or a typed script may be the traditional way to prepare notes for a presentation, but StarImpress offers you a better option — notes. The Notes feature enables you to print a copy of your slide on the top half of a page and your notes about that slide on the bottom half of the page. Having a copy of the slide on the same page as your notes means you don't have to turn around to look at the screen every time you refer to the slide content during your presentation — that can really help make your presentation more polished and professional. Although the Notes feature is designed for producing speaker's notes, you can use it to prepare annotated handouts, as well as other materials, for your audience.

To print your slides with accompanying notes, follow these steps:

1. **Open your presentation in StarImpress and choose View➪Master View➪Notes or click the Notes View button.**

   StarImpress displays your presentation in Notes view, as shown in Figure 14-5. Each slide appears on a separate page, and you use the tabs at the bottom of the screen to select a page to work on. The tabs are labeled as the slide tabs in Drawing View but with `(Notes)` added to the label.

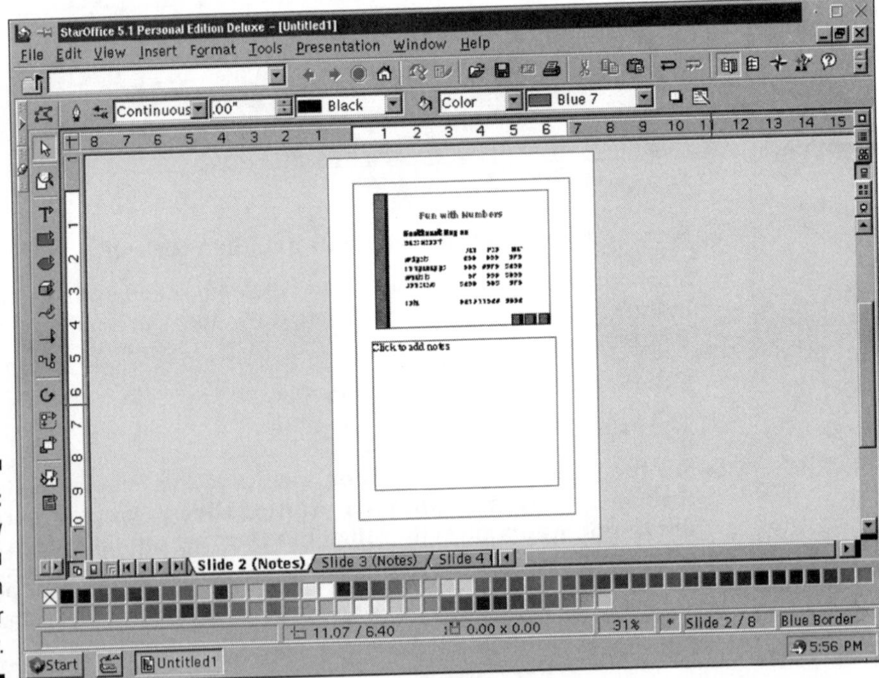

Figure 14-5: Notes view enables you to attach text for your eyes only.

2. **Select a slide notes page by clicking its tab.**

   Use the arrow buttons to the left of the tabs at the bottom of the screen to scroll through the list of available slide tabs. Click a tab to select the slide notes page.

3. **Click the** Click to Add Notes **text in the text box below the slide image and type your notes for the selected slide.**

When you click the Click to Add Notes text, the placeholder text disappears, a thick border appears around the text box, and the flashing text cursor appears in the text box. Type the text you want to appear on the Notes printout for the selected slide. If you're preparing speaker's notes, you can write whatever you want here — you're the only one who will see your notes. So it's okay to write *Look at audience. Smile*. After adding your text, you can click the page background outside the text box to deselect the text box and get a better preview of how the text appears on the notes page (but it's not really necessary).

4. **Repeat Steps 2 and 3 to add notes to additional slides.**
5. **Choose File⇨Print from the menu.**

   The Print dialog box appears.
6. **See the "Printing slides" section, earlier in this chapter. Follow Steps 2 through 5 of the procedure for printing slides, except in Step 4 be sure to check the Notes option rather than the Drawing option.**

   StarImpress closes the Print dialog box and prints notes pages for your presentation.

After StarImpress prints your notes, move them into a separate stack from your slides. You don't want to distribute your notes to the audience as handouts.

Part V
Scheduling Your Time and Tasks with StarSchedule

In this part . . .

Take charge of your hectic schedule with StarSchedule, StarOffice's appointment calendar and task manager. You can create to-do lists to prioritize and track your tasks. StarSchedule not only keeps track of your appointments, but also pops up a reminder to ensure that you make it to important events on time.

Chapter 15

Keeping Track of Tasks with StarSchedule

In This Chapter

- Creating a task list
- Scheduling tasks and due dates
- Tracking task completion
- Prioritizing and categorizing your tasks
- Adding links to tasks

Are you the sort of person who keeps to-do lists on little slips of paper stuffed into your pockets or bag? Do you lug around one of those heavy schedule binders with a zip-up leather cover but use it mostly to stick little pieces of paper into? If you are, StarOffice can help you with a tool called StarSchedule.

StarSchedule enables you to perform two general functions: Create a turbo-charged to-do list with the Tasks feature and enter appointments and recurring events using the Events feature. This chapter is about working with tasks. Skip to Chapter 16 for more information on working with events and using the scheduling functions.

Introducing StarSchedule

StarSchedule is a type of tool called a personal information manager (PIM). A PIM is a calendar program that allows you to keep both your to-do list(s) and your appointment schedule on the computer. You can set up prioritized task lists complete with due dates, reminders before important things happen, and appointments that recur daily, monthly, or even yearly. With a full-featured PIM such as StarSchedule, you have no excuse for neglecting important tasks or forgetting appointments . . . unless, of course, you don't turn on your computer very often.

Creating a New Task List

Obviously, you have to enter some tasks in order to use the Task feature of StarSchedule. If you only need one task list, you can simply use the one StarOffice creates automatically after you install the program. But you're not limited to one task list, either. You can set up as many as you need. If you want to keep a task list for work and a task list for home, go ahead. You can even keep a private task list and a task list available to other people on your network. StarSchedule works with whatever needs you have for your task lists.

If you want to use multiple task lists, you can create a new list by following these steps:

1. **Open the Explorer window, right-click on StarSchedule in the Explorer group, and choose New Task View from the pop-up menu that appears.**

   The New Task View dialog box opens. (Refer to Chapter 2 for instructions on using Explorer.)

2. **Click the General tab.**
3. **Type the name of your task list in the text box.**

   If you're going to keep more than one task list, make the name specific. You may call one task list "my work to-do" or another one "garden chores I need to do."

4. **Click the Data tab.**

   The Data tab has fields in which you can set information about who is allowed to read your task list. This only applies if you are using StarSchedule on a network and need to share task information.

   - Select the name of your server from the Data Source drop-down list box. If the server doesn't appear on the list, click Add and type the name of your server in the New Connection dialog box that appears and then click OK to close the dialog box and add the server to the list.
   - Select the appropriate user ID from the User drop-down list box.

5. **Click the View Options tab.**

   The View Options tab gives you several possible layouts for your task list. You can group your tasks by category, by participants, or by due date.

   You can also select filter options on this tab, choosing from None, Overdue, Due Today Only, or In Progress. If none of these options works for you, the tab also has buttons that take you to dialog boxes, which allow you to modify the options.

6. **Adjust the Layout and Filter settings as needed.**
7. **Click OK.**

   StarOffice adds a new task list to your system. A new item appears in the Explorer window with the name that you selected. (You may need to expand the StarSchedule branch of the tree in the Explorer group in order to see it.) If you prefer to open files from StarDesktop, click and drag your task list's name out of the Explorer window and drop it on the desktop to create an icon you can use to open the task list.

Opening the Task Window

After you create a task list, you can start to add tasks to it and rearrange it to your liking. After all, why go to the work of configuring a task list if you never add any tasks! You have two ways to open an existing task list. If you drag the list's name out of Explorer onto the StarDesktop, you can just double-click the icon on the StarDesktop. Otherwise, double-click on your schedule item in the Explorer window's Explorer group.

Either way, a task window opens, as shown in Figure 15-1, and you can begin to work with it.

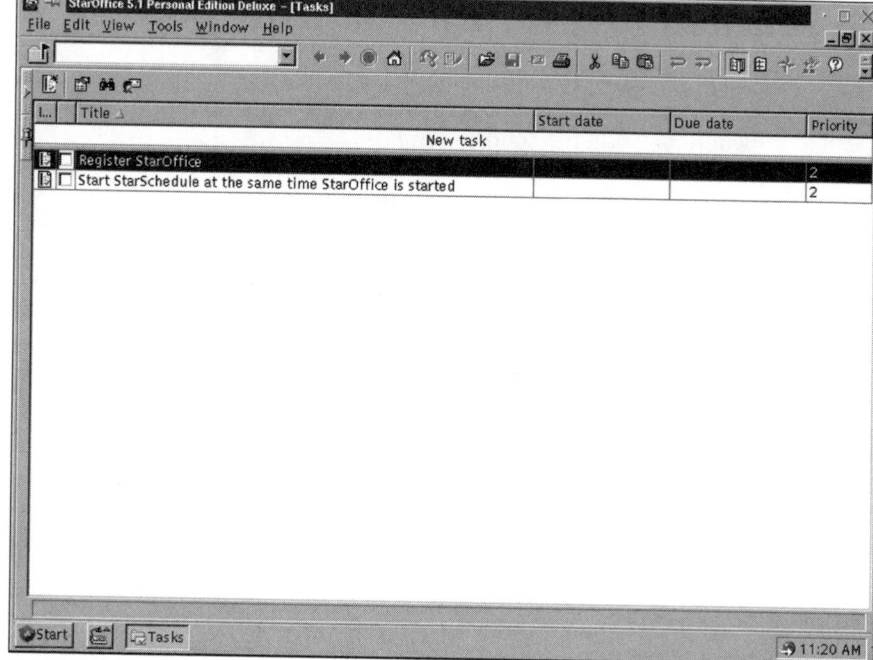

Figure 15-1: The default task list starts out nearly empty, but you soon fill it.

Using a To-Do List

You probably make hundreds of to-do lists in your life. Some people keep them on special paper with checkboxes, some people keep them in their daily planners, and other people scribble reminders on the back of receipts or scrap paper and stick them in a pocket or purse. The problem with all of these to-do lists is that they're not interactive. After you write a task down, nothing prompts you to actually do it!

StarSchedule adds the extra kick that gets you going on the tasks on your to-do list. Because you enter your tasks with due dates and priorities and all the sorts of things that give StarSchedule an idea of how important each task is, your to-do list becomes organized and clear. You can see that you have three top-priority tasks due by Wednesday or that you've finished the really critical stuff and can spend an enjoyable afternoon surfing the Web in the name of product research.

You can use the task list at whatever level of complication makes you happy. Some folks are fine with a plain list of tasks, while other people aren't happy until they prioritize and date everything on the list. You can probably find a middle ground that you can live with, which is the point of a good Personal Information Manager — you make it work for you.

Adding a task to the list

After you open the task window, you see a single line at the top of the task list separated from the rest of the list by a gray bar. This line is the New Task line, where you add new information.

To add a new task, click in the space under the heading Title and type the name of the task. It's that simple! A task can exist on your task list as nothing but a descriptive title. Actually, you probably want to add due dates and other information, but all that is optional. Click the task list outside the New Task line, and StarSchedule adds your new task to your task list. To edit a task in your task list, simply click the information you want to change and start editing.

Make your life easier — isn't that why you're using StarSchedule? — by keeping your task names clear and understandable. The task titles are what's listed in the task area of StarSchedule. No use wasting time trying to figure out what's on your to-do list.

Scheduling due dates

Of course you can live with a task list that's just a list of tasks, but you can do that with a pen and an index card. With StarSchedule, you can enter due dates into the task list. Then you can arrange the task list in order of due date so that you're working on time-prioritized items, if that's the best way for you to work.

Directly to the right of the Title column in the task list are two columns for Start Date and Due Date. Click in the Start Date or Due Date box of any task line to enter or edit the contents of that date box. You can enter a Start Date, a Due Date, or both for any task in your task list. You can also go back and edit those dates at any time.

You can either type the date into the Start Date or Due Date box in regular month/date/year format, or you can click the arrow button that appears at the right end of the box after it's selected. Clicking the arrow button opens a calendar. Use the arrow buttons in the calendar header to display different months. Just click the correct date in the calendar. The calendar disappears, and the date is inserted into your task list. This feature is great if you know something's always due on the last Friday of the month, but you're not sure of the date.

Prioritizing tasks

Due dates aren't always the best way to organize your tasks. Sometimes you just have to figure out what's the most important task to do, rather than what's due earliest. You can attach a priority to each task in your task list. Then you can sort your list by priority to show you what's the most important project to do each day.

To the right of the date fields in the task list, StarSchedule presents the Priority field. This field allows you to choose which tasks are the most important and which are not quite as important.

Be honest with yourself about priorities. Not everything on your list is a top priority, a do-it-now-or-else kind of task. Some people are really good at making you think their task is the most important thing in the world, when they just want you to think that they are important people. Don't make yourself crazy with a list full of high priorities.

To set a priority for a task, click in the priority field. Click the arrow that appears at the right end of the box and select a number from the drop-down list box that appears. The number 1 is the highest priority, 5 is the lowest priority. Assign a 5 to tasks that you have to do, but that don't have to be done by a certain time. Mowing your lawn is usually a 5, unless the city council is about to condemn your property because they can't see your house through the weeds. Getting to your IRS audit appointment is probably a 1.

Categorizing tasks

The final adjustment you can make to a task is to put it into a category. Categories enable you to group the same kinds of tasks together. If you use a Vacation category, for example, you can put all vacation-related tasks there, such as getting airplane tickets and hotel reservations or remembering to buy a bathing suit.

Select a task by clicking it and then click the Details button in the StarSchedule Object toolbar. Task details for the selected task appear in the lower half of the screen. You read more about details in the next section; at this point, just focus on categories.

On the left side of the screen, under the task name, you see the words Content, Details, and Participants. Click Details. The Details screen opens, as shown in Figure 15-2.

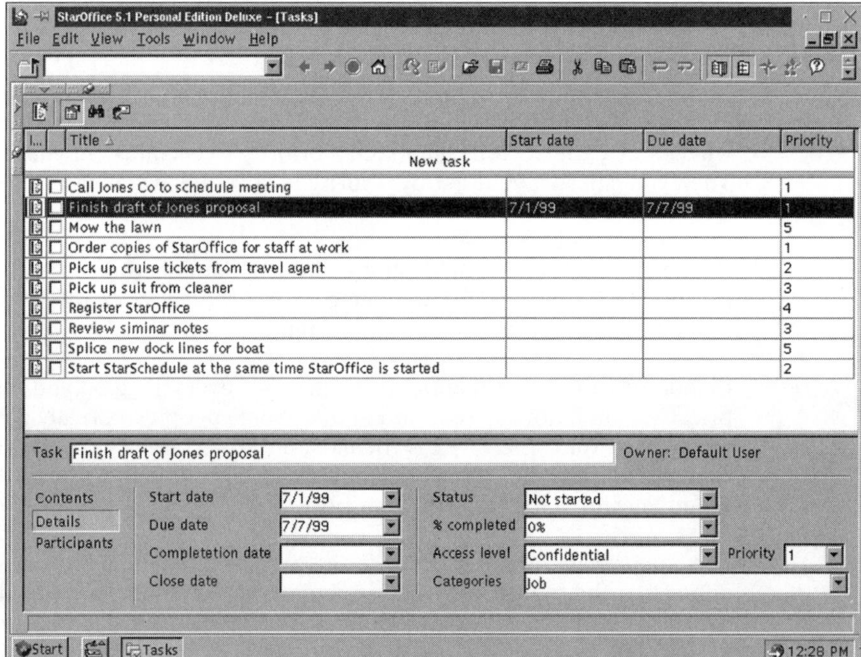

Figure 15-2: Viewing the Details of a task.

In the lower right-hand corner of the Details screen, you see a field for Categories. If you click the arrow, you see the default categories (Ideas, Job, Personal, Vacation). Select the one you want to apply to your category.

If none of the default categories meet your needs, you can add your own by simply typing the name of your new category in the Category area of the screen.

Working with task details

If you really like tinkering with your tasks, the Task Detail panel is for you. You can add all sorts of flags to each task that go beyond just Due Date, Priority, or Category.

Go to the Details panel by selecting a task and then clicking the Details button on the toolbar. The Details panel appears (see Figure 15-2). In the Details screen, you can tinker to your heart's delight. You can set or edit a number of flags. You can add extra dates to each task, such as Start Date, Due Date, Completion Date, or Close Date. You can also set the status of a given task, or show the percentage of the task that's been completed. If you share your task list over a network, you can set the access level for each task (public, private, or confidential).

If you didn't previously set a task priority or a category, you can always set those in this screen. No matter what sort of flags you choose to use, each of these functions allows you to control the way you access and sort your tasks.

Adding links to a task

Not all tasks are individual items. Sometimes you have a bunch of tasks that are all part of one project. If your particular task is part of a larger project or is related to another task, you can add a link between the tasks.

To link two tasks, open the Details panel. Under the task name, click the Content button to show the Content view of the selected task. In the Task List, choose a task to link to. Click and drag that task to the Also Refer To box in the Details panel (see Figure 15-3). If you want to move quickly from a task to its related task, you simply double-click the link. You can add links to documents and other files by dragging them from the Beamer window and dropping them in the Also Refer To box. (See Chapter 2 for information on using Beamer.)

Figure 15-3: Add links to related tasks and documents so that you can access them quickly.

Viewing the Task List

Obviously, as soon as you create a list of tasks, you want to look at them. StarSchedule lets you sort your tasks based on any of the flags you add. You can also just look at the straightforward list of tasks, but why bother after you add neat things to sort with?

Sorting and filtering tasks

You can sort and filter your task list using any of the detail information. Suppose you want a list of tasks in order of priority. That's easy — StarSchedule can do that for you. Or you can get a list of all the tasks that are due today. That's easy, too. (Just watch out. You can waste a lot of time playing with task sorting and filtering . . . and that's time you need to use to knock some of those tasks off the list.)

To sort your task list, open the list and click the header for the class you want to sort by. You can choose from Title, Start Date, Due Date, or Priority. Clicking Title arranges all the tasks in alphabetical order by title. Clicking Title again reverses the order. Clicking Start Date arranges the tasks by start date. And so on.

Filtering tasks is a bit more complicated. If you apply a filter to your task list, you choose which tasks you want StarSchedule to show you. Whereas the sorting feature rearranges all the tasks on your list, the filtering feature picks and chooses.

To apply a filter to your task list, choose View➪Define Task Filter. The Task Filters dialog box opens. This dialog box has three tabs:

- The Selection tab enables you to choose a pre-installed filter or create a new one.
- The Settings tab (shown in Figure 15-4) enables you to filter using Category, Title, Date, Priority, or Status.
- The More tab lets you define a condition that must be met in order for StarSchedule to display the task.

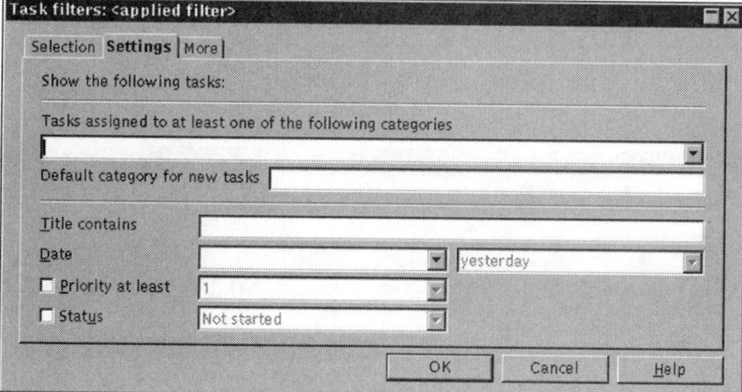

Figure 15-4: Define filters to determine what tasks appear in the task list.

After you select your settings, click OK, and the dialog box closes. The task list appears, displaying only those tasks that meet your filter criteria.

Grouping tasks

You can also use the various task flags to sort your tasks into groups. You may want to group all the tasks with a 2 priority or all the tasks that are 50 percent finished. You can use any of the flags discussed in this chapter to group your tasks.

To set up a task group, choose View➪Define Task Layout and select the Group tab (shown in Figure 15-5). The Group screen appears. In this screen, you can select an ascending or descending sort pattern. Then you can select up to three more layers of sub-sorts. Click OK to close the Task Layout dialog box and display your task list using the groups you specified (see Figure 15-6).

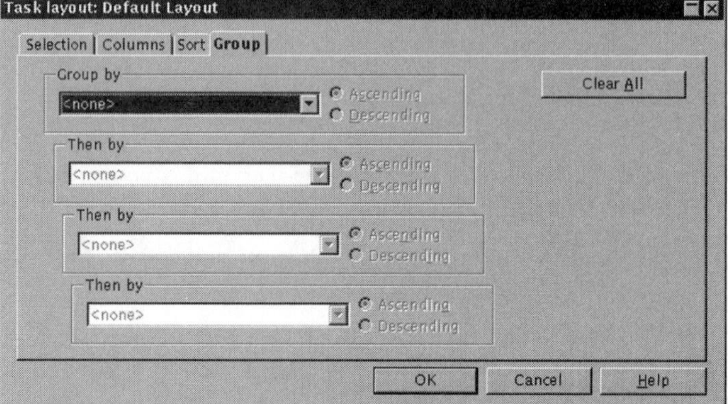

Figure 15-5: Display your tasks grouped by criteria you select.

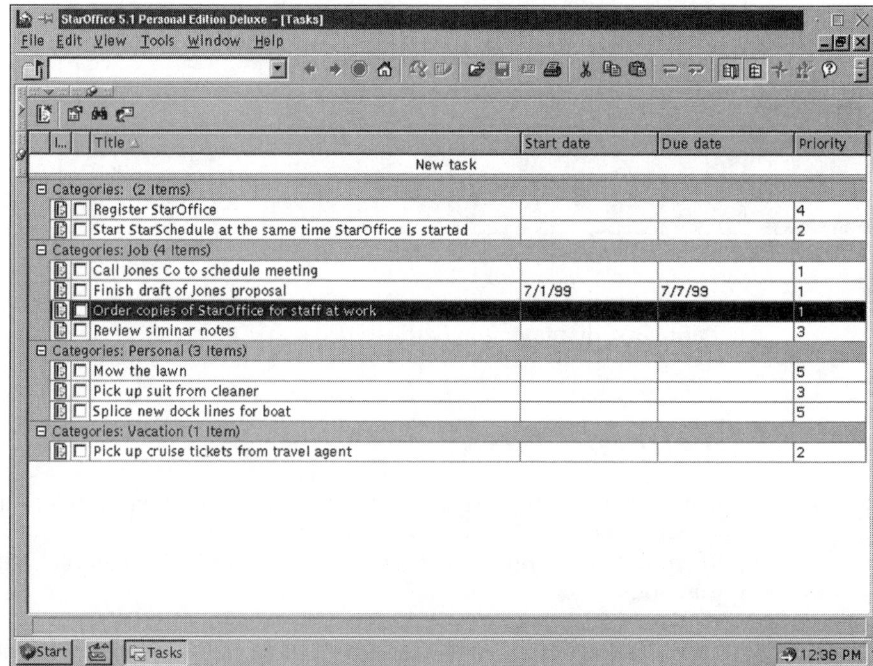

Figure 15-6: A task list sorted into groups.

Checking Off Completed Tasks

Nothing beats the feeling of crossing a task off your to-do list. You get a psychological boost when you look at a list of tasks with neat little checks next to the finished ones. And everyone needs a boost when tackling a complex list of things to do!

StarSchedule enables you to check off a task after you complete it. Just to the left of the task's title is a check box. Simply click the check box and a check mark appears. The status of that task changes to Completed.

You may eventually want to get rid of those completed tasks, so that you can see what you still have to do. You can set up a filter that only shows you the tasks in progress. That way you have a record of your completed tasks, but they're not cluttering up the display. If you really want to get rid of a task, you can delete it by selecting the task and pressing Delete, or by right-clicking the task and choosing Delete from the pop-up menu that appears.

Sharing Tasks with Other Programs

The cold hard fact of modern life is that not everyone uses the same Personal Information Manager. Some people use StarSchedule, others use Microsoft Outlook, the Symantec ACT, or one of tens of other similar programs. This variety can be a real pain if you want to share your task list. However, StarSchedule enables you to save your task list in a format that is compatible with many other calendar programs. This feature is particularly handy if you work with people who don't use StarOffice.

To share your task list with another Personal Information Manager, use File⇨Export. The Export dialog box appears. Give your task list file a name and select the file type you want to save it in. You can also use the radio buttons at the bottom of the screen to select the program in which you intend to use your saved task list file. If you only want to export certain tasks, you have the option of creating a filter at this point.

Chapter 16

Getting to the Church (or Meeting) on Time with StarSchedule

In This Chapter

- Creating an appointment calendar in StarSchedule
- Scheduling appointments
- Setting up recurring appointments
- Entering all-day events
- Displaying calendar options
- Sharing your calendar data with other calendar programs
- Printing out your schedule

Just what you need — an electronic secretary who tracks your appointments, lets you know what's high priority and what you can put off, and lets you see your upcoming events in a variety of views. StarSchedule lets you do all these things, and you only have to enter your data once.

Opening the Event Calendar

You can open the StarSchedule event calendar in one of two ways:

- Double-click the Events icon on StarDesktop.
- Open the Explorer window and double-click the Events item listed under StarSchedule in the Explorer group.

Either way, you see the StarSchedule event calendar screen, as shown in Figure 16-1.

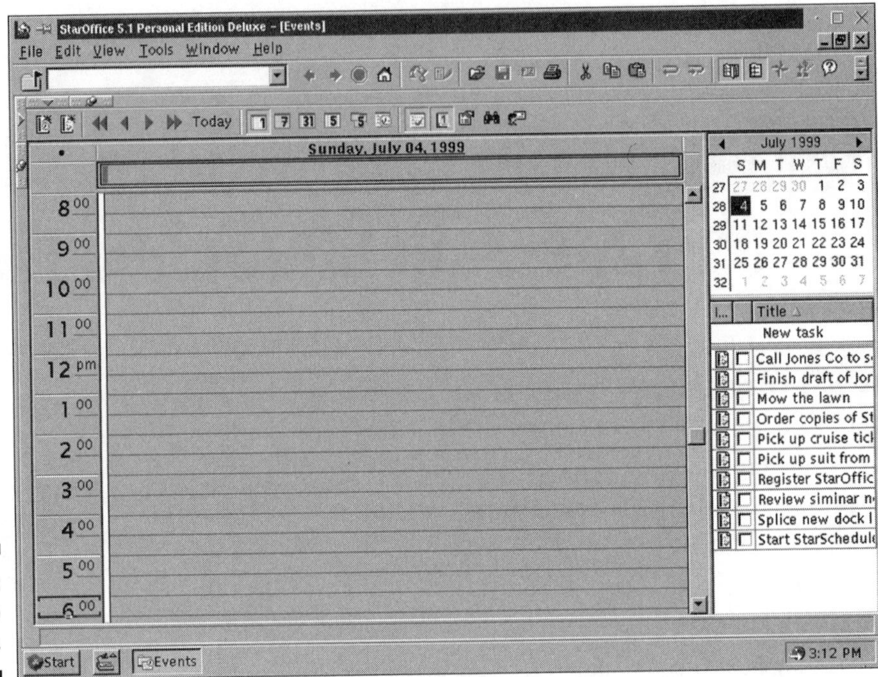

Figure 16-1: Welcome to StarSchedule.

The StarSchedule window is divided into three major parts, plus a toolbar. The largest part of the window is today's schedule, where StarSchedule displays information from your Events database. StarSchedule automatically displays the current day, divided into 30-minute blocks of time. If you need to see a part of your day that doesn't show in the main window, use the vertical scrollbars to slide up and down through the day until you find the right time.

In the top-right corner of the window, StarSchedule displays the current month. The current day — regardless of whether it's the day displayed in the main part of the screen — has a little box around it. The day that appears in that main area is colored blue in the month view. If you want to view a different day in the main area, just click that date in the month view.

In the lower-right corner of the window, StarSchedule shows you your task list. The task list is a place for you to write down and prioritize the important things that you need to do. I cover the task list thoroughly in Chapter 15.

You can click and drag the separating lines that form the borders of the events list, calendar, and task list to reallocate the space devoted to each part of the StarSchedule window. For example, you can click the vertical bar on the right edge of the time scroll bar and drag it to the left to reduce the width of the events list and increase the width of the task list and monthly calendars. This repositioning makes your task list much easier to read.

Navigating to the Desired Date

Because the point of a personal information manager (PIM) is to help you manage your life, you want to move around to different dates in StarSchedule. You may want to enter a conference date for next year or make sure that you get your mother-in-law's birthday right every year for the rest of your life. Not all of that stuff happens on one day (thank goodness!), and it's likely that none of it is happening today. So, you need to know how to navigate around the dates in StarSchedule.

Luckily, the StarSchedule Object toolbar provides a convenient set of buttons for navigating dates. This toolbar is located right above the main window, above the bar where the date is spelled out. Use these buttons to move around in the year:

- **Arrow buttons:** Move you backward or forward through the calendar. If you're showing days one at a time, the arrows move one day at a time. If you're showing full weeks in the main area, the arrows move one week at a time.

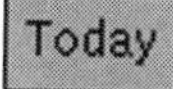

- **Today button:** Brings up the current date's schedule.
- **Day button:** Shows one day at a time in the main window.
- **Week button:** Shows one week at a time in the main window.
- **Month button:** Shows an entire month at a time in the main window.
- **Workweek button:** Shows one workweek at a time. The default workweek is Monday through Friday.

- **Multiple Workweek button:** Shows a full month at a time, but only workdays.

Scheduling Appointments

If you're like most people, you use a personal information manager mostly to manage appointments. An appointment isn't just a time that you set to meet with someone; an appointment can be a reminder, a TV show that you want to watch, or any other event that has a specific time and date.

Creating a new event

When you want to add an appointment to your schedule, you need to create a new event. When you create a new event, you block out the time period needed and give that time block a name.

To create a new event in the schedule window, follow these steps:

1. **Choose the correct day for the event in the calendar in the upper-right corner of the screen.**

   Make sure that you're in a schedule view that shows the daily schedule. This can be the one-day view, the one-week view, or the workweek view.

2. **Find the event's starting time in the window and click it. Drag your mouse to the ending time.**

   StarSchedule highlights the event's time block.

3. **Type a name for the appointment.**

   Make the name clear so that you know what the appointment actually is when you open StarSchedule later.

4. **Press Enter.**

   StarSchedule saved the event as part of your calendar. Figure 16-2 shows an event added to the calendar display.

Entering event details

You may want to store more information about a particular event than just its name and time. With StarSchedule, you can add various details to an event, just as you do to a task on your task list.

To add details to an event, first display the Details panel. Click the Details button on the Object toolbar or choose View⇨Details to split the StarSchedule window and show details of the selected event or task in the bottom section of the window, as shown in Figure 16-3.

To edit an event's details, select the event by clicking it. In the Details panel of the window, click the Details button on the left side of the screen under the task name. The Details options appear (refer to Figure 16-3).

The first details that you may want to edit are the start and end date and time of the event. The option boxes in this view enable you to type in times (such as 9:25) that you can't select by clicking and dragging across lines on the event list. Check the Day Event check box to create an event (such as a holiday or vacation day) that lasts all day instead of being tied to a specifictime. You can even set events (such as vacations or conferences) to last multiple days.

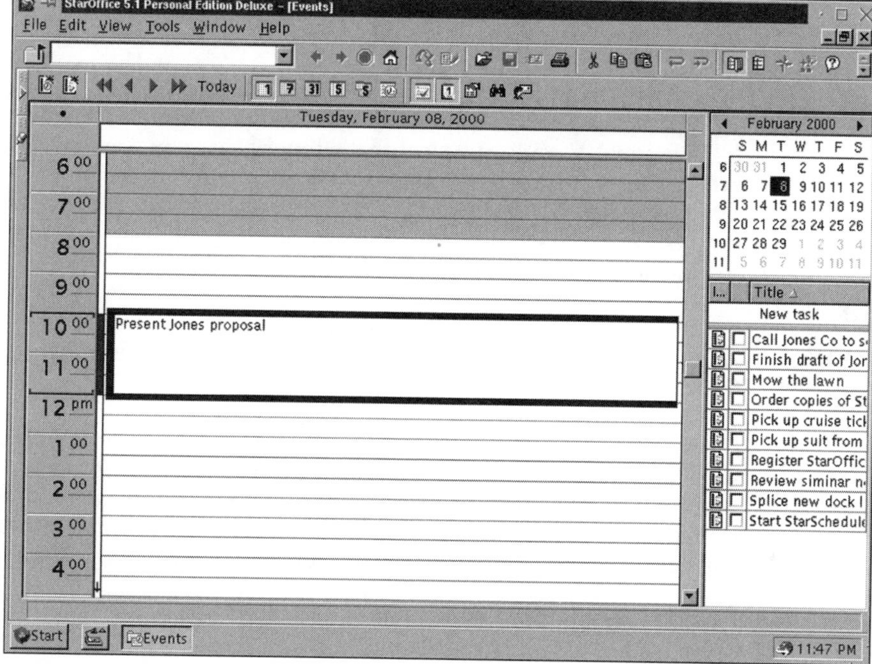

Figure 16-2: Add appointments directly to the calendar.

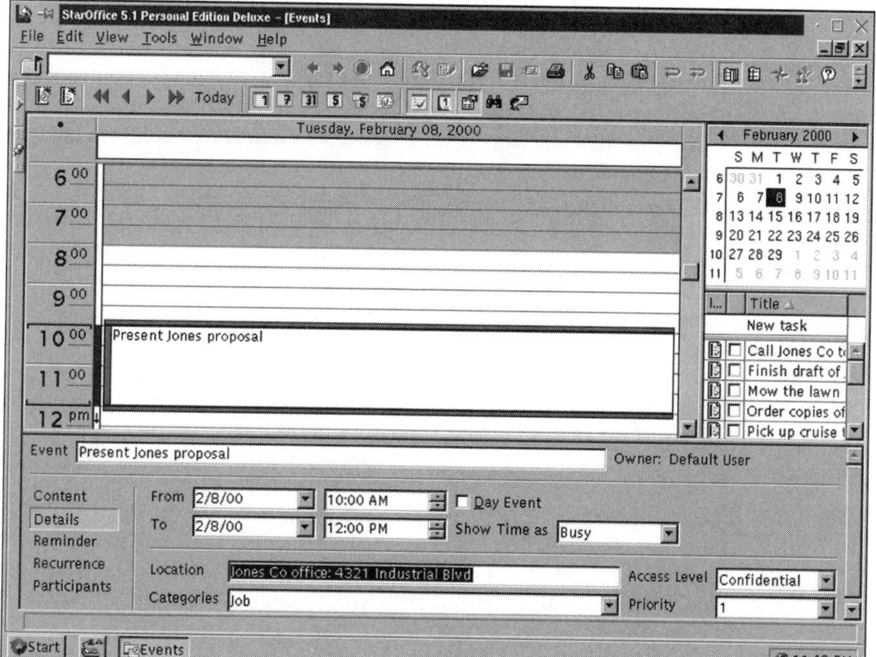

Figure 16-3: Get at all the details for an event in the Details panel.

You can also set a location for the event. And you can designate each event as Free, Busy, Tentative, or Out of Office.

Near the bottom of the window, you see a field for Categories. If you click the arrow, you see a drop-down list box showing the default categories (Ideas, Job, Personal, Vacation). Select the category that you want to apply to your event. These categories are the same ones you find in the task list. If you consistently assign categories to your events, you can define filters to select and display events based on their category. See the "Filtering calendar events" section later in this chapter.

If you need a category that's not included in the list provided by StarSchedule, you can make your own just by typing the category name in the text box.

If you share your schedule across a network so that other people can see what you're doing, you may want to set the access level for a given event. Not everyone in your office needs to know about your medical visits or personal errands. Although setting priorities isn't as important for events as for tasks, you can still set a priority level for an event while you're at this screen.

Click the Content button, which is on the left side of the Details view panel, to display a box for a longer description or notes for your event, and a box in which you can create links to related events and files. To link two events, just click and drag an event from the event list and drop the event into the Links box. You can also drag and drop tasks from the task list into the Links box or open the Beamer window and drag and drop document and file icons from the Beamer window into the Links box. (See Chapter 2 for more information on using Beamer.) Dragging and dropping enables you to create links to the documents that you may need for a meeting. When you want to examine the details of that meeting, you just double-click the link to access them quickly from StarSchedule.

You can leave the Details panel open if you want. Having it open can be a handy way to display detailed information about the selected event or task. But the Details panel takes up a lot of screen real estate. To close the Details panel, simply click the Details button in the StarSchedule Object toolbar.

Setting a reminder alarm

If you're the sort of person who loses track of time, then StarSchedule has a feature to help you. You can set a reminder alarm so that your computer displays a message or beeps when you need to get to a meeting or start some other scheduled event. You can also set StarSchedule to remind you via e-mail. The e-mail feature is especially useful when you need to remind other people about their appointment with you!

Here's how to set a reminder that shows up on your computer screen:

1. **Select the event that you need to be reminded about by clicking it in the event list.**

2. **Click the Details button on the StarSchedule Object toolbar.**

   StarSchedule displays the Details panel at the bottom of the window. (Skip this step if the Details panel is already open.)

3. **Click the Reminder button at the left end of the Details panel.**

   StarSchedule displays the Reminder options, shown in Figure 16-4.

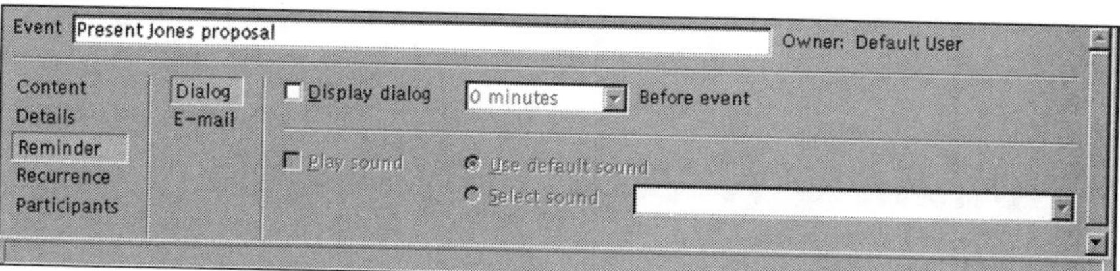

Figure 16-4: StarSchedule can remind you of your appointments.

4. **Click the Dialog button.**

   StarSchedule changes the Details panel to display the options for a dialog box reminder.

5. **Check the Display Dialog option and make a selection from the Before Event drop-down list box in order to specify the amount of advance notice you want StarSchedule to give you before the event.**

   You can set this time in a range anywhere from zero minutes ("The meeting is happening NOW!") to two days ("Don't forget to buy your dad a Father's Day gift").

   A small clock appears next to the selected event in the schedule. This icon indicates that StarSchedule has set a reminder for that event.

   If this is the first time that you've set a reminder, a window pops up asking you whether you want to start StarSchedule when you start StarOffice. Click Yes so that StarSchedule can deliver reminders to you as scheduled.

6. **If you want StarSchedule to play a sound when it reminds you, check the Play Sound option and select a sound.**

   Select Use Default Sound to set StarSchedule to play its own sound or select Choose Sound and enter the path and filename for a sound file of your choice.

7. **(Optional) Click the Details button in the StarSchedule Object toolbar.**

   StarSchedule closes the Details panel. This step isn't really necessary; it just helps clean up the on-screen clutter.

To set an e-mail reminder, follow the preceding steps but click the Email button in Step 4, instead of the Dialog button. StarSchedule changes the options that enable you to set how far in advance of the start time you want the message to go out and the e-mail address where you want the message sent. Normally, you want to select the Enter Address Manually option and supply one or more e-mail addresses for people you want to remind about the meeting (not much point to sending yourself an e-mail reminder). At the time that you set, StarSchedule sends an e-mail message to the specified people, reminding them of the date and time of the appointment.

Scheduling Recurring Events

One of the really great things about a personal information manager is that it can keep track of recurring events for you. A recurring event is anything that happens on a predictable schedule. If you get your hair cut every six weeks or you travel to Indiana to see your cousins every 18 months, you have recurring events. An event can recur every few days, months, weeks, or years.

StarSchedule takes the information that you provide when you enter a recurring event and sets up a schedule for you. No more counting Tuesdays to figure out when your next trip to the barber should be! StarSchedule sets your recurring appointments into the future. All you have to do is show up.

To set a recurring event in your schedule, you first need to create the event as a single occurrence. Then you can set the recurrence by following these steps:

1. **Create a new event or open an existing event for which you want to set up a recurrence schedule.**

   For more information, see the "Scheduling Appointments" section earlier in this chapter.

2. **Select the appointment and click the Details button.**

   Skip this step if the Details panel is already open.

3. **Click Recurrence in the Details window.**

   StarSchedule displays a column of radio buttons giving you a choice of recurrence frequency schedules. The choices are None, Daily, Weekly, Monthly, or Yearly.

4. **Select a recurrence frequency schedule.**

   If you want the event to recur every so many days, choose Daily. If the event should recur on certain days of the week, choose Weekly. If the event should recur on a certain day or date of the month, choose Monthly. For annual events, choose Yearly.

   StarSchedule displays a set of options enabling you to fine-tune how often you want the event to happen. The options vary depending on the frequency option that you chose. For example, Figure 16-5 shows the options for the Weekly schedule.

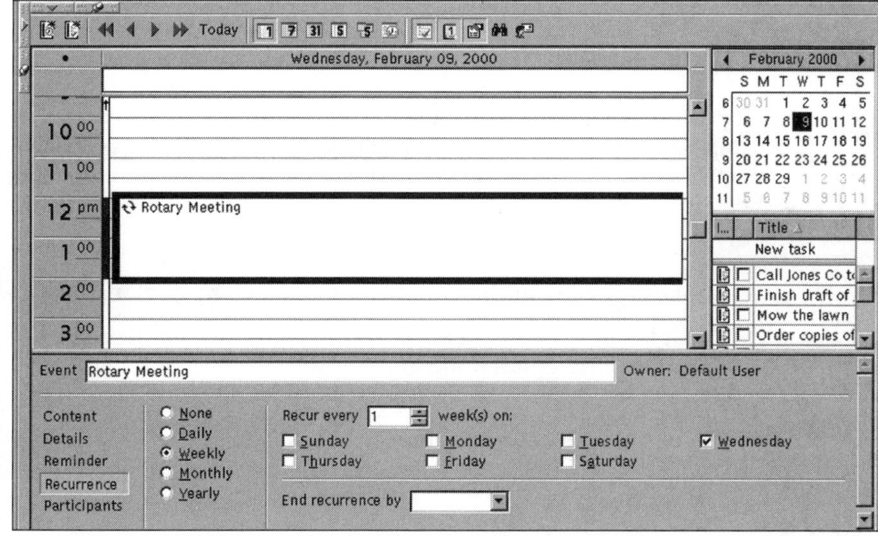

Figure 16-5: Tell StarSchedule how frequently the event occurs.

5. **Set the recurrence pattern for the event.**

   This step is where you specify the days on which you want the event to happen. For example, if you have a meeting every other Wednesday, enter **2** in the Recur Every box and check the Wednesday option.

6. **Set an end date for the recurring event in the End Recurrence By box.**

   Enter a date or click the arrow button in the End Recurrence By box to pop up a calendar and select the date from the calendar. If you don't put anything here, StarSchedule just keeps scheduling your event year after year after year.

7. **Click the Details button in the StarSchedule Object toolbar.**

   The Details panel closes. StarSchedule marks your recurring events with a circle made up of two arrows.

Suppose you have an exception. Maybe you have a recurring appointment to get your teeth cleaned, for example, but your dentist has gone scuba diving for the month of October. How do you change the event? If you need to edit a recurring event, you have to decide whether you want to edit every future occurrence of that event or just one occurrence.

If you want to change all future recurring events, follow these steps:

1. **Select the first occurrence of the event that you want to change.**
2. **Click the Details button.**
3. **Click Recurrence and change the settings as you did when you set up the recurrence schedule.**

   The changes affect all future occurrences of that event.

If you don't want to change every single future occurrence, but you just want to postpone one appointment from October 10 to October 15 (when you can get in to see the other dentist in the practice), you need to be a little more careful. To change one instance of a recurring appointment, follow these steps:

1. **Select the event that you want to change by clicking it once.**
2. **Right-click the event and choose Separate from Recurrence from the pop-up menu that appears.**

   The appointment becomes a new, stand-alone event. You can edit it to your heart's content without changing the future scheduled events.

Adding an All-Day Event

All-day events don't actually have times, but they need to appear in your schedule anyway. All-day events include birthdays, anniversaries, or Tax Day. An all-day event doesn't have to be one that happens regularly. A conference or an all-day seminar also qualifies as an all-day event.

Here's how to add an all-day event to your calendar:

1. **Choose the correct day for the event in the calendar at the upper-right side of the screen.**

   Make sure that you're in a view that shows the daily schedule — the one-day view, the one-week view, or the workweek view.

2. **Click the unnumbered line at the very top of the daily schedule, preceding the regular 30-minute time blocks.**
3. **Type the name of the all-day event and press Enter.**

Adding Holidays to Your Calendar

StarSchedule gives you the opportunity to import a list of holidays and events, which go straight into your calendar. To import StarSchedule's list of events, choose File⇨Import Holidays. An AutoPilot opens and helps you through the process of selecting and importing the holidays that you want to include, depending on your location in the world and the holidays you celebrate.

Changing the Calendar Display

Sometimes you really need to see the whole month at once, and sometimes you're focused on just getting through a single day. Ordinary paper calendars or day planners stick you with one kind of display, unless you enter all the same information again onto pages with another layout. Who has time for that?

With StarSchedule, you only have to enter your information once. You can see it displayed any way you want, and you can change that display instantly. If you like to start your week with a review of what's ahead for the next few days, show the workweek display. If you want to print out the monthly calendar and tape it up by your desk, you can do that and then revert to the daily view for a more specific look at your tasks.

Changing the calendar layout

StarSchedule offers several alternatives to the standard screen layout. If you prefer to see appointments for a week at a time, that's cool, StarSchedule can do that. If you want to get rid of the task list, StarSchedule can do that, too. The calendar layout changes as you click the following buttons in the StarSchedule toolbar, just above the main window:

- **Day:** Shows appointments for one day at a time in the main window. StarSchedule usually shows you your events this way. You see the full title of the event and a nice big display for the daily time blocks.

- **Week:** Shows one week at a time in the main window. Your events show up in each day's block, but in a shortened version, as shown in Figure 16-6. If you want to see what the shortened version stands for, just click that day and then click the daily view button. That day's schedule pops up, and you can see all the events for the day.

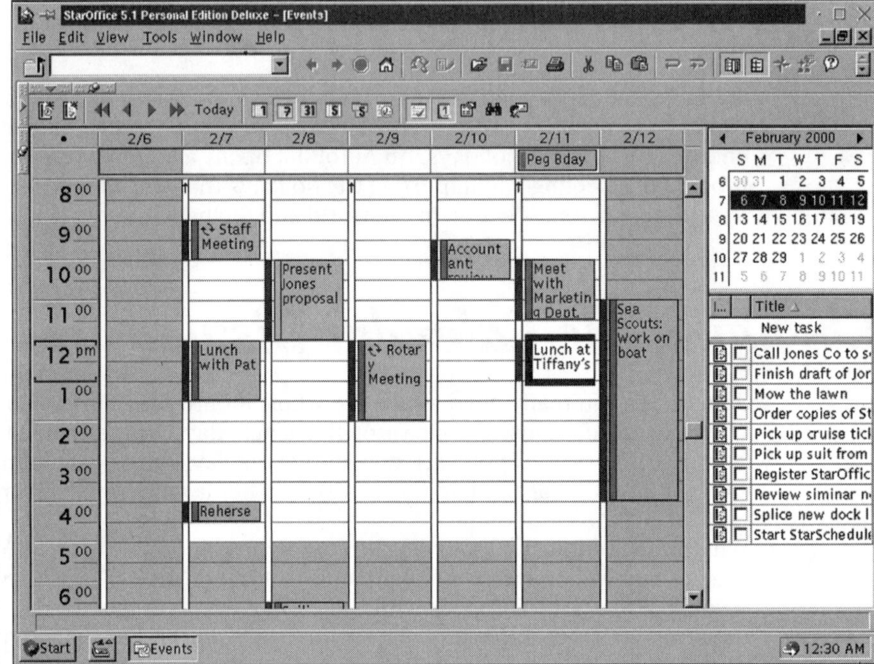

Figure 16-6: See a whole week's events at a time.

- **Month:** Shows an entire month at a time in the main window, as shown in Figure 16-7. The individual events are even shorter in the month view, but you can see which days are busier than others. Some people really like to print out the monthly or weekly view, so they have a paper copy to work with.
- **Workweek:** Shows one workweek at a time. The default workweek is Monday through Friday. If you don't schedule events on the weekends or you just don't enter them into StarSchedule, this view is good to use. It gives you slightly more room for each day, and you don't have to worry about putting an event into a weekend by mistake.
- **Multiple Workweeks:** Shows a full month at a time but only shows workdays. This is a super view for plotting out your next month's activities or for reconstructing a past month's activities for reporting what you did during work hours.
- **Details:** Displays or hides the Details panel at the bottom of the window. The Details panel shows detailed information about the selected event or task. This chapter includes several examples of the Details panel.
- **Tasks:** Enables you to display or hide the task list that normally appears in the lower-right quadrant of the StarSchedule window. Removing the task list makes room for more monthly calendars.

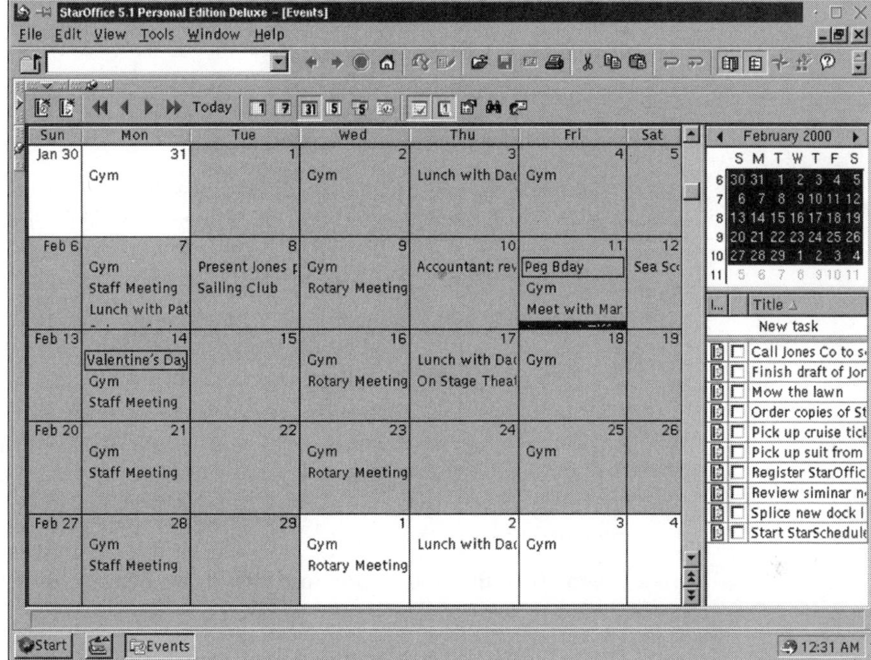

Figure 16-7: The Month view gives you a good overview of your schedule.

- **Calendar:** Enables you to display or hide the calendar that normally appears in the upper-right quadrant of the StarSchedule window. If you get rid of the calendar display, you have room for more tasks on the task list that normally appears below the calendars.

- **Address Book:** Opens the Beamer window and displays the StarOffice Address Book.

No matter how far afield you go with your calendar, you can always return to today's schedule by clicking the Today button in the toolbar.

Filtering calendar events

You can choose which events you see by applying a filter to your events. StarSchedule uses the filter to check each event to see if it meets the requirements that you set and shows you only those events that pass the test. You can set filters to show only work-related events, events on a particular date, or events with a given priority level.

To set a filter for your events, follow these steps:

1. **Choose View⇨Define Event Filter.**

   The Event Filters dialog box appears.

2. **Select or define a filter.**

   This Event Filters dialog box has three tabs:

   - **Selection:** Lets you name the current filter or select a previously defined filter. If you choose a filter that's already set up, the rules of the filter show on this tab. You can search through the filter options to find one with rules that fit your needs.
   - **Settings:** Lets you define a filter. You can filter your events based on the categories that you assigned in the Details screen, words in the title, due dates, start dates, or end dates. You can also filter based on priority levels.
   - **More:** Lets you define a filter that's more wide-ranging than the options available on the Settings tab. For example, you can set a filter that shows only events with a priority higher than 3, that use the word *Sales* in the title, and that started in April.

3. **Click OK to close the dialog box and apply the filter to the current StarSchedule view.**

   Only the events meeting the specifications of your filter appear in the events list in StarSchedule.

If you like to see your events through a filter, remember to look at your entire, unfiltered calendar once in a while. Filtering means that you're probably not seeing all of the events that you entered, and you can easily forget an event that you don't see. To remove the filter from your StarSchedule window, follow these steps:

1. **Choose View⇨Define Event Filter.**

   The Event Filters dialog box opens.

2. **Click the Selection tab and choose** `<none>` **in the Current Filter drop-down list box.**

3. **Click OK to close the dialog box.**

Sharing Calendar Data with Other Programs

If your office is networked and everyone uses StarOffice, you don't have to worry about saving and sharing your events. StarSchedule data is visible across the network because StarOffice functions as a schedule server —

assuming, of course, that your network system administrator installs the schedule StarOffice server option.

However, you probably already know that not everyone uses the same personal information manager. You may be the only person you know who uses StarSchedule, while your friends and coworkers use Microsoft Outlook or Palm Desktop or one of the many other programs that handle schedules and contacts. At times, keeping a computerized schedule may seem like more trouble than it's worth, especially when you want to share your schedule with other people. However, StarSchedule enables you to save your events list in a format that is compatible with many other calendar programs.

To share events from your schedule with another personal information manager, just follow these steps:

1. **Choose File⇨Export.**

   The Export dialog box appears.

2. **Give your event file a name and select Calendar events in the File Type drop-down list box.**
3. **Click Save.**

   StarOffice closes the Export dialog box and exports your event data to a file.

After you save a file in a format that is compatible with another person's personal information manager, you can send the file to that person as an e-mail attachment. Just open StarMail, click the paper clip button, and navigate to the events file that you just saved. StarSchedule attaches the file to your message, and you can send it off.

Printing Your Calendar

No matter how convenient an electronic schedule is, sometimes you need to see it on paper. If you carry a paper planner, you may want to print out your events pages and photocopy them to the proper size for filler pages. You may want to print out an appointment schedule for while you're on a trip and away from your computer. Or you may just like having a paper version of your schedule to scribble on while you're working during the day.

To print your StarSchedule calendar, just follow these steps:

1. **Choose File⇨Print (or press Ctrl+P) to open the regular print dialog box.**

   Just as any other time you print something from StarOffice, you can select the number of copies that you want to print or send specific information about your printer to the print manager.

2. **Click the Options button for some additional choices for printing in StarSchedule.**

   The Print Form dialog box appears, as shown in Figure 16-8, giving you all sorts of ways to print out your schedule:

   - **Day Overview:** Gives you a brief idea of your schedule for the day
   - **Week Overview:** Gives you a brief idea of your weekly schedule
   - **Month Overview:** Gives you a brief overview of your monthly schedule
   - **Event Overview:** Gives you an overview of all your scheduled events
   - **Detail View Events:** An event list with full detail on each item

3. **Select a form from the list or click the New Form button to launch an AutoPilot that leads you through the process of creating a custom form for printing your StarSchedule events and tasks.**

4. **After selecting the form, click OK.**

   The Print Form dialog box closes, and you return to the Print dialog box.

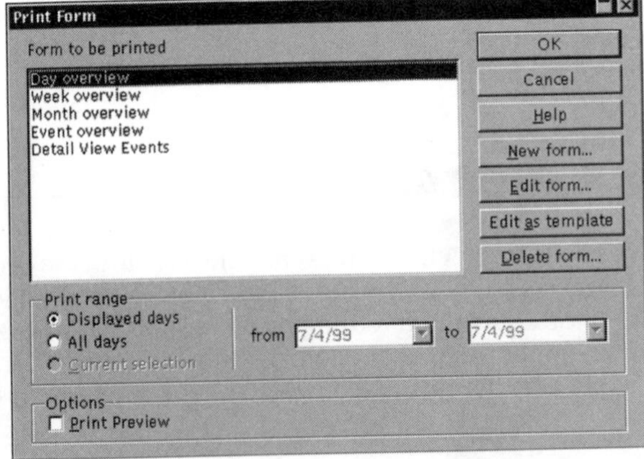

Figure 16-8: Select a form to use for printing your events and tasks.

5. **Click OK in the Print dialog box.**

   The dialog box closes, and StarSchedule sends the print job to your printer.

Part VI

Managing Your Data with StarBase

The 5th Wave
By Rich Tennant
©RICHTENNANT
WELL, OBVIOUSLY ONE OF THE CELLS IN THE NAVIGATIONAL SPREADSHEET IS CORRUPT!

In this part . . .

You need never lose an important address or phone number again — at least not if you keep track of them in StarOffice's built-in Address Book. Not only that, but the information in the StarOffice Address Book is instantly available and easy to insert into your StarOffice documents. The Address Book is an excellent example of StarOffice's database tool, StarBase, but that's not all you can do with StarBase. You can also create your own databases, complete with data entry forms and reports, to help you organize anything from a recipe list to a business inventory.

Chapter 17

Address Book: Database in Disguise

In This Chapter

- Getting acquainted with the Address Book database
- Looking into the little black book
- Updating Address Book data
- Finding names in the Address Book
- Putting Address Book information to good use

Keeping track of bits and pieces of information and retrieving them from time to time is a real chore for most human beings. But computers excel at this particular chore — provided they're equipped with a database program. StarOffice includes a powerful database called StarBase. This chapter introduces you to a StarBase database, StarOffice's built-in Address Book.

The StarOffice Address Book is a handy feature that enables you to maintain a list of contacts, complete with the usual assortment of name, address, and phone number data for each contact. The Address Book provides one of the key features of a personal information manager (PIM) program within StarOffice. In fact, when you combine the Address Book with StarSchedule (which I cover in Chapters 15 and 16), you have a very respectable PIM capability in StarOffice.

With the Address Book database, you can do the following:

- Maintain a list of your personal and business contacts.
- Search the Address Book database for contacts that match criteria that you select.
- Insert information from the Address Book into an open document.
- Go directly to the Web site of a contact in the Address Book.
- Automatically create an e-mail message addressed to a contact in the Address Book.

Best of all, the Address Book is part of the standard StarOffice installation. You don't need to create or configure the Address Book database yourself. You can just begin using it. The StarOffice Address Book even starts out with a handful of predefined contact records, so you have something to experiment with as you explore what the Address Book database can do.

Viewing Contact Records in the Address Book

You can view the Address Book database and the contact records that it contains a couple of different ways. One way is through the Address Book dialog box, as shown in Figure 17-1. To open this dialog box, choose Edit⇨Address Book from the menu bar. The Address Book dialog box displays information from the database for one contact at a time.

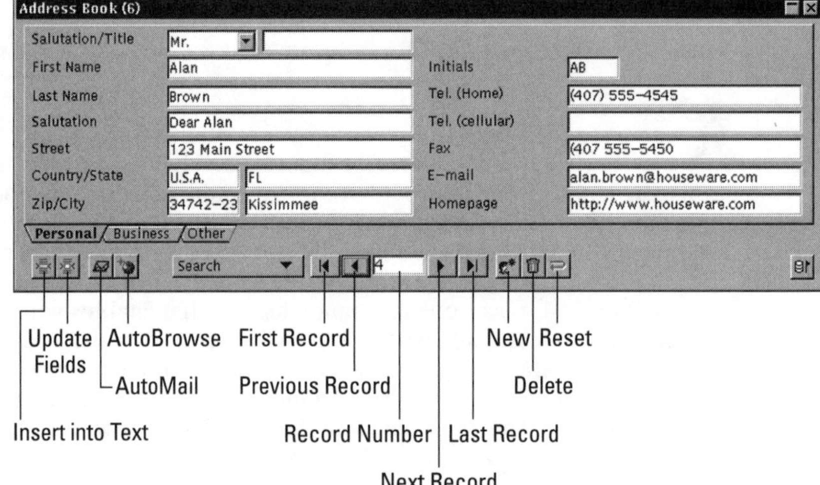

Figure 17-1: The Address Book dialog box displays one contact record at a time.

Here's a rundown on the navigation tools you will find in the Address Book dialog box:

- The number in parentheses after `Address Book` in the title bar is the number of records in your Address Book.
- If you know the number of the record that you want, type it in the Record Number text box and press Enter to go directly to that record.
- Use the Previous Record and Next Record buttons to browse back and forth through the Address Book.

- Use the First Record or Last Record buttons to move immediately to the beginning or end of the Address Book database.

- If the entry includes an e-mail address, click AutoMail to start the StarOffice e-mail tool with the address already filled in with the info from the Address Book.

- If the entry includes a URL, click AutoBrowse to go directly to the contact's Web site in the built-in Web browser.

If you want to leave the Address Book dialog box open but don't want it blocking your view of the document you're working on, double-click the title bar. The Address Book rolls up like a window shade. Double-click the title bar again to make the Address Book contents visible.

You can get more of an overview of the Address Book database by viewing the database as a table. In the StarOffice Explorer window, locate the Explore/Address book/Tables/address folder and double-click it. When you do, StarOffice displays the Address Book database in table form in a document window, as shown in Figure 17-2.

StarOffice 5.1 Personal Edition Deluxe - [Table Address book.address]

File Edit View Tools Window Help

file:///home/meadhra/Office51/e

PREFIX	FIRSTNAME	LASTNAME	TITLE	COMPANY	DEPARTMENT	ADDRESS	CITY	STATE
				Star Division Corp.		6515 Dumbarton	Fremont	CA
Ms.	Patricia	Fisher		PTH TV		2345 1st. St. NW	Washington	DC
Mr.	Alan	Brown		Houseware Inc.		123 Main Street	Kissimmee	FL
Mr.	Alan	Brown		Houseware Inc.	Controlling	123 Main Street	Kissimmee	FL
Ms.	Julie	Clark		ICM				
Mr.	Peter	Smith		Motor Works Ltd.	Sales	1234 Amsterdam .	New York	NY

Figure 17-2: The Address Book database displayed as a table.

In this view, each row of the table is a separate contact record. The columns represent the fields stored for each entry in the database. The advantage of the table view is that you can see data for multiple records at once, although you may have to scroll from left to right in order to see all the fields.

In database terminology, a *record* is all the information about one subject item in the database. *Fields* are the kinds of information stored in the database about each record. A record is made up of multiple fields, and a database *table* contains multiple records. In the Address Book database, the first name, last name, company, and city are all fields. The data in all those fields that pertains to a single contact entry constitutes a record. The database table contains all the records in the database.

Choosing View➪Current Database from within an open document window displays the Address Book database table in the Beamer window, as shown in Figure 17-3. The ability to show or hide the Beamer window means that your Address Book data can be readily available without cluttering up the screen when you're not actually using it. See Chapter 2 for the lowdown on how to use the Beamer window.

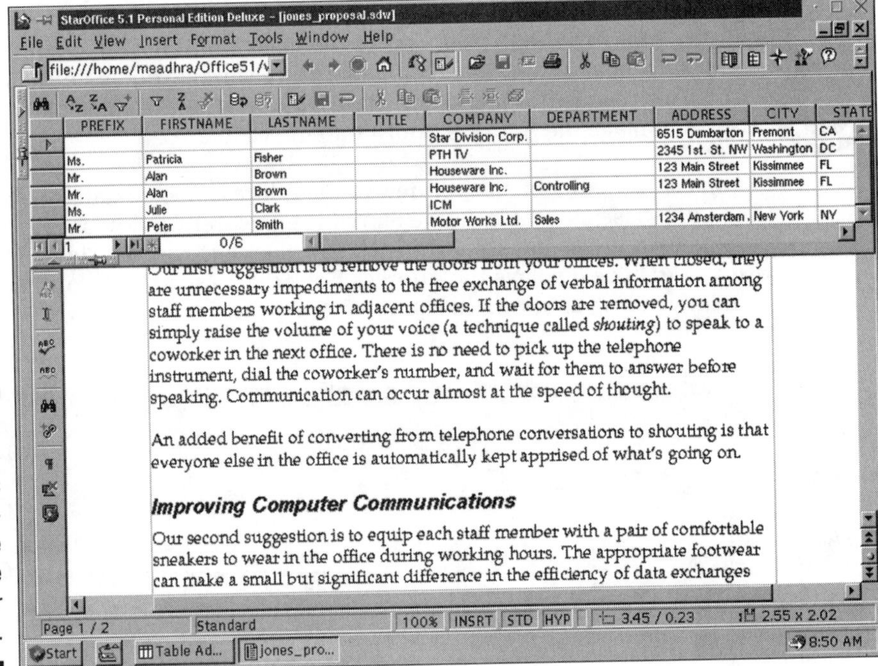

Figure 17-3: Viewing the Address Book database table in the Beamer window.

Adding and Editing Address Book Entries

The sample records that StarOffice installs in the Address Book database are fine for experimentation, but if you want to get any real use out of the Address Book, you need to add your own address entries.

To add a new record to the Address Book database by using the Address Book dialog box, follow these steps:

1. **If the Address Book dialog box is not already open, choose Edit➪Address Book from the menu bar.**

   The Address Book dialog box opens (refer to Figure 17-1).

2. **Click New.**

   StarOffice displays a new record in the Address Book dialog box. Nearly all the fields are empty, and the first field (Title) is selected.

3. **Type the information for your new contact in the text box.**

   Address Book asks for information, such as the following:

   - First Name.
   - Last Name.
   - Title. This is a drop-down list box containing `Mrs.` and `Ms.` Choose the one that's appropriate or type your own text into the field if you want something else.
   - Salutation. Use this field to indicate how you want to address this person in a letter or note. For example, enter **Dear Ms. Smith** or **Hey Bozo**.
   - Street.
   - Country.
   - State.
   - Zip.
   - City.
   - Initials.
   - Tel. (Home). This is a space for the contact's home telephone number. Business phone numbers are on the Business tab.
   - Tel. (cellular).
   - Fax.
   - E-mail.
   - Homepage. Enter the address of the contact's Web site.

4. **Press the Tab key to move the cursor to the next field.**

   Press Tab to move forward and Shift+Tab to go backward from field to field. You can leave fields blank if you want.

5. **Repeat Steps 3 and 4 until you've filled in all the personal information for the new contact.**

6. **Click the Business tab and repeat Steps 3 and 4 to fill in the business-related information for the new contact.**

   On the Business tab, Address Book asks for the following information:

   - Company.
   - Department.
   - Position.

- Tel. (Company).
- Tel. (Extension).
- Tel. (Other).
- Pager.

7. **Click the Other tab and repeat Steps 3 and 4 to fill in any remaining information for the new contact.**

   The Other tab includes four user-defined fields (space to put information of your choice) and a large Note field where you can type longer notes.

8. **Click the Next Record button to display a different record in the Address Book dialog box.**

   When you display another record in the Address Book dialog box, the StarBase adds the new information to its database. From there, you can browse the Address Book database, go back to Step 2 and begin adding another contact, or click the Close (X) button in the dialog box's title bar to close the Address Book dialog box.

The Address Book doesn't attempt to verify the validity of the data that you enter. For example, the Address Book willingly accepts *Fred* as an entry in the Zip Code field. Making sure that the information you've entered is accurate and useful is your job.

Editing an existing Address Book record is essentially the same as entering information for a new record. Just display the record that you want to edit in the Address Book dialog box and make the changes right there. Here are some tips on making those changes:

- Click once anywhere in a data field and use the normal typing and editing keys to enter or change the information.
- Double-click a field to select all the text in it. When all the text is selected, anything that you type replaces what's there already.
- When you press the Tab key or Shift+Tab in a field containing data, StarBase automatically selects that field as though you double-clicked it.
- If you've made a mistake while editing a record, click Reset to undo your edits and return the record's original data.

To delete a record from the Address Book database (one of the sample records, for example), display the record in the Address Book dialog box and then click Delete. StarBase deletes the record from its database and displays the next record in the dialog box.

Searching for Contacts in the Address Book

To find a contact record in the Address Book dialog box, you could click First Record and then keep clicking Next Record until Address Book displays the record that you're looking for. But that would be silly. Let the computer do the grunt work for you instead. Here's how:

1. **If the Address Book dialog box is not already open, choose Edit⇨Address Book from the menu bar.**

   The Address Book dialog box opens.

2. **Click Search and then choose Address Book from the drop-down list.**

   Address Book displays a blank record in which you can define a template for the search.

3. **Type the information that you want to search for into the appropriate field.**

   For example, if you want to search for all the Smiths in your Address Book, type **Smith** in the Last Name field. If you're interested only in Fred Smith, also type **Fred** in the First Name field.

   If you enter information into more than one field of the search template, Address Book searches for records that match *both* search criteria (or *all* the search criteria if you enter more than two items). In other words, in the preceding example, Address Book shows only those records for which First Name equals Fred *and* Last Name equals Smith, not all the records in which either the First Name equals Fred *or* the Last Name equals Smith.

4. **Click Start or press Enter to begin the search.**

   The title bar displays something like `Address Book (10/12)` to indicate that 10 of the 12 records in your Address Book meet your criteria — in other words, it displays the records that the search found. Information for the first record that matches the search criteria appears in the Address Book dialog box.

   Think of a search as a filter. While a search is active, Address Book shows you only the records that meet the search criteria that you provided. Use the navigation buttons described earlier to move back and forth through your Address Book. Address Book displays only the records that meet your criteria.

5. When you're done searching, click End.

Address Book reverts to displaying all the records in the database.

You can use wildcard characters to broaden or narrow your search. A question mark (?) can stand in for any single character, or an asterisk (*) for any group of characters. For example, say you can't remember how Fred spells his last name. Instead of `Smith`, you could enter `Sm*`. That search string locates all the Smiths, Smithes, and Smythes. Unfortunately, it also finds the Smathers, Smedleys, and whatnot as well. But search with `Sm?th*`, and Address Book displays only the records where Last Name starts with *Sm*, followed by any single character, followed by *th*, followed by any number of other characters.

Because Address Book doesn't format information like phone numbers or zip codes for you, pick a format that you like and stick with it. If you always enter phone numbers as (nnn) nnn-nnnn, you'll be able to do a search on area codes by using the parentheses as part of the search criteria. For example, to locate customers in southwest Ohio, you would do a search on phone numbers that match `(513)*`. If you aren't consistent about how you enter phone numbers, you won't be able to find them as easily, and you may inadvertently leave some of your best customers out of the search results.

Certain punctuation characters in a search string can result in error messages. For example, StarBase will fumble a search for a name that includes an apostrophe, such as O'Hara. Fortunately, you can easily work around the problem. Just use the `?` wildcard character in place of the problem character. A search for `O?Hara` should produce the desired results.

Using Address Book Entries in Other Programs

A stand-alone personal information manager (PIM) Address Book is nice, but when used in combination with other StarOffice tools — particularly StarWriter — it really starts to shine. You can copy selected text from Address Book and insert it into a document by using drag and drop, or you can insert entire Address Book entries into a document automatically.

Copying text with simple drag and drop

StarOffice enables you to insert information from the Address Book into a text document. This feature comes in handy if you want to write a quick letter to Aunt Jane to thank her for the birthday cookies that she sent you. Just follow these simple steps to insert selected Address Book information into a document:

1. **Create (or open) a StarWriter text document.**

   For example, begin composing your letter to Aunt Jane. Then position the insertion point cursor where you want to insert information from the Address Book.

2. **Choose Edit⇨Address Book from the menu bar if your Address Book isn't already open.**

   StarOffice displays the Address Book dialog box.

3. **Use the Search feature in the Address Book to find the person's record.**

   For this example, find Aunt Jane's record. See the "Searching for Contacts in the Address Book" section, earlier in this chapter, for instructions.

4. **Select the contents of any of the text boxes in the Address Book dialog box.**

   For the example, select the text in the Street text box.

5. **Drag and drop the selected text from the Address Book dialog box to your StarWriter document.**

   Aunt Jane's street address appears at the current cursor position in the letter that you're writing.

You can use essentially the same technique to copy information from the Address Book table displayed in the Beamer window. Instead of selecting text in a text box in the Address Book dialog box and dragging it to your document, just click the cell in the Address Book table in the Beamer window that contains the information you want to copy. Then drag that information to your document and drop it. StarOffice inserts the data from the Address Book database into your document. This technique works for copying individual bits of information, but if you want to copy an entire address record, you need to use a slightly different technique as described in the "Copying entire Address Book entries" section of this chapter.

This drag and drop technique isn't confined to Address Book and StarWriter. You can use it to copy information from Address Book into StarCalc, StarDraw, and other StarOffice tools as well. Keep the following points in mind as you work with Address Book and these StarOffice tools:

- **StarCalc:** You can drag selected text from Address Book text boxes to any individual cell in a spreadsheet.
- **StarDraw:** Dragging text from Address Book and dropping it onto the background of a StarDraw drawing creates a new text object (with whatever text defaults are currently in effect at the time) containing the text.
- **StarImpress:** This tool works like StarDraw. Dropping text from Address Book onto the slide background creates a new text object containing that text.

If you drag and drop text from the Address Book onto an open StarImpress text object, the text disappears from the Address Book. In effect, StarOffice performs a cut and paste rather than the copy and paste action you may expect. This is a problem because you're likely to want to insert Address Book information into the large text boxes that StarImpress uses to hold bulleted lists.

- **An HTML document:** Dragging text from Address Book to an HTML document works just like it does with a text document in StarWriter. As an added bonus, if you drag and drop e-mail addresses or Web page addresses, StarOffice automatically recognizes them and converts the text into an active hyperlink. Check out the Web site at `www.dummies.com/bonus/staroffice` for more information about working with HTML documents.

Copying text by dragging and dropping between Address Book and StarWriter (and the other StarOffice tools) works in reverse, too. You can select text in a StarWriter document, drag it to the Address Book dialog box, and drop it into a text box. So, if you've created a letter addressed to a new customer and decide that you want to create a new Address Book record for that contact, you can create the new record in Address Book and then drag and drop the address and other data from the letter instead of retyping it into the Address Book dialog box.

Copying entire Address Book entries

Simple drag and drop copying is great for little snippets of information, but what if you want to copy Aunt Jane's whole address from Address Book to a StarWriter document in one shot? Easy! Just follow these steps:

1. **Create (or open) a StarWriter text document and find the person's record in the Address Book dialog box.**

   Follow Steps 1, 2, and 3 in the preceding section of this chapter. As an alternative to opening the Address Book dialog box, you can display the Address Book in the Beamer window, scroll to Aunt Jane's record, and select it by clicking the row selector button at the left end of the row containing the desired record.

2. **Click the Insert into Text button in the Address Book dialog box.**

   Or, in the Beamer window, click the row selection button beside the desired record, drag it to your text document, and drop it.

   The Insert Database Columns dialog box appears, as shown in Figure 17-4.

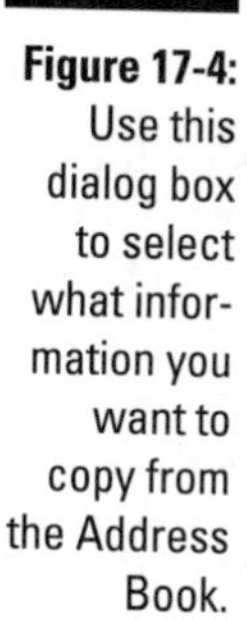

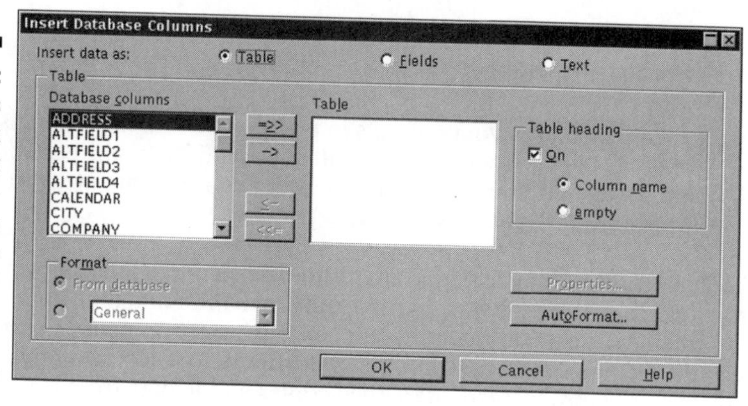

Figure 17-4: Use this dialog box to select what information you want to copy from the Address Book.

3. **Click the Text radio button next to** `Insert data as:`.

   This action tells StarOffice that you want to insert the data that you copy from the Address Book into your document as text.

4. **Locate the first information field that you want to copy in the Database Columns list and double-click it.**

   The field name appears in the text box to the right of the Database Columns list box. Note that you're selecting the database field names that contain the information you want. At this point, you can't see the information itself, but StarOffice will extract the information from the selected record when you complete the Insert in Text process.

   The Database Columns list displays field names as they're used to define the internal database structure. Those names don't always match the labels that appear beside the corresponding text boxes in the Address Book dialog box. You shouldn't have too much trouble figuring them out though. For example, STATEPROV is the field name for the information in the `State` text box, POSTALCODE is the real name for the `ZIP` field, and so forth.

5. **Repeat Step 4 as needed to select the other information that you want to copy.**

   The text in the box is editable, so you can add spaces or punctuation between fields and press Enter to insert line breaks into the information that you're copying.

6. **(Optional) Select a paragraph style from the Paragraph Style drop-down list box.**

   This step is optional. If you select a paragraph style, StarOffice automatically applies that style to the paragraphs of text that it inserts into your document. Select *none* if you don't want to use a paragraph style or if you prefer to apply styles later, in the text document.

7. Click OK.

The information that you've selected appears in your letter.

StarOffice remembers your settings in the Insert Database Columns dialog box until you change them again. So after you have the address information set up the way that you want to insert it into your documents, you don't have to start from scratch and redo it every time.

You can copy entire records from Address Book into a StarCalc spreadsheet, too. However, the process and the result are a little different from copying information into a StarWriter document. The Insert Database Columns dialog box doesn't appear to give you the opportunity to select what information you want to copy. Instead, StarOffice copies all the data from the Address Book record and inserts it into your spreadsheet automatically, placing data from one database field into one spreadsheet cell, starting with the current cell and progressing to other cells to the right.

Asking Address Book, "Who is that person?"

StarWriter enjoys a special relationship with Address Book. While working in a StarWriter text document, you can initiate a search for related information in Address Book with just a couple of mouse clicks. Here's how:

1. **In a StarWriter document, select the name of a person or company that you want to look up in the Address Book.**
2. **Right-click the selected text and choose Who Is? from the pop-up menu that appears.**

   StarOffice opens the Address Book dialog box, performs a search by using the selected text as the search criteria, and displays the results. StarOffice searches for the selected text in the Last Name field first, and if it doesn't find the text there, it searches in the Company field. If StarOffice can't find the selected text in one of those Address Book fields, it displays the message: `The address could not be found. Open address book anyway?` Click Yes to open the Address Book or No to return to your document.

Using this feature is a great way to look up more information about a person or company that you refer to in a StarWriter document. After the contact record appears in the Address Book dialog box, you can drag and drop information from the Address Book into your document.

Chapter 18

Creating a Database

In This Chapter

- Getting to know the StarBase database tool
- Creating your own database
- Working with a database table
- Working with data entry forms

Keeping track of bits and pieces of information is what a database is for. Perhaps you need to create a catalog of your music CD collection, keep a record of contributors and contributions to your charity project, or maybe maintain a membership list for an organization. StarBase is the StarOffice tool that addresses these needs — and many more besides. This chapter shows you how to set up a StarBase database and work with its tables and forms.

Introducing StarBase

StarBase, the StarOffice database tool, enables you to create and work with fully relational databases — databases that can include multiple tables of data and keep track of relationships between the data in those tables. If that doesn't mean anything to you, don't worry, you can do tons of useful database work without knowing what "relational" means.

Like all the other StarOffice tools, the StarBase database features are fully integrated into the StarOffice program. StarBase isn't a separate stand-alone program like the database programs in the other office suites.

You've probably already seen a StarBase database at work, although you might not have realized it. The StarOffice Address Book (see Chapter 17) is really a StarBase database. Even though the Address Book is just one example of the neat things you can do with StarOffice databases, the Address Book can help define some terms that you need to know to work with other databases:

- **Records.** The database term for all the bits of information about one contact is a *record.* A single record in the StarOffice Address Book, for example, contains the person's name, address, and phone number.
- **Fields.** You store the same kinds of information about each contact (the name, address, phone number, and such) — and those information categories are called *fields.* All the records in a database table contain the same fields (such as name), but each record can contain different data in that category (such as Steve, Jeanne, Sherri, or David).
- **Tables.** The standard way to store and view the information in a database is in the form of a *table* with one row for each record and a column for each field. A database can include multiple tables of related information, although simple databases (such as Address Book) are often composed of a single table.
- **Forms.** A *form* generally shows only one record at a time, cleaned up and presented in a more easily viewed format than raw data in a table. Often, you'll use a form to enter data into your database and to view individual records. The Address Book dialog box is a database form.
- **Queries.** The process of automatically selecting subsets of data from a database according to certain filtering criteria is called a *query.* The term *query* is often applied to the selection criteria, the selection process, and the resulting set of selected records. Clicking the Search button in the Address Book dialog box queries the database. You can use it to find all the contacts in your address book that live in a certain state.
- **Reports.** When you select, sort, and filter data from your database and pretty it up for easy viewing on-screen or on a printout, that's called a *report.* For example, you could create a personal phone book by generating a report that lists the names and phone numbers from the Address Book database.

If you're new to dealing with databases, you might want to read Chapter 17 and experiment with using the StarOffice Address Book before you try setting up a database of your own. When you're ready to set up your own custom database, StarBase provides the tools you need to do it. However, note that StarBase is just the toolkit for building a database. You also need a plan for building a database that stores and organizes your information in a usable format. That plan is entirely dependant on the kind of information you expect to store in your database and on how you expect to access and use that information.

Creating a Database File

The first thing you need to do to set up a custom StarBase database of your own is to create a new database file. You can do so by following these steps:

1. **Choose File⇨New⇨Database or right-click the StarOffice desktop and choose New⇨Database from the pop-up menu that appears.**

   The Properties of <Database> dialog box appears.

2. **Click the General tab of the Properties dialog box and enter a name for the new database in the text box.**

3. **Click the Type tab of the Properties dialog box.**

   The options shown in Figure 18-1 appear. Notice that the title bar of the dialog box now reads "Properties of" and the name you gave the database in the previous step.

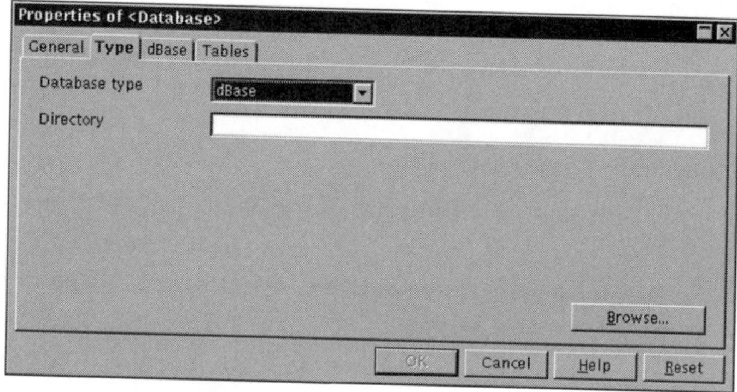

Figure 18-1: Selecting the proper database type is important.

4. **Select a file format for your database from the Database Type drop-down list box.**

   Normally, you will select the dBase type. It's the default format for StarBase, and it's widely supported by many other database programs. StarBase also supports ODBC, DB2, JDBC, and plain text formats, in case you need one of those formats. The choice you make here may affect some of the options available to you later.

   The Windows version of StarOffice gives you the option of creating your database file using a proprietary StarBase file format in addition to the formats supported by the other versions of StarOffice.

5. **Enter the directory where you want to create the database file in the Directory text box.**

   Instead of typing the directory name, you can click the Browse button to open the Select Directory dialog box, where you can browse the directory tree to locate the directory you want to use. Click OK to close the Select Directory dialog box and insert the selected directory name in the Directory box back in the Properties dialog box.

6. **Click OK.**

   StarOffice closes the Properties dialog box and returns you to the StarOffice desktop. A new database icon appears on the desktop with the name you gave it in the General tab of the Properties dialog box.

Creating a table

Creating a new database is just the beginning. The database alone isn't much use without any data in it. StarBase stores its data in tables that are part of a database, so before you can enter any data, you need to create a table to hold your information.

The simplest way to create a database table is to use the Table AutoPilot. Just follow these steps:

1. **Choose File⇨AutoPilot⇨Table.**

   StarOffice displays the first page of the Table AutoPilot, as shown in Figure 18-2.

2. **In the Database drop-down list box, select the database to which you want to add the new table.**

   Select the new database you created earlier if you wish to continue building your new database.

3. **Select either Business or Personal in the drop-down list box in the Table area.**

   The list of predefined table types in the lower list box changes to reflect your selection.

   - Select Business to display an assortment of business-related table types, such as Customers, Employees, Invoices, and Products.
   - Select Personal to list table types, such as HouseholdInventory, MusicCollection, and Recipes.

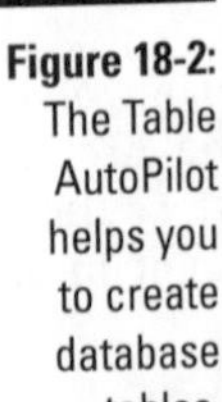

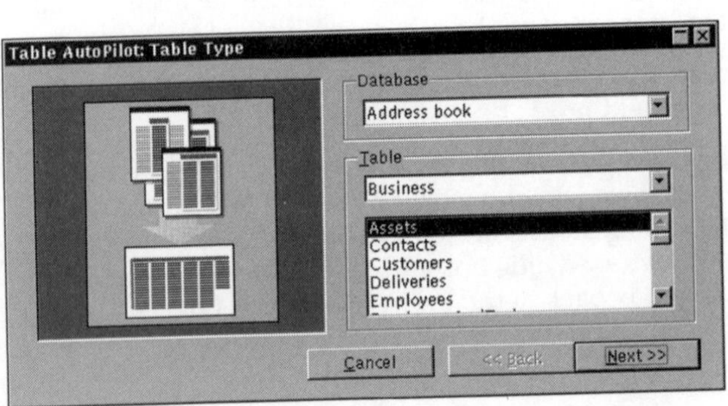

Figure 18-2: The Table AutoPilot helps you to create database tables.

4. **Select a table type from the lower list box in the Table area, and click Next.**

   The selection you make here determines what predefined fields the AutoPilot makes available for you to include in your new table. Don't worry if you don't see the exact table you want to create on the list. Just pick a table type that looks like it offers an assortment of fields that you need. For example, the Business Contacts or Personal Addresses table types offer fields such as name, address, phone number, fax number, and so on. The Business Assets table type, on the other hand, includes fields such as make, model, serial number, purchase price, and current value. You don't have to use all the fields that are available in a table type, and you can always change the details of your new table later. When you click Next, the AutoPilot advances to the next page, as shown in Figure 18-3.

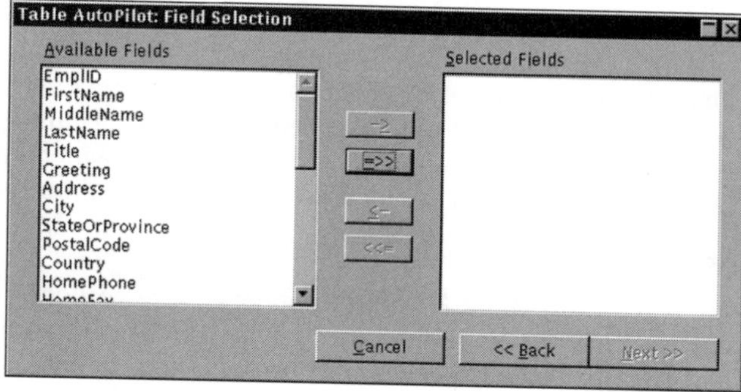

Figure 18-3: Select the fields you need in your table.

5. **Select the fields you want to include in your table from the Available Fields list.**

   To include a field in your table, click the field name in the Available Fields list and then click the -> button to add it to the Selected Fields list. To add all the available fields, click the => button. To remove a field from the Selected Fields list, click the field name and then click the <- button.

   Certain fields are set up to accept only certain kinds of data. For example, a PurchasePrice field is obviously designed to hold a number and display it as currency. StarBase won't let you type text into such a field, even if you rename the field to something like "Notes." When you select fields to include in your table, be sure to pick fields that are intended to hold the kind of data you plan to store in them. You can rename the fields in your table, but you can't easily change the kind of data the fields can store.

6. **When the list of Selected Fields is complete, click Next.**

   The Table AutoPilot displays the Customization page, as shown in Figure 18-4.

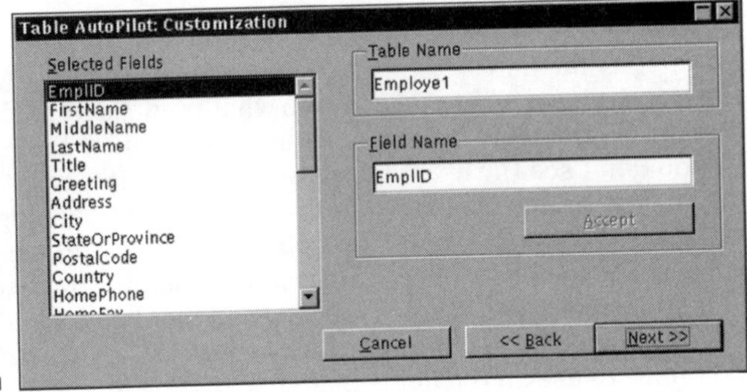

Figure 18-4: You can customize the field names added by the Table AutoPilot.

7. **Edit the contents of the Table Name and Field Name boxes for the selected fields, if you want.**

   To change the name of the table, simply edit the text in the Table Name box. To change the name of any of the selected fields, click the field name you wish to change in the Selected Fields list, edit the text in the Field Name box, then click Accept to record the change. For example, you might prefer just "State" to the default field name "StateOrProvince." As you change each field name, you see its name change in the Selected Fields list.

8. **Click Next.**

   The final page of the Table AutoPilot appears. Here you choose what you want to do with your new table once StarBase creates it. Your choices are: Insert Data in Table (in other words, begin adding data right away), Show Table (display your new table), or Do Not Show Table (create and save the table without displaying it).

9. **Make a selection by clicking a radio button and then click Create.**

   The Table AutoPilot creates your new database table according to your specifications.

   If you choose Insert Data in Table, the table is displayed and is ready for you to begin entering information. The new table is similar to the one shown in Figure 18-5, but the data area is blank with only one row of blank cells in the table. Skip ahead to "Entering records into a table" to find out how to proceed.

Displaying a database table

If you want to enter data into an existing table, or just view the contents of a database table, you need to open the table first. You can display a table by following these steps:

1. **Double-click the Database icon on the StarOffice desktop.**

   StarOffice opens the database and displays icons for Forms, Queries, Reports, and Tables.

2. **Double-click the Tables icon.**

   Icons for the tables in your database appear.

3. **Double-click the icon for the table you'd like to work with.**

   The table appears in a StarBase document window as shown in Figure 18-5. (The table in Figure 18-5 contains a few records for demonstration purposes.) Notice that the table looks like a spreadsheet grid of rows and columns with data cells at each row/column intersection. Each row represents one record in the database table. Each field appears as one of the columns in the grid with its field name at the top.

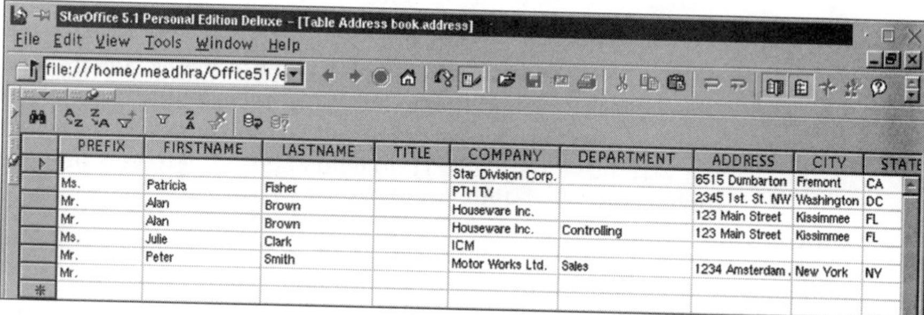

Figure 18-5: A StarBase database table open for view.

Sometimes, when you open a database table, StarBase displays the table in read-only mode, which means you can't edit or alter the table. Don't let this throw you — the read-only mode is not an indication of a problem with file or directory access permissions. You just need to click the Edit File button on the Function toolbar to switch from read-only mode to edit mode before attempting to alter the table.

Entering records into a table

When you're ready to begin adding records to your table, just follow these steps:

1. **(Optional) Click the Edit button on the StarOffice Function toolbar.**

   If a `(read only)` label appears in the Table's title bar, you need to switch to edit mode before you can enter data into your table. When you click the Edit button, the read only notation disappears and a new, blank row of cells (labeled with an asterisk [*] on the row button) appears in the table.

2. **Click the cell where you want to begin entering data, and type in your entry.**

   When you click a cell in the blank row of cells, the asterisk on the row button changes to an arrowhead to indicate the record is selected. When you begin entering data in one of the cells in the row, a pencil symbol appears on the row button to indicate that the record is being edited and a new blank row appears at the bottom of the table.

3. **Press Tab to move the insertion point cursor to the next cell to the right (or Shift+Tab to move the cursor to the next cell to the left) and enter data into that field.**

   Continue entering data into all desired fields in the record. Use the Tab and Shift+Tab keys to move the insertion point cursor from field to field. The table scrolls automatically to bring more fields into view. When you've entered information into the last field in the record, press Tab once more to go to the first field of the next record.

   Make sure you enter the appropriate kind of data into each field of the database record. StarBase displays an error message if you attempt to enter text into a field that is set up to accept only numbers, for example. StarBase can't actually validate the accuracy of the data you enter, but it can verify that data in certain fields conforms to certain general formats such as only text, only numbers, or a date.

4. **When you're done entering data, click the Save button on the Function toolbar.**

   StarBase records your changes in the database file. The database table remains open. If you want to close it, click the table window's Close (X) button.

Although these steps describe the process of adding new data to a database table, you can use exactly the same technique to edit existing data. When you click a cell in the database table that contains data, that data is highlighted. To replace it with new data, just begin typing. Click in the highlighted data again to get an insertion point cursor in the data cell that you can use to edit the existing text instead of replacing it.

Don't wait until you're finished entering a large amount of data before saving your work. Click the Save button or press Ctrl+S often while entering data into the table. I suggest saving after entering or editing each record. Saving only takes a second, and that way you won't lose any data if you have a power outage or software problem.

Creating a Data Entry Form

Viewing and entering data in a table isn't a bad way to get an overview of your information, but it's a pretty ugly way to work. That's why StarBase lets you create forms for entering, viewing, and editing your data tables.

The simplest way to create a form is that handy AutoPilot. Here are the steps to use:

1. **Choose File⇨AutoPilot⇨Form from the menu bar.**

   The first page of the Form AutoPilot appears. It looks very similar to the Table AutoPilot (refer to Figure 18-4).

2. **Select the database for which you want to create a form from the Database drop-down list box.**

   After you select the database, the AutoPilot shows the tables that are available in that database listed in the Data Source list.

3. **Select the database table to which this form will apply from the Data Source list box, and then click Next.**

   The Form AutoPilot advances to the Field Selection. Again, this page of the Form AutoPilot is very similar to its counterpart in the Table AutoPilot (refer to Figure 18-4).

4. **Select the fields you want to include on your form from the Available Fields list.**

   To include a field in your form, click the field name in the Available Fields list and then click the -> button to add it to the Chosen Fields list. To add all the available fields, click the => button. To remove a field from the Chosen Fields list, click the field name and then click the <- button.

5. **When the Chosen Fields list is complete, click Next.**

   The Field Alignment page of the Form AutoPilot appears, as shown in Figure 18-6.

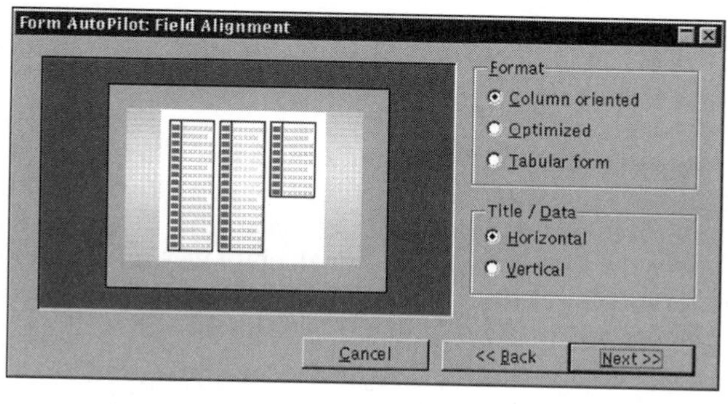

Figure 18-6: Select how you want the Form AutoPilot to arrange fields on your form.

6. **Select the Format (Column oriented, Optimized, or Tabular form) and Title/Data (Horizontal or Vertical) options you prefer.**

   The preview image at the left of the dialog box shows you the effect of your choices.

7. **When you're satisfied with your choices, click Next.**

   The Form AutoPilot advances to the Styles page shown in Figure 18-7.

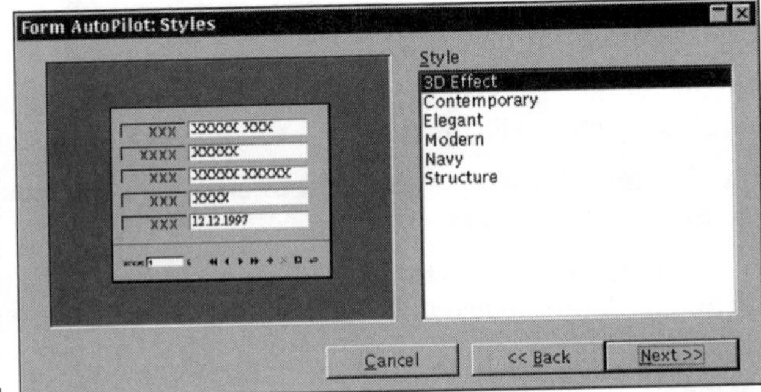

Figure 18-7: Select a style to determine the appearance of your form.

8. **Select a style for your form from the Style list box and then click Next.**

   Again, you get a mini-preview of your form on the left side of the dialog box that reflects your selection in the Style list. When you click Next, the final page of the Form AutoPilot appears.

9. **Edit the name of the form in the Document Title box.**

   This is your opportunity to give your form a different name if you don't like the default name StarBase came up with. Simply click in the Document Title box and type the new name.

10. **Select an option in the After Completion area and then click Create.**

    The After Completion options give you the choice of using your document right away or simply storing it for later use. Choose which you'd like to do; then click Create to finish creating your new form. The Form AutoPilot creates your new form according to your specifications. See Figure 18-8 for an example. Be patient — creating and loading a new form can take a while.

When you create a form for entering and viewing data in a table, the person using the form has access to only the fields that you've added. You don't have to include all the fields from your database table in a form. For example, you might have a data table that includes all employee information, but you could create forms that exclude sensitive fields like salary or home address and phone number for use by other employees.

Entering Records Using a Form

To enter new records into your database using a form, you first need to open the form, which is essentially the same process as opening a table. First, double-click your Database icon in the StarDesktop window. Next, double-click the Forms icon in the database window that appears, and finally, double-click the icon for the form you want to use in the Forms window. StarOffice opens the selected form, as shown in Figure 18-8.

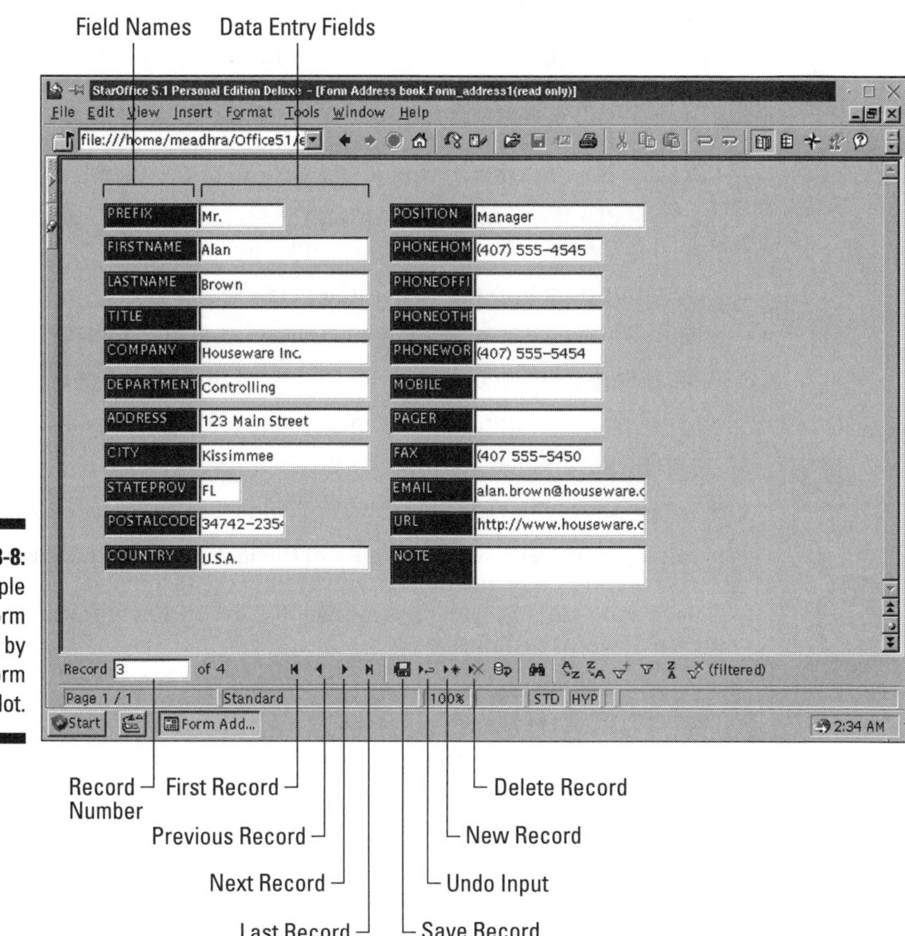

Figure 18-8: A sample form created by the Form AutoPilot.

Once you have the form open, you can use the form to

- View information in the data table one record at a time
- Edit the data records you view
- Add new records to your data table

Basically, you can do the same things with a database form that you can do with the Address Book dialog box. (See Chapter 17 for more information.) In fact, the Address Book dialog box is just a database form for the address book database that appears in a dialog box instead of a document window.

Use the First Record, Previous Record, Next Record and Last Record buttons to browse through records in your database table and display them in the form. To create a new record and add it to your database, follow these steps:

1. **Click the New Record button at the bottom of the form.**

   StarBase displays a blank record with the text insertion cursor positioned in the first field, ready to accept your data.

2. **Enter your data into the field, then press Tab or Enter.**

   StarBase moves the insertion point cursor to the next field.

3. **Repeat Step 2 as needed to enter data into the other fields of the form.**

   You can use Shift+Tab or Shift+Enter to move back to a previous field.

4. **Click the Save Record button.**

   StarBase saves the current record and adds it to your database table.

If you press Tab after entering data in the last field of a record, StarBase automatically saves the current record and creates a new record for you. This is equivalent to clicking the Save Record button followed by clicking the New Record button.

You can also edit the currently displayed record. Simply click any field and make any necessary changes, then click Save Record or move to another record with one of the navigation buttons to save your edits. If you make a mistake and want to start over, click Undo Input before you save or move to another record to have StarBase revert back to the original unedited data in the record.

Chapter 19

Reporting on Your Database

In This Chapter

- Constructing database queries
- Viewing and using a database query
- Performing quickie queries on tables
- Generating a report from your database
- Working with database reports

Storing information in a database is a smart thing to do. But information doesn't really do you much good tucked away out of sight in your database. Information is only useful when you can access it quickly and easily. This chapter shows you how to pull information out of your database using queries and reports.

Creating a Query

Database tables present the information stored in your database in raw format; the data's there, but hardly formatted for easy access. You would have to do a lot of scrolling back and forth and up and down to see all the fields and records in a typical database table. To make matters worse, many of the longer fields are truncated in the database table, which means that some information is hidden from view.

Forms aren't a much better solution for accessing information in your database. The information in each record is easier to see and work with in a form, but forms display only one record at a time and paging through each of the records in a large database is hardly an efficient way to find something.

A query enables you to ask a question about the contents of your database and view a subset of the information in it that answers your question. For example, you can construct a query to find all the contacts in your address book that live in the state of Indiana. The query searches all the records in your address book database table and filters out any records that don't have

Indiana in the State field. Then you can view only the records for those contacts that meet your search criteria. You don't have to go rooting through the database looking for those records yourself — just let a StarBase query do the searching and filtering for you.

You can create a query in StarBase that creates a special sub-table of your main data table, one that contains just the fields you want to view and only the records that meet the conditions that you specify. To create a query, follow these steps:

1. **Choose File⇨AutoPilot⇨Query from the menu bar.**

   StarOffice displays the first page of the Query AutoPilot, as shown in Figure 19-1.

Figure 19-1: The Query AutoPilot constructs a database query for you.

2. **Select the database you want to query from the Database drop-down list box.**

   The Query AutoPilot updates the Table Name list to show the tables in the selected database.

3. **Select the table containing the information you want to query from the Table Name list box, then click Next.**

   The Query AutoPilot displays the Field Selection page.

4. **Select the fields to include in the query.**

   All of the fields in your table are shown in the Available Fields list box on the left. If you want your query to display all of them, click => to put them all in the Chosen Fields list box on the right. You can select individual fields by clicking a field name in the Available Fields list box, then clicking -> to add it to the Chosen Fields list box. Click a field name in the Chosen Fields list box and click <- to remove it from the list.

5. **After selecting the fields to include, click Next.**

   The Filter page of the Query AutoPilot appears as shown in Figure 19-2.

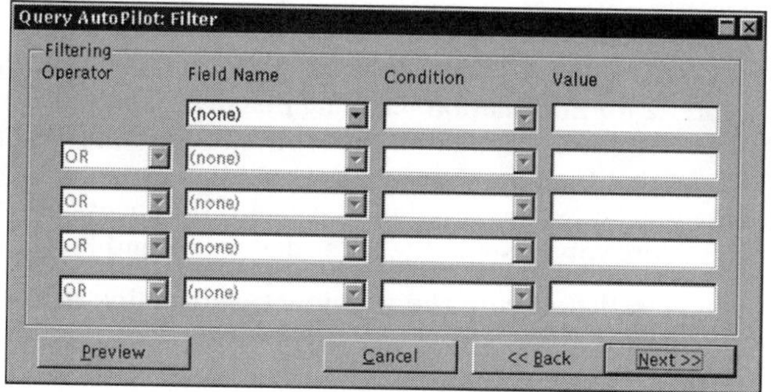

Figure 19-2: The filter criteria is what makes a query work.

6. **Define a filter criteria by selecting a Field Name and Condition from the respective drop-down list boxes and entering appropriate text or numbers in the Value box.**

   This page of the Query AutoPilot is where you set filters that limit the records that appear in your query. For example, to get a list of all customers in Indianapolis, choose City in the first Field Name drop-down list box, choose = as the condition, and type **Indianapolis** as the value. This tells StarBase to display only those records whose City field contains the word Indianapolis. The Field Name field is the database field you want the query to check. The condition determines how the contents of that field should compare to the value. Usually you choose equals (=) in the Condition box, but you have a choice of other mathematical expressions, such as <, >, =>, <> (not equal), and status conditions, such as like, not like, null (empty), and not null (not empty). The value is the text, number, date, or whatever the filter tests each field against.

   When StarOffice searches your database looking for matches to your query criteria, it's very literal about what matches and what doesn't. Abbreviations and misspellings of a search value fail the test and are excluded from the query results. If you abbreviate Indianapolis as *Indpls* or *Indy,* you have to add separate search criteria for those variations if you want them included in the query. If you use the like condition instead of =, you can use the ? and * wildcard characters in the search value. As a result, you can locate Indianapolis and its variations by using Ind* as the search value.

7. **Add more filters if needed.**

   You can build more elaborate queries by using additional filters. For example, to narrow our example query down to just those Indianapolis customers who have spent $10,000 or more with you this year, you add another filter with the word `AND` as the operator, YTD Sales as the Field Name, >= as the Condition, and **10,000** as the Value.

8. **Click Preview.**

   StarBase displays the results of your query in the Beamer window. (See Chapter 2 for information on using Beamer.) Only the records that match the filter criteria appear in the table shown in the Beamer window. Check to see that the query selects the data you expect (and doesn't select data you know you shouldn't be seeing). If necessary, modify or add to the filters you've set in the Filter dialog box and Preview again.

9. **When you're satisfied with the preview results, click Next to continue.**

   The Sort page of the Query AutoPilot appears, as shown in Figure 19-3.

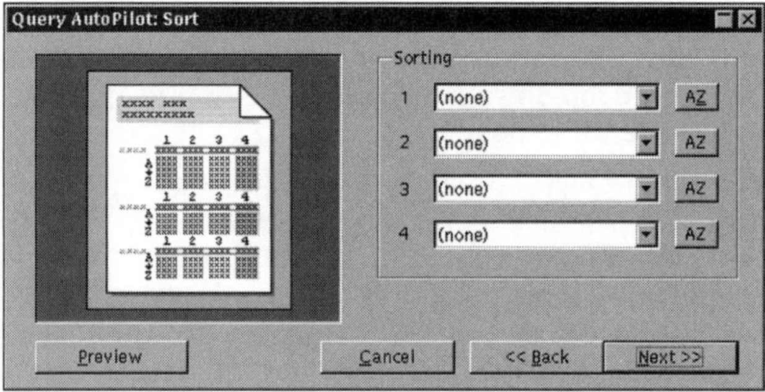

Figure 19-3: The Query AutoPilot enables you to sort the results of the query.

10. **Select the fields you want to sort and click the button beside each field list box to select ascending or descending order.**

    This determines the order in which your information is displayed. For example, to sort the query results according to the company name, choose Company in the first drop-down list box. To sort in reverse order, click the AZ button to change it to ZA. To apply multiple sorts (on Company Name and on Last Name, for example), choose additional fields and specify sort orders in the second through fourth Sorting list boxes. When the program encounters multiple records with identical values in the first sort field, it uses the values in the second through fourth sort fields to break the ties and to determine the order to display the query results. Click Preview at any time to check the results of your sorting selections.

11. **Click Next when you're finished setting sort options.**

    The final page of the Query AutoPilot appears.

12. **Edit the name of the Query in the Query title box and select a completion option.**

    In the Complete dialog box, give your new query a name in the Query Title text box. Try to keep the name short, but descriptive. It's usually easier to describe a query by its intended use (Custom mailing list) rather than by the query criteria. Then click the Execute query radio button to save your query and view it right away, or click the Store query radio button to save your query without using it.

13. **Click Create.**

    StarBase generates the query and stores it for future use. Depending on the option you selected in the After Completion area, StarBase applies the query to your database table and displays the results. The results appear as a database table except that only the records that match the filter criteria and the fields you specified on the Field Selection page of the Query AutoPilot appear in the table.

Displaying the Results of an Existing Query

After you've created a query, you can apply it to your database and view the results again at any time. StarBase stores the filters, sort order, and other options you chose when you created the query and reapplies them to the database each time you view the query.

Follow these steps to view an existing query:

1. **Double-click the database icon on the StarDesktop to open the database.**
2. **Double-click the Queries icon to see a desktop-like view of all the queries you've defined for the database.**
3. **Double-click the icon for the query you want to view.**

   StarBase applies the conditions you've set for the query and displays all the data that meets the query conditions in table format in a separate document window.

After the query appears on-screen, you can work with it just like a regular database table (see Chapter 18). You can scroll and view different portions of the query table. You can edit records, add new records, delete records, and anything else you can do with the main table. Any changes you make to the query table are reflected in the main database table. In effect, you are working with the main database table; the query just hides some of the records and fields from view, thus making it easier to work with a manageable sub-set of the data in the whole table.

Ad Hoc Sorting and Filtering Table Views

Any time you're viewing a database table or query (see Figure 19-4) or a database in Beamer, you can use the field name headers and toolbar buttons to temporarily sort the data. In effect, you can create ad hoc (quick, temporary) queries to filter and sort information in the table. This doesn't affect the actual data in the database table, it simply changes your current view of it. The following list summarizes what some of the toolbar buttons do.

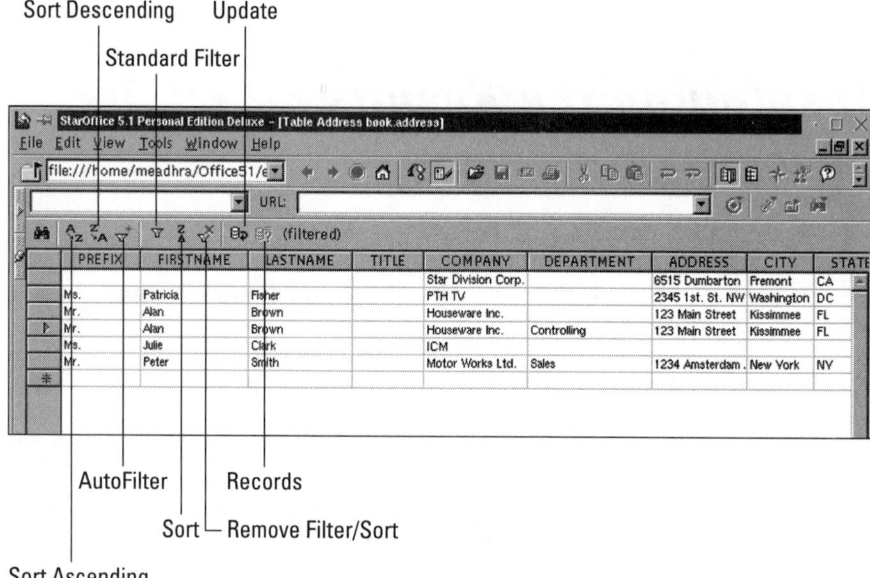

Figure 19-4: Sort and filter options in any database table window.

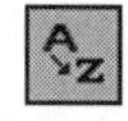

- **Sort Ascending:** Sorts the displayed information in ascending alphabetical order (A to Z).

- **Sort Descending:** Sorts the displayed information in descending alphabetical order (Z to A).

By default, StarBase performs the sort on the first field on the left. To sort on a different field, click its field name at the top of the column, then click Sort Ascending or Sort Descending.

- **AutoFilter:** Click any cell containing data and then click AutoFilter to have StarBase filter out records for which the chosen field's value doesn't match. For example, if you're viewing your customer list and just want to see customers located downtown, find any downtown customer, click the cell containing the customer's zip code, and then click AutoFilter. StarBase displays only the customers whose zip code matches the zip code you selected. You can repeatedly select data and click AutoFilter to further narrow the selection of displayed records.

- **Default Filter:** Brings up the Filter dialog box in which you can set more elaborate filters than are possible with the AutoFilter button (see Figure 19-5). If you select a cell before clicking the Default Filter button, StarBase pre-sets the search criteria in the Default Filter dialog box to match the contents of that cell. Modify or add to the criteria if you wish and then click OK.
- **Sort:** Brings up the Sort Order dialog box (see Figure 19-6) where you can set more specific sort conditions than you can with the other Sort buttons.
- **Remove Filter/Sort:** Removes any sort or filter criteria and displays all the records in the table.

Clicking the Remove Filter/Sort button when viewing a query not only removes any filters and sorts applied with the toolbar buttons, it also removes any query filter and sort criteria. StarBase displays *all* the data in the table.

- **Refresh:** Updates display from source data file. When you make changes, click this button to display the most recent information from the source data file.
- **Records:** Click this to update the display of the total number of records (this button is usually grayed out).

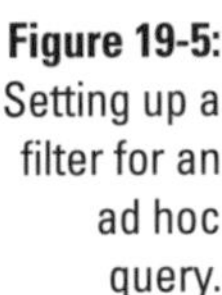

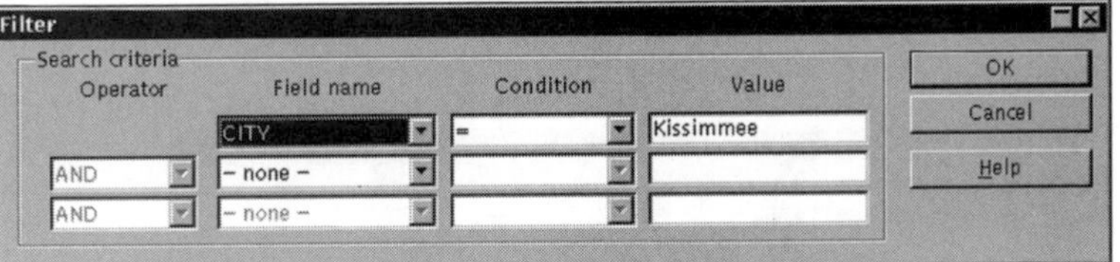

Figure 19-5: Setting up a filter for an ad hoc query.

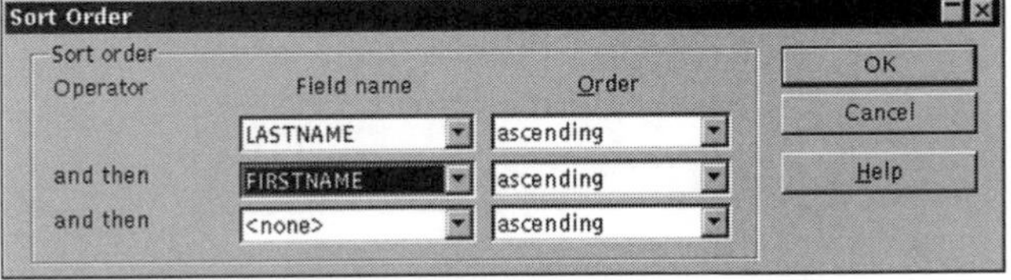

Figure 19-6: Defining an ad hoc sort on multiple fields.

Creating a New Report

The table view of your data is handy for getting a quick look, but it isn't polished enough for reports or presentations. StarBase reports let you view and print your information in much more polished and better organized form.

To create a report, follow these steps:

1. **Choose File⇨AutoPilot⇨Report from the menu bar.**

   StarOffice displays the first page of the Report AutoPilot.

2. **Select the database you want to report on from the Database drop-down list box.**

   The Report AutoPilot updates the Table Name list to show the tables in the selected database. Note that queries you've defined for this database appear in the list along with the tables. By choosing a query rather than one of the main tables, you can create filtered and sorted reports very easily.

3. **Select the table containing the information you want to report on from the Table Name list box, then click Next.**

   The Report AutoPilot displays the Field Selection page.

4. **Select the fields to include in the query.**

   All of the fields in your table are shown in the Available Fields list box on the left. If you want your query to display all of them, click => to put them all in the Chosen Fields list box on the right. You can select an individual field by clicking a field name in the Available Fields list box and then clicking -> to add it to the Chosen Fields list box. Click a field name in the Chosen Fields list box and click <- to remove it from the list.

5. **After selecting the fields to include, click Next.**

   The Outline page of the Report AutoPilot appears as shown in Figure 19-7.

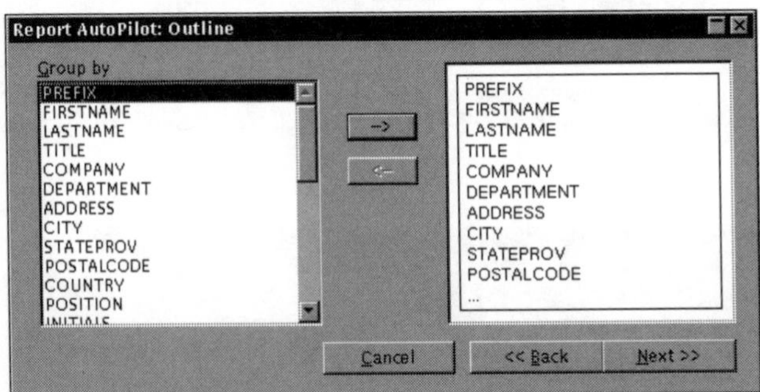

Figure 19-7: The outline page of the Report AutoPilot is where you organize the report into groupings.

6. **Select fields to use as outline groupings.**

   This page of the Report AutoPilot is where you create groups (or breaks) in your report. With no groups, the report includes each record in whatever order the record is listed in the data table. If you add groups to the report, the report generator creates a "break" every time the group field changes. For example, to list your contact database by city, click the click the City field, then click => to add a City group to the preview on the right. After doing this, your report displays a header for the first city alphabetically in the data table, with all of the contacts in that city underneath it, then another header for the next city and so on. You can add up to four groups to each of your reports.

Notice that as you add fields as groups, the field is removed from the main list of data to be displayed. Since the field appears as a header, there's no need to repeat it in the body of the report. This can make for more compact reports if you've got a lot of fields to squeeze into one report.

7. **When you're satisfied with your groups, click Next.**

   The Sort page of the Report AutoPilot appears. It looks and functions the same as the sort page in the Query AutoPilot (refer to Figure 19-3).

8. **Select the fields you want to sort and click the button beside each field list box to select ascending or descending order, then click Next.**

   The Report AutoPilot advances to the Style Selection page.

9. **Select an Orientation (Landscape or Portrait) and a Layout (Table or Column) for your report.**

   The preview on the left shows you approximately what your report will look like.

10. **Click Next.**

    The Format Style page of the Report AutoPilot appears, as shown in Figure 19-8.

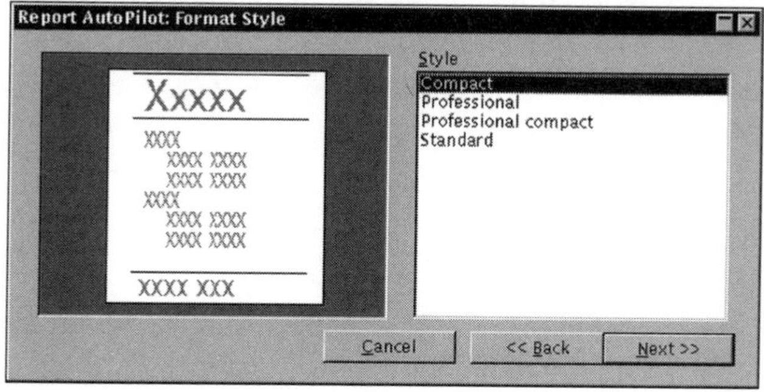

Figure 19-8: The Format Style page controls the page format of your report.

11. **Select a Style for your report, then click Next.**

    The final page of the Report AutoPilot appears.

12. **Edit the name of the report in the Report Name box and select a completion option.**

Type a Report Name (which will appear under the report's icon and as the report's heading) and choose either of the Show Report or Store Report radio buttons, depending on whether you would like to save your report and then view (or print) it right away or just save it for later use.

13. **Click Create.**

    StarBase stores the report settings for future use. Depending on the option you selected in the After Completion area, StarBase may also generate a report using the report definition you just created and display that report in a document window. Be patient, generating the report may take a while.

If you want to print your report, all you need to do is choose File⇨Print or click the Print button on the Function toolbar while the report is displayed on-screen.

Editing an Existing Report

Let's say you've created a really great-looking . . . well, almost great-looking report. To achieve total perfection, the report needs a few tweaks and adjustments. A graphic of your logo here, a headline moved there, that kind of thing. The report generator won't help you with that, but there's still a way (a pretty easy way, in fact).

To edit an existing report follow these steps:

1. **Display the StarDesktop window and double-click the icon for the database you want to work with.**

   StarOffice opens a new window and displays icons for the components of the selected database.

2. **Double-click the Reports icon.**

   StarOffice displays icons for all the reports associated with the selected database.

3. **Right-click the report you want to edit, then click Report Design on the pop-up menu that appears.**

   The StarBase report editor opens in a new document window, and looks suspiciously like a StarWriter document, which in fact it is. You can apply any style and formatting that you would apply in a regular StarWriter document.

4. **Edit and format your report using any of the normal StarWriter formatting tools.**

   See Chapters 3 and 4 for information on formatting documents with StarWriter.

5. **Choose File⇨Save As and rename the edited report in the Save As dialog box, then click Save.**

   This saves your report under a new name with a new icon that appears when you open the Reports section of your database.

Part VII
Getting on the Internet

"Would you like Web or non-Web?"

In this part . . .

StarOffice helps you make the most of your connection to the Internet or to a local intranet. The chapters in this part of a book show you how to browse the Web, send and receive e-mail, and participate in newsgroup discussions — all from within StarOffice.

Chapter 20

Browsing the Web

In This Chapter

- Getting connected — let me count the ways
- Telling StarOffice how to use your system's Internet connections
- Browsing the Web with StarOffice
- Adjusting the StarOffice Web browser's settings

Connecting a computer to a network — a local intranet or LAN, the Internet, or both — instead of having an isolated, stand-alone machine is increasingly common these days. StarOffice includes a number of built-in features that enable you to take advantage of the power of that network connection.

- The StarOffice Web browser enables you to view Web pages from the Internet, a local intranet, or HTML documents stored on your local hard drive.
- StarMail lets you send and receive e-mail over the Internet and on some of the most common LAN e-mail systems.
- StarDiscuss enables you to participate in Internet newsgroup discussions.
- StarWriter is an HTML document editor (in addition to being a full-fledged word processing tool) that you can use to create your own Web pages.

This chapter focuses on the StarOffice browser. See Chapter 21 for information on how to use StarMail and StarDiscuss. For information on using StarWriter to create HTML documents, see the bonus chapter on the Web at `www.dummies.com/bonus/staroffice`.

Configuring StarOffice for Internet Access

Before you begin using any of StarOffice's Internet access features, you need to tell StarOffice a little bit about how your computer connects to the

Internet. And how much you have to tell StarOffice depends on whether your computer is hooked up to an intranet or a LAN connected to the Internet, or whether your computer uses a dial-up connection to the Internet.

You, or whoever installed StarOffice, may have taken care of configuring the basic Internet settings, if you responded to the prompts from the Internet Setup AutoPilot that appear automatically when you first run StarOffice. If you skipped the Internet Setup AutoPilot when it first appeared, you can rerun it any time you want by choosing File⇨AutoPilot⇨Internet Setup. StarOffice opens the Internet Settings dialog box and begins prompting you for the information it needs. Simply make selections and enter information as requested by the AutoPilot, and then click Next to advance to the next page. Click Create on the last page of the Internet Setup AutoPilot to close the Internet Settings dialog box and record the settings.

The Internet Setup AutoPilot covers the basics of configuring StarOffice for Internet access and setting up e-mail and newsgroup accounts. You can also adjust the Internet access settings manually, which you may want to do if you need to customize some details not covered by the AutoPilot or you just don't want to go through the AutoPilot pages for e-mail and news to complete the Internet access setup.

Configuring for an intranet or LAN connection

If your computer is connected to an intranet or to a LAN that is connected to the Internet, then probably all that is necessary to enable StarOffice to connect to the Internet for Web browsing, FTP file transfers, and such, is to set a few Internet options in the Options dialog box. StarOffice can use your system's existing connection (which needs to be set up and operating properly before configuration in StarOffice).

Follow these steps to configure StarOffice's Internet settings.

1. **Choose Tools⇨Options from the menu bar.**

   The Options dialog box appears.

2. **Double-click Internet in the list box at the left end of the Options dialog box to expand that group, and then click Proxy.**

   The options shown in Figure 20-1 appear.

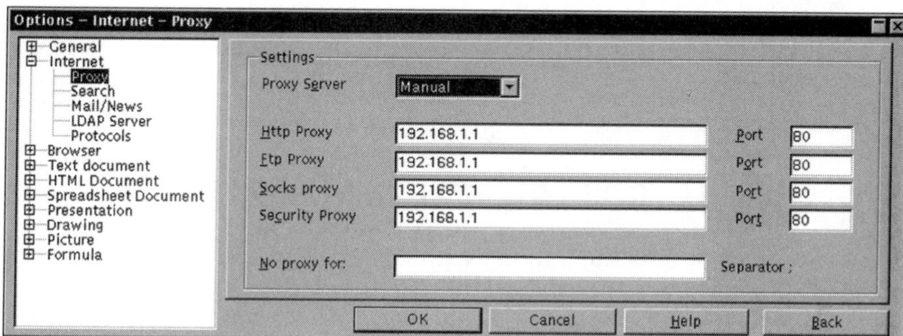

Figure 20-1: Proxy settings are important — if they apply to you.

3. **Adjust the settings on the Proxy tab according to instructions from your network administrator.**

   Check with your network administrator to learn whether you need to change the Proxy settings and what those settings should be. You don't have a network adminstrator? Great! You probably don't use a proxy server, so you don't need to worry about proxy settings. If you access the Internet via a dial-up connection using a modem and phone line, you probably do not go through a proxy server. In that case, select None from the Proxy Server drop-down list box.

4. **Click Search in the list box at the left end of the Options dialog box.**

   The search options appear.

5. **Select a preferred Web search site from the options provided in the Search In list box.**

   Unless you're very familiar with the way search strings are constructed, don't change anything else here.

6. **Click Protocols in the list box at the left end of the Options dialog box.**

   StarOffice displays the Protocol settings.

7. **Adjust the Protocol settings only if necessary.**

   Unless you have a specific reason for changing the Protocol settings, it's best to leave them set to their defaults. Your network administrator, if you have one, can advise you on whether you need to make any changes here. In particular, make sure the DNS server option is set to Automatic unless you have a specific reason for overriding your system's standard DNS server setting with a manual entry here. If you just have to change something, give yourself a few more FTP connections. You can often get more files downloaded in less time by downloading several files at one time. Each FTP session usually requires two connections, so it's best to increase this setting by two.

8. **Click OK when you're finished changing settings.**

   StarOffice closes the Internet Options dialog box and records the settings.

When you log in as a user on the local network, you are automatically connected through the local network to the Internet. StarOffice's Internet tools can use that network connection after they are properly configured.

Configuring for a dial-up connection

If you access the Internet via a dial-up connection over a modem and phone line, you may need to establish an Internet connection separately each time you want to browse the Web, send and receive e-mail, or do anything else requiring Internet access. The procedure you go through to establish a dial-up Internet connection varies depending on the hardware and software you use. StarOffice does not include dialing software or other utilities to handle dial-up Internet access. You need to use a separate utility program or the facilities built into your computer operating system to establish a dial-up Internet connection. After you establish an Internet connection, StarOffice uses that connection just as the program uses a network Internet connection.

If you're lucky, you have system software and utilities in place that can detect StarOffice attempting to access an Internet resource and automatically initiate a dial-up Internet connection for StarOffice to use. Otherwise, you may need to use a separate utility program to manually initiate a dial-up Internet connection before you attempt to access the Internet from within StarOffice. You may need to enter a username and password in order to log on to your Internet access account at your Internet service provider.

Linux users have a variety of options for manually starting a dial-up Internet (PPP) connection. In addition to the command line options, you can run the linuxconf configuration utility, then go to the Config⇨Networking⇨Client tasks⇨PPP/SLIP/PLIP tab, select your PPP connection, and then click Connect. If you use KDE, the Kppp utility does a nice job of handling dial-up Internet connections.

When running on the Windows platform, StarOffice uses Windows' built-in Dial-Up Networking (DUN) feature to connect to the Internet over a modem. If you have Dial-Up Networking configured to automatically connect to the Internet for other programs that need Internet access, StarOffice is able to use the same automatic connection feature. If you need to initiate a connection manually, open the Dial-Up Networking folder in the My Computer window (accessible by double-clicking the corresponding icon on the Windows desktop), and then select the icon for the DUN connection for your Internet service provider.

Viewing Web Pages in StarOffice

To view a Web page in StarOffice, simply type its address (called a URL) into the URL combo box on the StarOffice Function toolbar and press Enter. *URL* stands for Uniform Resource Locator. It tells your Web browser where to find just about anything that's available on the Net. It's the thing that starts `http://`.

When you type a Web page address in the URL box and press Enter, StarOffice displays the Web page in its own document window, as shown in Figure 20-2. That's all there is to it. You don't have to launch a separate Web browser program. The Web page viewer is built into StarOffice.

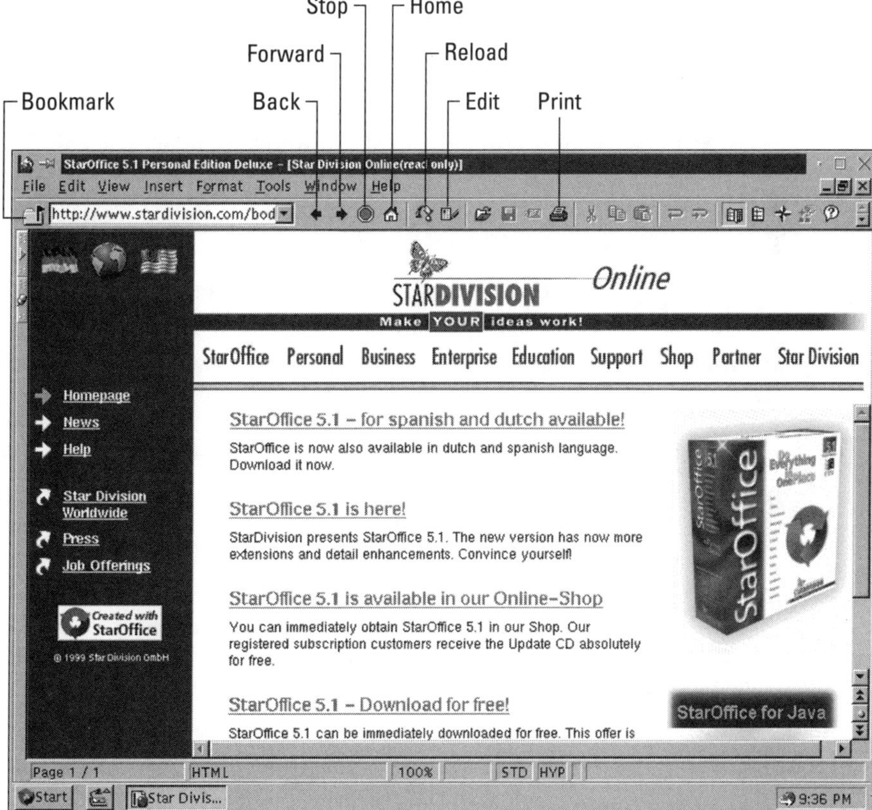

Figure 20-2: Browsing the Web from StarOffice.

A tour of the StarOffice Web browser window

After you get a Web page open for viewing in the StarOffice Web browser, you interact with the Web page in pretty much the same way you do in any other Web browser. If you've ever surfed the Web with Netscape Navigator, Microsoft Internet Explorer, or a similar Web browser, you probably already know how to use the StarOffice Web browser.

Hyperlinks usually show up as underlined text (unless the Web page designer did something different). When you point to a hyperlink, the pointer changes to a pointing hand instead of an arrow. Click a hyperlink to move from the current Web page to the Web page referenced by the link.

The StarOffice Function toolbar supplies the usual assortment of Web browser navigation tools. Here's a quick rundown:

- **Back.** Displays the previously viewed Web page.

- **Forward.** If you used the Back button to display previously viewed Web pages, clicking this button reverses the action and moves you forward again.

- **Stop.** Stops downloading a Web page before it is done. This is useful for aborting graphics-heavy pages that take forever to load.

- **Home.** Displays the Web page that is designated as your "Home" page. The default setting for the Home page is the Star Division corporate Web site, but you can change that to designate your own choice of Home page. (Flip to the "Setting Browser Options" section of this chapter to find out how.)

- **Reload.** Repeats the download and display of the current Web page. This button is useful when some graphics or other elements on the page failed to download or display properly on the first try.

- **Edit.** Opens the current Web page in StarWriter (in HTML editing mode). See the bonus chapter on the Web at `www.dummies.com/bonus/StarOffice` for information about creating and editing Web pages with StarWriter.

- **Print.** Sends the contents of the current Web page to the default printer.

Are you tired of waiting for graphics-heavy Web pages to download over a slow network connection? If you can do without the graphics, right-click the current Web page and choose Graphics Off from the pop-up menu that appears. The StarOffice Web browser thereafter ceases to display (and download) graphics. Text-only downloads are much faster. If you need to see graphics again, right-click the Web page and choose Load Images from the pop-up menu that appears. The StarOffice Web browser returns to normal operation and displays both text and graphics.

Other ways to call up Web pages

Typing a Web page address in the URL box isn't the only way you can open a Web document and view it in StarOffice. You can use several other techniques, most of them shortcuts, for returning to Web pages you've visited before. Here's a summary of the ones you're most likely to use:

- Most of the StarOffice programs recognize text that starts out with `http://` or `www.` as a URL and automatically format it as a Web link. When you click one of these links, the Web browser starts automatically and takes you to the Web site named in the link.
- You can also visit Web sites using the AutoBrowse feature in the Address Book. If an entry in the Address Book includes a URL, you can click AutoBrowse to go to the Web site.
- What if you want to view a Web page on your own hard disk? No problem. Just type the URL but start it with `file:///` instead of `http://` (yes, you counted right — that's three slash characters instead of the usual two). For example, to view the index.html Web page located in the ~/homepage/new directory you'd type **file:///~/homepage/new/index.html** into the URL box.

  Windows users can enter URLs for files stored on local disks using Internet-style slash characters (/) or DOS/Windows-style backslashes (\) — StarOffice converts the slashes for you.
- You can create link icons for frequently visited sites and store them on the StarDesktop (or in other folders); then just double-click the link icon to open the Web page.
- You can also create bookmarks (really just another link) and access them from the Explorer and Beamer windows. (See Chapter 2 for more info on using Explorer and Beamer.) To use a bookmark, open the Explorer and Beamer windows and select a folder under the Bookmarks heading in Explorer, and the bookmarks stored in that folder appear in the Beamer window. Choose and double-click the desired bookmark icon in the Beamer window to open the bookmarked Web page.

Follow these steps to create a link icon:

1. **Right-click the background of the StarDesktop and choose New⇨Link from the pop-up menu that appears.**

   The Properties of Link dialog box appears. (The Bookmark tab should be selected by default. If not, click the Bookmark tab to select it.)

2. **Type a name for the link in the Name box.**

   This name appears underneath the link's icon on your desktop.

3. **Type the full URL for the site in the Target URL text box.**

Some URLs are very long and hard to type without making errors. To avoid having to type a long URL, try this: Before starting to create the link, use the StarOffice browser to display the page you want to link to, select the URL in the address box on the Function toolbar, and then press Ctrl+C to copy the address to the clipboard. When you need to enter the URL into the Target URL box, you can simply press Ctrl+V to paste the address from the clipboard.

4. **Make sure there is a check in the Display in Explorer checkbox.**

5. **Click OK.**

   The new icon appears on the desktop.

To create a bookmark, follow these steps.

1. **Display the Web site you want to bookmark in the Web browser.**

   Make sure the URL for the site you want to bookmark appears in the URL box on the Function toolbar.

2. **Open the Explorer window and expand the Bookmarks heading to display the subfolders under Bookmarks.**

   Make sure that the folder where you want to store the new bookmark is visible.

3. **Click the Bookmark button on the Function toolbar and drag it into the Explorer window.**

   The pointer changes to a bookmark symbol as you drag.

4. **Release the mouse button to drop the bookmark into one of the folders under the Bookmarks heading.**

   StarOffice creates a new bookmark link to the current Web page address and stores it in the folder you dropped the bookmark in.

Setting Browser Options

For the most part, the default settings for the StarOffice Web browser work well, but if you'd like to customize them to better suit your own preferences, here's how easy it is:

1. **Choose Tools⇨Options.**

   StarOffice displays the Options dialog box.

2. **Double-click Browser in the list box at the left end of the Options dialog box to expand that group.**

   StarOffice has, by conservative count, 42 gazillion settings to choose from here. I'll skip the more esoteric stuff and mention only the ones you're most likely to want to change. When you've got some extra time on your hands, you might want to browse through the various Browser categories in the Options dialog box to get acquainted with what's here in case you need it later. Just click a category and then click the Help button for a brief explanation of the options available in that category.

3. **Click the Cache category in the list box at the left end of the Options dialog box.**

   The options shown in Figure 20-3 appear. Adjust the Memory Cache, Hard Disk Cache, and Verify Document settings as needed.

   The StarOffice Web browser temporarily stores Web pages as you visit them. This is called "caching," and if a page is cached, the browser can display it much faster the next time you view it. Here you can set the amount of memory and hard disk space StarOffice can use for caching. The Verify Document setting tells StarOffice when it should download a new copy of the requested Web page even though there is a copy available in the cache.

Figure 20-3: The cache settings let you balance memory usage against page reload speed.

4. **Click the Scripting category in the list box at the left end of the Options dialog box.**

   The scripting options appear. Check (or clear) the Enable option in the JavaScript area.

   This option lets you control whether or not StarOffice runs JavaScript applets on the Web pages you view. Other settings on this tab let you control StarBasic scripts (that's the macro language built into StarOffice). However, the StarBasic settings don't have much impact on Web pages.

5. **Click the Cookies category in the list box at the left end of the Options dialog box.**

   The options shown in Figure 20-4 appear. Select Accept, Ignore, or Confirm in the General Handling area.

   Cookies are little bits of data about you and your Web browsing habits that some Web sites collect. Generally, they're pretty harmless, and are actually necessary for sites that allow you to customize the content you view when you visit and for services such as online stores. Still, some folks hate 'em. If you're one of those folks, you can have the Web browser let you Confirm each request for cookies, or set it to Ignore all requests for cookies completely. If cookies don't bother you, let StarOffice Accept all cookie requests without bothering you.

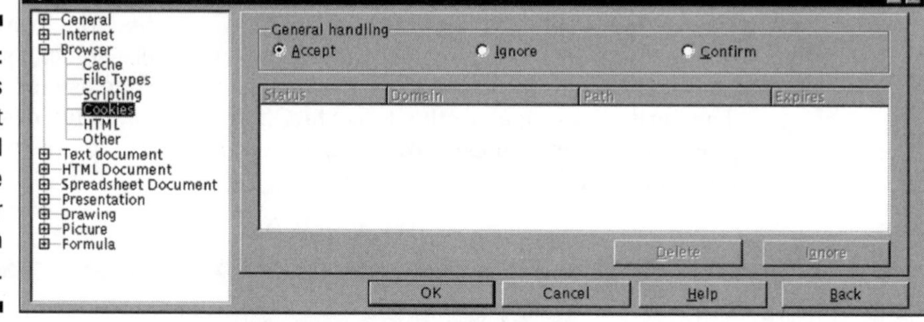

Figure 20-4: The Cookies settings let you control how the browser deals with cookies.

6. **Click the HTML category in the list box at the left end of the Options dialog box.**

   The options shown in Figure 20-5 appear. Adjust the Font Size preferences as needed.

   The settings in the Font Sizes area let you control what size text the StarOffice Web browser displays when it encounters type size specifications using one of the standard sizes. If you have trouble reading most Web pages because the text is too small, try increasing the setting in each of the Font Sizes boxes.

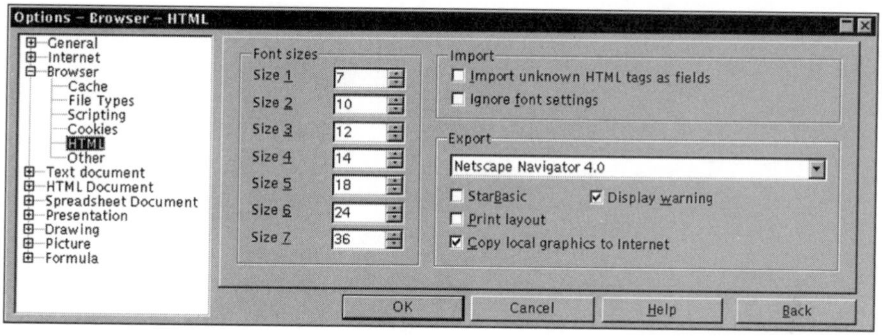

Figure 20-5: The HTML settings control font sizes and more.

7. **Click the Other category in the list box at the left end of the Options dialog box.**

   The options shown in Figure 20-6 appear. Here you can change the Homepage URL setting if you want.

   The Homepage URL setting controls what Web page the StarOffice Web browser displays when you click the Home button in the Function toolbar. You can replace the default setting (the Star Division Web site) with your own site or your favorite Web portal or search engine. You can also change a few other Java and Plug-in security settings here.

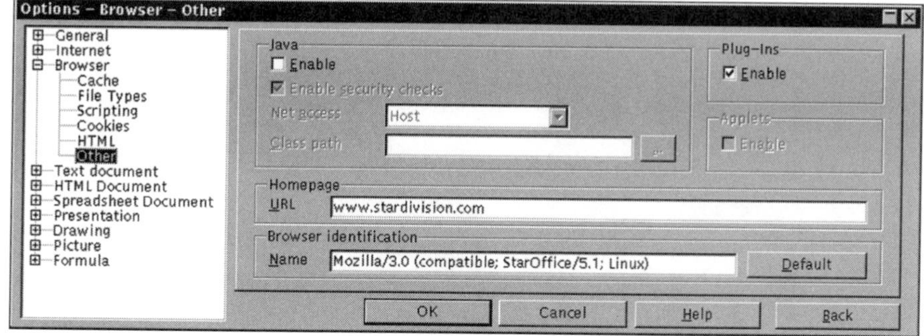

Figure 20-6: The Other settings let you control the default home page, among other things.

8. **Click OK.**

   StarOffice closes the Options dialog box and records the setting changes you made. The next time you view a Web page with the StarOffice Web browser, the new settings will be in effect.

Chapter 21

Communicating with E-mail and Newsgroups

In This Chapter

- Setting up your StarMail e-mail account
- Sending e-mail
- Reading e-mail
- Sending file attachments via e-mail
- Using StarDiscussion for newsgroups

If you've used *e-mail* (short for electronic mail), you know how much it speeds up communication. Shoot an e-mail off and in seconds the message arrives at its destination — whether that's down the street or around the world. Try that with the postal service! E-mail is a great way for families to keep in touch without high phone bills, or for workers to do part of their jobs at home and cut down on wear and tear on a car.

StarOffice can help you ride this electronic wave. StarOffice has an e-mail client called StarMail, an integrated set of features — not a separate program — designed especially to handle e-mail. Through StarMail you cannot only send and receive simple e-mail messages, but you can organize your mail however you want, attach files from your hard drive to send to other people, and keep your mail in a convenient place right inside StarOffice.

But wait: StarOffice has more! You can use a part of StarMail called StarDiscussion to communicate with people all over the world through newsgroups. *Newsgroups* are a part of the Internet that serve much like public bulletin boards, employing a variation on regular Internet e-mail to create online forums on a endless variety of topics. Send (or *post*) a message to a newsgroup address, and the message gets copied to servers around the world. You can make friends all over the world in a newsgroup, and with StarDiscussion, you can make these friends right from your computer.

Having StarMail and StarDiscussion together with your office suite is a great way to keep your Internet discussions handy. You can check your mail, or the newsgroups you read, while you're working — provided, of course, that the boss isn't looking over your shoulder.

Setting Up Your Inbox and Outbox

StarMail operates with an inbox and outbox that work just like the inbox and outbox you may have on your desk at work. Mail that's sent to you gets dumped into your inbox, and mail you send goes out through your outbox.

You need to tell StarMail how to handle your messages before you can start using it to read or send e-mail. This is not as complicated as it may look. All you need is some information about your account and about the provider's mail servers, and you're ready to go.

You need to collect the following specific information:

- The name of the incoming mail server. You might find this listed as a POP3 or IMAP mail server.
- The name of the outgoing (SMTP) mail server.
- Your e-mail address.
- The user name and password that you will use to access your e-mail account. (Often — but not always — this is the same user name and password that you use to log onto your Internet access account.)

Most ISPs (Internet service providers) give this info to you when you sign up, and the info is usually available on their Web page as well. If not, you can get the information you need from your ISP's help desk or the network system administrator for your local area network. Jot down this information somewhere convenient or print out the Web page with the information on it. Once you have all this together, you can set up your e-mail inbox and outbox in StarMail.

Setting up the inbox

First, you need to set up your inbox. This is the place where StarMail puts messages that are sent to you by other people, and this is where you go to check your e-mail every time you log on.

Your Inbox may already be set up if you responded appropriately to the prompts from the Internet Setup AutoPilot that runs automatically when you first install and run StarOffice. If you skipped the Internet Setup AutoPilot after installation but want to try it now, you can run it by choosing File⇨AutoPilots⇨Internet Setup. When the Internet Settings dialog box appears, select options and enter settings as prompted, and then click Next to advance to each new page in succession. Click Create on the last page to close the Internet Settings dialog box and apply the settings.

The Internet Setup AutoPilot can do the trick if you need a quick setup for Internet access, e-mail, and newsgroups. However, if you want to set up your e-mail account without messing with the other settings or you need access to some of the more detailed settings, you can use the manual technique described below.

The most common e-mail protocol on the Internet and on local intranets is POP3, so that's what I use as an example in the following instructions. However, StarOffice also supports the newer (but not yet dominant) IMAP protocol and the VIM e-mail standard that is used by a lot of LAN e-mail systems. If your mail server uses the IMAP or VIM protocol instead of the POP3 protocol, just substitute the appropriate option for your system everywhere POP3 pops up in this section. (For example, choose New⇨IMAP Account instead of New⇨POP3 Account to get things started for an IMAP account.)

To set up your inbox, follow these steps:.

1. **Right-click the background of the StarDesktop window and choose New⇨POP3 Account.**

   The Properties of POP3 Account dialog box appears with the Receive tab selected as shown in Figure 21-1.

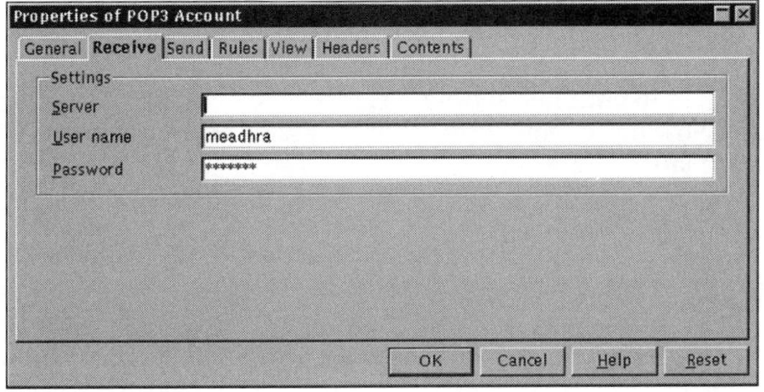

Figure 21-1: Start setting up your Inbox by defining your e-mail account.

2. **Type the name of your POP3 mail server in the Server text box.**

   This is probably a sequence of words separated by dots, like `pop3.email.org`. Sometimes your ISP gives you the e-mail server name as a series of numbers separated by dots, like `192.168.0.1`. This is called an IP address (the IP stands for *Internet Protocol*), and it works just like the names with words.

3. **Enter your User Name and Password in the respective text boxes.**

   Be sure to enter the user name and password for your e-mail account. They may (or may not) be the same as the login name and password that you use to log into the network when you access the Internet. Notice that the password appears disguised as a string of asterisks when you type it. This is a good thing, because it keeps people from snooping around and finding out your password, but it also means that you have to type it right the first time.

4. **Click the General tab at the top of the Properties of POP3 Account dialog box.**

   StarOffice displays the General options.

5. **Type a name for your e-mail account in the text box near the top of the General tab.**

   Now, you get to name your inbox. You could call it Wendy or Zorple if you wanted, but giving accounts names that show what they do or contain is usually a good idea. Try "In-box" or "My E-mail." This is the name that appears under the StarMail account icon on StarDesktop.

6. **Click OK.**

   StarOffice closes the Properties of POP3 Account dialog box and creates the new StarMail account. An icon for your StarMail account appears in the StarDesktop window. StarOffice also pops up a dialog box asking if you want to create an outbox.

7. **Click Yes or No.**

   Click Yes to continue setting up StarMail by configuring an outbox. (See the following section of this chapter.) Click No to postpone outbox setup until a later time.

Setting up the outbox

In addition to an Inbox for incoming e-mail, StarMail needs to know what to do with the mail that you send to other people. To set up your outbox, use this method (and yes, it looks a lot like setting up your inbox).

1. **Right-click the background of the StarDesktop window and choose New⇨Outbox, or click Yes in response to the** `Do you want to create an outbox?` **prompt in Step 7 of the procedure for creating an inbox (see preceding section).**

   A new dialog box shows up, called Properties of Outbox.

2. **Click the SMTP tab.**

   StarOffice displays the options shown in Figure 21-2.

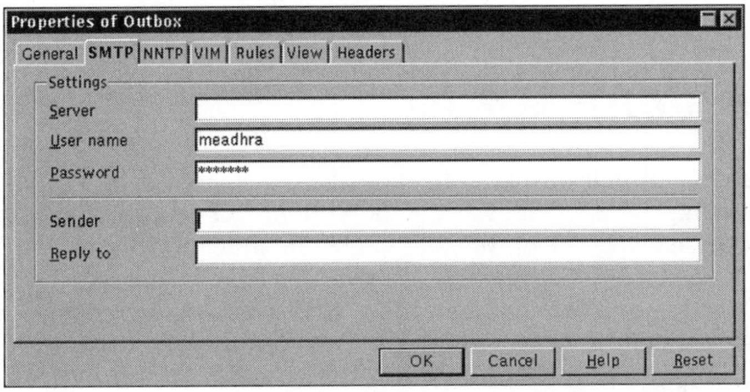

Figure 21-2: Setting up your outbox for outgoing mail.

3. **Type the SMTP server name in the Server text box.**

   The SMTP server name is part of the information you got from your ISP or system administrator. Like the POP3 server name, the SMTP server identification could be either in the form of a server name, such as `smtp.email.org`, or an IP address, such as `192.168.0.1`.

4. **Enter your User Name and Password in the respective boxes.**

   Make sure you enter the user name and password for your e-mail account, which are often — but not always — the same as the login name and password you use when you sign on to the network.

5. **Enter your e-mail address in the Sender and Reply To boxes.**

   This step is optional, but explicitly specifying your electronic return address often helps. StarOffice automatically enters into the Sender box the e-mail address you listed in the personal information when you installed StarOffice, but you can override that entry if necessary. The Reply To address is the e-mail address where you want correspondents to send replies to your e-mail messages; this address is usually the same as your regular e-mail address, but you can enter something else (if you have more than one e-mail address, for example).

6. **Click the General tab.**

   StarOffice displays the options on the General tab.

7. **Type a name for your outbox in the text box near the top of the General tab.**

   Like the inbox, you can name your outbox anything you want, but try to stick with something descriptive. "Outbox" is good. Unimaginative, perhaps, but good.

8. **Click OK.**

   StarOffice closes the Properties of Outbox dialog box and adds an icon for your new outbox to the StarDesktop window.

Checking Your Mail

Checking your mail with StarMail is real easy. No matter what tool or window you're using in StarOffice, you can pop open your inbox and check to see what's there using one of the following techniques:

- Open the Explorer window and double-click on the name of your inbox in the E-mail & News group.
- Double-click the inbox icon in StarDesktop.

The StarMail window opens (as shown in Figure 21-3) and StarMail automatically checks your e-mail account for new messages.

StarMail can only get your mail from your ISP or network server if you're logged onto the network! If you don't have an open Internet or network connection, StarMail won't be able to connect to your e-mail server to look for new mail messages. If you need to manually initiate a dial-up Internet connection, you should do so before opening your StarMail inbox.

The StarMail inbox window is divided into multiple sections or panes (window panes, get it?). You can use buttons on the toolbar to select different arrangements of window panes, but the default arrangement shown in Figure 21-3 is a good starting point.

If you have e-mail messages waiting, StarMail lists the name of the sender and the subject of the message in the pane that extends across the upper portion of the StarMail window. The panes in the lower portion of the StarMail window give you a preview of the message that is selected in the message list above. The message header appears in the left pane; a description of the message in the right pane; and the message text in the bottom pane.

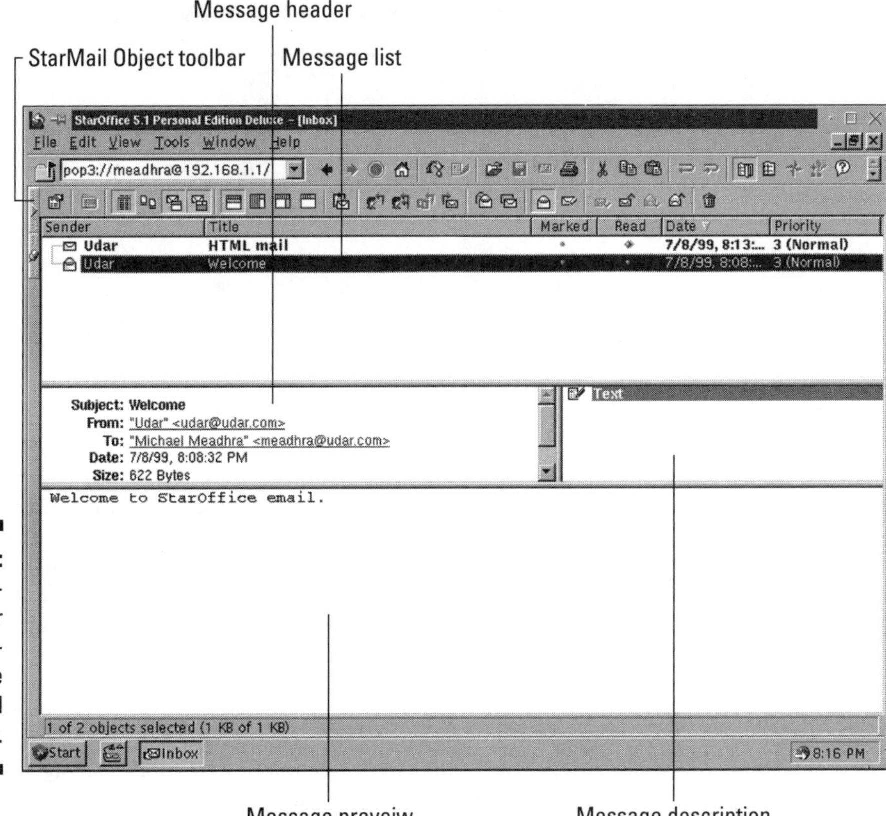

Figure 21-3: Take inventory of your e-mail messages in the StarMail window.

Reading E-mail

Once someone has been nice enough to send you some e-mail, you'll probably want to read it. That's what the message is for, after all. To read your e-mail in StarMail, first open your inbox either by opening Explorer and double-clicking your inbox's name or by double-clicking your inbox's icon in the StarDesktop window.

When the inbox opens, you'll see a list of the mail that people have sent to you. (Refer back to Figure 21-3.) You can simply select a message in the message list to see a preview of that message in the preview pane at the bottom of the StarMail inbox window. For short messages, that may be adequate, but you'll probably want to see a little larger view of your longer messages. You can right-click a message in the message list and choose Open from the pop-up menu that appears to open that message in a separate message window (see Figure 21-4).

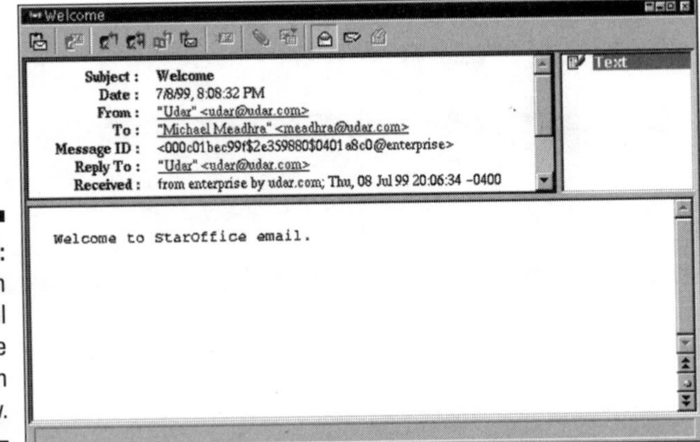

Figure 21-4: Reading an e-mail message in its own window.

Like the StarMail inbox window, the message window is divided into panes. The upper-left pane displays header information about the message, the upper-right pane lists any files or documents attached to the message, and the body of the message appears in the lower pane. If the entire message doesn't fit within the viewing pane, you can use the scroll bar on the right hand side to view and read different parts of the message.

Deleting e-mail when you're done with it is a good idea. Keeping mail in your inbox makes StarMail run more slowly, and the whole point of e-mail is that it's a fast alternative to regular mail. To delete an e-mail message from the StarMail inbox window, select the message you want to delete from the message list pane and press the Delete key, or right-click the selected message and choose Delete from the pop-up menu that appears. You can also delete a selected message by clicking the cute little trashcan (Delete) button on the StarMail Object toolbar.

When you delete a StarMail message it doesn't really go away immediately. Deleted items in StarOffice are stored in the Recycle Bin folder until you delete them permanently by emptying the Recycle Bin. If you make a mistake and delete the wrong message, you can salvage it by using Explorer and Beamer (see Chapter 2) to locate and display the contents of the Recycle Bin (it's in the Explorer group), then right-click the message in the Beamer window and choose Restore from the pop-up menu that appears.

You may want to save some messages for future reference, and yet, you don't want all those saved messages cluttering up your inbox. The answer to this dilemma is to create separate folders in which to store the messages you want to save. To create a folder for saved messages, follow these steps:

1. **Open the Explorer window and click the E-mail & News group.**

   StarOffice displays the contents of the E-mail & News group in the Explorer window.

2. **Right-click the background of the Explorer window and choose New⇨Folder from the pop-up menu that appears.**

   The E-mail & News dialog box appears.

3. **Type a name for the folder and then click OK.**

   StarOffice closes the dialog box and adds the new folder to the E-mail & News group in the Explorer window.

To save messages in the new folder, open the Explorer window and your e-mail inbox account window. Select a message in the message list in the e-mail window, the press and hold the Shift key as you drag the message icon from the e-mail window and drop it on the folder in the Explorer window. That's all there is to it. StarOffice moves the message from your e-mail account and stores it in the folder where you dropped it. Actually, the folder where you store e-mail messages doesn't have to be in the E-mail & News group — it can be in your Work folder or anywhere on your system that you want. To view a saved message, use Explorer and Beamer to display the contents of the folder in the Beamer window, and then double-click the message that you want to read. StarOffice opens a message window displaying the message.

Creating and Sending E-mail

Sending e-mail is as easy as reading it. To begin a new e-mail message, use any one of the following techniques:

- Choose File⇨New⇨Mail.
- Click the Start button in the StarOffice Task Bar and choose Mail from the pop-up menu.
- 

Double-click the New Mail icon on StarDesktop.
- Right-click the StarDesktop background and choose New⇨Documents⇨Mail from the pop-up menu that appears.
- 
Click the New Message button on the toolbar in the StarMail inbox window or in a message window.

Regardless of the technique you use to start creating a new mail message, the result is that StarOffice opens a message composition window, such as the one shown in Figure 21-5.

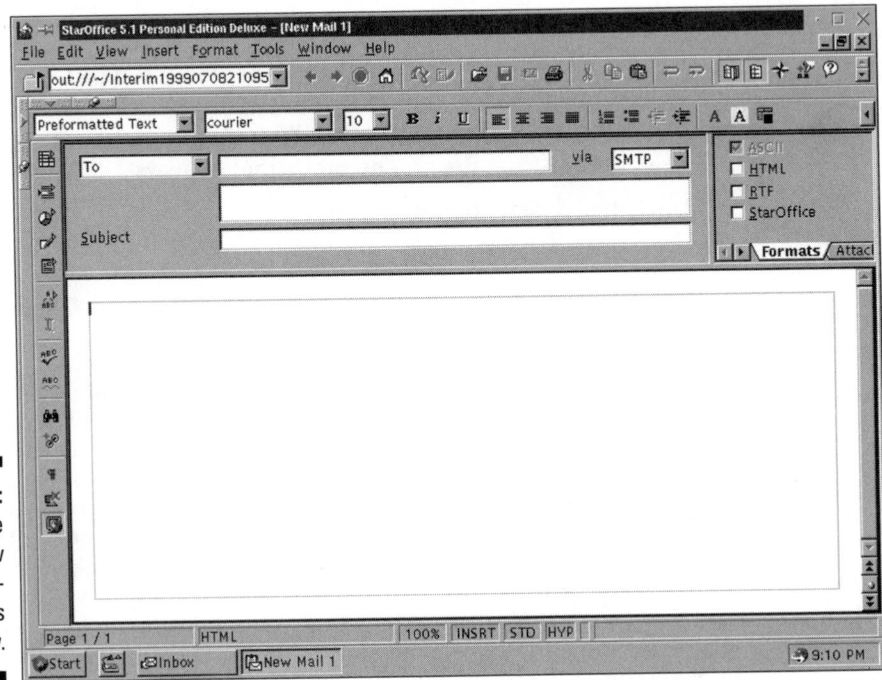

Figure 21-5: Compose your new e-mail message in this window.

The Mail window is divided into three panes. The big open pane along the bottom is for the text of your message, the pane in the upper left is where you type the e-mail address of the person you want to send the message to, and the pane in the upper right is where you can select the file format and add extras, like attaching a file.

Follow this method to create an e-mail message.

1. **Choose File⇨New⇨Mail.**

   You can use any of the techniques listed above to start a new mail message. StarOffice opens a mail composition window, as shown in Figure 21-5.

2. **Select To from the first drop-down list box in the Headers pane, at the upper left.**

   The header type `To` is already showing.

3. **Select SMTP from the Via drop-down list box to the right of the address line box.**

   That tells StarMail that you're creating an Internet e-mail message as opposed to a newsgroup article or VIM-mail message.

4. **Click in the text box to the right of the To box and type the e-mail address of the person you want to receive your e-mail, then press Enter.**

   StarOffice transfers the completed address line to the list box in the middle of the header pane. You can repeat Steps 2 to 4 to add more addresses to the message if needed.

   If the Address Book is open in the Beamer window, you can click and drag an e-mail address from the Beamer window and drop it on the address line in your e-mail message. See Chapter 17 for information on working with the Address Book and how to display it in the Beamer window. I cover using Beamer in Chapter 2.

5. **Type a subject label for the message in the Subject box.**

   What you type in this line shows up in the recipient's e-mail program as the one-line description of the mail. When you're done entering header information, check the headers to be sure they're correct. If you need to, you can edit them before moving on.

6. **Click in the big text entry box at the bottom of the screen.**

   The flashing vertical bar cursor indicates the insertion point in the text message area. The Object toolbar changes to offer an assortment of formatting tools. However, you can just ignore these tools; e-mail generally doesn't need to be formatted like a word processor document, and many e-mail clients don't understand StarOffice styles anyway.

7. **Type your message in the text entry area.**

   Keep your messages short and to the point.

8. **Click the Formats tab in the upper-right pane and select a message format.**

   The safest choice is ASCII, or plain text. Use plain text if you don't know what kind of e-mail reader your recipient has. HTML lets you use special tags, so that your e-mail message can look and act like a Web page, complete with live hyperlinks. StarOffice uses special StarOffice formatting codes. Don't use either of these if you don't know for sure that your recipient can read them, otherwise they may just get screens full of garbage.

9. **Click the Send button in the StarOffice Function toolbar.**

   The program doesn't have a menu option for sending mail, for some reason, so you have to use the button. (A duplicate button appears on the StarMail Object toolbar.) StarOffice sends your e-mail message to the StarMail outbox and from there to the outgoing e-mail server. If you're not connected to the Internet when you send the new message, StarMail saves the message in the outbox and sends it the next time you connect to the Internet.

Sending Documents as E-mail

Some people really hate writing e-mail messages in the mail editor and want to write everything in a word processing tool like StarWriter first. Other people write letters in StarWriter and then realize that sending the letters via e-mail is easier than postal mail. You can write a message in StarWriter and then have StarMail send it as the text of a message if you use this procedure.

1. **Create a new StarWriter text document (or open an existing text document) and compose your message.**

   See Chapters 3 through 6 for information on how to use StarWriter.

2. **Save the StarWriter document.**

3. **Choose File⇨Send⇨Document As E-mail.**

   StarOffice opens the Send Mail dialog box as shown in Figure 21-6.

Figure 21-6: How would you like that sent?

4. **Select As Mail Content and click OK.**

   The Send Mail dialog box disappears and StarOffice opens a new mail message window with the contents of the StarWriter text document inserted as the message text.

5. **Address the message normally.**

   See steps in the preceding section for info on creating a new e-mail message. Pay particular attention to Step 8, selecting a format for your message. The format defaults to StarOffice because the StarWriter document contains StarOffice formatting codes. Unless you're sending the message to another StarOffice user, you should uncheck the StarOffice format option.

6. **Click the Send button in the StarOffice Function toolbar.**

   StarMail sends your message on its way via the StarMail outbox and the outgoing e-mail server for your e-mail account.

Attaching Files to E-mail Messages

StarOffice makes attaching all kinds of files to an e-mail message very simple. When you attach something, the attachment goes along with the e-mail without being part of the message. (Imagine your attached file as a big sticky note that's stuck to a letter.) The recipient sees both your regular message and a note that the message has an attachment. You can attach a file from any StarOffice program, and attachments can include pictures, sound files, or just about anything!

Whether or not the recipient can successfully open and read the attached file depends on whether the program required to work with that kind of file is available on the recipient's system. Ask first! Also, some people have limits on the size of an e-mail message they can receive. Be sure you don't blow out someone's inbox because you sent them a huge attached file.

To attach a file to a StarMail message, just use these simple steps.

1. **Create an e-mail message, complete with address, subject, and message text.**

   See the "Creating and Sending E-mail" section of this chapter for instructions on creating an e-mail message.

2. **Click the paperclip button in the toolbar.**

   The Open dialog box appears; this is the standard Open dialog box you use to open StarOffice files for editing.

3. **Select the file you want to attach to your e-mail.**

   You may have to navigate through your folders to find the right file.

4. **Double-click the filename or select the file and click Open.**

   StarOffice closes the Open dialog box and the selected filename appears on the Attachments tab in the upper right pane of the StarMail new e-mail message window. If you right-click on the filename with your mouse, a dropdown menu appears. Use the dropdown menu to do things like change the name of the file or delete it from the e-mail message.

5. **Click the Send button on the StarOffice Function toolbar.**

   StarMail sends the message and its attached file to the recipient.

Once the filename has appeared in the attachments area, the file is stuck, or attached, to your e-mail. When you send the message, your attached file goes along for the ride.

Setting Up Newsgroup Access

Technically, StarDiscussion is a *newsreader,* a software client designed specifically for reading and posting to newsgroups. (By long-standing tradition, messages on a newsgroup are called *articles* or *posts,* and sending an article to a newsgroup is called *posting* the article.) StarDiscussion shows you posts in the newsgroups that you read and *threads* them for you. *Threading* collects an article and all the articles posted as a reply to the original article, and all the replies to those replies, and so on, and groups them together in sequence so they make sense as a sort of dialog. Some newsreading clients don't do this, and they make newsgroups a lot more confusing than they have to be.

If you're not familiar with newsgroups and how to locate newsgroups on topics that interest you, you may want to read more on the subject. A good resource for this (and many other Internet-related topics) is *The Internet For Dummies,* by John R. Levine, Carol Baroudi, and Margaret Levine Young (published by IDG Books Worldwide, Inc.).

Before you can use StarOffice to access newsgroups, you have to tell it where to find news. Setting up news access is just like setting up your mailboxes. You have to get the name of the news server from your ISP, but that's all you need.

1. **Right-click the StarDesktop background and choose New⇨News.**

   The Properties of News dialog box pops open.

2. **Click the Receive tab.**

   StarOffice displays the Receive options.

3. **Enter the name of your news server in the Server box.**

   This will be something like `news.yourisp.com` or `nntp.yourisp.com`, or might possibly be an IP number such as `192.168.0.1`. Like your e-mail account information, you should be able to get this information from your ISP's help-desk or Web site, or from your network system administrator.

4. **Enter your User Name and Password in the corresponding text boxes.**

   In most cases, you can skip this step. Most newsgroup servers don't require you to enter a user name and password in order to access the newsgroups on the server.

5. **Click the Subscribe tab.**

   This is where you choose the newsgroups you want to subscribe to. Lots and lots of newsgroups exist, and if your ISP carries anything even remotely resembling a full newsfeed, downloading all of the names takes quite a while. (Of course, you must be connected to the Internet in order to access the newsgroup server for this information.) When they're finally loaded, the group names appear in the large list box that dominates the Subscribe tab.

6. **Select the newsgroups to which you want to subscribe.**

   Use the Filter line at the top of the Subscribe tab to help locate newsgroups you're interested in. Subscribe to a group by clicking in the checkbox to the left of the group's name. You can subscribe to as many groups as you want, but remember that some of these groups get hundreds of messages a day!

7. **Click the Subscribed tab at the bottom of the newsgroups window.**

   This removes all the groups that you're not subscribed to from the list. (You can always click the All tab if you want to see unsubscribed groups, too.)

8. **Click the View tab.**

   This gives you some options that control how the newsgroups are displayed. You can select which groups you'll see, and the type and number of messages to be displayed.

9. **Adjust the settings as needed.**

10. **Click the General tab.**

11. **Enter a name for your newsgroups.**

    Something like "My Newsgroups" is fine.

12. **Click OK.**

    StarOffice closes the Properties of News dialog box and a new icon for your newsgroups appears on StarDesktop.

Reading the News

After you have set up your news access, it's time to read some news. Be aware, though, that most of the stuff posted in newsgroups isn't actually news as we define it. Instead, the postings are usually about hobbies or theories or arguments about life on Mars, not the sort of stories you would see on your local newscast. Newsgroups can seem really confusing if you're new to them, so you should familiarize yourself with the basics before you jump in with both feet.

One of the first newsgroups you should read is one called `news.newusers.questions`. Just like the name says, `news.newusers.questions` is designed especially for people who are new to the whole newsgroup thing and who have questions. One of the great features of `news.newusers.questions` is that FAQs are posted frequently.

What's an FAQ? A document that answers Frequently Asked Questions, like "What's this group for?" The answers to these questions are combined into one document that's posted regularly. Most newsgroups have FAQs, and it is always a good idea to read the FAQ before you start posting to the group.

So, you've got the name of a newsgroup that you want to read, and you're excited about seeing what's available — maybe a group about *Star Wars,* or an antiques group, or someplace to discuss that old Amiga computer you have out in the garage. Let's get you set up to enter the world of newsgroups! Here's how:

1. **Double-click your newsgroups icon in StarDesktop.**

   A window opens with the names of the newsgroups you subscribed to in it (see Figure 21-7). Newsgroups that have their names in boldface type have unread news in them.

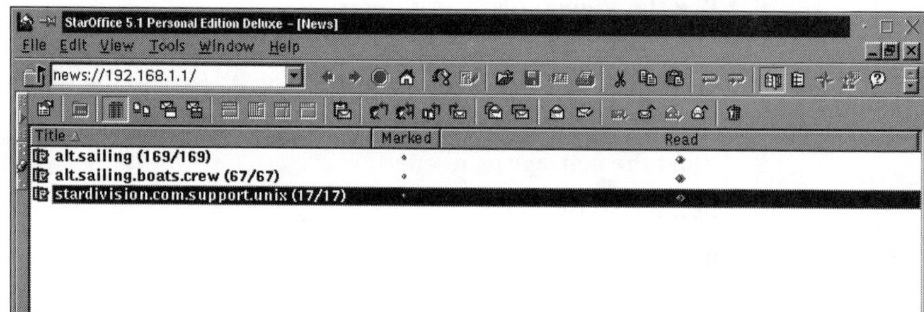

Figure 21-7: Check out the list of newsgroups.

2. **Double-click a newsgroup name.**

   The newsgroup names are replaced by a list of threads in the selected newsgroup. A little plus sign next to the thread name means follow-ups to the post are shown. If you click on the plus sign, the tree expands so you can see the other posts. (This is not as complicated as it sounds. You'll get the hang of it quickly.) If, instead of an author's name, you see a folder icon, that means that thread is a long one.

   Theoretically, threads are about the same subject, but newsgroup threads often undergo topic drift when people start replying to tangential comments made in other posts. So don't be surprised to find posts about turnips or auto parts in a thread called Rutabaga.

3. **Click on a particular article in the list.**

   StarDiscussion displays the selected article in the panel below (see Figure 21-8). It may take a couple of minutes for the article to show up.

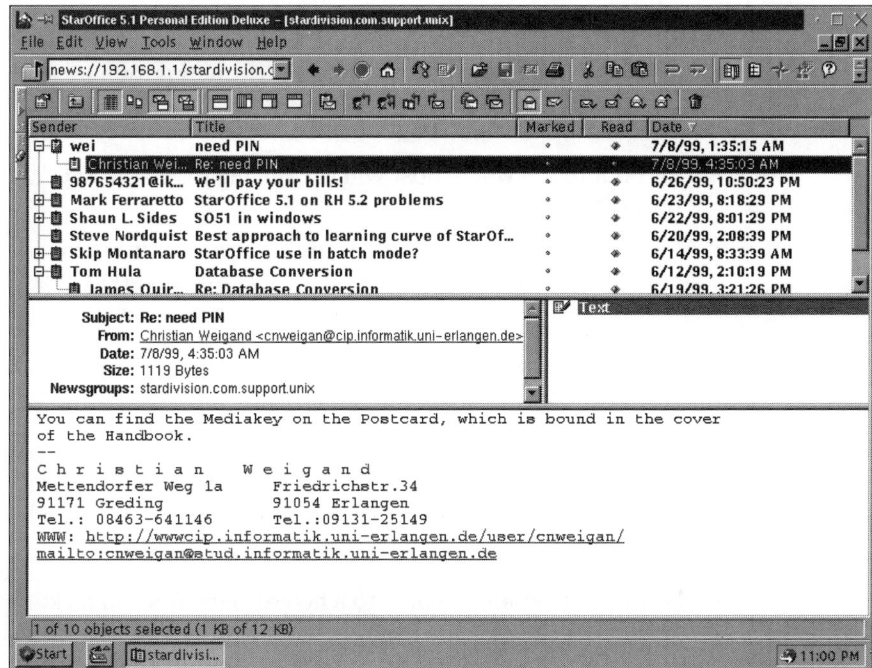

Figure 21-8: Reading the news.

You can resize the panels within the StarDiscussion window by clicking and dragging the borders until you get an arrangement you're happy with. The text of the message appears in one panel, and the message headers (lines which contain information about the message, author, server, and so on) appear in another. Some messages have attachments as well as text content, which are listed in another panel. You can switch between the attachments by clicking on the one you want. For most messages, though, only the word "Text" will be in that panel.

As you read articles, the names in the top panel change from bold to normal type. This means that they have been read. You can also use the two icons at the right end of the Newsgroups toolbar to mark articles and threads as read. Why would you want to? Well, if you don't read an article, StarDiscussion thinks you want to read it later and keeps on showing it to you.

Posting News Articles

Once you have read newsgroups for any length of time, you're going to want to reply to something you read. That's the way newsgroups work; they're discussion groups, and it's expected that people who read them will contribute to the discussion. People who just read, and don't post, are called *lurkers*. Being a lurker isn't wrong, but participating and becoming known in the group is just more fun!

Here are some basic guidelines for posting to newsgroups:

- Make sure that you're posting to the right newsgroup for your topic — don't post a question about guns to alt.collecting.beanie-babies, and don't post a question about Beanie Babies to rec.sport.pro-wrestling.
- Don't quote the whole post you're replying to, just to say "Me too!" down at the bottom.
- Most of all, just pay attention. If you've read the group for a few days, and you've found and read the FAQ, you'll have a good idea of the group's "feel."

Newsgroup articles are really just e-mail messages that are addressed to the newsgroup and posted for all to see instead of being a private message addressed to an individual. So, you shouldn't be surprised that you compose newsgroup articles in the same StarMail message composition window you use for e-mail messages. Everything works the same as when you create an e-mail message except for the way you create a newsgroup article compared to an e-mail message.

Follow these instructions to post to a newsgroup. You can make several kinds of posts, so read through the list to figure out what you want to do.

- If you want to post a follow-up article (that is, post an article in reply to a newsgroup article that is addressed to the group so that everyone can read it), click the Post Reply icon (two pieces of paper with an up-and-to-the-left arrow) while reading the article you want to reply to. The message composition window appears with the text of the original post inserted in the text area, preceded by a '>' character at the beginning of each quoted line. Edit the original post to just the material you want to reply to, type your reply, then send the post just like sending an e-mail message.

- If you want to make a new post (that is, a post which is not a reply to anything), click the New Mail icon while reading articles in the newsgroup to which you want to post. The message composition window appears with the address of the newsgroup already filled in. Compose and send your message as normal — just like an e-mail message.

- If you want to send a reply to an article (that is, send an e-mail directly to the author of the article you're reading instead of posting a reply on the newsgroup), click the Reply icon. The message composition window opens and you can write and send your message as normal.

Just from looking at the screen, telling whether you are writing a newsgroup post or an e-mail message is difficult. Be very careful about what you're doing, or you could have a private message sent all over the world. When in doubt, look at the Header field marked "via." If the field says "NNTP," you're writing a newsgroup post. If the field says "SMTP," you're writing e-mail.

Part VIII
The Part of Tens

"I failed her in algebra but was impressed with the way she animated her equations to dance across the screen, scream like hyenas, and then dissolve into a clip art image of the La Brea Tar Pits."

In this part . . .

This part is where you find a collection of tips and techniques for sharing information — sharing information between the various StarOffice tools and also sharing documents and files between StarOffice and Microsoft Office and other programs.

Chapter 22

Ten (or So) Things about Sharing Information between StarOffice Tools

In This Chapter

- Placing images in your documents
- Working with spreadsheets, presentations, and drawings
- Charting a plan for sharing charts
- Copying and pasting across tools
- Pasting with special flair
- Editing shared objects

The StarOffice tools are a tightly integrated set of document-creation tools, not just a collection of separate programs bundled together to form an office suite. Nowhere is this synergy more evident than in the way you can use the StarOffice tools together to create *compound documents* — documents that you create with one tool but contain elements or objects created with a different tool. For example, a compound document can be a report or proposal that is a text document and also contains a StarCalc spreadsheet, StarImage pictures, and StarChart charts. This chapter gives you an assortment of tips and tricks for creating compound documents.

By the way, the *document* in *compound document* frequently means a text document into which you insert other elements. However, a compound document can also be a StarCalc spreadsheet that contains a StarChart chart, or a StarImpress presentation that contains a diagram drawn with StarDraw, or just about any other combination you can imagine. Not all the StarOffice tools can create compound documents, but most of them can, and those that can't play host to objects from other StarOffice tools can create objects that you can insert into documents generated with other tools.

Inserting Pictures into Documents

You can insert a picture into a document four different ways: (I cover these techniques in more detail in Chapter 6.)

- Choose Insert⇨Picture⇨From File to open the Insert Picture dialog box. Select the picture file that you want to import and click Open. StarOffice adds a copy of the selected image to your document.
- Choose Insert⇨Picture⇨From Image Editor to create a new image on the spot.
- Choose Insert⇨Object⇨OLE Object to open the Insert OLE Object dialog box. Select Create From File, specify a StarImage file, and click OK. This trick enables you to insert a copy of an existing image file into a document and still have it appear as an editable object, like the images that you create on the spot.
- If you have a scanner, choose Insert⇨Picture⇨Scan⇨Acquire to access your scanning software and begin scanning an image. If you can't use the Acquire command to scan directly into your document, you can always scan a picture and save it as a file and then use the Insert⇨Picture⇨From File command to insert it into your document.

Inserting Spreadsheets and Other OLE Objects into Documents

You can insert a StarCalc spreadsheet into a StarWriter text document or a StarImpress presentation and tap into all of StarCalc's calculation capabilities. The difference between a simple table and a spreadsheet object is that when you create (and edit) the spreadsheet, you have access to StarCalc's menus, toolbars, and features. It's a full-fledged spreadsheet, right there in your document. When you're not editing the spreadsheet, a "picture" of the spreadsheet appears in your document.

Inserting spreadsheets into text documents works, courtesy of a technology called *OLE — Object Linking and Embedding.* The spreadsheet is a self-contained object, complete with its own special characteristics and editing tools, that is embedded in the text document container. Embedding objects into a document enables you to add features to that document that you can't create with the document's normal editing tools. And spreadsheets aren't the only OLE object types that you can insert into documents. You can also embed charts, drawings, and other object types.

To insert an OLE object into a document, follow these steps:

1. **Choose Insert⇨Object⇨OLE Object to open the Insert OLE Object dialog box.**
2. **Select Create New and then select one of the following object types that you can add to your document:**
    - **StarOffice 5.1 Spreadsheet:** Adds a StarCalc spreadsheet to the document
    - **StarOffice 5.1 Presentation:** Adds a StarImpress presentation to the document
    - **StarOffice 5.1 Chart:** Adds a StarChart chart to the document
    - **StarOffice 5.1 Image:** Adds a StarImage picture to the document
    - **StarOffice 5.1 Formula:** Adds a StarMath (equation editor) formula to the document
    - **StarOffice 5.1 Draw:** Adds a StarDraw drawing to your document
3. **When you're finished, click OK.**

   StarOffice closes the Insert OLE Object dialog box and adds an object of the selected type to your document.

Your document remains visible in the background, but the menus and toolbars change to give you access to the full set of tools for creating and editing the selected object. For example, if you insert a spreadsheet object, the StarCalc menus and toolbars appear when you select the spreadsheet for editing. When you click outside the object, the normal menus and toolbars return. Note that you're not creating a separate file; the object is created and saved in the compound document.

Inserting Charts into Documents

After pictures and spreadsheets, charts are probably the most common StarOffice object that you can insert into another document. Charts show up frequently in text documents, such as reports and proposals, and in many StarImpress presentations. You can insert a chart into your document by using either of the following techniques:

- Choose Insert⇨Object⇨OLE Object, select StarOffice Chart in the Insert OLE Object dialog box, and click OK. StarOffice inserts a StarChart chart based on the standard default chart data. Edit the chart type and chart data as needed to create the chart that you need.

- If you have an existing table in your document that contains data you want to use as the basis for a chart, select the data in the table and then choose Insert➪Chart. StarOffice opens the Chart AutoFormat dialog box with the table selected as the data source. This technique is similar to adding a chart to a spreadsheet, which I describe in Chapter 10.

Copying and Pasting between Documents

If you have existing information in one StarOffice document that you want to use in another StarOffice document, you can simply copy the information from one document and paste it into the other. Here's how:

1. **Select the information that you want to copy.**
2. **Choose Edit➪Copy or press Ctrl+C.**
3. **Open the document that you want to paste the information into.**
4. **Place the insertion point cursor at the correct place, and choose Edit➪Paste or press Ctrl+V.**

If both the source and destination documents are the same type — for example, both are StarWriter text documents — then the information from the clipboard is inserted into the destination document as if you had typed it in.

However, if the document types are different, StarOffice inserts the information from the clipboard as an OLE object. This technique is essentially the same as using the Insert➪Object➪OLE Object command to insert that type of object into your document and then copying the selected information into the object.

Using Special Pasting Options

When you copy information from one StarOffice document and paste it into another type of StarOffice document, you may not always want to insert that information into the new document as an OLE object. For example, if you copy part of a spreadsheet into a text document, you may want it to appear as plain text that you can edit with StarWriter instead of as a StarCalc spreadsheet object.

StarOffice gives you several options for how you want to insert copied information when you choose Edit➪Paste Special. For example, if you choose Paste Special after copying some spreadsheet information to the clipboard, the Paste Special dialog box appears with the following options available:

- **StarCalc Spreadsheet:** Inserts the information from the clipboard as a StarCalc spreadsheet object. This feature is the same as the regular Paste command.
- **GDI Metafile:** Inserts a picture of the information in the GDI Metafile format (a versatile graphics file format).
- **Bitmap:** Inserts a picture of the information in the bitmap format.
- **HTML:** Inserts the information as HTML formatted text or table. (HTML is the format used for Web pages.)
- **Unformatted Text:** Inserts the information as plain, unformatted text.
- **Formatted Text:** Inserts the information as text formatted using the RTF file format (text that retains formatting information, such as font selections, paragraph spacing, alignment, and such).

Depending on what kind of information you copied to the clipboard, the Paste Special dialog box may present different options. However, the preceding options are fairly typical.

Editing OLE Objects

After you create an OLE object, either by creating it in your document from scratch or by copying and pasting information, you can edit that object with ease. But you don't edit the object with the tools of the host document.

When you click an OLE object, selection handles appear around it, just like the selection handles around a picture. At that point, you can move and resize the object in the same way that you move or resize a picture.

To edit the contents of an OLE object, follow these steps:

1. **Double-click the object.**

   In addition to the selection handles, a gray outline appears around the object to indicate that you're in object-editing mode. The menus and toolbars from the object's own StarOffice tool replace the menus and toolbars of the host document.

2. **Edit the object.**
3. **Click anywhere in the host document outside the object to return the normal menus and toolbars to the screen.**

After editing the OLE object, you should save your work. Since the OLE object is embedded in the host document, it's a part of the host document file, not a separate file. To save updates to the embedded object, simply save the host document by choosing File➪Save, clicking the Save button in the Function toolbar, or pressing Ctrl+S.

Chapter 23

Ten Ways to Share Information with Others

In This Chapter

- Using Microsoft Office documents in StarOffice
- Working with word processing documents
- Sharing spreadsheets
- Powering presentations from PowerPoint to StarImpress
- Looking out for Outlook schedules
- Imagining images everywhere
- Weaving a Web of HTML

Often, you may need to share documents and files with coworkers, family, and friends. If those folks don't happen to use StarOffice, you face some special considerations in how to deal with different file formats that other programs use and what kinds of files those other programs can open. The same considerations come into play if you use a different office suite or program at the office and need to take files home to work on them in StarOffice.

Other programs aren't likely to be able to use your StarOffice files, but StarOffice can handle the translation chores needed to exchange files and documents with a variety of other programs. StarOffice is particularly adept at exchanging files with Microsoft Office. This chapter is a collection of tips and techniques for doing just that.

Importing Microsoft Office Documents

One of the most common scenarios that you as a StarOffice user may face is the need to open and work with a batch of files received from a Microsoft Office user. (In fact, you may be the Microsoft Office user yourself, and the files may be a project that you brought home from the office.) StarOffice includes a special utility that enables you to convert a batch of Microsoft Office files to StarOffice format all at once. It's called the Microsoft Office Import AutoPilot.

The Microsoft Office Import AutoPilot can import Microsoft Word documents and templates, Microsoft Excel spreadsheets and templates, and Microsoft PowerPoint presentations and templates. It can automatically locate all the target files in a given directory, make copies of those files in the corresponding StarOffice file format, and store the StarOffice files in the directory of your choice. Using this utility is a great way to transform all the files for a project from Microsoft Office files into StarOffice files so that you can work with them in your favorite office suite.

To use the Microsoft Office Import AutoPilot, follow these steps:

1. **Choose File⇨AutoPilot⇨Microsoft Import.**

   StarOffice opens the Microsoft Office Import AutoPilot dialog box. The first page of the AutoPilot just gives general instructions on its use.

2. **Click Continue.**

   The Microsoft Word import options appear, as shown in Figure 23-1. Note the three buttons below the banner at the top of the dialog box. These buttons enable you to access separate settings for importing Word, Excel, and PowerPoint files.

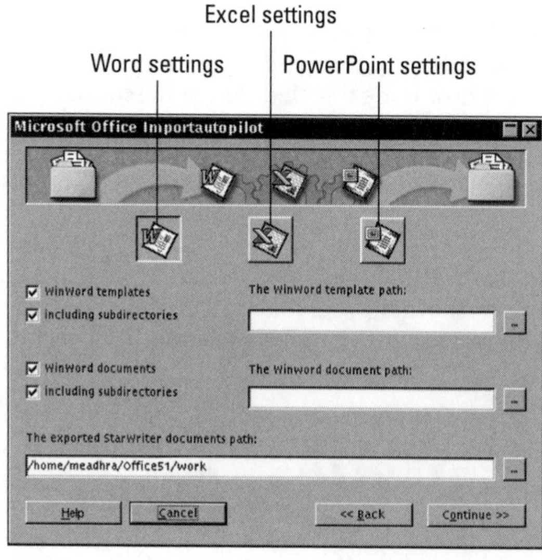

Figure 23-1: The Microsoft Office Import AutoPilot can convert all the Office files in a directory — and its subdirectories.

3. **Check the import options and fill in the directory information for importing Word documents.**

   You can choose whether you want the AutoPilot to import Word documents or templates and whether to include documents and templates located in subdirectories of the specified directories. You need to supply a directory name to indicate where the AutoPilot should look for documents to import and a separate directory for template files. (You can type the directory name into the text box or click the ... button beside it to open the Select a Directory dialog box and locate the directory that way.) By default, StarOffice puts the converted files in your Work folder, but you can change that setting by specifying another directory in the box at the bottom of the dialog box.

4. **Click the Excel settings button.**

   The Excel import settings appear. You have the same options available for importing Excel files as you have for importing Word files.

5. **Adjust the Excel import settings as needed.**

6. **Click the PowerPoint settings button.**

   The PowerPoint import settings appear. Again, you need to supply the same information as you did for importing Word files.

7. **Adjust the PowerPoint import settings as needed.**

8. **Click Continue.**

   The final page of the AutoPilot appears, as shown in Figure 23-2. The AutoPilot shows a summary of import tasks that it will perform and lists the template groups where it will store the imported templates.

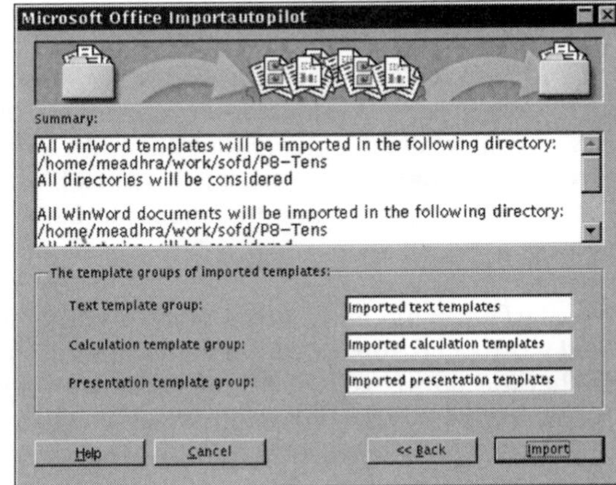

Figure 23-2: Check the summary page before proceeding with the import.

9. Review the information and then click Import.

The AutoPilot displays status messages informing you of its progress as it reads, converts, and saves the files that you selected for import. When the import process is complete, the Microsoft Office Import AutoPilot dialog box disappears. The imported files are now available for use as regular StarOffice files.

Exchanging Documents with Microsoft Word

Exchanging documents with Microsoft Word is no problem because StarOffice can read and write Microsoft Word document files using the StarWriter word processing tool. StarWriter can open files created by Word 97, Word 95, and Word 6.

You can also save a StarWriter document as a Microsoft Word document file so that a Word user can open and edit the file. Basically, you can open or save a Word file using the same technique you use to open or save a StarWriter file. You just need to make sure you select the correct Word file format in the File Type drop-down list box. I explain the process in detail in Chapter 3.

Exchanging Documents with Other Word Processing Programs

StarOffice doesn't read and write word processing document files using the native file format of word processing programs other than Microsoft Word. But that doesn't mean you can't exchange document files with someone using another word processing program. The trick is to find a file format that both programs support and exchange documents using that file format. You have the following choices:

- **Microsoft Word** — StarOffice and many other word processing programs can read and write Microsoft Word document files. Consequently, you can often use that format to exchange documents with other word processing programs as well as with Microsoft Word. You can use the other word processing program's export feature to create a Microsoft Word document file, which you can then open in StarOffice. To go back in the other direction, save your StarWriter document as a Microsoft Word file and then use the import feature of the other word processing program to open the Word document.

- **RTF** — If the other word processing program with which you want to exchange files doesn't support the Microsoft Word document format, you can try *RTF* (Rich Text Format) — a file format designed for exchanging formatted text documents between programs. StarOffice supports it, so see if the other word processing program does, too.
- **Text** — The lowest common denominator is a plain-text file. StarOffice supports several variations of text files as used on various platforms, so you can read and create text files compatible with just about anyone else's system. The problem with text files is that you get the text of your document but no formatting whatsoever.
- **HTML** — One of the other file formats to consider for sharing documents between word processing programs is HTML. This file format is used for Web pages, and it's not really designed for transferring documents between word processing programs. However, with the immense popularity of the Web, most newer word processing programs can create Web pages using the HTML format. And, of course, StarOffice speaks HTML fluently. So, the odds are good that StarOffice and the other word processing program have the HTML file format in common. Converting a word processing program document to HTML may not be the cleanest way to transfer it, but the technique supports more formatting and graphics than a plain-text file.

Exchanging Spreadsheets with Excel

Exchanging spreadsheet files between StarOffice's StarCalc tool and Microsoft Excel is easy because StarOffice can read and write Microsoft Excel files using the normal techniques for opening and saving spreadsheet files. To open or save Excel files, just select the appropriate file format in the File Type drop-down list box in the Open or Save As dialog boxes. StarOffice supports Excel 4.0, Excel 5.0, Excel 95, and Excel 97 file formats. You can find more detailed information on opening and saving spreadsheets in Chapter 7.

Exchanging Spreadsheets with Lotus 1-2-3

In addition to exchanging files with Microsoft Excel, StarOffice can exchange spreadsheet files with Lotus 1-2-3 to a limited extent. StarOffice can read and write some Lotus 1-2-3 spreadsheet files. To use the feature, you simply select the Lotus 1-2-3 format in the Open or Save As dialog boxes — just like opening or saving an Excel spreadsheet file.

The hitch is that StarOffice supports only a couple of older Lotus 1-2-3 spreadsheet file formats, so you probably can't open a file created by a recent version of Lotus 1-2-3 and stored in its native file format. In fact, you'll probably have better luck saving your StarCalc or Lotus 1-2-3 spreadsheets in one of the Microsoft Excel file formats and using that as the translation medium between the two spreadsheet programs.

Exchanging Presentations with PowerPoint

The ability to exchange presentations between StarImpress and PowerPoint is an important part of the compatibility between StarOffice and the Microsoft Office suite. StarOffice can read both presentation and template files from PowerPoint 97 by simply selecting the appropriate format in the Open dialog box's File Type drop-down list box. Similarly, you can save a StarImpress presentation as a PowerPoint 97 file by selecting that format in the Save As dialog box.

Exchanging Schedules with Outlook and Organizer

Exchanging schedule information between StarSchedule and Microsoft Outlook or Lotus Organizer is not as straightforward as exchanging text documents between StarWriter and Microsoft Word; it's not as simple as opening a document file.

To import data from Outlook or Organizer, follow these steps:

1. **Export the information from Outlook or Organizer using that program's import/export utility.**

   You must export tasks and events as two separate files. Use the export feature of Outlook or Organizer and export the data as comma-separated values (Outlook) or text (Organizer) files.

2. **Open the StarSchedule window and choose File⇨Import.**

   The Import dialog box opens.

3. **Choose the appropriate file format and information type in the File Type drop-down list box.**

4. **Select the file that you exported from Outlook or Organizer, and click Open.**

   StarSchedule imports the data.

To export schedule data from StarSchedule, follow these steps:

1. **Choose File⇨Export to open the Export dialog box.**
2. **Select vCalendar events (*.vcs) from the File Type drop-down list box, give your file a name, and select a directory.**
3. **Click Save to create a data file containing information about your StarSchedule events.**

Now you can use the import/export feature of Outlook or Organizer to import this data into the other program. You can export StarSchedule events this way, but not tasks.

Exchanging Images with Almost Anyone

StarOffice's image editor, StarImage, can read and write a large variety of file formats. With the ability to open all the file formats on the following list and save images in most of the formats, StarImage ensures compatibility with just about any other image viewer or editor you may want to use. StarImage supports the following file formats:

- BMP — Windows bitmap
- GIF — Graphics Interchange Format (the standard format for Web graphics)
- JPG — Joint Photographic Engineering Group or JPEG (the standard format for photos on the Web)
- PBM — Portable Bitmap
- PCD — Photo CD (open only)
- PCX — Zsoft Paintbrush (open only)
- PGM — Portable Graymap
- PNG — Portable Network Graphics (an emerging alternative to GIF)
- PPM — Portable Pixelmap
- PSD — Adobe Photoshop (open only)
- RAS — Sun Rasterfile
- TGA — Truevision TARGA (open only)

- TIF — Tagged Image Format (often used for scanned images)
- XBM — X-Consortium (open only)
- XPM — X Pixel Map

Exchanging Drawings

Like StarImage, StarDraw offers compatibility with a large assortment of file formats. In addition to StarDraw's own files, StarOffice opens the following file formats in StarDraw:

- CGM — Computer Graphics Metafile
- DXF — AutoCAD Interchange
- EMF — Enhanced Windows Metafile
- EPS — Encapsulated PostScript
- MET — OS/2 Metafile
- PCT — Macintosh PICT
- WMF — Windows Metafile

StarDraw saves drawings in its own file format when you use the File⇨Save As command. But when you choose File⇨Export, you have the following options available in the Export dialog box. Note that some of the file formats are bitmaps (raster files), which automatically convert your drawing from a vector drawing to a bitmap image in the export process. Others are vector drawing formats that retain the characteristics of your StarDrawing and the ability to edit individual objects in the drawing. Refer to Chapters 11 and 12 for more information on bitmaps and vector drawings and the differences between the two.

- BMP — Windows bitmap (exports as bitmap image)
- EPS — Encapsulated PostScript (exports as vector drawing)
- GIF — Graphics Interchange Format (exports as bitmap image)
- JPG or JPEG — Joint Photographic Engineering Group (the standard format for photos on the Web) (exports as bitmap image)
- MET — OS/2 Metafile (exports as vector drawing)
- PBM — Portable Bitmap (exports as bitmap image)
- PCT — Macintosh PICT (exports as vector drawing)

- PGM — Portable Graymap (exports as bitmap image)
- PNG — Portable Network Graphics (exports as bitmap image)
- PPM — Portable Pixelmap (exports as bitmap image)
- RAS — Sun Rasterfile (exports as bitmap image)
- TIF — Tagged Image Format (exports as bitmap image)
- WMF — Windows Metafile (exports as vector drawing)
- XPM — X Pixel Map (exports as bitmap image)

Exchanging Web Page Documents

Exchanging Web page documents with another Web page editor requires no special techniques beyond the normal file open and file save operations. When you create a Web page in StarOffice, you save it as an HTML file. Because HTML is the standard file format for Web pages, any Web browser or Web page editor should be able to open the file without requiring any special translation or conversion. Naturally, the same rule works in reverse. StarOffice can open and view or edit any standard HTML file created by another Web page editor.

Appendix
Installing StarOffice

Obviously, you can't use a program like StarOffice until you first install it on your computer system. If you haven't done that yet, read on. This appendix shows you how to acquire, install, and register your copy of StarOffice.

StarOffice is available in versions for several popular computer platforms including Linux, Windows 95 or 98, Windows NT, Solaris, OS/2, the Mac OS, and Java clients. Most of the StarOffice installation and registration process is the same, regardless of the computer platform on which you install the program. Naturally, a few platform-specific differences exist, but they're minor. In keeping with the title of this book, I use the StarOffice for Linux installation as the basis for the following instructions. Because the Windows version of StarOffice is also very popular, I note the differences between the Linux and Windows installation steps where they occur. (Note the Linux and Windows icons marking the paragraphs describing those differences.)

I don't include specific instructions for installing StarOffice on other platforms besides Linux and Windows, but users who have previous experience downloading and installing software for their chosen computer systems can probably adapt the following instructions easily. The main platform-specific differences show up in the procedures for expanding the compressed archive files you download from Star Division and in how you start the installation program.

Acquiring StarOffice

Unlike Linux, StarOffice is a commercial software product, not a freely distributed open-source program. The StarOffice program is tightly controlled by its developers, Star Division. Although StarOffice is commercial software, it's not widely available in computer stores and mail order catalogs. (At least, that's the case as I write this.) A trial version of StarOffice is included in collections of Linux applications that are packaged with some Linux distributions and may be available from other sources as well. However, if you want a current version of StarOffice, you probably need to get it directly from Star Division.

StarOffice is very reasonably priced. In fact, individuals and students can download and license the software for personal use for free. Corporate users are required to pay a license fee for using StarOffice, but it's very inexpensive compared to other office suites. You can download StarOffice from the Internet, or you can order StarOffice on a CD, complete with printed documentation. Star Division also offers an assortment of support and upgrade subscriptions.

The StarOffice program is normally available as a fully functional, 30-day free trial. You must register the software to continue using it beyond the 30-day trial period.

Full details about current pricing, online orders, downloads, and more are available at the Star Division Web site: `www.stardivision.com`.

Ordering a CD

Perhaps the simplest way to get StarOffice is to order the Deluxe version of the software. It's not free like the downloadable version, but you get printed copies of the Setup Guide and Getting Started guide, along with a CD containing the StarOffice software plus an assortment of extra fonts and clip art images that aren't included in the downloadable version of the program.

The convenience of having the StarOffice setup files available on a CD instead of having to download and expand them yourself can be well worth the modest cost of StarOffice Personal Deluxe (about $40 as I write this). In fact, ordering the Deluxe version on CD may be the only practical way to get StarOffice if you don't have a reliable (and fast) Internet connection. (Downloading StarOffice can take several hours at typical modem speeds, which makes downloading the program impractical for many people with dial-up Internet access.)

To order a StarOffice CD online, go to the Star Division Web site (`www.stardivision.com`) and follow the links to the online shop; from there, head to the Personal version and to the computer platform of your choice. If you're a noncommercial user and want the CD version, be sure to order *StarOffice 5.1 Personal Deluxe.* You must pay by credit card. Fill in the on-screen form with your contact information and credit card number and submit your order. Star Division confirms your order via e-mail and ships you a copy of StarOffice.

You can also order a copy of StarOffice by phone by calling (510) 505-1470.

Downloading files from the Internet

In order to get the latest version of StarOffice direct from Star Division for free, you must download it from Star Division's Web site (www.stardivision.com). Just follow the links to the free download area for the personal version of StarOffice.

Star Division requires you to fill out an on-screen form providing registration information (name, address, phone number, and such) before you can download the software. After submitting your registration information, the Star Division Web site responds by assigning you a customer number and registration code. Be sure to make a note of these numbers and your registration information; you need them later when you install the software. (Star Division also sends the information to you in an e-mail if you provide an e-mail address in the registration information.)

The simplest way to make a note of the registration information is to just use your Web browser's print command to print that page before you move on to the next page.

After you complete the registration screens, you can pick a download location and begin downloading the compressed StarOffice file. All the StarOffice setup files are compressed into a single file for download. Be prepared for a long download, because it's a very large file!

StarOffice is a large program, and receiving it over the Internet means downloading a very large file — 50 to 70MB, depending on which computer platform version you need. Although downloading a file of this size may not be a problem if you have a high-speed Internet connection, it can require several hours to download the file using a typical dial-up Internet connection over a standard modem. Many people find it difficult (if not impossible) to maintain a continuous Internet connection for long enough to download StarOffice. To improve your odds of being able to successfully download StarOffice, avoid downloading during peak network traffic periods, such as late evening. If you can't download the program successfully, order the Deluxe version on CD.

Expanding the compressed files

The StarOffice download file is a single large file that contains all the necessary StarOffice setup and configuration files in a compressed archive file format. Before you can install StarOffice, you must first expand the contents of the downloaded archive file so that the setup files are available on your system at their original size for use in the installation process. The archive file format varies depending on the computer platform on which you'll install StarOffice. Therefore, the technique for expanding the compressed archive file varies depending on which platform-specific version of StarOffice you downloaded.

Extracting Linux Setup files

The StarOffice download file for Linux (and other Unix systems) is a tar archive. You need the tar archive utility (or one of its variants) to extract the setup files from the archive file. Start by moving or copying the StarOffice download file to a temporary directory on your system. Make sure that the temporary directory is empty of other files and that you have full access permission to the directory. Then change to that directory and use the following command (or its equivalent for your preferred archive utility) to extract the setup files from the archive:

```
tar xvf filename.tar
```

Substitute the full filename of the file you downloaded for *filename* in the command preceding. The tar utility extracts the StarOffice setup files from the downloaded archive file and stores them in the temporary directory along with the download file.

Unzipping the Windows Setup files

The download file for the Windows 95 or 98 version of StarOffice is a self-extracting archive. (The download file is an executable program with an EXE extension.) You don't need to have a special utility program on hand to extract the setup files from the archive. Simply copy or move the StarOffice download file to a temporary folder on your hard drive (preferably, a folder containing no other files), and then open that folder in an Explorer window and double-click the download file's icon. The extraction program built into the download file runs and automatically extracts the compressed setup files from the archive.

Installing StarOffice

After you receive your StarOffice CD or download the StarOffice archive file and extract the setup files from it, you're ready to install StarOffice. Obviously, you must make sure that you have the correct version of StarOffice for your computer platform. Also, confirm that you have your registration information, customer number, and registration number; or a media key number (for a CD); or a campus registration number (for a school or corporate installation). You need at least one of these numbers in order to install StarOffice.

Starting the Linux installation

Before you launch the StarOffice for Linux setup program, log in to your Linux system using your regular login name — the one you plan to use when running StarOffice. Do not install the single-user version of StarOffice as the root or superuser. (System administrators should consult the read me files and setup documentation files for instructions on installing StarOffice on a network for use by multiple users.)

Make sure that you have adequate permissions to read and execute files in the directory where the StarOffice setup files are located. If you're installing StarOffice from a CD, make sure that the CD is in the CD-ROM drive and properly mounted. (You may need to temporarily switch to superuser mode or request the assistance of the system administrator in order to mount the CD.)

After the preliminaries are out of the way, follow these steps to start the StarOffice for Linux setup program:

1. **If necessary, issue the startx command to start the X-Window System.**

   StarOffice and the StarOffice setup program are X-Window applications and must run under the X-Window System Graphical User Interface. If your system doesn't automatically start X-Window system, you need to start it manually before installing StarOffice. The startx command is the most common way to launch X-Window System. However, you should substitute the appropriate command to start X-Window if your system uses something different.

2. **Open a terminal window using xterm or a similar terminal program.**

   The terminal window enables you to interact with the Linux command line from within the X-Window System.

3. **Type the command —** /pathname/setup **— on the command line in the terminal window and then press Enter.**

   Substitute the full path to the directory where the StarOffice setup files are stored in place of *pathname* in the preceding command. For example, if the setup files that you extracted from the downloaded archive are in the /home/meadhra/temp/Star_dl/ directory, then the command would read: `/home/meadhra/temp/Star_dl/setup`. If you're installing StarOffice from a CD mounted at /mnt/cdrom, then the command would read: `/mnt/cdrom/linux/office51/setup`. (The files are stored in the /linux/office51/ subdirectory on the CD.)

   Linux loads and runs the StarOffice setup program. Be patient; it may take a moment or two to read all the necessary files and display the first screen of the setup program.

After the StarOffice setup program screen appears, you're ready to proceed with the installation. See the instructions in the "Continuing the installation" section of this appendix for more information.

Starting the Windows installation

To start the StarOffice setup program from Windows, follow these steps:

1. **Open an Explorer window (double-click the My Computer icon on the Windows desktop) or run Windows Explorer (choose Start➪Programs➪ Windows Explorer).**

   Windows opens a folder browser window.

2. **Navigate to the drive and folder where the StarOffice setup program files are stored.**

   For example, if the setup files that you extracted from the downloaded archive are in the \Temp\Star_dl folder on the C drive, then you need to display the contents of the `C:\Temp/Star_dl` folder. If you're installing StarOffice from a CD in the E drive, you need to display the contents of the `E:\windows\office51` folder.

3. **Double-click the icon for the Setup.exe file.**

   Windows loads and runs the StarOffice setup program. Be patient; it may take a moment or two to read all the necessary files and display the first screen of the setup program. The Windows version of the StarOffice 5.1 Installation is remarkably similar to the Linux version.

After the StarOffice setup program screen appears, you're ready to proceed with the installation. See the instructions in the "Continuing the installation" section of this appendix for more information.

If your Windows system is configured to allow multiple users to maintain separate Start menus and desktops, you want to make sure that you're logged in under your regular user ID when you install StarOffice. The installation program adds StarOffice to the Start menu that is in use during the installation. Later, you can add StarOffice to the Start menu for other users, but you have to do so manually.

Continuing the installation

After you start the StarOffice setup program on your computer system, the rest of the installation process is the same regardless of what computer platform you're working on. To continue the StarOffice installation, follow these steps:

1. **Click Next to proceed with the installation.**

   StarOffice Installation displays the Enter the Key Code dialog box, as shown in Figure A-1.

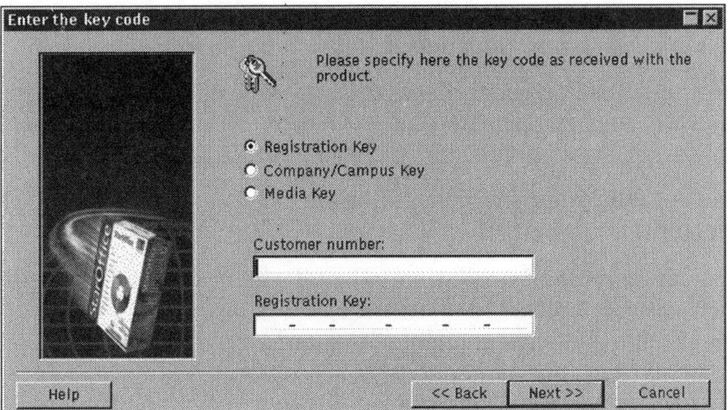

Figure A-1: You must enter the correct code before you can install StarOffice.

2. **Select the kind of key code you have (Registration Key, Company/Campus Key, or Media Key), enter the key in the text box, and then click Next.**

   If you've already registered your copy of StarOffice (such as completing the registration form when you downloaded the archive file), select Registration Key and enter your Customer Number and Registration Key number in the text boxes provided.

   If you received a Company/Campus Key number from your system administrator, select Company/Campus Key, enter the key number in the text box, and then click Next to proceed.

   If you purchased StarOffice Deluxe on a CD, select Media Key and enter the Media Key number that you received with the CD in the text box provided. After entering the key, click Next to proceed.

   The Enter User Data dialog box appears.

3. **Enter your name, address, and other user data in the text boxes provided, and then click Next.**

   The information you enter in this dialog box is (or will be) tied to your StarOffice Registration Key number. If you've already registered StarOffice and entered your Registration Key number in the preceding dialog box, the registration information that you enter here must match what you submitted when you registered the program; otherwise, the Registration Key number won't work. If you haven't registered yet, be sure that the information in this dialog box is what you want to submit when you register the program. StarOffice also uses the User Data from this dialog box to do things such as automatically create return addresses for your envelopes. You don't have to fill in all the boxes if you don't want to, but you must supply at least a first and last name, street, city, and zip code.

   After you click Next, the Installation program displays another dialog box confirming the user data you entered.

4. **Read the information in each of the next three dialog boxes and click Next in each one to proceed to the next page.**

   You have the opportunity to confirm your user data, read an installation update, and read the StarOffice license agreement. Then the installation program displays the Select Installation Type dialog box.

5. **Select either Standard Installation, Custom Installation, or Minimum Installation, and then click Next.**

   Select Minimum Installation to install the basic StarOffice components without the normal assortment of accessories and support files. Normally, you want to select Standard Installation to install all the StarOffice components, help files, and sample files, plus a standard assortment of input and output filters. If you select Custom Installation, the installation program displays another dialog box where you can pick and choose which StarOffice components and support files you want to install.

   After you click Next, the installation program displays the Select Installation Directory dialog box.

6. **Confirm (or change) the directory where the setup program will install StarOffice, and then click Next.**

   Normally, the default StarOffice installation directory works just fine. If you want to change it, simply type a new directory name in the text box. After you click Next, the installation program displays the Start Copying dialog box.

7. **Click Complete to begin copying StarOffice files to your system.**

   StarOffice 5.1 Installation begins copying the StarOffice files to the specified directory on your hard drive. Depending on your system configuration, an additional dialog box may appear asking you to confirm the availability (or absence) of some Java files before proceeding. Unless you know the location of some Java files that the installation program was unable to find, just click OK to close the dialog box and proceed with installation.

   StarOffice 5.1 Installation keeps you informed of its progress by updating a bar chart and clock in the lower-left corner of the screen, as shown in Figure A-2. Copying all the StarOffice files takes a while, so this may be a good opportunity to go get a cup of coffee. After it finishes copying files, the installation program displays the Installation Complete dialog box.

8. **Click Complete.**

   This action closes the Installation Complete dialog box and the StarOffice 5.1 Installation program window. StarOffice is now installed and ready to use.

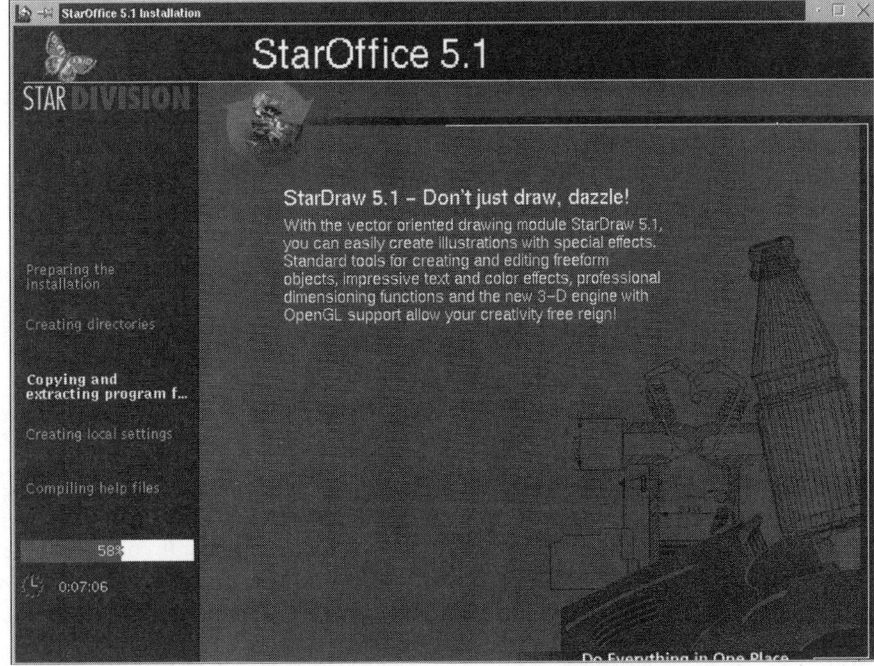

Figure A-2: You can read about some of the StarOffice features while you wait for the installation program to copy files.

If you're installing StarOffice for Windows, you must restart your computer after installing StarOffice. The installation program automatically adds StarOffice to the Windows Start menu at Start⇨Programs⇨StarOffice 5.1⇨StarOffice 5.1.

Registering StarOffice

You must register your copy of StarOffice if you want to use it beyond the initial 30-day free trial period. Registering the software for private, noncommercial use is free, but you must complete the registration process or the software quits working after the time limit expires. If you have not yet registered your copy of StarOffice, you see a reminder to do so every time you start the program.

Registering StarOffice is easy, and you can do it all online. You submit your user data (name and address), and in return, you get a customer number and registration number. Then you enter those numbers into the software to remove the time limit that would disable the program.

If you downloaded your copy of StarOffice directly from the Star Division Web site, you registered the software by submitting your user data before the download. Entering your customer number and registration number and your matching user data during installation completed the registration process. You're done. You don't need to go through a separate registration process.

However, if you installed StarOffice from a CD, you must submit a separate registration (even though you may have furnished similar information about yourself when you placed the order for the CD). To register your copy of StarOffice, follow these steps:

1. **Click Register Now in the registration reminder dialog box that appears when you start an unregistered copy of StarOffice.**

   Alternatively, you can choose Help➪Registration. StarOffice displays the page shown in Figure A-3, which lists your registration options.

2. **Click the Online Registration link.**

   You can also submit your registration via fax or mail, or by using any Web browser, but online registration is fastest if you have Internet access. StarOffice displays the user data you entered during installation.

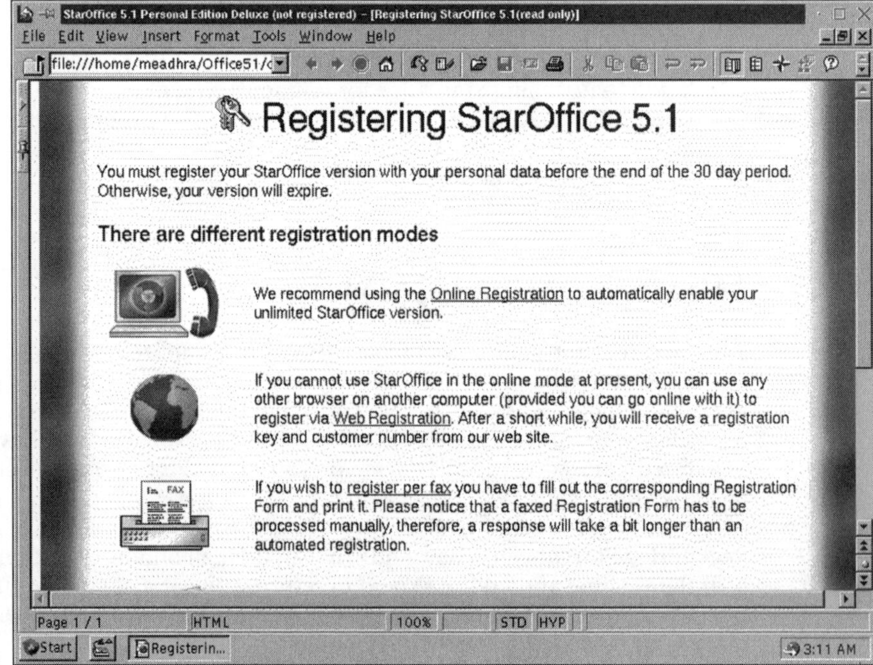

Figure A-3: StarOffice gives you plenty of options for submitting your registration.

3. **Click Submit Data.**

   StarOffice connects to the Internet and submits your user data to Star Division. If the connection is successful, StarOffice displays a document listing your customer number, registration number, and other pertinent information. (I suggest printing a copy of that document.)

   Depending on your system configuration, you may need to establish an Internet connection using a separate utility before clicking the Submit Data button.

That's all there is to it. The registration numbers are automatically recorded in your StarOffice program.

Installing Fonts and Printers in StarOffice

The StarOffice installation process automatically installs an assortment of fonts for use by StarOffice and configures StarOffice to use your default printer queue. In addition to its own fonts, the program can use many of the existing PostScript fonts that you have installed on your Linux/X-Window system as well as new fonts that you may add. But first, you must tell StarOffice where to find those fonts and the font metrics files that go with them. You can also select a different printer driver to use with StarOffice. To install printer drivers and fonts in StarOffice, follow these steps:

1. **Double-click the Printer Setup icon on StarDesktop.**

   StarOffice opens the Printer Installation dialog box, as shown in Figure A-4.

2. **(Optional) Select a printer driver from the Existing Printer Drivers list and click Add New Printer.**

   The selected printer appears in the Installed Printers list. If you want to change the default configuration for the printer, select the printer from the Installed Printers list and click Configure to open the Configure dialog box. Adjust the settings in the dialog box as needed, and then click OK to close the Configure dialog box and return to the Printer Installation dialog box.

3. **(Optional) Select a printer from the Installed Printers list and click Default Printer.**

   The selected printer appears in the Default Printer area at the top of the Printer Installation dialog box. StarOffice uses this printer as the default selection when you print your documents.

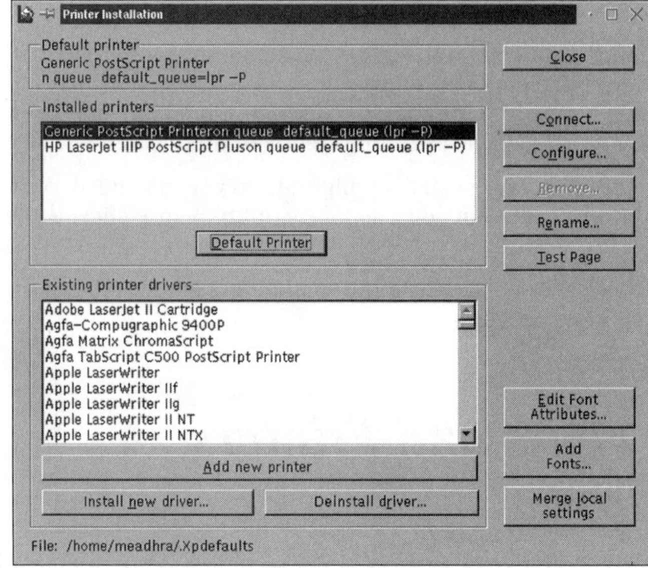

Figure A-4: This dialog box is where you configure printers and fonts for use in StarOffice for Linux.

4. **(Optional) Click Add Fonts.**

   The Font Path dialog box appears, as shown in Figure A-5.

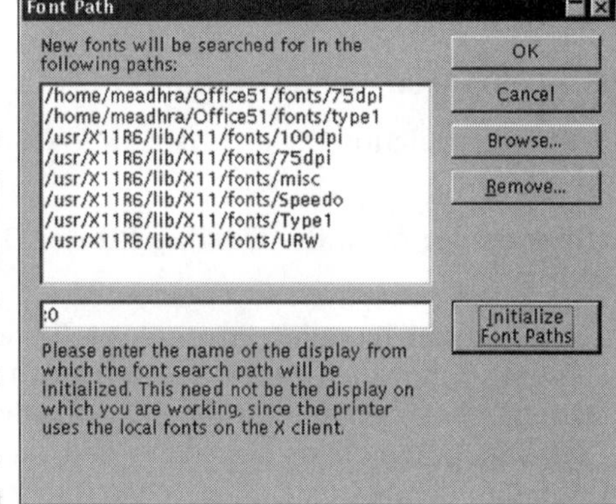

Figure A-5: You need to tell StarOffice where to look for font files on your system.

5. **Click Initialize Font Paths.**

   The recognized font paths (from X-server and StarOffice) appear in the list box. If you want to manually add a font path, click Browse to open the Select Directory dialog box, and then type the pathname for your font directory in the Directory text box and click OK.

6. **Click OK.**

   The Printer Installation utility scans the specified directories searching for font files (PFB) and corresponding format files (AFM) and installs the fonts for which it finds matching font and format files. You may need to click OK to acknowledge some status messages or dialog boxes.

7. **Click Close.**

   The Printer Installation dialog box closes. The new fonts and printer settings are ready for use in StarOffice.

You don't need to go through the procedure above to use fonts in StarOffice for Windows. StarOffice, like other Windows programs, can automatically locate and use any of the regular Windows printers and fonts installed on your system. You don't need to perform any separate procedure to install the printers or fonts in StarOffice or otherwise make them available for StarOffice.

Index

• Symbols •

• A •

• B •

• D •

(continued)

• E •

• G •

• H •

• I •

• N •

• P •

• Q •

• R •

• T •

(continued)

• U •

• V •

• W •

IDG BOOKS WORLDWIDE BOOK REGISTRATION

We want to hear from you!

Visit **http://my2cents.dummies.com** to register this book and tell us how you liked it!

- Get entered in our monthly prize giveaway.
- Give us feedback about this book — tell us what you like best, what you like least, or maybe what you'd like to ask the author and us to change!
- Let us know any other *...For Dummies*® topics that interest you.

Your feedback helps us determine what books to publish, tells us what coverage to add as we revise our books, and lets us know whether we're meeting your needs as a *...For Dummies* reader. You're our most valuable resource, and what you have to say is important to us!

Not on the Web yet? It's easy to get started with *Dummies 101*®*: The Internet For Windows*® *98* or *The Internet For Dummies*®, 6th Edition, at local retailers everywhere.

Or let us know what you think by sending us a letter at the following address:

...For Dummies Book Registration
Dummies Press
7260 Shadeland Station, Suite 100
Indianapolis, IN 46256-3945
Fax 317-596-5498

BESTSELLING BOOK SERIES FROM IDG